U0942998

编辑委员会

《符号与传媒》2020 年秋季号，总第 21 辑

中国知网（CNKI）来源集刊　中文科技期刊数据库来源集刊
超星数字图书馆来源集刊　万方数据库来源集刊

符号与传媒
Signs & Media

主编　赵毅衡
四川大学符号学-传媒学研究所　主办

总第21辑

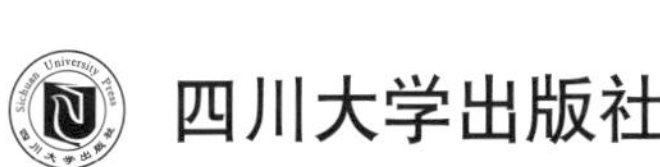

项目策划：黄蕴婷
责任编辑：黄蕴婷
责任校对：毛张琳
封面设计：墨创文化
责任印制：王　炜

图书在版编目（CIP）数据

符号与传媒. 21 / 赵毅衡主编. — 成都 : 四川大学出版社, 2020.9
ISBN 978-7-5690-3390-8

Ⅰ. ①符… Ⅱ. ①赵… Ⅲ. ①符号学－文集 Ⅳ. ①H0-53

中国版本图书馆 CIP 数据核字（2020）第 166576 号

书名　符号与传媒（21）
Fuhao yu Chuanmei (21)

主　　编	赵毅衡
出　　版	四川大学出版社
地　　址	成都市一环路南一段 24 号（610065）
发　　行	四川大学出版社
书　　号	ISBN 978-7-5690-3390-8
印前制作	四川胜翔数码印务设计有限公司
印　　刷	郫县犀浦印刷厂
成品尺寸	170mm×240mm
插　　页	2
印　　张	17.5
字　　数	323 千字
版　　次	2020 年 9 月第 1 版
印　　次	2020 年 9 月第 1 次印刷
定　　价	70.00 元

扫码加入读者圈

◆ 读者邮购本书，请与本社发行科联系。
电话：(028)85408408/(028)85401670/
(028)86408023　邮政编码：610065
◆ 本社图书如有印装质量问题，请寄回出版社调换。
◆ 网址：http://press.scu.edu.cn

四川大学出版社
微信公众号

编者的话

符号学的探索始终充满活力，一方面不断拓展新的理论领域，另一方面也不断深化对自身理论基础的理解和阐释。在本辑“哲学符号学”中，作者们重访经典符号学家的思想或概念，从中获取新的启示：张智庭回顾了巴尔特的话语符号学及其概念史，托尼·贾皮从皮尔斯的“直接对象”概念出发，说明符号过程的目的性因素；奥古斯托·庞齐奥则在伦理符号学的观照之下，讨论“倾听”这一人类元符号学活动的关键环节；孙金燕讨论了贡布里希对图像与现实关系的辩证思索及其背后的理性原则。

文字不仅是表意的工具，也是文化的根本元素。“汉字符号学”中，孟华以语音中心主义为概念框架讨论了文字的“向心”与“离心”；陈永生以古埃及象形文字为例分析其图像与语言的互动关系；匡景鹏则从绘画入手讨论文人画中的汉字性构意法则。

作为常设专辑，“传播符号学”依然汇集了学者们对多种传播现象的独到思索：魏伟从波德里亚理论视角对商品社会语境下的奥运会进行了分析；宗争对中西方游戏研究历程和脉络进行了系统梳理并展望了游戏学研究的发展方向；蒋诗萍等从双轴关系出发讨论了品牌跨界中存在的问题；赵禹平、刘娜对电影、娱乐人设做了精彩讨论。“广义叙述学”中，王欣讨论了创伤叙述中的真实、情感与类型问题，倪爱珍论及图像叙述的图与事，王长才提出了“双层区隔”理论可能面临的挑战；伏飞雄等重新审视广义叙述的定义问题。我们始终关注这些领域，呈现其中理论与应用的探索争鸣。

Editor's Note

The exploration of semiotics is always full of vitality. It constantly expands into new theoretical fields and deepens the understanding and interpretation of its theoretical basis. In the section on "Philosophical Semiotics", the authors revisit the thoughts and concepts of the classical semioticians to obtain new inspiration. Zhang Zhiting reviews the concepts in Roland Barthes' semiology of discourse, and their history. Tony Jappy starts with the "immediate object" of Peircean semiotics to explain purpose and intentionality in semiosis. Basing his discussion on semioethics, Augusto Ponzio discusses "listening", which is key to metasemiosis. Sun Jinyan works on Gombrich's dialectical thinking on the relationship between image and reality and the potential principle behind it.

The written character is not only a vehicle of signification but also an essential element of culture. In the section entitled "Semiotics of Chinese Characters", Meng Hua discusses the "endocentric" and "exocentric" nature of characters, with phonetics as the conceptual framework. Chen Yongsheng takes ancient Egyptian hieroglyphics as an example to analyse the interaction between images and language. Kuang Jingpeng ponders the laws of the construction of Chinese characters in literati paintings.

The regular section "Semiotics of Communication" brings together scholars' unique thoughts on various communication phenomena. Wei Wei analyses the Olympic Games in the context of the commodity society from the perspective of Baudrillard. Zong Zheng systematically examines the course of Chinese and Western game studies and looks ahead to the further development of ludology. Jiang Shiping discusses problems with brand crossover from the perspective of biaxial relations. Zhao Yuping and Liu Na provide invaluable insights into film and character settings in entertainment. In the section "General Narratology", Wang Xin explores truth, affect and mode in trauma narratives. Ni Aizhen talks about the image and object in pictorial narratives. Wang Changcai puts forward possible challenges to the "double framing" principle. Fu Feixiong and his colleagues re-examine the definition of general narrative. We pay attention to all of the above fields and note with great interest the connections and conflict between these theories and their applications.

目　录

哲学符号学

汉字符号学

传播符号学

广义叙述学

综述与书评

Contents

Philosophical Semiotics

Semiotics of Chinese Characters

Semiotics of Communication

General Narratology

Review

哲学符号学

话语符号学：从韩蕾《论巴尔特》谈起

张智庭

摘　要：本文从韩蕾博士《论巴尔特：一个话语符号学的考察》谈起，首先肯定作者的观点，即巴尔特话语符号学为超语言学并在总体上与其新修辞学有同质关系，同时就“话语符号学”这一概念在法国的出现与当前状况做了介绍，一并以全新的资料厘清了结构符号学、叙述符号学、修辞学及叙述学等相关问题之间的关系，也指明了法国符号学今后发展的方向。

关键词：话语符号学，结构符号学，叙述符号学，修辞学，陈述活动

Semiology of Discourse: A Review of Han Lei's *On Roland Barthes*

Zhang Zhiting

Abstract: Starting with the reading of Dr. Han Lei's monography *On Roland Barthes: An Exploration of Semiology of Discourse*, in this article the present author completely agrees with her on defining Barthesian semiology of discourse as equal with his translinguistique and la nouvelle rhétorique in general considering the homogeneity among them; meanwhile, this article serves as an introduction of the emergence and current situation of semiotics of discourse in French academia; it clarifies the relationship among structural semiotics, narrative semiotics, rhetoric and narratology with recourse to new materials and points out the future direction of the development of French semiotics.

Keywords: semiotics of discourse, structural semiotics, narrative semiotics, rhetoric, enunciation

DOI: 10.13760/b. cnki. sam. 202002001

一、书名引起的思索

韩蕾博士的这本《论巴尔特：一个话语符号学的考察》（下称《论巴尔特》）出版于2019年6月，随后，她给我寄来了样书。看到书后，我一方面是高兴，因为我总是乐见年轻人的研究成果问世，另一方面这本书的书名一下子就抓住了我：巴尔特曾经在叙事分析和话语语言学方面做过阐释和努力，但他形成过确定的话语符号学吗？书名中的“考察”二字，是否具有商榷的意味呢？我一时难以获得明确的答案。依据我的认知，在法国的符号学研究史中，虽然有列维-斯特劳斯（Claude Lévi-Strauss，1908—2009）的“叙事分析”、福柯（Michel Foucault，1926—1984）的“话语实践”，但形成定见的是，“话语符号学”这一名称及内涵的确立及正式进入法国大学的教学体系，应该是作为法国符号学研究之主流学派的“巴黎符号学派”（École de Paris）的努力成果。这一学派也产生于法国20世纪50年代根据索绪尔结构语言学和其他几位语言学家的理论而形成的结构主义之中。在其创始人格雷马斯（A. J. Greimas，1917—1992）于1966年出版《结构语义学》（*Sémantique structurale*）之后，这一学派便逐渐与在此之前长时间存在的“sémiologie”在研究方法和内容上明显地出现了不同，并且该学派参照国际符号学学会采用“semiotics”一词，于70年代初最终采用“sémiotique”来定名自己的符号学研究，以便与“sémiologie”在名称上也区别开来。现在，我们已经知道，格雷马斯的总体符号学构想就是在参照了本维尼斯特（Émile Benveniste，1902—1976）的相关论述后，依据美国语言学家乔姆斯基（A. N. Chomsky，1928—　）“生成语法”的伟大启示而建立起来的：“上个世纪70年代，阿尔吉达·朱利安·格雷马斯主张根据乔姆斯基的语法，将符号学理论的全部构成部分组织成唯一的生成模式；各个层级，从最抽象到最具体，从意指过程的基础结构到表层叙述结构，都做了层递排列。”（Fontanille，2011，p. 4）这其中自然包括“话语符号学”。可以概括地说，巴黎符号学派的话语符号学就是一套完整的层级生成系统，具有可以称得上是科学的组织机制。较长时间以来，人们曾经费劲地在“sémiologie”与“sémiotique”两个词之间做着区分，其实，我们如果把前者称为“结构论符号学”，把后者称为“叙述论符号学”（也有称为“生成符号学”的），就很容易把两者区分开来。我将在后面介绍这种定名的依据。“叙述论符号学”已经不再考虑符号及其性质和系统，而是专注符号之间的联系：“sémiotique 的计划在于建立有关意指系统的总体理论……在巴黎符号学派看来，符号是已经被构建的对象。”（Coquet，1982，p. 5）随后，格雷马斯便一直致力于构建这种符号学的叙述语法，到了 20 世纪 70 年代中期和 80 年代才提出了相对清晰的“话语符号学”概念，随后才有了作为雏形的《叙述与话语符号学》（J. Courtés，*Sémiotique narrative et discursive*，1976）、《符号学赌注（I、II 卷）》（A. Hénault，*Les enjeux smiotiques*，*I et II*，1979，1983）、《文本的符号学分析》（Entreverne research team，*Analyse sémiotiques des textes*，1979）等叙述符号学基础读物的出版，而科凯（亦译高概，Jean-Claude Coquet）的《话语与主体》（*Le discours et son sujet*，*I et II*，1984，1985）则是对于话语符号学中的“主体”和“主体性”的更为深入的研究成果。到了 20 世纪 90 年代才有了比较全面的话语符号学成果，例如：《话语分析符号学》（J. Courté，*Analyse sémiotique du discours*，1991）、《话语符号学》（J. Fontanille，*Sémiotique du discours*，1999）等书籍。这是因为，按照巴黎符号学派最概括的看法，“我们可以将话语概念与符号学过程概念等同看待，并将位于言语活动组合关系轴上的所有符号学现象（关系、单位、操作等）都看作属于有关话语的理论”（Greimas & Courtés，1979，p. 102）。“叙述论符号学”是在“结构论符号学”之后发展和形成的，它们显然代表着法国符号学研究的不同阶段。无可否认，罗兰·巴尔特是“结构论符号学”时期的代表性学者，他的研究成果曾经启发过格雷马斯的探索，但他在巴黎符号学派“话语符号学”建立之初就已去世，那么，他的“话语符号学”又是怎样的情况呢？

二、《论巴尔特》对“巴尔特话语符号学”地位的确定

我带着不少的问号进入了对于《论巴尔特》的阅读。不想，该书作者在其开篇的导论中也首先提出了一系列问题：是否存在“巴尔特的话语符号学”？巴尔特的话语符号学“是否有理论反思与文本验证？巴尔特的话语符号学能否应用于分析典型的话语活动——文化对话？……巴尔特的话语符号

学发展前景怎样？”

作者在导论中引述符号学鼻祖索绪尔在不同版本的著述中对“符号学”（sémiologie）一词的阐述，强调指出索绪尔有关“sémiologie”的定义最初就包含着动态的“符号生命”的意义，并列举了后来的多位符号学名家对索绪尔有关“符号学”概念的诠释，说明了其定义中原本就包含着系统与过程两个方面，其中的过程就是涉及组合关系的。而巴尔特则在这两个方面均有所建树。但是，巴尔特的“话语符号学”是分散的，涉及的范围非常广泛，从这一点上，又可以说巴尔特并没有建立起属于自己的“话语符号学”。但是，作者认为，巴尔特在《符号学基础》的引言中“将对于索绪尔语言学与符号学的逆转，及其在《符号学基础》中对于叶姆斯列夫内涵符号学的吸收混合在一起，成功地在索绪尔‘sémiologie’传统下发展出一套既包含索绪尔符号学，也容纳统一后的叶姆斯列夫内涵符号学的新符号学。通过正文的讨论，笔者将会证明，这一套符号学正是他的‘话语符号学’”（韩蕾，2019，p. 6）。作者又说，因为巴尔特的话语符号学思想分散于20世纪60年代至80年代初的作品中，“他自己也不曾直接地讨论过作为一套完整的理论体系存在的‘话语符号学’。从这一观点来看，作者的工作由于是建构性的，因此有很大难度，但是这一工作是必要的，且有其特殊的价值。建构巴尔特的话语符号学，对我们重新阐释巴尔特在法国符号学史上的定位极为关键，同时也能够帮助我们得以反观其他学者对符号学的建设”。我赞同作者的这一观点，并且随着阅读，我欣喜地看到了作者付出的巨大努力获得了可喜的成果。

作者首先告诉我们：巴尔特的符号学及其知识体系都来自一个特殊的话语空间的塑形作用，“是文化，是无数的知识与对话的集合……简单说来，就是互文文本”，于是，作者总结说，巴尔特“是话语符号学思想的读者也是贡献者……巴尔特的话语符号学，从理论到时间跨越性都更强，他不但活跃于文学研究，也为文化研究、影像媒体研究甚至音乐、戏剧研究提供分析典范”。（p. 13）这种情况既为作者对巴尔特的话语符号学的重构准备了大量的研究材料，自然也带来了巨大的困难。不过，作者对于完成她这部书的既定任务还是有足够信心的：她认为“基本能在符号学学科发展承续脉络中定位巴尔特的话语符号学的地位，一并探讨巴尔特自己对话语符号学的批判性书写实践”（p. 19）。

三、《论巴尔特》对于巴尔特话语符号学的重构

全书由四章和一个结论组成。第一章介绍了巴尔特话语符号学的思想渊

源与理论基础，从中可以看出，作者为确立她的论题做了较长时间的系统研究。第二章论述了巴尔特话语符号学的对象领域、基本内涵与模式演进，是作者对巴尔特话语符号学重构的核心内容，我们就从这一章谈起。

作者首先从巴尔特的《叙事作品结构分析导论》（Introduction à l'analyse structurale des récits）开始了她的潜心研究，认为这一重要的文章反映的是巴尔特话语符号学初期的容貌。作者认为，巴尔特的叙事分析有结构分析与文本分析之分，并尝试在话语符号学这一更为宽阔的领域内整合二者，将其统一为对叙事话语的意指活动的符号学分析。作者赞同巴尔特的看法，认为每一种叙事作品都是索绪尔意义上的言语，这种叙事在句子之上的范围活动，“属于第二语言学即超语言学的领域。因此，我们研究巴尔特的超语言学（也即我们定义的话语符号学），他的叙事话语结构分析是一个不可忽视的部分”（p. 112）。作者看重巴尔特的这篇《叙事作品结构分析导论》，是因为这篇文章不仅较为集中地体现了巴尔特的叙述学思想，也可以让我们从中提炼出一些在讨论话语符号学思想时必须仔细研究的主题。作者认为，巴尔特在吸收了俄国形式主义者普罗普的“功能说”之后指出，各种功能之间的联系是靠指示词（后来又扩展成了“催化作用”概念）来维系的。这样，功能之间的句段关系就有了与之相配合的聚合关系，功能单位之间的关系是“分配式的”，而指示词之间的关系是“整合性的”。于是，巴尔特的话语单位结合理论便从索绪尔的组合与联想两轴关系、雅各布森的组合与聚合两轴关系、叶姆斯列夫的关系与关联两轴关系，过渡到了自己的句段与系统两轴关系，从而让我们更好地理解叙事作品中的结构组成。而这样的结构关系，也指导和培养了读者横向的阅读能力和纵向的对于超功能即超语言学的阅读能力。概括说来，“巴尔特对叙事作品的结构分析以‘功能’层、‘行动’层和‘叙述’层展开……他指出了话语符号学视域下对于叙述话语的认知，以及话语符号学所配置的叙事话语的分析方法”（p. 126），而在这一过程中，巴尔特接受了本维尼斯特的主张，讨论叙述者而非故事人物的声音，尤其是讨论第一人称叙述的问题。作者认为，巴尔特热情地拥抱了本维尼斯特在其《普通语言学问题》中所阐述的原则，说他“全盘接受了本维尼斯特有关人称的分析，尤其是本维尼斯特有关人称与非人称的分类，以及他对人称代词的极性、人称中存在的时位、人通过‘我’在现在时中占为己有而标注自己为主体等问题的分析”（p. 130）。这种认识，也帮助了巴尔特后来在自己的作品中极富创造性地让人称发挥了绝妙的产生全新意指的作用。根据作者的介绍，笔者认为，巴尔特从这个时期开始已经接受了本维尼斯特有关“主体”和“主观性”（subjectivité）的理论，也接受了作为本维尼斯特对于语言学贡献最大的有关“陈述活动”（énonciation，作者译为“陈述行为”）的论述，从而进一步丰富了他自己主张的“话语符号学”的内涵与操作手段。

作者认为，正是在本维尼斯特的影响之下，巴尔特在1970年发表的《话语语言学》（Linguistique du discours）中确立了自己的话语符号学的框架，“巴尔特所谓的‘话语语言学’的对象同时包含着话语产物（texte de l'énoncé）与陈述行为，后者是前者的外观。这也是话语分析（l'analyse du discours）、文本语言学（linguistique textuelle）的范围”（p. 144）。巴尔特将话语语言学的对象——话语，“界定为言语的有限领域，（该领域）从内容来看是一致的，都是被第二级的交际目的发送并结构化，同时也被语言系统之外的其他因素文明化”（Barthes，p. 612）。巴尔特认为，可根据两种必要原则来构建话语语言学：一是话语语言学要明确超语言学而取代语言学的方式：由于话语语言学必然要承担对于语境或情境的研究，所以，它的任务便是为指涉对象编码，而赋予编码的手段则是几个世纪以来同样是在为言语建立编码的修辞学；二是返回语言学，因为话语系统与有关句子的系统一样，也涉及同一层面要素之间的替代（substitution）及分配关系和每一个层次各单位在更高层面的一个单位中的整合。因此，可以不仅把话语看作一种分配关系集合体，而且看作一种被整合的集合体。整合原则包括两方面的内容：首先是结构作用，因为这种作用从理论上可以描述意义；其次是总体的作用，因为这种作用赋予系统的界限一种描述性地位。在此，结合作者的论述，笔者想指出两点：

第一，巴尔特明确地说明了话语符号学的对象：一是话语产物，二是陈述行为（或“陈述活动”），这与一般对于这一概念的看法（包括巴黎符号学派）相一致：“我们可以把话语看作陈述语段（énoncé），或者在考虑说话人和谈论情境的人的情况下，将其看作陈述活动（énonciation）”（Rey-debove，1979，p. 49）。第二，巴尔特一直在说，话语符号学属于超语言学，他在这里又告诉我们，在经过超语言学阶段后，还要返回语言学，这就明显地承认，他又调整了自己对语言学与符号学之间关系的看法，那就是符号学包含着语言学，而不再是相反，亦即实现了第二次“逆转”。《论巴尔特》作者在这里提到了巴尔特在这篇文章中第一次使用了巴黎符号学派使用的“sémiotique du discours”，请注意，其中的“符号学”一词使用的是“sémiotique”（叙述论符号学）。作者认为，这是因为巴尔特受到了本维尼斯特的影响，或是接受了当时学界对“sémiologie”与“sémiotique”的化约。笔者也注意到了这

《符号与传媒》征稿启事

《符号与传媒》，是四川大学符号学-传媒学研究所主办的学术集刊，目前由四川大学文学与新闻学院赵毅衡教授任责任主编，每年分春秋两辑出版。自2008年创办以来，《符号与传媒》已与国内外符号学团队合作共推出多个颇具影响力的学术研究专题。为适应刊物进一步国际化、专业化的需求，本刊自2014年春季号起全面改为中英文双语版，并严格执行国际同行评议制度。

本着兼容并包、不拘一格的开放性学术理念，本刊努力将符号学方法与理论系统地扩展至新闻传播学研究、文学文化研究、叙述研究、中国文化典籍研究、艺术研究等众多研究领域，拓宽符号学运动的锋面。本刊所征收的稿件不仅涵盖社会、历史、文化、经济等科学范畴，更着重于将思想的触角延伸至人类科学的各种门类，各种活动。本刊希望通过不同形式的探索，为符号学提供一片广阔的沃土。

思想无疆界。我们相信大作能为符号学与传媒学的理论与应用提出新的想法，我们衷心期待您的文章。

赵毅衡

《符号与传媒》编辑部

投稿邮箱：semiotics_ media@163.com

联系电话：028-85412121

传　　真：028-85412710

官方论坛：www.semiotics.net.cn

官方微博：http://e.weibo.com/semioticsscu

官方微信：符号与传媒

地　　址：四川省成都市武侯区望江路29号

四川大学文学与新闻学院，符号学-传媒学研究所

邮　　编：610064

Signs & Media Calls for Papers

*Signs & Media*is a bilingual (English-Chinese), peer-reviewed academic journal, founded in 2008 by the Institute of Semiotics & Media Studies (ISMS), Sichuan University. *Signs & Media*, dedicating itself to the interdisciplinary research on semiotics and media studies, has collaborated with many semiotic research teams from all around the world, publishing professional papers or special sections.

Under the editorship of Professor Henry Yiheng Zhao, *Signs & Media* endeavors to systematically expand semiotics to all fields of human sciences, covering, notably, communication and media studies, cultural studies, art and literature, as well as narratology, stylistics, discourse analysis, cognitive science in the semiotic perspective, and, in particular, reinterpretations of Chinese traditional semiotic heritage.

Signs & Media welcomes contributions on any topics, so long as they, in a way, help illuminate the theoretical foundation and widen the sphere of applicability of semiotics.

Henry Yiheng Zhao
Editor, *Signs and Media*

Email address: semiotics_ media@ 163. com
Phone: +86 -28 -8541 -2121
Fax: +86 -28 -8541 -2710
Website: www. semiotics. net. cn
Official Microblog: http: //e. weibo. com/semioticsscu
Official Wechat: semiotics2008
Postal Address: Institute of Semiotics & Media Studies,
Sichuan University,
No. 29 Wangjiang Road,
Chengdu, 610064
China

种用法，但想在下面的文字中做出更多的阐释。

那么，什么是巴尔特要建立的话语符号学呢？《论巴尔特》的作者告诉我们，“要研究巴尔特的话语符号学，即超语言学，就必须对其修辞学思想进行深入的了解”（p. 150）。我认为，作者对于巴尔特《旧修辞学》一文的阐释，则是全书最为详细精到的部分。按照巴尔特的主张，旧修辞学为话语分析提供了分析方法，旧修辞学与后来的话语语言学是话语符号学的两个阶段，前者是话语符号学的基础，并为其提供了操作指南，“从旧修辞学中借用的话语分析模式，依然可以沿用于新的话语分析”，超语言学与修辞学具有“同质关系”，因此，“话语修辞学是他用以替代旧修辞学的新修辞学”。（p. 153）巴尔特对旧修辞学的研究开始很早，他在 1964 年发表的《图像修辞学》（Rhétorique de l'image）一文中就说道：“有可能在结构主义视域中研究旧修辞学……因为这一研究将使得它有可能建立一种总体修辞学，即内涵系统之特征的语言学”，这种努力的结果，便是“使得以自然语言为基础的语言学模式对符号系统的分析，能够包括对于非自然语言在结构上类似的结构/系统的分析”。作者也借助巴尔特这篇文章，详细地介绍了柏拉图、亚里士多德等人的修辞学主张和巴尔特的批判思想，使我们对这一领域有了更为深刻的认识。对于巴尔特在修辞学方面的建树，《符号学词汇》（*Lexique sémiotique*）一书给出的结论是：“在巴尔特看来，修辞学就是内涵要素的形式。”（Rey-debove，1979，p. 125）这似乎可以帮助我们对巴尔特的修辞学理论做进一步的理解。

书的第三章《自我反射式的书写对话语符号学的实践反思》，是分析了《巴尔特自述》和《恋人絮语》（作者使用的译名是《爱的言谈——片段集》）两书中巴尔特话语符号学的展现；其第四章是《作为方法论的话语符号学对比较文学的模构：案例分析》。这两章都展现了巴尔特的话语符号学在“陈述语段”（或作者使用的“陈述结果”）亦即在“形态研究”方面的成果。这些对于我们都具有很大的启发作用，并进一步印证了作者对于巴尔特话语符号学重构的成立。

似乎我们可以用下面的话来概括作者为巴尔特总结出的话语符号学：话语符号学就是超语言学研究，这种研究有层次衔接，它从总体上讲与修辞学具有“同质关系”，具有很强的可操作性。这部书并不是在汇总性地介绍巴尔特已经存在的话语符号学思想，而是从其多个方面的符号学论述中总结和概括出属于巴尔特“话语符号学”的理论构架和内容。这自然是一项艰巨和富有意义的工作。而且，由于巴黎符号学派在 20 世纪 70 年代之后很快就成了法国符号学研究的主流，在至今的长时间内，人们甚至基本不再谈论“结构论符号学”的贡献，也不谈巴尔特，那么在这个时候，系统地研究“结构论符号学”的代表学者巴尔特的话语符号学，就更显示出其特殊的意义。

四、对几个相关问题的浅见

我们当然是围绕着罗兰·巴尔特和他的符号学活动来谈。

（1）关于“sémiologie”与“sémiotique”的译名。我曾根据《结构主义史》（*Histoire du structuralisme*，1992）一书对“sémiologie”内涵的阐释和主张，将其在汉语上定名为“结构论符号学”，放进了我编写的长文《法国符号学概论》中，该文后来被收进了由北京大学出版社出版的《法国符号学研究论集》一书。当时这样定名，我就遇到了在汉语中如何定名“sémiotique”一词的问题，可是由于缺乏足够的资料，我最后还是采用了“巴黎符号学派符号学”的名称。后来我想到，这种符号学以“叙述语法”为其研究的主要内容，便觉得似乎为其定名为“叙述论符号学”比较合适，以方便区分和记忆，但这要找到相关论述作依据。不久，我又想到，在20世纪60年代末和70年代初，这两个名词是经常互用的，比如，格雷马斯在1973年发表的文章《一个叙述符号学问题：价值对象》（Un problème de sémiologie narrative：les objet de valeurs）照样使用了“sémiologie”作为“符号学”的名称，但这同一篇文章在被收进其《论意义 II》（*Du sens*，*II*，1983）时，就将“sémiologie”改为了“sémiotique”。这不，这里已经出现了“sémiotique narrative”的称谓，这就更强化了我的想法。前不久，我在我过去的一位学生为我提供的一篇参考文章中也找到了支持。那是格雷马斯的祖籍国立陶宛的维尔纽斯大学的尼乔勒·盖尔斯伊特（Nijolé Keršyté）先生用法文写的《话语的相互作用：在叙述论符号学与叙述学之间》（Les interactions discursives：entre sémiotique narrative et narratologie），那是发表在《波罗的海沿岸国家协同》杂志上的一篇文章（2008年第5期，第85-104页）。所以，我认为，把两个名称分别定为“结构论符号学”和“叙述论符号学”是符合各自内涵的——尽管后者在本质上也是“结构论的”。然而，没有想到的是，就在我有了上述认识之后，2017年5月30日至6月2日于巴黎的联合国教科文组织（UNESCO）总部举办的“今天的格雷马斯：结构的未来——纪念格雷马斯100周年诞辰（1917—1992）”的国际研讨会的宣传材料中，巴黎符号学派也承认在现时的“sémiotique”研究中，仍然有“sémiologie”的研究内容，并且该学派也以名词加形容词的“结构论符号学”（sémiotique structurale）自居，只是其中的名词是“sémiotique”，而不是“sémiologie”，并称今天的巴黎符号学派是对当年结构主义的真正继承。在认真思考之后，我认为，这是法国符号学研究不同学派在几十年的纷争之后于认识上的一种趋同。这样一来，自然就需要把我认定的两个名称做一下变动。我的想法是，在汉语上将“sémiologie”称为“结构符号学”，将“sémiotique”称为“叙述符号学”，它们都去掉一个“论”字，而在这两个名称之上人为地设立一个统一的上位词——“结构论符号学”，这就不会再引起理解上的困扰了。而相对于法国符号学今后的发展，“结构论符号学”正包含着两种有着一定差异的符号学研究的一个大的阶段。至于法国符号学今后的名称，我在我的书中提出了自己的看法：法国符号学将会是在统一的“sémiotique”名下，对符号、符号性质、符号系统和符号之间的关系亦即“词语显现”的一种总体研究，就像我们在汉语中对于“符号学”这一学科的理解那样。

（2）巴尔特在文章《话语语言学》中，于结尾之前采用的都是“sémiotique”这个词。我认为，巴尔特在此可不是混用两个名称。一位曾经在20世纪70年代于法国高等研究院（EHESS）聆听过巴尔特和格雷马斯讲课、现在从事法国符号学史研究的美国学者托马·布罗登（Thomas Broden）在纪念格雷马斯100周年诞辰研讨会上，以《结构主义的另一条道路：格雷马斯与巴尔特的合作》（Une autre voie du structuralisme：la collaboration Greimas-Barthes）为题做了发言，谈及两个人过去30年中有过的三次密切合作：第一次是在1950—1955年期间，格雷马斯曾劝说巴尔特与他一起进行词汇学研究，并注册索邦大学的博士学位，后来由于巴尔特忙于写作和解决生计问题而未能继续下去；第二次是在1955—1968年期间，两人针对雅各布森与列维-斯特劳斯对于波德莱尔诗歌《猫》（*Les chats*）进行形式主义分析，决定共同却各自地致力于对话语结构的意指和社会功能的研究，但在后期两位学者出现了较大分歧；第三个阶段则是在1968年之后，两个人又都表示出在研究方面相互靠拢的意愿（Broden，pp. 214-227）。巴尔特的《话语语言学》一文正好发表在这个时期中的1970年；而格雷马斯也在此期间与之相向而行，并在由他和库尔特斯合编的《符号学：言语活动理论的系统思考词典》中于词条“sémiologie”名称下肯定了几位先行者做出的努力，也赞许了巴尔特的著述，例如《符号学基础》和《服饰系统》（*Système de la mode*）做出的成绩与贡献，还在巴尔特去世后写出了几篇在思考方式上并不是特别严格的属于审美方面的文章，以《不完善性》（*De l'imperfection*，1987）为名出版，算是两个人在思想上和研究方法接近的表示和对两人友情的纪念。（Broden，pp. 214 - 227）更何况，1969 年在巴黎成立的国际符号学学会的名称采用的是“sémiotique”。这也再一次证明，巴尔特是善于学习别人和随时修正自己观点的谦虚学者。不过，需要指出的是，这篇文章在最后还是使用了“sémiologie”的形容词形式“sémiologique”。我的解释是，巴尔特认为，话语符号学也还是离不开结构符号学，因为他在论述其总体作用之后就说，这种作用“同时以结构符号学的（sémiologique）术语（这一点很重要）来定名该系统与社会和历史衔接的时刻：一种尊重整合性原则的叙述符号学具备有效地与一些外在结构符号学例如历史学、心理学或美学进行合作的任何机会”（Barthes，p. 616）。这里，显然涉及原本属于“sémiologie”符号学研究的一些内容。巴尔特没有说错，笔者在 2016 年年底至 2017 年年初于法国做短期学术访问期间，曾有幸与当时的法国符号学学会会长德尼·贝特朗（Denis Bertrand）教授会面，他当时让我看了他与名誉会长雅克·丰塔尼耶（Jacques Fontanille）一起为纪念格雷马斯 100 周年诞辰而起草的国际研讨会资料，标题是《今天的格雷马斯：结构的未来》（Greimas aujourd'hui：l'avenir de structure）。这份材料把格雷马斯的研究仍然归为结构主义运动，并对其贡献做出了评价，指出，“格雷马斯……在其对于意指的分析中以最为稳定的方式展示了结构主义的原理与方法……他的研究工作在于以这位学者特有的纯真来过问意义的出现和塑造我们对世界的感知方式”。材料中提出了研讨会的思想讨论主题：一是“一项在时间延续中的科学计划：继承、后续和转换”，主要探讨 20 世纪 60 年代作为一项科学计划的结构主义的后续研究工作并对其做出评价。笔者惊异地看到，该材料对于所涉及的单独学科的符号学仍然使用了“sémiologie”一词，这说明现在以“sémiotique”来命名自己符号学研究方法的巴黎符号学派已不像 20 世纪 70 年代那样尽力使自己与前者分开，而是也接受、继承了前者。我当时只有两个月居留签证，无法参加于当年 5 月 30 日—6 月 2 日的研讨会，便请当时还在那里学习的天津外国语大学的李双老师为我拿到了会上发言的摘要汇编本。有关这次研讨会的情况，大家可参阅李双老师在《语言与符号》第 4 期上发表的文章。

（3）《论巴尔特》的作者把巴尔特话语符号学的最后内容放在了巴尔特研究过的修辞学方面，是值得称赞的，因为这正与法国符号学的发展远景相一致。我们都熟悉热奈特对修辞学研究做的贡献，他曾把巴尔特为阐述“二级符号”所绘制的层级式图表直接用来阐释修辞格与总体的修辞学。他说：“有关修辞格的修辞学的雄心，就是建立文学内涵的一种规则。”（Genette，

p. 220）他后来进行的叙事话语的研究，也是与修辞学紧密关联的。可以说，热奈特为之奋斗的诗学（包括叙述学［narratologie］）就是对修辞学的延展和深化。在此，我想就叙述学与符号学的关系，说一说几十年后人们的观点。上述美国学者托马·布罗登2019年于法国符号学两年一次的研讨会上，宣读了他对20世纪60年代的叙述理论研究的成果，他把“叙述学”与格雷马斯的“叙述符号学”放在了一起，作为那个时期有代表性的符号学的两种叙述理论研究，这获得了与会学者们的赞同。这种情况，有益于我们国内学者调整看法，原因是，热奈特与托多罗夫曾经说过，叙述学是对于话语文本“词语显现”（manifestation verbale）的研究，它不属于具备语言学背景的“sémiologie”和与语言学不分的“sémiotique”，而这样的表述一旦翻译成汉语，就成了“叙述学不属于符号学”，因此，也就造成了我们国内学界理解上的某种偏移。

后来在修辞学上做出深入研究和重大贡献的学者，当属上面提到的德尼·贝特朗先生。贝特朗认为，修辞学早已突破了其作为对于语言的文学使用的定义，有关修辞学的符号学研究的革新自21世纪初已经开始，并成为符号学学科研究的重要事件。在文学符号学领域，这种革新的首要成绩似乎是使修辞学摆脱了文体学（stylistique）并将其放在更为宽泛的维度中进行重新考虑。问题的关键已不再仅限于修辞格的使用和“文体效果”的显示，而是关于处在行动中的言语活动的包括说服性和操纵性在内的可分享的效能（efficience）。现在，人们应该将话语的修辞学空间放进有关长时值的大的符号学研究工程之中来重新定义，“在我看来，符号学的最宏伟计划之一，将是被设想为对于修辞学的一种当然的替换”（张智庭，2019，p. 226），即是说，未来的修辞学就等同于符号学。这种放大修辞学的研究领域和其与风格（style）相脱离的理论主张，无疑是需要我们认真关注和研究的。我们在肯定巴尔特具有远见卓识的同时，也不禁为《论巴尔特》一书的作者认可巴尔特的这种观点拍手叫好。

结束语

我向韩蕾博士送上诚挚的祝贺，她的研究成果让人们更为深入地了解了法国符号学研究史上的重要学者巴尔特。如果要我提一点意见的话，那就是在术语的使用上，最好多采用现在比较一致的译名；此外，巴尔特在对“阅读”和“听”等属于“陈述语段”方面的论述，也具有非常重要的认知作用，亦可在这方面再着一点笔墨；再就是，书名中的“一个话语符号学”中的“一个”可以考虑改动一下，因为这样的量词似乎不适合用在“符号学”这种概念名词前面。总之，《论巴尔特》是一部研究巴尔特的重要著作，我希望有更多研究巴尔特的著作问世。

引用文献：

韩蕾（2019）. 论巴尔特：一个话语符号学的考察 . 成都：四川大学出版社 .

张智庭（2019）. 法国符号学研究论集 . 北京：北京大学出版社 .

Barthes, R. (2002). Œuvres *complètes. Tome III.* Paris: Seuil

Broden, T. (2017). Retrieved from http://afsemio.fr/wp-content/uploads/AFS_ Actes. 2017. pdf, 214-227.

Coquet, J. -C. (1982). *L'École de Paris.* Paris: Classique Hachette.

Fontanille, J. (2011). *Corps et sens.* Paris: PUF.

Genette, G. (1972). *Figures III.* Paris: Seuil.

Gremas, A. J., Courtés, J. (1979). *Sémiotique. Dictionnaire raisonné de la théorie du langage.* Paris: Hachette Supérieur.

Rey-debove, J. (1979). *Lexique sémiotique.* Paris: PUF.

作者简介：

张智庭，笔名怀宇，南开大学外国语学院法语系教授，天津外国语大学语言符号应用传播研究中心专职研究员，法国符号学译者和研究者。

Author:

Zhang Zhiting, professor from the Department of French, College of Foreign Languages, Nankai University, a full-time researcher of the Research Centre for Linguistic Semiotics, and a translator and scholar on French semiotics; some of his works were published under the pen name of Huaiyu (怀宇).

Email: zhangshuono3@163.com

Semioethics and Philosophy of Language as Recovery of Listening

Augusto Ponzio

Abstract: Semioethics is the vocation of semiotics, because responsive understanding is the original vocation of the sign, where responding is not limited to the word, or to any type of identification interpretant. Listening is *encounter*, going towards the other, *hospitality*, responsiveness not as initiative by the person responding, responsibility without alibis. Human semiosis is characterized by *metasemiosis*: the capacity to reflect on signs, to suspend responses and deliberate, beyond immediate semiosis undistinguished from the response to it. Human semiosis is characterized by *metasemiosis*: the capacity to reflect on signs, to suspend responses and deliberate. This capacity involves an inescapable responsibility from the human animal towards life over the whole planet.

Susan Petrilli's book begins with a question, in the title of the first chapter, concerning the relation between "Semiosis and Life": *What lies in their future?* Her response: our present is the *future perfect of semiotics.* The problem is not simply of the theoretical order, given that semiotics is also implicated as semeiotics, as symtomatology. The relation between semiotics and the question of the health of life at the planetary level is not only of the historical order, ensuing from the connection of semiotics today with medical *semeiotics*, symptomatology, beginning with Hippocrates and Galen. The human being as a "semiotic animal" is the only animal responsible for semiosis, for life, even more so the professional scholar of signs.

Keywords: encounter, humanitas, listen, literary writing, methaphor, philosophy of language, other, semioethics, silence, similarity, taciturnity, translation.

DOI: 10.13760/b.cnki.sam.202002002

Ⅰ. Semioethics as the Vocation of Semiotics

Signs, Language and Listening: the first, *Signs,* are the specific object, or rather the theme, of semiotics; the second, *Language*, if understood as verbal language, is the object or theme of linguistics, and in any case both verbal and nonverbal languages are the object, theme of semiotics, where linguistics is part of semiotics as the general science of signs. And *Listening*?

Listening is not to hear, nor is it limited to the verbal. It does not concern understanding in the sense of recognition, identification, but as *responsive understanding*, where responding is not limited to the word, or to any type of identification interpretant; nor is it a question of interpretants of the pragmatic order.

Listening is *encounter*, going towards the other, *hospitality*, response not as initiative by the person responding, but as *responsibility* that cannot be avoided; not simply *saying* to the other, but *gifting* (Levinas, 2020; Ponzio, 2019a), *owing the other* something, in a relationship that does not ensue from free choice. As to the subtitle of the book we are presenting: *Semioethic perspectives,* they enter via listening.

A second perspective that invests semiotics, concerned with signs and language, is that offered by *philosophy of language* (Petrilli, Ponzio, 2016).

That semiotics, the general science of signs, cannot avoid philosophy of language, is explained by Umberto Eco in his book *Semiotics and Philosophy of Language* (1984, pp. xii - xiii). The different special semiotics can fail to interrogate their philosophical foundations, but not so for general semiotics. The nature of general semiotics is philosophical; philosophical discourse is *constitutive* of semiotics. In particular, the relation of semiotics to philosophy is the relation to *philosophy of language.*

But as recites the subtitle of Susan Petrilli's book, the perspective of semiotics here is *semioethics*. Consequently, via *listening* (associated in the title of the book to *Signs* and *Language*), the relation of semioethics with philosophy of language (a theme announced in the title of the first section in the first chapter) is such that the latter invests semioethics, as anticipated in the first section of the second chapter, with the character of *art of listening*.

To orient semiotics in the sense of semioethics implies a great responsibility for the semiotician, the scholar of signs, because it confers upon the sign science a commitment that supercedes the limits of *theoretical reason* (though coherently deriving from it) to concern *practical reason*.

This commitment in fact is of the *ethical* order and concerns the *health of life*, today more than ever put at risk in this "global village" that is our planet, rendered such by the global market, by the need to expand the market into its current form known as *globalization* (Petrilli, 2020a).

The relation between semiotics and the question of the health of life at the planetary level is not only of the historical order, ensuing from the connection of semiotics today with medical *semeiotics*, symptomatology, beginning with Hippocrates and Galen. The relation between semiotics and health also derives from identification of *semiosis* (any sign process) and *life*, considering recent studies in *biosemiotics* as a result of broadening the "semiotic field" with Thomas Sebeok's *global semiotics* (2001). But the relation of semiotics to the health of life at a planetary level is due especially to the *objective involvement of human life with all of life over the entire planetary ecosystem.*

Life is a specifically *human* problem insofar as it is an ethical problem; responsibility towards life over the planet is human responsibility. In fact, the human being is the only *semiotic animal*, that not only lives on signs, but reflects on them, accounts for signs and life, even at the cost of one's own life.

Human semiosis is characterized by *metasemiosis*: the capacity to reflect on signs, to suspend responses and deliberate, beyond immediate semiosis undistinguished from the response to it. Another term for metasemiosis is *semiotics*, distinct and at once connected to *semiotics as the name of the general science of signs*, an expression of *human understanding*.

This special meaning of "semiotics", as a human species-specific capacity, is closely connected with "semiotica" understood as a *discipline*, which now is also *semioethics*, the highest level of human awareness of the inescapable responsibility without alibis towards life over the planet.

II. Semioethics and Philosophy of Language as the Art of Listening

The fundamental problem of philosophy of language in its close relation to semiotics, also "doctrine of signs" (Sebeok), is the problem of the other, which is the problem of the word, the word as voice, recognized as the demand for listening. *Philosophy of language is here understood as the art of listening.*

Listening is not external to the word, an addition, concession, initiative by the listener, it is not a choice, an act of respect towards the other. Listening is a *constitutive element of the word.* As Mikhail Bakhtin says in "The Problem of the Text" (1986 [1959 -61], pp. 103 - 131), listening derives from the very nature of the word, which demands listening, responsive understanding, new understanding beyond immediate understanding in an unending process. Insofar as it flourishes on listening, the word is a dialogical relationship, it calls for listening, understanding, for a response and in turn responds.

Listening is the *art of the word,* its peculiar task, attitude, prerogative, way of being. Absence of listening, of interlocutors is the worst that can happen to a word—non *taciturnity*, which is the condition of listening, but *silence.*

Philosophy of language concerned with listening is *philosophy of alterity* which, compared to philosophy of identity—widespread, shared, thus dominant—is no doubt a minority trend, traceable in a few authors, like Mikhail Bakhtin and Emmanuel Levinas, and in certain presentday orientations and projects concerning signs and language.

Dialogism presupposes corporeality and intercorporeality. Dialogue is not possible without the body and intercorporeal co-implication.

To dialogism of the word, evidenced by Bakhtin at a maximum in Dostoevsky's polyphonic novel, there corresponds dialogism as intercorporeality of the "grotesque body" as revealed in "grotesque realism", described by Bakhtin (1965) in his analyses of *Gargantua et Pantagruel,* by François Rabelais. After all, the grotesque appears in the "novelistic" genre, the most dialogical literary genre, therefore in Dostoevsky's polyphonic novel. For this reason Bakhtin, in the second 1963 edition of his monograph on Dostoevsky (1st ed., 1929), includes a new chapter (the IVth) on the relation between the "novel" genre and grotesque realism in carnivalesque folklore, showing how the novel has its roots in grotesque realism.

Dialogism and *intercorporeality* are two faces of the same coin. They belong to the real, material, biosemiotic interconnection among living bodies. "Life by its very nature is dialogic. To live means to participate in dialogue" (Bakhtin, 1963, Eng. trans. 1984 [1961], p. 293) . We can speak of *Bakhtinian dia-logic*, juxtapposed by Bakhtin, implicitly and explicitly, on various occasions (from the original 1929 edition of his monograph on Dostoevskij through to his writings of the 1970s) to Hegelian dialectics and the dialectical materialism of real socialism. The Bakhtinian vision is subtended by a *dialogics of nature*, a *dialogics of life* which today would be expressed in terms of "biosemiotics".

Dialogue not only exists in *communication semiosis*, where the interpreted is already itself an interpretant response oriented to being interpreted as a sign by another external interpretant. Dialogue also subsists in *semiosis of symptomatization*, where the interpreted is an *interpretant response* (symptom) not oriented to being interpreted. And dialogue also subsists in *semiosis of information*, where an inanimate object acts as sign only because it receives an interpretation from a living being (Petrilli, Ponzio, 2002, 2007). In any case, interpretation, the response to the "interpreter", is dialogical in nature (Ponzio 2006b). Hence dialogue does not begin with the signaling behaviour of a sender who intends to communicate something to a receiver about some object.

All of semiosis is a dialogical process. The logic of semiosis is *dia-logic*. The interpretant, the sign we use to interpret something else transforming it into a sign, is as such "a disposition to respond".

Ⅲ. Linguistics of Silence and Philosophy of Language

In "From Notes Made in 1970 –71", Bakhtin (1986 [1970 –1971], pp. 132 – 158) distinguishes between *listening* and *wanting to hear* and establishes a relationship, respectively, between *listening* and *taciturnity*, on the one hand, and *silence* and *wanting to hear*, on the other.

Silence is the absence of noise and condition for the perception of sound, for understanding-recognition of the verbal sign, the sentence, the repeatable elements of discourse (in the *langue* distinct from *langage*). Taciturnity is only possible in the human world. It is constitutive of the "logosphere", a necessary condition to understand the word's sense, which is unrepeatable, through which language participates in historical unrepeatability, and in the unfinalized totality of the logosphere. Therefore, each element of discourse is perceived on two levels: that of the repeatable sentence, of the *langue*, which calls for silence as a condition; and of the *unrepeatable utterance*, which instead calls for taciturnity. Silence enables perception of sounds and of the distinctive traits of language (phonemes), therefore *recognition*, *identification* of the *repeatable elements* of discourse, the elements forming *langue*, at the level of phonology, syntax, semantics. Instead, taciturnity is the condition for understanding the sense of the *single utterance* in its *unrepeatability*. Silence is connected to physical entities, to sound, and to abstract units of the *langue* as a system: phonemes, morphemes, propositions, sentences; taciturnity concerns concrete verbal communication, the utterance in its unrepeatable aspects.

To deal only with the elements of the *langue* and of the sentence means to recognise silence as the only condition of the verbal sign. This tells of the incapacity to enter the space of *taciturnity*, which is the space of the utterance in its unrepeatability, and of the interpretant of responsive understanding: the space of intertextuality and of the dialogic of utterances.

Philosophy of language distinguishes itself from linguistics which takes the *langue* and the sentence as its objects. The objects of linguistics stand out against the background of silence, which enables perception of sounds and identification of verbal signs. Silence is not only the condition for objects to be taken into account by linguistics; it is also their limit, with respect to which all that presents itself as other is not relevant and is excluded.

Both taxonomical and generative-transformational linguistics (Noam Chomsky)—which shifts its attention from the elements of language (*langue*) and of the sentence to the relations that generate sentences—are part of the same orientation, one that neglects the relation of responsive understanding among utterances and their sense (for a critique of Chomskyian linguistics, see Ponzio, 1992, 2012); utterances and sense, unlike sentences and their meaning, do not have silence as their condition of possibility, but require taciturnity instead as the condition of their very production.

Consequently, taxonomical and generative-transformational linguistics is unable to account for the *utterance*, for its dialogical character, its essential destination to responsive understanding. This also means they do not account for the different forms of taciturnity, for indirect, deferred, allusive, parodical, ironical speaking, for ambiguity and polysemy, implicit sense, the capacity for shifting sense; even less so for *literary writing* which is construed on forms of taciturnity: the writer, as Bakhtin says in his essay, "From Notes Made in 1970 –71", does not use language directly, but has the gift of indirect speaking, of taciturnity.

Based on the notions of systems of rules and codes, and moving only in the space that goes from sound to sign, identified phonologically, syntactically, semantically, that is, the space of silence, this type of linguistics, linguistics of the code, is *linguistics of silence.*

Mutual exchange in methodological and terminological terms between linguistics of the sentence and mathematical information theory is not incidental. The expression "code linguistics" recalls this exchange. As information theory, this type of linguistics only recognizes "noise" as the obstacle disturbing interpretation of verbal signs, which is interpretation reduced to de-codification, recognition, identification. Once the utterance is reduced to a relation between code and message, proper to signals, "noise" (in the sense of information theory) is the only disturbance possible, deriving from an imperfection in the communication channel, or interference from the external context, or lack of restrictive rules between code and message leading to ambiguity. Fundamentally, "noise" is interruption of silence, which is the condition of perception of the signal.

The problem of sense goes beyond the limits of code linguistics, the linguistics of silence, to concern linguistic reflection that is not limited to language considered as a code, nor to linguistic relations among the elements forming the system of language, or among elements of a single utterance, or among sentences, and their transformational processes (from "deep structures" to "surface structures").

Instead, linguistics based on listening, linguistics of the utterance, addresses dialogical relations among verbal signs, as utterances and interpretants of responsive understanding. The background of these dialogical relationships is taciturnity. Instead, silence, the absence of noise, constitutes the physical condition of the utterance, the minimal condition that concerns the dimension of signality, the dimension of recognition and identification; but this minimal condition is not sufficient for the utterance to subsist as a sign and be endowed with sense. Taciturnity is both the situation, the position at the origin of the utterance, and the situation, the position of its reception.

The condition of the word's freedom is taciturnity, a choice made my the speaker; it foresees violation of taciturnity and not simply violation of silence; the word's freedom presupposes *taciturnity as a listening position.*

From taciturnity at the origin of the utterance as free choice, to taciturnity that the utterance demands, to which it turns, to which it entrusts itself and which welcomes the utterance in listening: this is the movement of the utterance. Between these two positions in taciturnity there is no substantial difference: taciturnity at the origin of the utterance takes a listening position; and the utterance is effectively a response, an interpretant of responsive understanding. Vice versa, if listening is effectively to be achieved, taciturnity, a listening position, is in turn the beginning of responsive understanding which, if verbal, takes the form of an utterance.

"Linguistics of silence" corresponds to a *social communication system dominated by silence.* As code linguistics, it is the expression of real centripetal forces in the social. Monologism, the tendency to univocality, lowering of the sign to the level of signality, according to a relation of equal exchange between signifier and signified, belong to the linguistics of silence only in a secondary sense: *in the first place they belong to the social system that has chosen silence as the background of speaking,* of which linguistics of silence is only an expression.

Homologation of the communicative universe reduces listening to wanting to hear, it reduces the spaces of taciturnity, in which *freedom of listening is as necessary as freedom of the word*: consequently, homologation of the communicative universe invests the verbal sign solely with the conventional characteristics of the signal, or with the natural characteristics of sound.

Closed in a universe of silence and of the obligation to speak according to certain laws, conventions, habits, the sign loses its capacity for challenge, provocation, with respect to identity, to the closed totality; it loses the possibility of questioning what would seem to be solid, definitive, as though it were natural. Instead, this is what the sign can do thanks to its taciturnity, by its not collaborating with the *closed universe of discourse*, by withdrawing from monologism, by its excess with respect to the logic of equal exchange between signifier and signified, between interpreted and interpretant.

Taciturnity is only possible in the *human world*, as Bakhtin says, in the passage cited "From Notes Made in 1970 - 71", referred to above. To limit the sign to the space of silence, separating it from taciturnity and freedom of listening, listening open to polysemy, deprives the sign of its *human* character, thus rendering it mechanical and pseudonatural, making it oscillate between *conventionality of the signal* and *naturalness of sound*, *naturalness of what makes no claim to sense*.

Philosophy of language in *semioethic perspective* keeps account of the connection between *Signs*, *Language* and *Listening*, as in this book by Susan Petrilli. As such, for what concerns the verbal, it recovers those aspects of language and communication that the "linguistics of silence" expels, thus expelling the relation to the *other*, the *alterity* relationship, costitutive of the life of the word. Understood in a semioethic key, philosophy of language considers the forms and practices of verbal language that most showcase dialogism, listening, hospitality, the welcome towards the word of the other.

Ⅳ. Listening to the Other: Literary Writing and Translating

As an utterance, the word expresses that which is not already thematized in signs, in other words, neither the object nor the objective of the message, understood as a postal package passing from sender to receiver.

Linguistics of the utterance benefits from the contribution that may come from literary texts, where the utterance is depicted at its best, and from translation, even among different languages (dialects, special languages, etc.) within the same historical-natural language, in addition to translation *across* different historical-natural languages, where the aim is to say "almost the same thing" (Eco, 2003), or, achieve a text recognizable as "the same other" (Petrilli, 2001, 2012a, pp. 231 - 285; 2020b).

Under this aspect, the practices of *literary writing* and of *translation* are particularly interesting (see in the book we are here presenting, § 3, "Writing as the Play of Musement", in chapter II, "Inventing New Worlds", and chapter VII, "Listening, Otherness and Translation").

Taciturnity is the condition of listening—the taciturnity of listening speaks—reached at the highest degree in literary writing. As Bakhtin avers, to valorize listening as the art of the word, we need *verbal art*, literary taciturnity, "secondary" "complex" discourse genres, the genres of the indirect, objectified, depicted word; with respect to "primary and simple genres of everyday discourse, we need the *writer*, the *écrivain* (Roland Barthes distinguishes between *écrivains* and *écrivants*)".

This is where philosophy of language as the art of listening, linguistics of the utterance and literary writing encounter each other (see Petrilli, 2007).

Functional, productive, necessary and necessarily oriented language "institue pour l'écrivain une condition déchirée" (Barthes, 1953, vol. 1, p. 218). "La Littérature devient l'Utopie du langage" (*ibid.*, p. 224): the closing line in *Le degré zéro de l'écriture.*

Writing evades the arrogance of discourse: arrogance that imposes itself even in claims to the "natural" "obvious", to "being right" (*ibid.*, p. 202). The only action *other* from the arrogance of assertive discourse is the transition from discourse to writing, the practice of *writing*: the Neutral of writing, desire of writing. Writing is a movement of escape from the *ideosphere*, from dominant ideologic; because it does not assert a conviction, idea, thought, but writing itself, writing as writing. This is what the writer calls "working", but in an unproductive, "perverse" sense, an intransitive *nonfunctional* sense. With Blanchot this is the time of the "other night" with respect to the time of the "madness of the day", a function of the ever expanding reproduction of the identical (Levinas, 1975).

All concepts, as Barthes says in *Le Neutre* (2002), arise as *identification of the non-identical.* He defines the concept as *force reducing difference.* To refuse this reduction, we must say no to the concept, not use it. How then to speak? Barthes's response: "*Par métaphores.* Substituer la métaphore au concept: écrire". Barthes's own work is inseparable from reflection on writing, on the *writer-scrivener* relationship.

Metaphor is not only a rhetorical figure—as already claimed by Giambattista Vico, in *La scienza nuova* (1725) —but the motor that re/generates sense. Vico establishes a connection between metaphor and "logique poétique" (Ponzio, 2006c, 2010, 2016). He avers that tropes are the corollary of poetic logic, of which metaphor is the most luminous, necessary and frequent (Vico, *Principi di scienza* nuova, Chapter 2).

But a connection can also be made with César Chesneau Dumarsais's conception of language (Petrilli, Ponzio, 2019). In his *Traité des tropes* (1730), Dumarsais asserts that metaphor is the "figure" that prevails in inventive speech and imagination; he observes that "figure" here is already a metaphor in itself. "Bien loin", as he claims, "que les figures s'éloignent du langage ordinaire des hommes, ce serait au contraire les façons de parler sans figures, qui s'en éloigneraient, s'il est possible de faire un discours où il n'y eût que des expressions sans figures". The idea is that "poetic logic" (Vico) is present in ordinary language, as also claimed by Bakhtin and members of the Bakhtin Circle (cf. Ponzio, 2014), who describe a relation of similarity between "discourse in life" and "discourse in poetry", by contrast with the Russian formalists who juxtapose ordinary language and poetic language.

Semiotics according to the tradition delineated by John Locke, Charles Peirce, Victoria Welby (whom Susan Petrilli duly reestablishes in the sphere of sign and language studies), Giovanni Vailati (on the relation between Welby and Vailati, see Ponzio 1990), and more recently Charles Morris, Roman Jakobson, Thomas Sebeok, Ferruccio Rossi-Landi, contributes to evidencing the role of metaphor, therefore the iconic dimension of sign in innovative thinking (Petrilli, Ponzio, 2010, 2012). Vico's influence on semiotics in the twentieth century is examined by Sebeok (2000); and for what concerns linguistics by Marcel Danesi (2000).

In Sebeok and Danesi's terminology, *similarity* in metaphor is not "cohesive similarity", but "connective similarity", also named *elective similarity*, *similarity by affinity*, *attraction* (Petrilli, Ponzio, 2018). Similarity in this case does not concern what presents itself as belonging to the same category, as identical, but, on the contrary, it concerns that which is different, recalcitrant to cohesive form, that cannot be assimilated, that in the relation remains irreducibly other: this is similarity in *alterity*, something altogether different from similarity through identity.

As regards the relation between concept and metaphor, we distinguish therefore between two logics: on the one hand, cohesive, assemblative logic of the concept, which proceeds through genres and species, paradigms and oppositions, assimilating what cannot be assimilated (singularity); and, on the other hand, connective logic, association by attraction, Vico's *poetic logic*, which flourishes through metaphor.

With Peirce metaphor is an expresison of "iconicity" and "firstess", it is founded in the "agapastic" relation (Petrilli, 2012a, pp. 190 – 231). In the logic of elective affinity, "agapasm" (Peirce), similarity leaves the terms of the relation in their alterity, in their irreducible singularity.

The relation between language and utterance, *langue* and *parole*, is not a direct relation, a dualistic relation; nor is communication reduced to a dualistic relation between "sender" and "receiver". Both relations, that between *langue* and *parole*, and between "sender" and "receiver" pass through discourse genres. Every utterance, every verbal text necessarily belongs to a discourse genre. Not only do we always speak in a given language, but also in a given discourse genre.

In "The Problem of Speech Genres", Bakhtin (1986 [1952 – 53], pp. 60 – 102) analyzes discourse genre and had planned on writing a book on the topic. He distinguishes between primary and secondary genres, the genres of everyday life (official representation, social reality, roles, everyday interpersonal relations, the functional and objective word) and secondary genres, indirect or complex genres, that portray the former: these are the genres of literary depiction (*izobrazenie*), genres of the indirect word. Secondary genres evidence the word in its openness to the other's word, revealing how one's own word lives and flourishes thanks to the word of the other, thanks to reception of the other's word, its interpretation and transmission, to responsive understanding.

This is the reason why philosophy of language and "metalinguistics" (by comparison to "official linguistics"), a linguistics of listening, call for the relation with literary writing, in all its genres, and not only the novelistic genre. Reduction of Bakhtin's interest solely to the novelistic genre is another big limitation on interpretation of Bakhtinian thought.

The worst thing that can happen to the word, as stated above, is the lack of listening, the word subjected to wanting to hear, to interrogation. Instead, literary writing, an allusive, parodical, ironical form of taciturnity, a form of laughter, is perhaps today the form of writing that best asserts the rights of alterity, against homologation with identity as imposed by dominant communication. Literary writing, with its gaze "from the outside" (from an extralocalized, *exotopic* standpoint with respect to contemporaneity, in the time specific to literature, what Bakhtin calls the "great time"), by virtue of this distancing precisely, valorizes proximity, unindifference (Petrilli, 2012b). The writer not only participates in life, but loves it from the outside, with the love we all recognize as *true* love, love in its total nonfunctionality.

Literary writing and translation resemble each other because both involve oblivion of self and a great sense of hospitality as required of language, whether one's own or the others, not for self, but for others, the *other-author* in the case of the translator, the *other-hero* in the case of the writer.

The translator, as maintained by Susan Petrilli in *Lo stesso altro* (2001), does not employ indirect discourse to say what the other says, indirect discourse which, as a form of reported discourse, involves dominating over the other's word with one's own word; nor does the translator use direct discourse, which would simply mean to introduce the other's discourse with an "he says": and report the other's discourse word by word, in this case in the same historical natural language.

Instead, the translation speaks *as if* s/he were the other, in the form of indirect speech (because translation is interpretation) "masked", as claimed by Petrilli (2001), "as direct discourse". The relation between the original text and the target text is one of similarity, but that type of similarity that Peirce indicates as *iconic*. The iconic character of translation which Petrilli (2006, 2008, 2010) has contributed to evidencing in her writings on the theory and practice of translation (this is the character of icon which as in sacred images renders visible that which is invisible, precisely because the author has stepped aside) is effectively an essential aspect of the translational process, one that cannot be set aside to understand the rather complex relationship between a translation and the original.

Translation carries out an important role in the face of literary writing, that of making the writer visible, the writer who as a writer has chosen through taciturnity to make him/herself invisible; and, paradoxically, the writer is rendered visible by another who has also chosen *invisibility*, to not speak in his/her own name, the translator.

V. Listening, Tuning in

This is a matter of listening to the other, of tuning in: the recurring message in this book by Susan Petrilli.

Listening thus described concerns *symptoms* in presentday globalisation, that serve to identify different aspects of illness (in social relations, international relations, in the life of single individuals, in the spread and increase of different aggressive and pervasive forms of anthropization of the environment, of life generally over the planet). Petrilli looks towards a future for globalization as openness to the other, not based on the humanism of identity *which excludes the other's rights from human rights* (Petrilli, 2019b, 2019c), but on the *humanism of alterity* (Levinas), in full contrast to globalization devoted to its own destruction.

Susan Petrilli's book begins with a question, in the title of the first chapter, concerning the relation between "Semiosis and Life": *What lies in their future?* Her response: our present is the *future perfect of semiotics* (the title of a book by Caputo, Petrilli, Ponzio, published in 2006). The future of semiotics is decided today, not only the *science*, but also the *human species-specific capacity to use signs to reflect on signs and decide as a consequence.*

The problem is not simply of the theoretical order, given that semiotics is also implicated as semeiotics, as symtomatology. The life of signs and the signs of life, continuity of semiosis over the planet is decided today—never before has responsibility for the future and at once our capacity for destruction been so great. The human being as a "semiotic animal" is the only animal responsible for semiosis, for life, even more so the professional scholar of signs. Paraphrasing Terence: "As a student of signs, nothing in the life of signs is alien to me." (see Petrilli, 2012a, pp. 1 – 16)

As a unique event, as encounter, the utterance with its *dissymmetry* and *anarchy* resists unification, communion, community affiliation to partial, ethnic, national identities; it resists universalization with respect to the maximum, total, omnicomprehensive identity, that as *human race.*

Somebody is always "more human" than others and somebody "less human", "inhuman," as occurs in George Orwell's *Animal Farm*, where everybody is equal, but some are more equal or less equal than others. *Umano troppo disumano* (Human too inhuman) is the title of a book edited by me with Fabio de Leonardis (2008). *Humanitarian* wars, *humanitarian* military interventions: here, "human" and "humanitarian" derive from *homo*, a kind, class, system.

But another etimology, it too from Giambattista Vico, has "human" derive from *humanitas*, not from *homo* which while uniting us all, at once establishes the *human/inhuman* opposition. Instead, like *humilitas*, humility, *humanitas* can be made to derive from *humus*, earth.

This etimology does not defer to kind as in humankind, bringing us all together, eliminating singular differences, singularities, thus achieving a "uniform" "general" "official situation": not incidentally three military terms. In contrast to humanitarian military intervention and preventive war, *humanitas* appeals to the possibility, to the human commitment to *preventive peace* (Levinas, cf. Ponzio, 2009c).

Deriving from *humus*, *humanitas* evidences involvement, implication, absence of the boundaries that divide each single individual from the "natural" and "social" environment: use of inverted commas indicates a fictitious difference which we continue to establish because of habit, inertia, for reasons of convenience and opportunity.

The *human* sciences, those which most interest us here, including linguistics, should remember this second etimology. And semiotics should remember it, even if as *global semiotics* (Sebeok, 2001) it does not fail to address nonhuman signs beyond the human. *The human being is a semiotic animal*: consequently, semiotics could be indicated *as the most human of sciences*, not to glorify oneself, but to underline the semiotician's *enormous responsibility* as a student of signs.

(Translation from Italian into English by Susan Petrilli)

References:

Bakhtin, M. (1929). *Problemy tvorčestva Dostoevskogo.* Leningrad: Priboj; now in Bachtin e il suo circolo 2014: 1053 – 1423.

— (1963). *Problems of Dostoevsky's poetics.* (C. Emerson, Ed., Trans.). Minneapolis: University of Minnesota Press, 1984.

— (1965). *Tvorrčeestvo Fransua Rable i narodnaja kul'tura srednevekov'ja i Renessansa.* Moscow: Chudozevennaja literature; *L'opera di Rabelais e la cultura popolare* (M. Romano, Trans.). Turin: Einaudi, 1979; *Rabelais and His World* (H. Iswolsky, Trans.). Bloomington: Indiana University, Press, 1984.

— (1986). *Speech Genres and Other Late Essays* (V. W. McGee, Trans.). In C. Emerson & M. Holquist (Eds.). Austin: University of Texas Press.

Bakhtin, M. e il suo circolo (2014). *Opere 1919 – 1930*, ed., comment, Intro., vii – xlviii (A.

Ponzio, Trans. in collab. L. Ponzio). bilingual Russian/Italian edition. Milan: Bompiani.

Barthes, R. (1953). *Le degré zero de l'écriture.* In Barthes, *Œuvres completes* . Vol. I. Paris: Seuil.

—(2002). *Le Neutre.* Cours et séminaires au Collège de France (1977 – 1978). Paris: Seuil.

Caputo, C., Petrilli, S., & Ponzio, A. (2006). *Dieci tesi per il futuro anteriore della semiotica.* Milan: Mimesis.

Chomsky, N. (1985). *Knowledge of language.* New York: Praeger.

Eco, U. (1984). *Semiotica e filosofia del linguaggio.* Turin: Einaudi.

— (2003). *Dire quasi la stessa cosa.* Milan: Bompiani.

Danesi, M. (2001). *Lingua, metafora, concetto.* Intro. A. Ponzio, 7 – 22. Bari: Edizioni dal Sud.

Deely, J., Petrilli, S., & Ponzio, A. (2005). *The semiotic animal.* Ottawa: Legas.

De Leonardis, F., Ponzio, A. (Eds.). (2008). *Umano troppo disumano.* Rome/Milan: Meltemi and Mimesis.

Levinas, E. (1975). *Sur Blanchot.* Montpellier: Fata Morgana; *Su Maurice Blanchot*(A. Ponzio, Trans., Intro.). Bari: Palomar, 2015.

— (2020). *La filosofia del linguaggio.* J. Ponzio (Ed.). Lecce: Pensa Multimedia.

Locke, J. (1690). *Essay concerning human understanding.* Milano: Bompiani, 2004.

Petrilli, S. (Ed.) (2001). *Lo stesso altro.* Rome/Milan: Meltemi and Mimesis.

— (2006). Meaning, metaphor, and interpretation: modeling new worlds. *Perspectives on metaphor. Semiotica* 161 – 1/4, 75 – 119.

— (Ed.) (2007). *Philosophy of language as the art of listening.* Bari: Edizioni dal Sud.

— (2008). Iconicity in translation. On similarity, alterity and dialogism in the relation among signs, *sign crossroads in global perspective. The American Journal of Semiotics.* Intro. & Ed. by John Deely, Volume 24.4, 237 – 302.

— (2010). Translation, iconicity, and dialogism. In C. Ljungberg et al. (Eds.), *Signergy*, 367 – 386. Amsterdam: John Benjamins.

— (2012a). *Expression and interpretation in language.* New Brunswick: Transaction.

— (2012b). *Altrove e altrimenti. Con Bachtin.* Milan: Mimesis.

— (2016). *The global world and its manifold faces. Otherness as the basis of communication.* Bern: Zurig, Peter Lang.

— (2019a). Peirce and welby: For an ethics of the man-sign relation. In T. Jappy (Ed.), *Bloomsbury Companion to Contemporary Peircean Semiotics*, 359 – 390. London: Bloomsbury.

— (Ed.) (2019b). *Diritti umani e diritti altrui.* Milan: Mimesis.

— (2019c). Citizenship between identity and alterity. For a semioethic analysis of the European Constitution. In M. Ellis (Ed.), *Critical global semiotic. understanding sustainable transformational citizenship*, 84 – 95. London: Routledge.

— (2020b). Translation, Ideology and social practice. In C. Ji, & S. Laviosa(Eds.), *Oxford handbook of translation and social practices*. London: Oxford University Press.

Petrilli, S., Ponzio, A. (2000). *Philosophy of language, art and answerability in Mikhail Bakhtin*. Ottawa: Legas.

— (2001). *Thomas Sebeok and the signs of life*. London: Icon Books.

— (2002). Sign vehicles for semiotic travels: Two new handbooks. *Semiotica*, 141 – 1/4, 203 – 350.

—(2003). *Semioetica*. Roma: Meltemi.

— (2005). *Semiotics unbounded*. Toronto: Toronto University Press.

— (2007). Semiotics today. From global semiotics to semioethics, a dialogic response. *Signs-International Journal of Semiotics*, November 2007, 29 – 127.

— (2010). Iconic features of translation. In J. Queiroz, & D. Aguiar(Eds.). *Applied semiotics/ Semiotique appliquée* 24, 9 *Translating culture / Traduire la culture*.

— (2012). Iconicity, otherness and translation. *Chinese Semiotic Studies*, 7, 1, 11 – 26.

— (2016). *Lineamenti di semiotica e filosofia del linguaggio*. Perugia: Guerra.

— (2018). "Difference and similarity in the I-Other relation." Plenary lecture delivered at International Conference *Differences and Similarities*, "Semiosis in Communication" series, Southeast European Center for Semiotic Studies, University of Bucharest, 14 – 16 June 2018, forthcoming in relative Proceedings.

— (2019a). *Dizionario, Enciclopedia, Traduzione tra César Chesneau Dumarsais e Umberto Eco*. Paris. L'Harmattan; Alberobello (Bari): AGA.

— (2019b). *Identità e alterità. Per una semioetica della comunicazione globale*. Milan: Mimesis.

— (2019c). Identity and alterity of the text in translation. A semioethic approach", *International Journal of Semiotics and Visual Rhetoric*, 3, 1, January – June, 46 – 65.

Ponzio, A. (1990a). *Man as a sign* (S. Petrilli, Intro., Trans., Ed.). Berlin: Mouton de Gruyter.

— (1990b). Theory of meaning and theory of knowledge: Vailati and Lady Welby. In Walter Schmitz (Ed.), *Essays in Significs*, 165 – 178. Amsterdam: John Benjamins.

— (1990c). Bakhtinian alterity and the search for identity in europe today. In R. Barsky, & M. Holquist (Eds.). *Bakhtin and otherness. Discours social*, 1 – 2: 217 – 228.

— (1992). *Production linguistique et idéologie sociale*. Candiac (Canada): Editions Balzac.

— (1993). *Signs, dialogue and ideology* (S. Petrilli, Trans., Ed.). Amsterdam: John Benjamins.

— (2004). *Elogio dell'infunzionale*. Milan: Mimesis.

— (2006a). The I questioned: Emmanuel Levinas and the critique of occidental reason, *Subject*

Matters, vol. 3, 1, 2006: 1 – 42, texts by A. Z Newton, M. B. Smith, R. Bernasconi. G. Ward, R. Burggraeve, B. Bergo, W. P. Simmons, A. Aronowicz, 43 – 127.

— (2006b). *The dialogic nature of sign.* Ottawa: Legas.

— (2006c). Metaphor and poetic logic in Vico. In F. Nuessel(Ed.), *Perspectives on metaphor. Semiotica.* 161 – 1/4: 231 – 248.

— (2009°). *Da dove verso dove. La parola altra nella comunicazione globale.* Perugia: Guerra Edizioni.

— (2009b). *L'écoute de l'autre.* Paris: L'Harmattan.

— (2009c). *Emmanuel Levinas. Globalisation ad Preventive Peace.* Ottawa: Legas.

— (2010°). *Rencontres de paroles.* Paris: Alain Baudry & Cie.

— (2010b). Metaphoric image and iconic likeness. *Semiotica* 181 – 1/4, 275 – 281.

— (2011). *La filosofia del linguaggio. Segni, valori, ideologie.* Bari: Giuseppe Laterza.

— (2012). *Línguistica Chomskyana e ideología social.* Curitiba (Brasil): Editora Ufpr (Univesidad Federal do Paranά, Brasil).

— (2014). *A revolusão bakhtiniana.* Saô Paol (Brasil): Contexto.

— (2015). *Tra semiotica e letteratura. Introduzione a Michail Bachtin.* Milan: Bompiani.

— (2016). Language, mind, and culture. In L. Tateo(Ed.). *Giambattsia Vico and the new psychological science*, Foreword by Jaan Valsiner, 151 – 171. New Brunswick: Transaction.

— (2018). *Il linguaggio e le lingue.* Perugia: Guerra.

—(2019a). *Alterità e identità. Con Emmanuel Levinas.* Milan: Mimesis

— (2019b). Logic and dialogic in Peirce's conception of argumentation. In T. Jappy(Ed.). *Bloomsbury companion to contemporary peircean semiotics*, 235 – 252. London: Bloomsbury.

Ponzio, L. (2020) (Ed.). *La persistenza dell'Altro.* Lecce: Pensa Multimedia.

Sebeok, T. (1990) *I think I am a verb: More contributions to the doctrine of signs.* New York and London: Plenum Press; *Penso di essere un verbo*(S. Petrilli, Trans., Ed. & Intro), 11 – 18. Palermo: Sellerio.

— (2000). Some reflections of vico in semiotics. In D. G. Lockwood, P. H. Fries, & J. E. Copeland (Eds.). *Fuctional approaches to language, culture and cognition.* Amsterdam: John Benjamins, 555 – 568.

— (2001a). *Signs*, Toronto: Toronto University Press; *Segni* (S. Petrilli, Trans., Ed. & Intro.), 11 – 43. Rome: Carocci, 2003.

— (2001b). *Global semiotics.* Bloomington: Indiana University Press.

Sebeok, T., & Marcel, D. (2000). *The forms of meaning.* Berlin: Mouton de Gruyter.

Vailati, G. (2000). *Il metodo della filosofia*, intro. A. Ponzio, v – vli. Bari: Graphis.

Vico, G. (1999). *Scienza nuova*, in *Opere (Vol. 1, 2)*. In A. Battistini (Ed.). Milan: Mondadori. [published as *Principi di scienza nuova.* In F. Nicolini, & C. Ricciardi(Eds),

1953; ried. Turin: Einaudi, 1976.]

Author:

Augusto Ponzio, Italian semiotician, Professor Emeritus in philosophy and theory of languages, University of Bari Aldo Moro. His research interests are Semiotics, Marxist semiotics, etc.

作者简介：

奥古斯托·庞齐奥，意大利符号学家，巴里大学语言哲学荣休教授，研究兴趣包括符号学、马克思主义符号学等。

Email: augustoponzio@ libero. it

无法与无需抵达之象：贡布里希艺术思想核心理念讨论

孙金燕

摘　要：贡布里希的艺术研究坚持再现逻辑与理性原则。他认为艺术不是对世界的像似，也非对制作者内心世界的描绘，而是对符号原型功能主义的再现。在此理念下，他创立了艺术图式、错觉主义、等效性等典范性概念，阐释艺术与现实的双向辨认关系，以此为柏拉图模仿说阴影下的艺术正名，且对放弃艺术图式、非理性的现代艺术的价值，表达了他的质疑。

关键词：贡布里希，功能主义再现，图式－矫正，双向辨认

An Unreachable and Unnecessary Image: On the Core Concepts of E. H. Gombrich's Artistic Thought

Sun Jinyan

Abstract: E. H. Gombrich insists on the logic of representation and the principle of reason in his artistic research. He advocates the idea that art is neither a resemblance of the world nor a depiction of the composer's inner world, but a functionalist representation of the sign's prototype. Following this basic idea, he proposes such classic concepts as artistic schema, illusionism and equivalence, and expounds on the bidirectional recognition between art and reality, to reclaim the value of art concealed under the shadow of Plato's theory of "imitation". In addition, he queries the value of "irrational" modern art that has abandoned artistic schema.

Keywords: E. H. Gombrich, Functionalist representation, Schema-correction,

Bidirectional recognition

DOI: 10.13760/b.cnki.sam.202002003

有一件关于马蒂斯的逸事可以概括这一切，贡布里希在《艺术与错觉》中也引用了这段逸事。一位妇人看过这幅肖像后告诉他这个女人的手臂太长，他回答道："夫人，您弄错了，这不是女人，这是一幅画。"（贡布里希，2015a，p. xxi）

贡布里希似乎格外偏爱这一逸事，除在《艺术与错觉》中特别示例，事实上，他在其他著作中也反复援引过这一案例，以讨论图像与符号的关系和心理定向问题（贡布里希，2013a，p. 144；2016，p. 217）。究其原因，概源于他认为艺术只在艺术的范围之内抵达。这可以从两个层面来理解：其一是关于艺术制作的认知，艺术不创造自然，只创造（图像）符号，固然这种符号能引发关于世界"真实"的错觉；其二是关于艺术欣赏的契约，逼真必须在媒介的范围之内实现，一旦越出了这个框架，我们就在艺术的范围之外了。

诚如马蒂斯关于肖像与女人关系的辩解，贡布里希的反复提示，同样希冀说明艺术图像与自然之象之间属于无法且无需抵达的关系，这与他在众多的研究实践中以艺术图式、错觉主义、等效性等典范性概念所彰显与坚持的艺术理性原则与再现逻辑，是一以贯之的。

一、从"如画"到"入画"：符号原型的功能主义再现

"没有艺术这回事，只有艺术家而已"（贡布里希，2015b，p. 15），这是贡布里希最广为关注的一句论断，可视为这位艺术史家的研究立场：相比于艺术的起源及价值等，他更关心与艺术家相关的艺术的具体生产。并且，他坚持一种观念，即艺术家制作形象与他看待世界的方式有关，而不同时代语境下，艺术家看待世界的方式受不同文化压力的支配，也即意味着艺术家所制作的艺术品在视觉特征上与特殊的文化需求相关。

下文引用的贡布里希关于东西方艺术的线性梳理，或许有将复杂多元的艺术发展纳入简单逻辑的嫌疑，但对于理解其艺术思想却具有效性。

> 埃及人大画他们知道（knew）确实存在的东西，希腊人大画他们看见（saw）的东西；而在中世纪，艺术家还懂得在画中表现他感觉（felt）到的东西。（贡布里希，2015b，p. 165）

追逐永恒的埃及艺术，几乎三千年坚守“概念性”原则，绘制对世界的知识记忆，不只呈现人和自然的形象，还呈现这些形象的意义，如在形式上，避开不能一眼即明的角度，赋予形象侧面图以保证所呈现对象的信息完整。希腊艺术则起步于对埃及艺术的矫正，信任眼睛的“发现”，不断进行获取逼真效果的视觉实践，由此带来光线表现、空间征服、立体外形塑造乃至人物内心的刻画，最具代表性的希腊雕像又呈现充满生气的人体的全部优美，造型力图展现心灵的活动。基督教入主欧洲的中世纪艺术，则重新返回对“概念性”的追求，重在讲述基督神圣故事，手法上多以头部有层次的光线和色彩暗示圣徒的虔敬心境，以弯曲的线条和衣衫的皱褶暗示圣徒受到灵感激励时的激动等，以求直观表达神圣谦抑的要义。

贡布里希以所知与所见为主线来勾勒艺术的发展脉络，细数其在历史的上下文中的运行规律，主要是为了标明艺术在实用原则的支配下对社会文化需求的反应，也标明艺术的再现不是建立在相似性的基础上，而是缘于其承担的功能。如在木马游戏中，棍棒与马的共同因素是功能而不是形式，“图像只是作为替代物意义上的‘再现’”（贡布里希，2018，pp. 17－18）。

艺术与木马游戏相类。埃及艺术及中世纪艺术依据对世界的知识而记录形象，与法术和宗教有关，图像是具有神力的现实替代物，而非现实的虚像；希腊艺术家对自然的理想化（idealizing）呈现，是在平衡类型化形象与个别化形象的前提下才有的结果，“倒不是因为希腊人比别人健康，比别人美丽——那样想毫无道理——而是因为当时的艺术已经达到那样一种境界”（贡布里希，2015b，p. 105），可理解为是对美的觉醒的境界。

这种功能主义的再现，可以得到更广范围的证明。追溯至原始文化，则有如萨满教之鼓①上的符号使其具有便携式祭坛的功能，“通过这些图画萨满对天人、属灵祖先或辅助神发出恳求”（米哈伊·霍帕尔，2020，p. 44）；中国巫祝盛行的殷商时期，“铸鼎象物”是为了“通过控制敌人的图像来控制敌人”（谢清果，张丹，2018，p. 81）；《周易》卦画取象能指示“现实中某种事物的运行发展规律”，缘于它是神意的替代（苏智，2018，p. 120）；延展至当下，仍有如三岁小儿一本正经的线条涂鸦，或许是对自己日常所享用糖果、糕点等的手账式记录，甚而有时也意味着那就是他的妈妈。

功能主义主导下的图像制作，其绘制路径依据记忆中的知识，不能与外

---

① 萨满鼓，鼓面圆如宇宙，上以太阳、月亮、金星等指示天宇，下以冥界之王的七个黑色铁头儿子指示下界，中以十字纹为区隔，标志着祭祀仪式迷狂之旅的起点。

界世界做一一对应的联系，甚至不是制作者内心世界的描绘（贡布里希，2018，pp. 13－19）。与之相对，形式上的相似显得并不那么重要。希腊历史学家希罗多德（Herodotus）即发现埃及人将潘神（Pan）再现为长着山羊的头和腿，然而它只是被制作成它现在所示的样子，因为埃及人并不相信它会看上去不同于其他诸神（贡布里希，2013a，p. 141）。而马奈《隆香赛马》（1865）中的斑点，也与马的外形相去甚远。

当然，这也并不意味着艺术是在肆无忌惮地凭空捏造。艺术家对艺术品的制作需在符号原型的象征域内进行，道理如同乐队演奏所依循的乐谱需依据乐谱系统制成，日常交际语需在话语系统内才能被理解一样。在绘画艺术中，风景画可对此做出较好示例。

面对如画风景，画家以其眼睛取景并将其转换至画布，调色板上的颜料依次转化为画布上的明暗色域，但摹写再现之景就是画家眼前的景物吗？借用温斯特·丘吉尔对此的理解，可以较为清晰地辨析其中的区别："它已从光线转为颜色。它传给画布的是一种密码。直到它跟画布上其他各种东西之间的关系完全得当时，这种密码才能被译解，意义才能彰明，也才能反过来再从单纯的颜料翻译成光线。不过这时候的光线已不再是自然之光，而是艺术之光了。"（贡布里希，2015a，p. 34）

艺术的形式是基于对功能的适应产生的，贡布里希曾以康斯特布尔的《达德姆溪谷》（1802）来细致印证视觉"暗示"（suggesting）提供象征"关系"（relationships）以达到映射自然的魔法（贡布里希，2015a，pp. 31－34）。符号原型经由艺术代码处理后仍能被辨认，缘于艺术代码为信息理解提供视觉暗示，比如作品所再现的是此世界可能存在的物体、可能被观看的角度、可能发生的情境等，再现之景与眼前之景或许不同，但它们都提供关于这个世界特征的正确信息。也就是说，艺术的功能性再现为自然编码，是让我们辨认出现实，而非回忆现实。

二、是否可以信任我们的眼睛：艺术图式与马奈的目光

艺术关于可见世界的知识，似乎是其一切难题的根源。在坚持古典文化传统的贡布里希看来，希腊艺术无疑是人类精神文明的高峰，而最为他津津乐道的是，希腊艺术对眼睛所见世界的关注，看上去像是一场对概念化制像的知识运作的逃离，尽管事实上，知识一直如影随形。诸多理论家为此专门提出，要将知识置之度外，让眼睛行使记录世界的职能，从而使得大自然能

自陈身世，比如约翰·拉斯金关于“纯真之眼”（the innocence of the eye）的表述：

> 绘画的全部技术效果倚靠我们恢复不妨称为眼睛的纯真的东西；也就是说，恢复的是对那些平面色迹的儿童般的知觉，这种知觉仅限于色迹本身，不要意识到它们的寓意所在——就像一个突然被赋予视力的盲人看见它们一样。……由于我们已经得出一些结论，涉及某些色彩的含义，我们就总是以为自己实际看见了其实仅是我们所知的东西，对自己已经知道如何解释的那些符号的真实面貌几乎毫无意识。（贡布里希，2015a，pp. 261－262）

轻装上阵，初见世界，当然会是一趟视知觉的惊奇之旅，但“纯真之眼”真的可靠吗？贡布里希给出的答案是否定的。至少在两个层面上，知识必然介入观看：

其一，观看并非单纯的色觉刺激，视网膜对信息的处理受知识的矫正。贡布里希依据光学学者的实验对此做出提示：视网膜并非通过单独的光线刺激来捕获视觉印象，而是对光线的相互关系做出反应，这个过程需要信息分类，经由知识的改造。我们或许都有相关的经验，当戴上粉红色眼镜时，出于对世界假设的冲突，视觉会使用对立的色调来平衡，企图重建正常颜色，于是当脱下粉红色眼镜时，我们会发现世界短暂地染上了绿色（贡布里希，2013a，p. 113）。与此相类，若没有对传入信息基于知识的登记、归档、分类，那个突获视觉的盲人体验到的不过是一个混沌的世界。并且，即便真有所谓的“纯真之眼”，那在他观看下的绘画艺术，便非阳光下的青黄色草地，而应是黄绿色的颜料。

文学亦可对此提供例证。毛姆的《月亮和六便士》以后印象派画家高更的逸事来讲述理想和现实的取舍问题，小说如此命名，正因为在大多数人的视觉归类中，月亮和一枚六便士的银币大小相当；再如伍尔夫的经典小说《墙上的斑点》，“我”之所以能将斑点视作旗帜、红色的骑士、夏天的玫瑰花瓣、古冢、钉进墙里已经两百年的钉头等，缘于知识的引领，事实上，那不过是一只蜗牛。

其二，艺术的创作过程受知识的影响。贡布里希将其归纳为艺术的图式，是时代语境下的艺术的惯例。艺术家以一种积极的态度在惯例中绘制世界，在既有的图式范围内对其吸收与修正，情况类似于 T. S. 艾略特以“容器”(receptacle)[①]（艾略特，2012，p. 7）一词指示诗人的个人才能在传统中的作为，主要是将个人化的体验纳入不断在调整和发展完善的艺术的整体体系当中，去延续一种历史，而并非为了创造一种传统，“因为对艺术描绘的研究至少表明了以下这一点：你无法凭空创作出一个忠实的图像。只要你在其他图画中看见过，你就必定已经学会了这种诀窍”（贡布里希，2015a，p. 74）。

考察自然主义艺术传统中的西方艺术，会发现一系列至高无上的技术公约——短缩法，透视原则，对光、空间、质感的表现，甚至包括对人类情感的掌握等（Gombrich，1969，pp. 68 - 104），它们让艺术行为不断回溯传统中的经典标准，比如莱奥纳多、拉斐尔、米开朗琪罗的艺术成就受益于乌切洛、马萨乔的艺术技巧，而乌切洛、马萨乔又受到了乔托的影响，乔托亦非横空出世，在他那里仍能看出契马布埃的手法的影子。每一件伟大的艺术品，甚至是每一位伟大的艺术家，都是艺术传统锁链中的一环，虽然导向未来，但也回顾过往。

这当然让艺术避开知识而复制自然无异于天方夜谭，但印象主义艺术常常被视为其中较为成功的叛逆者，贡布里希甚至将印象派的探索与希腊艺术相提并论，“马内（即马奈，编者注）及其追随者在色彩处理方面发动了一场革命，几乎可以媲美希腊人在形式表现方面发动的革命”（贡布里希，2015b，p. 514），但他们果真能摈除知识的视觉改造吗?

如果说过去的艺术倾向是看见他要画的，那印象派画家则宣称要画他所看见的。为此，以马奈为代表的印象派画家采用相对纯粹的色彩、特殊的光照与亮度形式等，以处理运动的形象、户外的色彩等，标示其绘画的立场是“画其所见”。

马奈的这种绘画特点为受现象学影响的福柯所关注。1971 年，米歇尔·福柯专门在突尼斯做了一场讲座，对马奈的 13 幅绘画作品进行评论，“因为在对绘画的历史或深化包装习以为常的眼光下，现在的表象具有某种唐突、震撼的东西，它要求一个被还原为‘是其所是’的世界。马奈用前所未有的努力提出的，是诸物的沉默、不透明和神秘的在场，当在场回归本质时，绘画就指明这种在场”（福柯，2009，p. 69）。如同现象学所强调的，必先看到显现的东西所给出的现象，才可能声称“面对实事本身”（倪梁康，2006，

---

① 原文：The poet's mind is in fact a receptacle for seizing and storing up numberless feelings, phrases, images, which remain there until all the particles which can unite to form a new compound are present together.

p. 21)，福柯所说的“在场”当然有多重指向，其中之一必然与马奈对“所见”的尊重有关。

但马奈的诸种突破，在绘画史上同样有迹可循。《草地上的午餐》(1863）的经典三角稳定构图，取自马尔坎托尼奥·拉伊蒙迪《帕里斯的裁判》(约1515)；《阳台》(1868—1869）对户外强光隐没室内形象的探索，则多像是对戈雅在其《阳台群像》(约1810—1815）中所做试验的深入。贡布里希将其对传统艺术图式的习得梳理得更为清晰：“他有意识地从前拉斐尔派画家所摈弃的大师的传达传统中寻求灵感，那个传统开始于威尼斯画派大师乔尔乔内和提香，经过委拉斯克斯到19世纪的戈雅成功地在西班牙坚持下去。”(贡布里希，2015b，p. 514)

可以说，宣称记录当下所见世界的印象派只是更换了探索再现自然的角度，却并没有从根本上偏离古希腊即已确立的制像传统，驱除知识不过是一种错觉，或想象。

三、观看的本分：对再现的功能主义的恰当体认

既然图像是对世界的功能主义再现，那观看者如何从艺术作品提示的信息中提取恰当的解释，也便成了贡布里希的艺术研究较为关注的话题。观看需要沉浸，以愿意相信眼前的一切都是真的为前提，只有这样才能顺利读解艺术家的意向。对此，贡布里希信任文化史家约翰·赫伊津哈在《游戏的人》中提供的“游戏”契约，并将其理解为是一种“内部逻辑”：“在游戏中，与外部环境的一致性检验被故意免除了，游戏创造了一个封闭环境……在游戏的兴头上外部世界消退到我们意识之外。”（贡布里希，2013a，p. 115)

约翰·赫伊津哈的《游戏的人》讨论文化的游戏成分，而非文化中的游戏成分，他企图在非常广阔的范围内寻找游戏的表现形式，但他也认为与造型艺术的创作过程相比，游戏更适用于艺术的接受过程：“如果从总体上说，游戏因素在造型艺术中没有在被我们称为音乐艺术或缪斯艺术中那么明显，当我们从艺术创作转向艺术在社会中的接受方式时，问题会立即发生变化。”(赫伊津哈，1997，p. 188）原因是，造型艺术的接受过程相对而言更符合游戏的以下形式特征：其一，是自主的，即不是因被迫而强制模拟沉浸其中，明知道这是假的，但假装认为是真的；其二，按照固定规则或有秩序的方式，进入一个暂时的、有别于现实真实生活的时空；其三，它具有隔离性与有限

性，在特定的时空中演出，并包含它自身的过程和意味。（赫伊津哈，1997，pp. 9－13）

确实，在玩游戏时，谁都愿意做个懂行的，而不愿成为一个扫兴的人被驱逐出游戏。一幅画本质上首先是涂满颜料的二维平面，其次才被视为神秘的蒙娜丽莎、威文荷公园的草地，甚或是阿姆斯特丹射击手们的夜巡事件，将目光锁定在二维平面画布及画框的人，永远无法读解画中的笔触游戏。莫奈的《日出·印象》引导观画者将一幅充满雾霭的海上晨景投射入这些色块中，观画者则需要心甘情愿地对莫奈的暗示做出相应反应，否则这场看与被看的游戏，无异于夏虫语冰。

贡布里希认为，是“把偶然的形状读解为什么形象，取决于从它们之中辨认出已经存储在自己心灵中的事物或图像的能力”（贡布里希，2015a，p. 162），这也是观看者的本分。读解图像依据的基础是传统，然后才是相应的心理投射与预测，也就是说，观看的本分依然是对再现的功能主义的体认，而非出于对形式相似性的信任。

观看是对可见世界的记忆的唤起。艺术家不会在作品中给出明确指示，如近处是屋舍，远处是牛羊。要将画中显示出来的形象看成它意指的对象，需要的是观者对物体外形及相对位置和大小的推断。这个空间合理化的过程，调动了观者对于可见世界的记忆，并将其投射到画布上点、线、色块构成的图案之中，推断并解释出那个拿着长矛准备投掷向猎物的是猎人，胯下奔驰的是马，而那匹看上去尤其小的马，则是由于它已奔跑至了远处。

观看也是对从艺术观念中习得的艺术图式的运用。首先，是常识问题。艺术观念在文化中建立起一个知识库，使观看能按图索骥，“一幅画的主题，其答案可能在某篇原典里，这时你就得知道去看那篇原典并把它和画联系起来……所有这些都是我所说的常识，即你该在什么地方找出一种说明或一种答案的直觉”（贡布里希，1998，p. 112）。如王维在画论《山水论》中总结中国传统绘画造型为：“远人无目；远树无枝；远山无石，隐隐如眉；远水无波，高与云齐。”（周积寅，2016，p. 427）教会观看者将无目之人、无枝之树、无石之山、无波之水置于心灵的一个类目中，从而在观看作品时将其辨认为远人、远树、远石与远波。

其次，是情境逻辑的想象。观看者以艺术家自居，想象创作者创作时的情境，以虚拟重建这一情境，让观看的技能与艺术家暗示的技能相匹配，将画布上的二维图像解释为艺术家意向的记录。这个过程可以被描述为：观看者在愿意相信艺术家的造型总有其合理性的基础上，经由其自身对再现的功能主义的体认，对造型技术的一致性进行检验，即便面对“鸭兔图”这种具有“阐释漩涡”（赵毅衡，2011，p. 238）的多义性图像，也能将不同的形状投射进同一轮廓中以消除解释的冲突，获取关于造型艺术内部信息连贯性的读解错觉。

艺术家在其作品中提示的信息是繁复的，观看者的解释也可以是多元的，但并非每一种都是恰当的，需要观看者对自我关于可见世界的记忆的唤起，以及常识的支撑与情境逻辑的想象，它与对艺术再现的功能主义体认是分不开的。那么，观看的本分被打破的界限在哪里？或者说，读解的错觉在何种情况下会被终止？贡布里希曾对这个问题进行追问（贡布里希，2013a，p. 116），目的是为了从相反的方向确认观看在其契约内顺利维持一致性。

文学作品对观看和被看的本分的不确定性进行讨论的经典案例，最著名者莫若皮兰德娄的荒诞剧《六个寻找作者的剧中人》，而其短篇小说《蝙蝠》通过演员、剧作家、观众、导演对一只闯入剧场的蝙蝠的不同反应，同样提示出，所谓的艺术内部逻辑的一致性，是可以轻易就被现实世界的来客“蝙蝠”扰乱的，它不受控制，且“无法预知”。[①]（皮兰德娄，2002，p. 102）

与其相类，艺术作品如玛格利特的绘画作品《这不是一只烟斗》等，也曾引起观看者的不安。这不安缘于画家在画框中将一只精心绘制的烟斗图像与一行“这不是一只烟斗”的文字并置[②]（福柯，2012，p. 3），正是文字符号的介入打破了传统绘画以图像符号无声言说的封闭现象。“它”当然不是一只立体的烟斗，只是烟斗的二维图像，这应该是不言自明的，文字的解说似无必要。但是，文字符号在画框内，观看者就必须将其纳入读解图像的“内部一致性”，对指称性的“这”进行否定性的判断，也就意味着打开了一切可能，此时，“这”就不再是“这”，观看者将随它一起陷入无方向的读解的眩晕。

玛格利特的探索，如其致福柯的信中所言，是在图像的相似和仿效的辨认中，为其自在的图像即可见的思想正名（福柯，2012，pp. 81 - 83）。但关

① 小说从现实世界到剧中世界对这只“蝙蝠”提示了四种态度：其一，害怕蝙蝠的女演员小加斯蒂娜认为，既然艺术要创造现实，那么现实世界蝙蝠的闯入也就可以带来剧本的改动；其二，剧本作者佩雷斯认为这个提议无异于毁了他的作品，因为那只蝙蝠，是自己钻进了演戏的舞台，却不是钻进他的剧本里；其三，当首演舞台上，那只蝙蝠对准女演员小加斯蒂娜冲过去并将其吓晕时，这逼真的晕厥，让沸腾的观众以为剧情就是这样的；其四，无论是首演前还是首演后，剧院团长都一再拒绝捣毁那只蝙蝠窝。

② 此处仅讨论玛格利特绘制于1926年的“简单”版本，他为《远方的黎明》一书制作插图的另一版本，在读解上更为复杂。

于此点，观看者既不能从可见世界的记忆中唤起相关经验，也无法从既往的艺术观念提供的艺术图式中寻求答案，此时，观看与被看的契约只能被截断。这也反向地证明了，观看的界限正在于观看者的错觉一致性能否与艺术家的艺术一致性相统一，当艺术家做出暗示的技能与观看者领会的技能相匹配，观看的本分才能顺利实现，观看者才能沉浸于艺术的游戏。

四、艺术与现实的双向辨认：贡布里希对柏拉图模仿说的重新阐释

不唯哲学也包括美学，谁都没有逃离开柏拉图模仿说的影响的焦虑，希冀能以各种方式肯定它、否定它或限定它。贡布里希的艺术研究也没有避开柏拉图，几乎在他的每一部研究著作中都能发现他对柏拉图模仿说的讨论与批评。《偏爱原始性》以专门一章讨论“柏拉图的偏爱”，以此回应哲学家怀特海的格言：整个西方哲学史不过是柏拉图理论的一系列注脚（贡布里希，2013a，p. 11）；《图像与眼睛》以马克思·利贝曼劝说被画人“这张画，我亲爱的先生，比你自己更像你”的逸事，回应柏拉图思想的继承者对恒定的追求（贡布里希，2013b，p. 126）；《艺术与错觉》则援引柏拉图的多篇对话，尤其在谈到《克拉底鲁篇》中有关图像是规定性符号还是真实世界的模仿问题时，他甚至希望自己就是那个对话者，可以与苏格拉底进行一次在场的辩论，“哎呀，苏格拉底，我们现在知道，它们也绝不敢指望其画面上的颜料能跟一片阳光照耀的现实风景等量齐观。但是，一片片阳光照耀的风景已经画出来了，你认为不可能的事情业已发生了” （贡布里希，2015a，p. 320）；诸如此种，不一而足。

就像纳博科夫在其所有小说的序言中表达对弗洛伊德及其追随者的精神分析理论的否定，会让读者认为纳博科夫所有小说即是证明精神分析不可靠的写作实验一样，柏拉图在贡布里希艺术研究中的频频出场，也势必会引起一种读解的猜测：贡布里希的研究是对柏拉图的肯定、否定，还是限定？

无人不知，柏拉图是反艺术的，尤其是反对同时代的造型艺术，如希腊的绘画、雕塑等。他在《理想国》中以“三种床”[①] （柏拉图，2015）论说了艺术何以是对理念的模仿的再模仿，终与永恒不变的理念相距甚远。但贡

① 第一种是自然本有的、永存不变的理念之床，第二种是木匠据理念制造、享有理念之床真实性的现实之床，第三种是画家据现实之床绘制的形象之床。

布里希提出了不同的意见，他认为木工与画家的位置应该互换："许多床都是首先经过设计，制出蓝图，然后才着手制作。遇到这种情况，柏拉图就不得不让设计者进入他的理想国，因为设计者也是模仿床的理念，并非模仿什么骗人的现实。"（贡布里希，2015a，p. 87）这种先设计后制作的案例在艺术与现实中都比比皆是，比如画家的写生图，或家具商场提供的床的图像目录，既可以理解为是床的设计图样，也可以理解为是已经制作好的床。

柏拉图所指认的制作和模仿的区别，在贡布里希看来，界限是非常模糊的，他将其原因解释为："因为人的世界不仅仅是一个事物的世界；人的世界也是一个象征符号的世界，在这个世界里现实和假装之间的区别本身就是不真实的"（贡布里希，2015a，p. 88），自然和象征符号之间存在着过渡甚至是转换，所以现实与虚像的区分也便成了无意义。

艺术不是对现实的模仿，而是与现实的相互辨认，"所有的艺术发现都不是对于相似性的发现，而是对于等效性的发现；这种等效性使我们能按照一个图像去看现实，而且能按照现实去看一个图像。与其说这种等效性的基础在于成分的相似性，不如说在于对于某些关系所产生的反应的同一性"（贡布里希，2015a，p. 305）。艺术创作与观看都是在图像和现实之间不断地相互解读，并最终获取等效认同。在堆雪人时，孩子们觉得就是在用雪来制作人，而不是制作人的虚像，然而摆弄雪团的过程，难道不是以对人的记忆或理念为依据在进行，最终抵达对人的象征？而人们在发出"风景如画"的感叹时，不正是从现实向图像的反向辨认（inverted recognition）（贡布里希，2013b，p. 30）？

也就是说，艺术也不是直接模仿理念。新柏拉图主义认为艺术家是有神圣天赋知觉之人，能觉察永恒原型本身，在贡布里希看来，这不过"是以自我欺骗为基础的。对于不是画一株个体的树而是画一株树，不是画一个个体的人而是画一个人的这样一种素描艺术……它给予的是一个有些华而不实的哲学光环"（贡布里希，2015a，p. 138）。艺术家所体悟到的原型或共相，不过是艺术的图式："我所说的'图式'是共相"（贡布里希，2015a，p. 135），是一代又一代艺术家积淀下来的创作典范，它并非永恒不变的，而是在"图式－矫正"模式下不断推进的。经由对传统艺术图式的继承，并在新时代图像功能的不同需求下对其进行修正，艺术家才能制作出一幅令人信服的画面（贡布里希，1987，p. 359）。

柏拉图模仿说对艺术的批评，表达了对艺术绘制视点所见而非永恒的功能，将人们引入对琐碎细节的担忧；更重要的是，希腊艺术拟真"瞬间"现实，会使人们诉诸想象去辨认图像的可见与不可见，与他对理性的追求是相悖的，就像论文一开始引用的画家马蒂斯的逸事，有着不成熟心灵的“夫人”们，难免陷入将现实与艺术混为一谈的误区。贡布里希虽坚持为艺术正名，却也深刻认同柏拉图的理性原则。

可以说，理性原则是贡布里希对艺术生产的解释、艺术批评及艺术史研究的基本原则，也是他与现代艺术分野的重要原因。在他看来，立体主义、超现实主义等现代艺术运动，打破了艺术发展的图式逻辑，是“缺乏图式、缺乏再现、缺乏模仿、缺乏情感和缺乏创造”，是“与社会上的任何功能都不相关的为艺术本身而进行的活动”（贡布里希，1989，p. 82，p. 58）。这些作品以视觉双关与蓄意的模糊歧义“蔑视理性”（Gombrich，1991，p. 161），流于晦涩而漫无目标，“（《面部幻影和水果盘》，达利，1938 年）反映了个人的迷惑难解的梦，我们茫茫然不得要领”（贡布里希，2015b，p. 594）。

当然，贡布里希没有回避这一切都是时代使然，他曾明确指出：“如果不是生在当今这个时代，当代画家和雕塑家中一定有一些已经做出了为时代增光生色的事业。”（贡布里希，2015b，p. 596）并且事实上，作为一位理性的艺术史家，贡布里希也必然意识到，他无法拒绝这些现代艺术实验终有一部分将进入经典，成为艺术图式的一部分，但这些都不妨碍他对经典准则的坚守。

这或许正是贡布里希与柏拉图的殊途同归之处。

五、结语

贡布里希对图像与现实之间的关系，有着他一以贯之的坚守。在他看来，这是为艺术正名的重要一步，如同他在《艺术与自我超越》一文的最后所表述的：“我想不出比这（指艺术在时代的动荡中对精神的抚慰，笔者注）更好的例子来说明在现实世界中价值的地位。”（贡布里希，2013c，p. 121）然而，“历史由我们的历史构成，因此我们永远不可能对自己和自己的历史有一个中立的完整的图像”（温特，2019，p. 204），贡布里希也只是复杂时代的一部分，他的诸多观念尤其是对现代艺术的观点，或许在当下会备受诟病，但谁能预料当下之后会怎样。历史难道不曾告诉我们：正确的答案绝不止一个？

引用文献：

艾略特，T. S.（2012）. 传统与个人才能（卞之琳，译）. 上海：上海译文出版社.

柏拉图（2015）. 柏拉图文艺对话集（朱光潜，译）. 北京：商务印书馆.

福柯，米歇尔（2009）. 马奈的绘画——米歇尔·福柯，一种目光（谢强，马月，译）. 长沙：湖南教育出版社.

福柯，米歇尔（2012）. 这不是一只烟斗（邢克超，译）. 桂林：漓江出版社.

贡布里希，E. H.（1987）. 秩序感——装饰艺术的心理学研究（杨思梁，徐一维，译）. 杭州：浙江摄影出版社.

贡布里希，E. H.（1989）. 艺术与人文科学：贡布里希文选（范景中，编译）. 杭州：浙江摄影出版社.

贡布里希，E. H.（1998）. 艺术与科学：贡布里希谈话录和回忆录（杨思梁，等译）. 杭州：浙江摄影出版社.

贡布里希，E. H.（2013a）. 偶发与设计（汤宇星，译）. 杭州：中国美术学院出版社.

贡布里希，E. H.（2013b）. 图像与眼睛——图画再现心理学的再研究（范景中，杨思梁，徐一维，译）. 南宁：广西美术出版社.

贡布里希，E. H.（2013c）. 理想与偶像——价值在历史和艺术中的地位（范景中，杨思梁，译）. 南宁：广西美术出版社.

贡布里希，E. H.（2015a）. 艺术与错觉——图画再现的心理学研究（杨成凯，李本正，范景中，译）. 南宁：广西美术出版社.

贡布里希，E. H.（2015b）. 艺术的故事（范景中，译）. 南宁：广西美术出版社.

贡布里希，E. H.（2016）. 偏爱原始性——西方艺术与文学中的趣味史（杨小京，译）. 南宁：广西美术出版社.

贡布里希，E. H.（2018）. 木马沉思录——艺术理论文集（曾四凯，徐一维，译）. 南宁：广西美术出版社.

赫伊津哈，约翰（1997）. 游戏的人（多人，译）. 杭州：中国美术学院出版社.

霍帕尔，米哈伊（2020）. 民族符号学——文化研究的方法（彭佳，贾欣，译）. 北京：社会科学文献出版社.

倪梁康（编）（2006）. 面对实事本身——现象学经典文选. 北京：东方出版社.

皮兰德娄（2002）. 皮兰德娄精选集（吕同六，等译）. 济南：山东文艺出版社.

苏智（2018）. 符码特征与《周易》取象的意义建构. 符号与传媒，2，115－124.

温特，赖纳（2019）. 自我意识的艺术——文化研究作为权力的批判（徐蕾，译）. 重庆：重庆大学出版社.

谢清果，张丹（2018）. 观象制器：夏商周时期青铜器图像的文化符号表征. 符号与传媒，2，77－92.

赵毅衡（2011）. 符号学. 南京：南京大学出版社.

周积寅（编著）（2016）. 中国画论辑要. 南京：江苏美术出版社.

Gombrich, E. H. (1969). The evidence of images II: The priority of context over expression. In Charles S. Singleton (Ed.). *Interpretation: Theory and practice*. Baltimore, MD : Johns Hopkins University Press.

Gombrich, E. H. (1991). *Topics of our time: Twentieth century issues in learning and in art*. London, UK: Phaidon.

作者简介：

孙金燕，博士，云南民族大学文学与传媒学院副教授，主要研究领域为符号学、中国现当代小说。

Author:

Sun Jinyan, Ph. D. , associate professor of School of Literature and Media, Yunnan Minzu University. Her research mainly focuses on semiotics, modern and contemporary Chinese Literature.

Email: 08yan08@ 163. com

Semiosis as a Model of Purpose-driven Representation

Tony Jappy

Abstract: The paper examines a particular aspect of the way semiosis models complex anthroposemiotic activity as exemplified by the "persuasion path" implicit in any source or origin of intentional influence in human communication. Now, in theory, we should be able to account for every stage in the process of semiosis, and this ability has a bearing on the way signs are to be classified according to the nature of their immediate objects. The topic is a pretext, consequently, for exploring the stages in semiosis from the dynamic object to the sign via the immediate object in selected pictorial examples of purpose and intentionality in semiosis, since, to be understood successfully—indeed, to function at all—any such persuasive or influential activity depends upon the formal organisation of its representation. The paper thus presents one possible explanation of the role of the immediate object in cases of evident intentionality. However, in view of the fact that Peirce never developed a clear idea of semiosis, it is necessarily speculative and abductive.

Keywords: Peirce, semiosis, sign, purpose-driven representation, intentionality, immediate object

DOI: 10.13760/b.cnki.sam.202002004

A purpose is merely that form of final cause which is most familiar to our experience.

CP 1. 211 (1902)

Ⅰ. Introduction

The paper examines the contribution of a sign's immediate object to the way semiosis models the type of complex anthroposemiotic activity exemplified by the series of formative stages implicit in, for example, Edward Bernay's (1947) apology for "scientific" persuasion—what he referred to, apparently without cynicism, as "the engineering of consent" and, of course, by any other source of influence. Since, for Peirce's theory of signs to be a viable scientific proposition we have to be able to account for every stage in the process of semiosis, such an ability will necessarily require at some point that signs should be classified according to the nature of their immediate objects. The topic is a pretext, therefore, for exploring the stages in semiosis from the dynamic object to the sign via the immediate object in selected examples, since any persuasive or influential activity requires the formal organisation of its representation and there can be no communication without representation, irrespective of the nature of the "agents"—human or otherwise—involved. While not all representations are purpose-driven—those with an existent dynamic object can be shown to be causal rather than intentional—the paper presents one possible illustration of the role of the immediate object in cases of conspicuous intentionality. Note, finally, that Peirce never used the term "intentionality", he referred instead to "purpose" or "intention" (the latter generally in the restricted, technical sense of "first intention" "second intention").

The paper is organized as follows: in view of developments in his theory of signs over the ten years at the beginning of the last century, chronology is the backbone or framework of any investigation of Peircean semiotics. Initially, then, a brief review of the well-known ten-class system from the syllabus of 1903 accompanying Peirce's Lowell lectures on logic precedes a description of the post-1903 hexadic system of sign-action, in which the sign comes to be defined as a medium and which also leads to the definition of semiosis in 1907. This is followed by discussions first of semiosis itself, and, subsequently, of the implications of Peirce's statements concerning the immediate object. Since his changing conception of the ways in which signs are to be classified is characterized by a gradual move from phenomenology to a form of ontology as the basis of the analysis of classificatory divisions into subdivisions, a section is devoted to this important theoretical decision. Finally, discussion in two case studies of intention-driven representations present the hypothesized function of the immediate object in the development of the deliberative stages leading from conception to representation.

Ⅱ. Peirce's Evolving Theory of Signs

i. The Sign as Medium

In the course of the Lowell lectures of 1903 Peirce had defined the sign in the following manner, in which the continuing influence of his conception of phenomenology is clearly visible:

> A Sign, or Representamen, is a First which stands in such a genuine triadic relation to a Second, called its Object, as to be capable of determining a Third, called its Interpretant, to assume the same triadic relation to its Object in which it stands itself to the same Object. (CP 2. 274, 1903)

This definition involving three correlates, namely sign, object and interpretant, enabled him to establish a typology formed of three divisions. These were a division for the sign, one concerning the relation between sign and object, and, finally, a division concerning the sign and its interpretant. With his three categories of Firstness, Secondness and Thirdness, he was able to subdivide these divisions and combine the resultant subdivisions as represented on Figure 1 so as to derive only ten classes of signs from a potential twenty-seven.

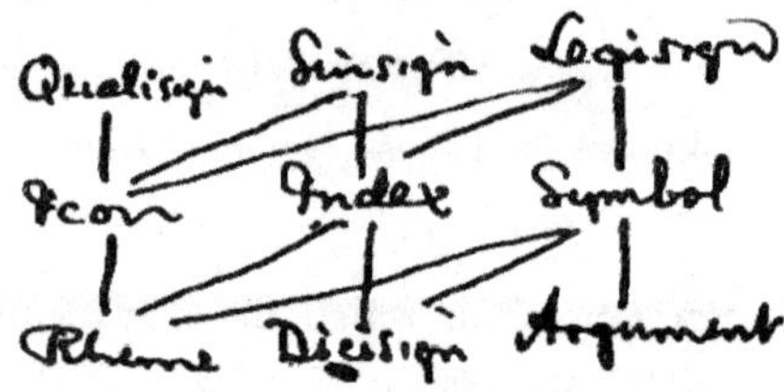

Figure 1 Peirce's Table of Compatibilities between Subdivisions

The scheme on Figure 1 indicates the categorial affinities holding between the subdivisions of these three trichotomies. The vertical columns correspond to the three categories leading from Firstness on the left to Thirdness on the right, while the horizontal entries correspond to the Sign, Sign-Object and Sign-Interpretant trichotomies. The "rules" drawn by Peirce on Figure 1 are simple. First, two vertical lines associating three subdivisions of the same phenomenological complexity form one class. For example, the first, least complex class, the qualisign, is obtained by tracing the leftmost pair of vertical lines linking subdivisions partaking of Firstness from qualisign to rheme through icon. Since a qualisign cannot combine with a subdivision of greater phenomenological value such as an index (Secondness) or a symbol (Thirdness), there is no need to mention the icon and the rheme in the class label: the terms are redundant, hence, simply, "qualisign". Similarly, another vertical trace associating the subdivisions partaking of Thirdness leads from legisign to argument through symbol, yielding the tenth, most complex class, the argument. As the vertical line shows, a Thirdness can only be preceded by another Thirdness, so there is no need to specify the association with legisign and symbol.

A second "rule" allows a downward diagonal trace from right to left, going from the phenomenologically more complex subdivisions to the less. For example, it is possible to trace a class from sinsign to icon, which necessarily leads to rheme. This yields the iconic sinsign, another case where mention of the rhematic status of such a sign is superfluous. By combining subdivisions in this way Peirce obtained ten classes of signs (Figure 2), which he numbered according to increasing phenomenological complexity, and in which the terms not indicated in bold can be omitted from the class label.

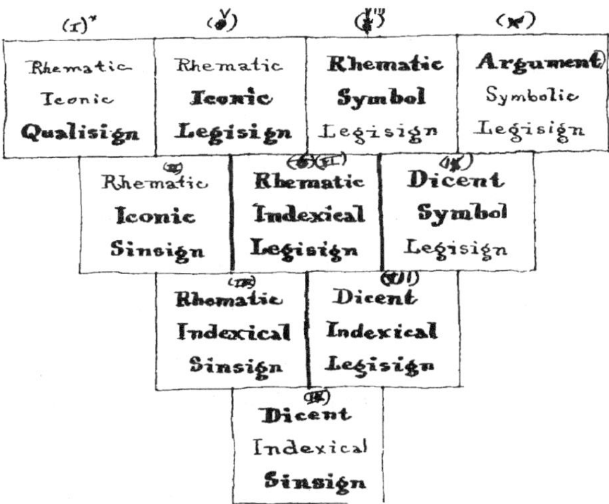

Figure 2 Peirce's Ten Classes of Signs from the Syllabus of 1903 (R 549 16; EP 2 296)

However, in the period 1905 – 1906, no doubt partly as a consequence of the expanded set of correlates, he was led to specify the role of the sign more completely than before, and, in the course of integrating two objects and three interpretants in his conception of representation, explicitly attributed to the sign itself a more precisely defined mediating role, as we see in the following extract from manuscript RL 463, a draft letter to Lady Welby dated 9 March 1906:

> I use the word "*Sign*" in the widest sense for any medium for the communication or extension of a Form (or feature). Being medium, it is determined by something, called its Object, and determines something, called its Interpretant. In order that a Form may be extended or communicated, it is necessary that it should have been really embodied in a Subject independently of the communication; and it is necessary that there should be another subject in which the same form is embodied only as a consequence of the communication. (EP 2 477, 1906)

As can be seen from the quotation, the 1906 draft insists upon the fact that the sign is a medium for the communication of a "form". Just what sort of entity is this form that the object communicates to the sign via the immediate object? Peirce suggests an explanation for this in a variant page 3 of another contemporary manuscript, R 793:

> [That] which is communicated from the Object through the Sign to the Interpretant is a Form. It is not a singular thing; for if a Singular thing were first in the Object and afterward in the Interpretant outside the Object, it must thereby cease to be in the Object. (R 793 5, 1906)

Clearly, if what was communicated from the object to the sign were an existent, singular entity it would cease to be located in the object once it had been communicated to the sign and would cease to be in the sign as soon as it had been communicated in turn to the interpretant. The form communicated by the dynamic object to the sign via the immediate object is therefore necessarily qualitative, quality being described as the "monadic element of the world" (CP 1.426, c. 1896) and consequently the only category of being that can simultaneously be "the same form" embodied in sign, objects and interpretants. In the course of normal human communication, for example, signs—media—as defined by the 1906 statement above simply need to be perceivable and to accommodate such forms emanating, of course, from the dynamic object. Potential media, then, according to this view, are the artist's canvas, cinema-, computer- or TV-screens, neon hoardings outside department stores, metal panels on roadsides, old-fashioned school blackboards, and even human skin. As for the form communicated, it is tempting to consider it as the form of the immediate object.

ii. Semiosis Defined

A new stage comes with the document entitled "Pragmatism" (Prag) of 1907. This is manuscript R318, a 698-page document consisting in various drafts of letters to editors, all of which were rejected. Parts of the manuscript are reproduced in CP 5.465 - 496 and parts in EP 2 398 - 433, a delicate situation as it tends to highlight, as in the case of the CP selections concerning the logical interpretant, for example, concepts which are thought to be important from their prominence in the *Collected Papers* but never appear again after 1907. The variants in the manuscript, which really requires to be read in full, show that Peirce now saw the nature of the association of the three foundational constituents of semiosis or "semiosy", as he also called it (CP 5.473, 1907), as being the dynamic action involving the "cooperation" of three subjects, namely a sign, its object and its interpretant:

> It is important to understand what I mean by *semiosis*. All dynamical action, or action of brute force, physical or psychical, either takes place between two subjects [whether they react equally upon each other, or one is agent and the other patient, entirely or partially] or at any rate is a resultant of such actions between pairs. But by "semiosis" I mean, on the contrary, an action, or influence, which is, or involves, a coöperation of *three* subjects, such as a sign, its object, and its interpretant, this tri-elative influence not being in any way resolvable into actions between pairs. (CP 5.484, 1907)

In the same manuscript, Peirce, no doubt aware of the immensity of the task, defines "semiotic" in a novel manner and announces the need for future research into the identification in logic of what he saw as all possible varieties not so much of classes of signs, but of *varieties of possible semiosis*, thereby establishing a necessary theoretical relation between class of sign and class of semiosis:

> I am, as far as I know, a pioneer, or rather a backwoodsman, in the work of clearing and opening up what I call *semiotic*, that is, the doctrine of the essential nature and fundamental varieties of possible semiosis; and I find the field too vast, the labor too great, for a first-comer. (R 318 119, 1907)

Such a relation would have been inconceivable in 1903, since the classes of signs were not directly linked to the action in which the sign was engaged: the only correlate so linked was, necessarily, the sign itself, since at this time it was both the determination of the object and the determinant of the interpretant, while the ten classes of signs involved neither of the other two correlates but, rather, *relations* between the sign and the two correlates. The statement is important, then, in two ways: first, it establishes that there is not one form of semiosis, but many different types. Second, it implies that to each distinct type of semiosis there corresponds a distinct class of signs; conversely, each distinct class of signs is necessarily the result of a distinct type of semiosis. Consider, furthermore, the following example of a sign that Peirce offers in the same manuscript:

> Suppose, for example, an officer of a squad or company of infantry gives the word of command, "Ground arms!" This order is, of course, a sign. That thing which causes a sign as such is called the *object* (according to the usage of speech, the "real," but more accurately, the *existent* object) represented by the sign: the sign is determined to some species of correspondence with that object. In the present case, the object the command represents is the will of the officer that the butts of the muskets be brought down to the ground For the proper outcome of a sign, I propose the name, the *interpretant* of the sign. The example of the imperative command shows that it need not be of a mental mode of being. (R 318 51 – 53, 1907).

The interesting features of this example are, first, that the object can now be the will of the officer, a case of intentionality in semiosis which confirms the potential for such a semiotic determinant to be found in an earlier description of the immediate (intentional) interpretant in the 1906 draft (EP 2 478) mentioned above as a determination of the utterer, and second, that the interpretant—here the existential interpretant and elsewhere referred to in manuscript R 318 as the "energetic" interpretant—can not only be a thought or habit but also an action. In the draft of 9 March, 1906, Peirce seemed still to consider the sign's object as what the sign represented immediately—the model in a photograph, for example. In the pragmatism manuscript of 1907, however, the object of the military command is the *source of the imperative utterance*, namely, the officer's will, not the implicit grammatical subject *You*, the ground and the muskets. In 1907 he thus identifies the dynamic ("real") object of the military command "Ground arms!" as the will of the officer, a theoretical decision which makes the dynamic object the locus or source of, amongst other things, intentionality, purpose and persuasion.

iii. Universe or Category?

Over the course of the years between 1903 and 1908, beginning probably in 1906 with the publication of "Prolegomena to an Apology for Pragmaticism" (cf. CP 5. 544 - 5. 546), Peirce was led to adopt a different set of values enabling him to subdivide the trichotomies of the ten-division systems he had begun to derive in the summer of 1905. A universe, Peirce claimed in 1906 (CP 4. 545), is not the same as a category, and he continued:

> Let us begin with the question of Universes. It is rather a question of an advisable point of view than of the truth of a doctrine. A logical universe is, no doubt, a collection of *logical* subjects, but not necessarily of metaphysical Subjects, or "substances"; for it may be composed of characters, of elementary facts, etc. (CP 4. 546).

Instead of the categories of Firstness, Secondness and Thirdness from 1903, in 1908 he explicitly employed three "universes of experience" as described in "A Neglected Argument for the Reality of God" (CP 6. 452 - 6. 493, 1908). These were subsequently defined modally to be composed of possible, existent and necessitant entities (including signs, objects and interpretants) and became the means of subdividing trichotomies in his December 1908 three-division, six-division and ten-division typologies (EP 2 478 -491).

In a manner which clearly parallels the way he began his description of speculative grammar in the intended Syllabus of 1903 (EP 2 267 -272) and in the letter to Lady Welby of 1904 with its six divisions of signs (CP 8. 327 - 8. 333) by means of an introduction to phenomenology and the three categories, Peirce prefaced the definition of the innovative hexadic process of signification in 1908 by a thorough and explicit association of three modally-defined universes with semiosis, by which he established the subdivisions within each of six new trichotomies:

> It is clearly indispensable to start with an accurate and broad analysis of the nature of a Sign. I define a Sign as anything which is so determined by something else, called its Object, and so determines an effect upon a person, which effect I call its Interpretant, that the latter is thereby mediately determined by the former[...] I

> recognize three Universes, which are distinguished by three Modalities of Being. One of these Universes embraces whatever has its Being in itself alone[...] I denominate the objects of this Universe *Ideas*, or *Possibles*, although the latter designation does not imply capability of actualization[...] Another Universe is that of, 1st, Objects whose Being consists in their Brute reactions, and of, 2nd, the Facts[...] I call the Objects, Things, or more unambiguously, *Existents*, and the facts about them I call Facts[...] The third Universe consists of the co-being of whatever is in its Nature *necessitant*, that is, is a Habit, a law, or something expressible in a universal proposition. (EP 2 478 –479, 1908)

These universes of experience were later to become a single universe of existence in his correspondence and drafts to William James. In the following extract from a draft letter to James composed a month after the one to Lady Welby in which the twenty-eight and sixty-six classes of signs were first mentioned, Peirce offers the following definition of the sign and an innovative development in his conception of the dynamic object detailing a number of cases where the sign's dynamic object corresponds to or identifies a "universe of existence" (EP 2 492 –493, 1909). In other words, the dynamic object is, or determines, an ontology:

> A Sign is a Cognizable that, on the one hand, is so determined (i. e., specialized, *bestimmt*) by something *other than itself*, called its Object (or, in some cases, as if the Sign be the sentence "Cain killed Abel" in which Cain and Abel are equally Partial Objects, it may be more convenient to say that that which determines the Sign is the Complexus, or Totality, of Partial Objects. And in every case the Object is accurately the Universe of which the Special Object is member, or part), while, on the other hand, it so determines some actual or potential Mind, the determination whereof I term the Interpretant created by the Sign, that that Interpreting Mind is therein determined mediately by the Object. (EP 2 492, 1909)

By identifying the dynamic object as the universe itself, rather than the earlier typological conception in which the dynamic object is referred to one of three universes in the classification of signs, Peirce has simplified the theoretical framework considerably, if only briefly, but shows a certain hesitation in his verbocentric examples as to what the object of a sign really is. Note that in a letter to James dated 14 March 1909 he did subsequently refer to a three-universe system (EP 2 497).

As seen above, we have Peirce discarding the phenomenological framework mentioned in his intended syllabus for the Lowell lectures five years earlier and in the letter to Lady Welby of 12 October 1904, adopting instead what in this paper is referred to as an ontological one, i. e. one in which Peirce has specified domains of possible, existent and necessitant entities and relations among them. There are a number of possible explanations for such a move, but the reader is reminded that the choice of three universes as opposed to the earlier phenomenological categories as the means of establishing the subdivisions of the various trichotomies is dismissed as irrelevant by certain Peirce specialists, who claim that the concepts that Peirce has been referring to in the texts above are nothing more than another term for the categories, that, in fact, the phenomenology, or "phaneroscopy" as he had been calling it since 1904, still provided in 1908 the principles for subdividing the divisions of his typologies (Savan, 1988, p. 53; Anderson, 1995, p. 140; Freadman, 2004, p. 160; Houser, 2005, p. 459 and Bellucci, 2018, p. 335, for example). There are several arguments against such a claim.

There witll be a process of any kind which involves the dynamism necessary for the determination of a sign that is "percussive", for example the case where the dynamic interpretant **Id** is an existent on Table 1, and produces an action such as bringing musket-butts to the ground, the categories are clearly inapplicable: a category is a type of predicate or descriptive term concerning phenomena and is incapable of materially organizing a sequence of correlates resulting in musket-butts being brought to the ground. We know, too, that Peirce derived the single sign, the two objects and the three interpretants at the time when he was still working with his categories, and that he claimed in 1907 that it was the categories that defined the three interpretants (R 318 281). Since there is no way in which he could have derived such a one-two-three correlate system using the universes of the sort described in 1908, universes must be logically and functionally distinct from categories. In any case, it would be difficult for defenders of the "category = universe" thesis to assimilate a category of any sort to the single universe of *existence* as Peirce described it briefly to James in the draft of February 1909 (EP 2 492), even though he did subsequently refer James to a three-universe system (EP 2 497). Finally, in view of Peirce's strictures on the ethics of terminology and given the fact that he was still presenting work elsewhere on his phenomenology, now termed "phaneroscopy", if he mentions universes as classification criteria in the

1908 letter and drafts and in subsequent letters and drafts to William James, an extract of which was quoted above (EP 2 492, 497, 1909), it can reasonably be assumed that he meant universes and not categories. The distinction is important as many non-specialist readers of Peirce from other disciplines can easily be misled into thinking that semiosis is somehow based upon phenomenology. See Chapter Three of Jappy (2016) for a longer discussion and references.

Ⅲ. Semiosis

In 1908, in a letter to Lady Welby, Peirce describes the six-correlate process of semiosis as the following sequence:

> It is evident that a possible can determine nothing but a Possible, it is equally so that Necessitant can be determined by nothing but a Necessitant. Hence it follows from the Definition of a Sign that since the Dynamoid Object determines the Immediate Object,
>
> which determines the Sign itself,
> which determines the Destinate Interpretant,
> which determines the Effective Interpretant,
> which determines the Explicit Interpretant.
>
> The six trichotomies, instead of determining 729 classes of signs, as they would if they were independent, only yield twenty-eight classes; and if, as I strongly opine (not to say almost prove) there are four other trichotomies of signs of the same order of importance, instead of making 59049 classes, these will only come to sixty-six. (SS 84 -85, 1908)

Standardizing the interpretants, the process can be represented quite simply by Figure 3. Note that not every authority agrees on the order given below as the explicit interpretant is sometimes taken to be the immediate and the destinate to be the final.

Od > Oi > S > Ii > Id > If

Figure 3 The Linear Order of Semiosis (SS 84, 1908, interpretants standardized)

Since these correlates are organized in logical, linear order, we see that signs have a "history" originating first in the dynamic object and continued by the immediate. This history can be traced from the following table (Table 1), in which the order of divisions has been labelled to show the linear structure of semiosis as described above. There are three points to note concerning semiosis and the order of divisions as represented on Table 1:

Table 1 The Six-division Typology of 1908 Reflecting the Order of Semiosis

(semiosis)	Subject				
	Od →	Oi →	S →	Ii →	Id →
Universe					
Necessitant	collective	copulant	type	relative	usual
Existent	concretive	designative	token	categorical	percussive
Possible	abstractive	descriptive	mark	hypothetical	sympathetic

· Since the order of the correlates occurring in the determination sequence corresponds to the order of divisions or trichotomies forming the typology, any discussion of semiosis naturally involves the typology and vice versa.

· The passage from an intentionality such as the officer's order emanating from the dynamic object to its representation by the sign is shown not to be immediate: we must therefore theoretically be able to identify aspects of the immediate object in order to classify the sign.

· To be perceivable at all by, say, a human interpreter, the sign must be an existent—a token or an instance of a type—but the immediate and dynamic objects can both be necessitant. In short, both can be of greater modal complexity than the sign. On the "cut-down" table, Table 2, the sign represents an intentionality (a necessitant **Od** and a formal structure (a necessitant **Oi** more complex than itself).

Since these correlates are organized in logical, linear order, we see that signs have a "history" originating first in the dynamic object and continued by the immediate. This history can be traced from Table 2, in which the order of divisions corresponds to the linear structure of semiosis as described above (Table 1). It should be noted, however, that in all his numerous tabular typologies Peirce never set out his divisions horizontally as on Table 1 but, rather, vertically down the page. Moreover, he never set out a six-division typology based solely on the correlates.

Table 2 The Three Divisions from the Dynamic Object to the Sign

(semiosis)	Subject		
	Od →	Oi →	S →
Universe			
Necessitant	collective	copulant	type
Existent	concretive	designative	token
Possible	abstractive	descriptive	mark

> The Mediate Object is the Object outside of the Sign; I call it the Dynamoid Object. The Sign must indicate it by a hint; and *this hint, or its substance,* is the Immediate Object. (SS 83, 1908, emphasis mine)

One way to determine the nature of the immediate object and to show how it communicates to the sign form from the dynamic object is by adopting the definition from 1906 given earlier and treating the sign *strictly* as a medium—airwaves, a page in a book, a piece of canvas or an oak panel, a computer of cinema screen, even human skin[...] This is the method adopted here: *any sign determining its series of interpretants is the fusion of the form-bearing immediate object and a medium.*

This hint or substance constituting the immediate object raises a theoretical problem to be considered concerning the two major ways proposed by Peirce of classifying and analyzing the same sign: the 1903 Syllabus version and the post-1906 semiosis-based conception of the sign as medium in a dynamic process. Consider (1), the transcription of a spoken utterance and (2) and its written version:

(1) [ðis ru: mz veri kʊld]

(2) This room is very cold.

Utterances (1) and (2) constitute a simple example of diamesic variation: the same assertion expressed in two different media. In the case of the spoken utterance, the medium is the air which transmits its particular form as the sequence of troughs and peaks of the airwaves conveying the message. In the second case, it is the paper and the series of ink marks on it on the written page of this journal that constitute the medium, but the assertion could just as easily be conveyed by other media, a computer screen, for example, or a classroom blackboard. In each case the intentionality of the dynamic object is the same, but the two distinct media have been formed—informed—by distinct immediate objects.

Now, on analysing the signs within the phenomenology-based system of 1903 we find that both are replicas of dicent symbols, one of the ten classes of signs obtained from the three divisions that Peirce derived in his syllabus for the Lowell lectures, namely the sign division, the sign-object division and the division concerning the relation between sign and interpretant. It is important to notice that neither the dynamic object nor the immediate object is involved explicitly in the classification, which must perforce, therefore, be considered as static. As the following definitions suggest, the three divisions were obviously based upon a theory in which the action of the sign is dependent upon a conception of determination which is only *implicitly* dynamic—a conception in which, rather, the notion of triadicity is uppermost:

> Every sign stands for an object independent of itself; but it can only be a sign of that object in so far as that object is itself of the nature of a sign or thought. For the sign does not affect the object but is affected by it; so that the object must be able to convey thought, that is, must be of the nature of thought or a sign. (CP 1. 538, 1903)

My definition of a representamen is as follow:

> *A REPRESENTAMEN is a subject of a triadic relation TO a second, called its OBJECT, FOR a third, called is INTERPRETANT, this triadic relation being such that the REPRESENTAMEN determines its interpretant to stand in the same triadic relation to the same object for some interpretant.* (CP 1. 541, 1903)

Such definitions and others like it from the Lowell lectures suggest that at the time Peirce was less interested in the action of the sign as a process than in the classification of signs, now that he had developed his phenomenology and had thus developed the conceptual framework required to establish his divisions and to subdivide them. The dynamism implicit in the three-correlate definitions of 1903 like those above were only really made explicit five years later in the "post-scriptum" addressed to Lady Welby in a draft of December 28, 1908.

The system developed on Figure 4 (RL 463 144; EP 2 490 - 491; 28 December, 1908) from is completely different from that of 1903 (Figure 2), since it is the correlates themselves that constitute the divisions of the classification and not the sign and two sign-correlate divisions of 1903. Moreover, since it is always the

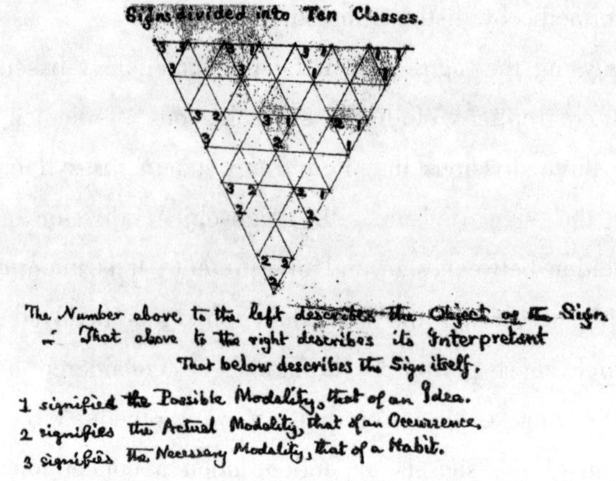

Figure 4 The "Post-scriptum" Ten Classes of Signs with Peirce's Explanations

dynamic object situated top-left in each of the classes that is the most complex of the three correlate divisions if one correlate is more complex than the other, and that it is always the interpretant which is the least complex of the three if there is one correlate less complex than the others, we can consider the classes to be based on the process of semiosis described on Figure 3. But even with this form of "cut-down" semiosis composed solely of **Od** → **S** → **If**, there is no immediate object to inform the sign with the intentionality of the dynamic object: there is no immediate object to "implement" the formal organization of the sign as medium, in other words.

Within the ontology-based system of 1908, on the other hand, where these two variants (1) and (2) of the assertion would be classified as instances or tokens of a collective copulant type (interpretant divisions omitted for simplicity). This system, as described by Peirce to Lady Welby in the letter of 23 December 1908 *does* have an immediate object that communicates to the sign form inherited from the dynamic object, a property which makes Peircean semiosis a possible model for intention-based representation. With this in mind we examine two illustrations of the principles involved.

Ⅳ. Two Case Studies

As a final discussion of the way the hexadic system of 1908 with its inclusion of an immediate object differs from the Syllabus conception of signs of 1903 which doesn' t, we examine two contrasting examples of how the immediate object informs the sign.

ii. A Studio Portrait

Consider, first, the photograph of a studio portrait in Figure 5.

Figure 5 Portrait of a Young Chinese Girl

To begin with, it is convenient to review two definitions from the 1902 - 1903 period as these will make clear the differences between a semiotic system that doesn' t have an immediate object and one that does:

> We say that the portrait of a person we have not seen is *convincing*. So far as, on the ground merely of what I see in it, I am led to form an idea of the person it represents, it is an Icon. But, in fact, it is not a pure Icon, because I am greatly influenced by knowing that it is an *effect*, through the artist, caused by the original's appearance, and is thus in a genuine Obsistent relation to that original. (CP 2.92, 1902)
>
> A man's portrait with a man's name written under it is strictly a proposition, although its syntax is not that of speech, and although the portrait itself not only represents, but is, a Hypoicon. But the proper name so nearly approximates to the nature of an Index, that this might suffice to give an idea of an informational Index. A better example is a photograph. The mere print does not, in itself, convey any information. But the fact, that it is virtually a section of rays projected from an object *otherwise known*, renders it a Dicisign[...] It will be remarked that this connection of

> the print, which is the quasi-predicate of the photograph, with the section of the rays, which is the quasi-subject, is the Syntax of the Dicisign; and like the Syntax of the proposition, it is a fact concerning the Dicisign considered as a First, that is, in itself, irrespective of its being a sign. Every informational sign thus involves a Fact, which is its Syntax. (CP 2. 320, 1903)

These quotations offer useful explanations as to how we are to understand the difference between sign and object within the classification theory of 1903, in which two of the three divisions are relational. The first shows how for Peirce, the object of the artist's sketch on Figure 5—a simple crayoned likeness which, he claims, most observers familiar with the person portrayed elevate to the semiotic status of an index—is simply the young model, while the crayon lines on the artist's sheet constitute an iconic sinsign. The second quotation, dealing with photographs and for which the human and non-human elements to be found in the studio are the determinants of the section of rays composing the "subject" half of a propositional sign of which the predicate half is the print, explains why the studio and its human and non-human elements constitute the object of the photograph, a dicent sinsign. In neither definition, nor in any other from the period, is the intentionality responsible for the bringing into being in any identifiable way of the portrait or of the photograph of the sketching of the portrait.

The structure and linear functioning of semiosis as described to Lady Welby in 1908 does makes it possible to identify such an intentional origin and to understand how this origin determines the way a pristine artist's sheet is modified by the lines and forms crayoned upon it. The dynamic object on Figure 5 is, we may be sure, the sitter's desire to be commemorated in the sketch by or for her parents, otherwise she wouldn' t be sitting there in the first place. In other words, to distinguish herself from the millions of selfie-takers, she or her parents have deliberately elected to immortalize the moment by means of a crayon representation on the sheet of a studio artist's sketch-pad clipped to an easel. Such deliberation is the object of the sketch: an object, therefore, intentional in nature. The medium, is composed of a sheet of paper and the accompanying non-randomly distributed crayon marks. The dynamic object is thus necessitant and the sign is classified in this division as collective. As a pictorial representation, the sketch itself offers no proof of the existence of its object. It is nevertheless understood to have been contracted to represent an individual, and the represented properties of the young sitter—lines, shapes, colours—function as the immediate object. As a class of signs, the image on its own would be classified as a collective, designative token as shown on Table 3.

Table 3 Classification of the Studio Portrait of a Young Girl

(semiosis)	Subject				
	Od →	Oi →	S →	Ii →	Id →
Universe					
Necessitant	collective	copulant	type	relative	usual
Existent	concretive	designative	token	categorical	percussive
Possible	abstractive	descriptive	mark	hypothetical	sympathetic

ii. A Donor Portrait

Within the system of 1903, and without a caption, Memling's panel is an iconic sinsign. With the caption, the panel is multimodal and becomes a replica of a dicent indexical legisign. Hypoiconically, it is diagrammatic, as there are conventional contrastive relations holding, for example, between the positions and sizes of the protagonists.① It is indexical by virtue of the proper names in the caption ("the 'referents' are like this"), and as these are verbal signs it is also a legisign. It is dicent because caption plus image (indices + icon) form, as mentioned in the second (1903) quotation reviewed above, a type of proposition.

According to Wikipedia "A donor portrait[...] is a portrait in a larger painting or other work showing the person who commissioned and paid for the image, or a member of his, or (much more rarely) her, family". At the time of the painting, the commission of many religious paintings was a form of commercial transaction between patron and artist, the patron supervising many aspects of the finished work, even paying for expensive pigments such as ultramarine. In the case of a donor portrait the donor was included in the painting. Such portraits were organized in a conventional manner, where the donor was represented kneeling and often depicted on a smaller scale than the accompanying holy figures, here the Virgin Mary and Saint Anthony Abbot; the latter is recognisable by his attributes, namely the staff

① For a description of Peircean hypoiconicity the reader is referred to Chapter Five of Jappy (2013).

Figure 6 Hans Memling, *Virgin and Child with St. Anthony the Abbot and a Donor*

and the little pig by his right foot. Since the relation between donor and Virgin corresponds to a difference in secular *vs.* holy status it is represented by relative size, where secular status is shown as reduced, and also by differences in stance, with the secular element kneeling while the Virgin and child are standing. These differences in status are further deliberately indicated by the Virgin and child's occupation of the centre of the image with the donor to the side, and by the Virgin's being depicted in splendid colour while the donor is in lowly sub hues.

The dynamic object here is principally the donor's desire to be commemorated for posterity in the painting but this desire is necessarily combined with contemporary artistic conventions—Memling no doubt had his own Flemish conception of how to paint portraits. And it is this combination which determines the features characterizing the structure and contents of the image: the dynamic object is thus necessitant and the sign classified in this division as collective. Memling's complex sign considered simply as a *medium* or vehicle in the artistic sense is composed of oils and an oak panel. It is thus existent and as a medium is classified as a token What the immediate object, the "hint" or "its substance" of the dynamic object in the sign, imparts to this medium is the peculiar and unique distribution and disposition of colours and shapes in the painting identified above from the point of view of their hypoiconic values, arranged to signify the contrast in status (holy vs. secular) and identity (Virgin, saint, donor) of the various figures. This means that the organization of the portrait is not determined, as in the portrait of the young girl on Figure 5, according to the physical features of the model, or here, according to those of the donor, but according to a complex system of contractual determinants: unlike the portrait of the young girl, which is an image hypoicon, Memling's image is diagrammatic; that is, it operates semiotically on a more complex hypoiconic level determined by the contract between painter and donor. The immediate object communicates this complex combination of values—donor's desire and artistic conventions—as a diagram in the Peircean sense.

The difference in hypoiconic values in the two types of portrait can be seen at the **Oi** stages on Table 3 and Table 4. In the first case, the immediate object, which organizes the medium according to salient physical features drawn from the young girl, is thus existential, the hypoiconicity is that of the image and the sign is classified as *designative* in this division, whereas on Table 4 the immediate object is necessitant, communicating to the medium representative features of convention, contract and personal wishes—factors more complex than actual physical appearance—structuring the sign diagrammatically, for which reason the sign is classified as *copulant* in this division. In short, since they involve contracts, such donor portraits necessarily present contractually and deliberately significant aspects of the immediate object, this being the conspicuous evidence of the way the donor and artist had agreed on the contents and organisation of the portrait. As a class of signs, the donor portrait would thus be classified as a collective, copulant token (Table 4).

Table 4 Memling's Donor Portrait Classified

(semiosis)	Subject				
	Od →	Oi →	S →	Ii →	Id →
Universe					
Necessitant	collective	copulant	type	relative	usual
Existent	concretive	designative	token	categorical	percussive
Possible	abstractive	descriptive	mark	hypothetical	sympathetic

V. Conclusion

In view of the widespread employment of the concept of semiosis, it is surely a theoretical necessity to be able to identify and characterize the nature of each stage in the process, and not simply for classification purposes. The paper has sought to treat as media such signs as two portrait paintings in an attempt to determine the exact semiotic status of the various immediate objects composing the representation of the intentionalities in which they originate; to determine, that is, their status within the three-universe classification system advanced by Peirce in 1908. In order to do so the field chosen was that of obvious intentional activity glossed broadly as purpose-driven representation.

By isolating significant aspects of the immediate object—comparing the simple structure of the studio portrait with Memling's formally more complex donor portrait, for example—the paper has sought to identify aspects of the immediate object's role in semiosis that take its definition further than the blanket description of "object inside the sign". The operating principle adopted took at its face value the hexadic definition of semiosis advanced by Peirce in his letter to Lady Welby of 23 December 1908 and isolated the sign as a simple medium as an artist might. This made it possible to hypothesize as the contribution to semiosis the arrangement of the elements composing two pictorial media as the form communicated by the immediate object, which can thus be seen to function as a filter of the intentional influence of the sign's dynamic object.

To what extent would Peirce have agreed with the methods employed and resultant findings concerning the immediate object mentioned above? He probably would not, since his definitions of the immediate object are strictly logic-oriented and his examples most often logocentric. More to the point, he would never have indulged in analyses of case studies such as those discussed above, as he was more interested, he tells William James (EP 2 500), in discovering all possible types of signs rather than in analyzing actual cases. Nevertheless, since he never exploited empirically his conception of semiosis, the paper has sought to investigate one aspect of its heuristic potential.

References:

Anderson, D. (1985). Peirce on metaphor, *Transactions of the Charles S. Peirce Society*. XXI (4), 453-468.

Bellucci, F. (2018). *Peirce's speculative grammar: Logic as semiotics*. London: Taylor and Francis.

Bernays, E. (1947). The engineering of consent. *Annals of the American Academy of Political and Social Science*, 250, 113-120.

Freadman, A. (1996). Peirce's second classification of signs. In Colapietro & Olshewsky, (Eds.). *Peirce's doctrine of signs: Theory, applications, and connections*. New York: Mouton de Gruyter, 143-159.

Houser, N. (2005). The scent of truth. *Semiotica*, 153(1/4), 455-466.

Jappy, T., (2013). *Introduction to Peircean visual semiotics*. London: Bloomsbury Academic.

Jappy, T. (2016). *Peirce's twenty-eight classes of signs and the philosophy of representation: Rhetoric, interpretation and hexadic semiosis*. London: Bloomsbury.

Peirce, C. S. (1931-1958). *Collected papers of Charles Sanders Peirce* (8 Volumes). C. Hartshorne, P. Weiss, & A. W. Burks, (Eds.). Cambridge, MA: Harvard University Press. (CP)

Peirce, C. S. (1998). *The essential Peirce* (Vol. 2). Peirce Edition Project (Ed.). Bloomington: Indiana University Press. (EP2)

Peirce, C. S., & Welby-Gregory, V. (1977). *Semiotic and significs: The correspondence between C. S. Peirce and Victoria Lady Welby*. C. S. Hardwick (Ed). Bloomington: Indiana University Press. (SS)

Savan, D. (1988). *An introduction to C. S. Peirce's full system of semeiotic*. Toronto: Toronto Semiotic Circle.

Author:

Tony Jappy is Professor Honoraire of University of Perpignan Via Domitia, France. He has published widely on Peircean semiotics and linguistics, iconicity theory and visual semiotics. His current research is concerned with Peirce's late semiotic system.

作者简介：

托尼·贾皮，法国佩皮尼昂大学荣休教授，出版成果涉及皮尔斯符号学与语言学、像似性理论、视觉符号学等领域，现在研究方向为皮尔斯后期符号学理论。

Email：tony@ univ-pepr. fr

汉字符号学

文字符号的向心和离心

孟 华

摘　要： 汉字符号学主要研究文字的超符号性质。超符号指超越自身而内部隐含、外部关联了其他异质符号的符号。超符号关系主要是语言符号与非语言符号的关系，集中表现为语言与文字和语言与图像（包括实物符号）的关系。本文主要通过汉字的分析，讨论了两种超符号关系方式：以语言符号为中心的向心方式和以非语言符号为中心的离心方式。

关键词： 向心，离心，超符号，汉字符号学

Endocentric and Exocentric Approaches of Character Signs

Meng Hua

Abstract: Research on the semiotics of Chinese characters mainly focuses on the trans-sign properties of Chinese characters. The term "trans-sign" refers to a sign that transcends itself, then internally implicates and externally associates other heterogeneous signs. The trans-sign relationship is predominantly a relationship between linguistic signs and non-linguistic signs, which is primarily a question of the relationship between language and text, and between language and image (including physical signs). Based on the analysis of Chinese characters, this paper discusses two approaches to trans-signs: an endocentric approach, centred on linguistic signs, and an exocentric approach, centred on non-linguistic signs.

Keywords: endocentric, exocentric, trans-sign, semiotics of Chinese characters

DOI: 10.13760/b.cnki.sam.202002005

溪水急着要流向海洋，浪潮却渴望重回土地。 ——席慕蓉

一、关于文字的向心和离心

百余年来，东方农耕文明的奇葩——表意汉字急着要流向世界文字拉丁化的海洋，西方海洋文明激进的思想浪潮却开始批判语音中心主义的拼音文化，思考着用汉字之“药”疗治字母之“病”。这是对“以谁为中心”的文化秩序的反思：汉字走向拉丁化，意味着对海洋文明的“向心”而对农耕文明的“离心”；拼音文化的自我批判则象征着自身的离心倾向而重估汉字文化的价值。当然西方后现代主义的自我离心倾向并不意味着要重建一个东方中心，而准确地说是“移心”：消解东方和西方两个中心之间此消彼长的对立。

“中心”这个词在结构主义符号学中有两个含义（肖锦龙，2004，p.7）：一是“中心主义”，如“逻各斯中心主义”“语音中心主义”“弥赛亚主义”“官僚主义”等，它是一种主观性的文化思想体系或理论立场；二是“中心性”，它是事物得以构成的自然因素，是一种客观现实，是组织和统辖某种结构的核心要素，雅各布森叫作“主导”①，如在电视 MTV 中主导的符号是音乐而不是画面，古汉语文言文的中心要素是汉字而非口语中的词，官本位体制下的中心要素是官员，等等。

任何进入书写阶段的语言都有一个言文关系（“语言和文字关系”的简称）中以谁为中心的问题，这个中心便是一个现实存在的“中心性”的概念，这个中心是某种客观存在的文字制度形成的终极目的和原因。如汉字是以无声的视觉方式迂回地表达有声语言，在言文关系中以“文”或“字”为中心；拉丁字母则尽力隐藏文字的视像性以唤出声音的直接出场，在言文关系中以“语”或“音”为中心。这两个中心范式其实是两种符号化方式——

① 罗曼·雅各布森：“对主导可以这样下定义：一件艺术品的核心成分，它支配、决定和变更其余成分。正是主导保证了结构的完整性。”转引自赵毅衡（2004，p.8）。

东西方文化使用不同文字符号来表达语言，描述世界的集体智能，也可以分别称之为“字本位”和“语本位”[①]（或称“文本位”和“言本位”）方式。

作为文化思想概念的“中心主义”，则是一种“以谁为中心”的哲学文化思潮或理论主张：主观上区分出中心和边缘两个要素，建立一种人为的等级制格局。德国学者白瑞斯将语音中心主义文字观表述为：

> 文字系统的一个普遍性特征，就是要利用相互区别的符号来表示包含在整体流动的语言之下的这些较小的单位。因此，文字和语言之间首要的且是最为重要的连接点，便是语言的声音要素……音素，才是与文字系统发生关联的主要成分。（转引自黄亚平等，2009，p. 4）

上述引文蕴含着一个以表音素为中心的文字学思想，由此产生一个向心的等级制：向心程度以表音素的程度为标准，即以文字是否与音素这一级语言单位关联为标准。只有最接近记录音素的文字，才是最好的向心文字。在西方语言学中，语言被描述为一个双层的分节装置。第二分节单位是音素层，第一分节是符号层，又具体包括语素、词、词组和句子。从音素到句子这五级单位中，越是接近音素的文字越是向心而文明的，与音素中心的距离越远便越是离心的、野蛮的或原始的（卢梭，2003，p. 27）。显然，以拉丁字母为代表的拼音字母记录的是语言的音素单位，因此是向心文字的最高符号范式，而汉字记录的是汉语的语素和词这一级单位，相对而言是离心的。向心性文字以表音性为旨归，所以也可表述为“口治性”文字；离心的汉字则可表述为“目治性”或“表意性”文字。

就汉字自身而言，近百余年来在某种程度上也经历了一个以拼音文字为认同坐标的向心化过程，这是西方文化中心主义或语音中心主义对古老的农耕文明冲击的结果。20 世纪的汉字拉丁化运动[②]，就是对汉字离心性符号化范式的自我批判和走向拼音文化的向心化思潮。不可否认的是，就全世界的

---

① 中国大陆的字本位语言理论的代表人物是徐通锵、潘文国。参见（孟华，2008，p. 17，p. 28）

② 明嘉靖以后，西方基督教传教士即对汉字进行注音，形成了最早的汉字拉丁化。清朝末年，开始发动创制拼音文字的运动——切音字运动。到了五四时期，又形成新的高潮，先驱者于门不满足于有一套汉字笔画式的注音字母，明确提出“汉字革命”，甚至主张“废除汉字”、全盘西化。1918 年中华民国教育部公布第一套法定的 37 个民族字母形式的注音字母方案。1928 年中华民国教育部公布第一套法定的拉丁化拼音方案——国语罗马字（简称国罗）。1958 年，中华人民共和国公布的第二套法定的拉丁化拼音方案，使用了 26 个拉丁字母，用符号表示声调。直到 20 世纪 80 年代，汉字拉丁化运动才逐渐消息。

文字符号等级制谱系而言，其中心毫无疑问是以拉丁字母为代表的拼音文字体系。拼音字母通过任意性原则记录最为抽象和形式化的音素单位，追求形音一致的向心性。符号学的任意性也叫作无理据性，即字母的形体结构中不包含任何人的主观动机和外部世界的客观信息。由于切断了文字与文化意义世界的理据联系，字母文字成为跨民族、跨语言传播的普适符号，使得拉丁字母成为世界交流的文化公器。据统计，大约有 100 种主要的语言、120 个国家以及将近 20 亿人口使用拉丁字母（萨克斯，2008，p. 9）。

本文主要是在“语音中心主义”这个概念框架下讨论文字的离心和向心的：就文字系统背离或趋近音素中心的状况而言，这种文字观认为背离表音素倾向的文字是离心的，如汉字；趋近表音素倾向的文字是向心的，如拉丁字母。

二、言文关系和语象关系的向心和离心

文字的向心和离心，在语言文字学那里涉及的是言文关系范畴，而在符号学看来，它们同时也是一对语象（语图）关系范畴。汉字符号学就是希望通过汉字的言文关系分析而获得一种关于语象关系的符号学范式。

在今天的杂语化时代，“所有的符号系统都与语言纠缠不清”（巴尔特，1999，p. 3）。符号学的热点由指示关系（语言与概念或现实的关系）、言文关系（书写与语言的关系）逐渐转向语言与图像、语言与非语言符号的关系。当语言遭遇非语言符号时，就会产生向心和离心两种关系的博弈。

（一）言文关系和语象关系的向心化

首先看言文关系的向心化或表音化趋势。汉字的拉丁化和汉语的白话文运动，跟着读书语气走的传统句读改为跟着语言语法结构走的现代标点符号，繁体汉字的简化或汉语中的音译外来词，传统小学转变为语言文字学、汉语学由文法研究走向语法研究……这些都反映了表意的汉字逐步向语言靠拢、走向表音的趋势。

语象关系的向心化则表现为图像符号向语言靠拢的趋势。艺术家徐冰的“地书”用 三个连缀的具象图符表达一个句子：“他爱她。”这就是图像的向心化：图像符号转换为表词单位或象形文字。网络上盛行的图像性表情包几乎成为语言的第二书写系统，这也是目治性图符走向口治性字符的表现。图像的向心化即图像的语言化、概念化自古有之，不仅中国传统写意画以及

欧洲中世纪的宗教画充满了诗性和言说性，贡布里希甚至称古埃及绘画艺术是“概念艺术”：“他们在图画中再现已知而非所见的一切的方法”（米歇尔，2006，p. 34），即古埃及艺术家是根据既有的语言概念而不是凭视觉经验去进行绘画创作。图像的概念化、语言化也是现代艺术创作的重要特征之一：绘画的原型直接来自语言符号负载的语词概念、思想主题或程式化观念，而非实际存在物。譬如毕加索的《格尔尼卡》是根据新闻报道创作的，而非他亲眼所见的事件。另一位西班牙现代主义大师米罗的画作《女人·鸟》中，女人和鸟已经结合为一个巨大的黑色形体，隐喻着二者的相似性。“在米罗看来，女人就是鸟，鸟就是女人，因为女人与鸟有着共同的特征：她（它）们都有诱人的色彩、柔和的外表，都使人迷恋……”（鲍诗度，1993，p. 320）。显然，在这幅作品中，视觉形象是为语言概念服务的，是大写的象形字。

（二）言文关系和语象关系的离心化

（包括文字在内的）任何符号强调自己异质于语言、独立于语言的符号性质则是离心关系。

（1）就言文关系而言，汉字是离心性较强的文字符号系统。

索绪尔就认为汉字没有字母文字那样的“令人烦恼的后果”。因为汉字与语音无关：“对汉人来说，表意字和口说的词都是观念的符号；在他们看来，文字就是第二语言。”（1980，p. 51）当汉字成为独立于语言的符号时，它就破坏了言文之间的向心关系而强调了文字自身视觉符号的离心性质，所以德里达说：“中文模式反而明显地打破了逻各斯中心主义（按：即表音中心主义）。”（1999，p. 115）言文关系的向心化和离心化之间的张力运动，是贯穿中国现代性文化建设的一大主题。五四新文化运动提倡汉字拉丁化和白话文，可以称为“去汉字化”或“向心化”运动，此后直到20世纪80年代一直是中国学术和文化界的主流意识形态。80年代起，去汉字化或向心化所造成的传统断层越来越受到关注和批评。不断有学者强调表意汉字与记音的字母之间的文化差异，认为汉字是独立于汉语的符号系统，要求对汉字的视觉性文化特性重新评估，提出艺术、文学创作的会意性“字思维”（石虎）或汉字书写原则的“春秋笔法”（曹顺庆），认为中西哲学的差异在于“写”和“说”（杨乃乔），汉语语法的本质是文法而不是语法（申小龙），中西语言基础单位的差异在于“字”和“词”（徐通锵），汉字不是附属品而具有与汉语同样的地位（潘文国），汉字与汉语之间不是脚与靴子的关系而是瓜皮和瓜瓤的关系（苏新春），汉字是看待汉语的意指方式而非语言的简单记录工具（孟华）……这种“再汉字化”的思潮就是言文关系的离心化（申小龙、孟华，2014，p. 1）。

（2）就语象关系而言，离心性突出地表现为两个符号领域：一是图像的去语言（文字）化，二是文字的图像化。

①语象之间的离心化首先表现为图像的去语言（文字）化。这是一种极性思维：在图像与语言文字的对立、分治中确立前者的视觉符号特性，在目治和口治之间划出一道非此即彼的边界。德国文艺批评家莱辛就以绘画和诗歌为例强调了图像与语言之间的对立、分治关系：“时间上的先后承续属于诗人的领域，而空间则属于画家的领域。”（莱辛，2006，p. 107）这显然涉及语象两种对立性的编码原则：语言的线性、时间特征和图像的非线性空间特征。这种离心化是一种等级制格局：图像的性质是建立在它不是语言或者对图像自身的语言因素予以抑制、排斥基础上的。这种极性思维认为，图像性的可见和语言性的可读、可说是互相排斥的，如福柯所谓“在视觉中被封口，在阅读中被隐形”（福柯，2012，pp. 22 - 23）。去语言化的离心图像观表现于文字起源研究领域，就是在图像和文字之间划一道非此即彼的边界，图像的归图像，文字的归文字。认为史前的图像符号如抽象记号、图案、图画不属于文字，因为它们不记录固定的言语单位，只有到了表词的象形字阶段，人类文字文明才开始，前者叫作史前文明，后者才是有史文明。当然，从史前的图像到象形字，中间存在一个亦文亦图的过渡阶段，叫作图画文字（伊斯特林，1987，p. 27）、文字画或初期意符（沈兼士，1986，p. 207）。但即使这些过渡性文字符号，也要划清与图像的界限：图画是与语言无关的具体艺术形象，而图画文字是“图示性的约定图像”，后者已经在一定程度上记录固定的言语单位，比如印第安人在一幅画中画了野牛、海獭、绵羊、猎枪等符号，“这几种动物的图像不是供艺术欣赏，而是用来表示、规定事先在言语中表达的交换条件”（伊斯特林，1987，p. 21）——显然这幅画中的动物图符代表某些言语单位，构成了一个由图画文字记录的贸易文本，阅读取代了观看。

然而，到了德里达的中性语象观那里，史前图像和图画文字、象形字之间泾渭分明的边界被消解了，它们都被认为是广义的“文字”或书写①。

②语像之间离心化的另一种表现是文字的图像化，即发掘、呈现文字符号中所隐含的被遮蔽和压制的视觉图像特性，揭示隐藏在文字中的离心化元素，恢复文字符号所具有的语象双重编码的复合性质。德里达生造了一个“différance”来表达“异延”这个概念，以揭示文字所具有的语象双重编码特性：空间的差异（图像）和时间的延宕（语言）的中介化。“différance”（异延）是由“différence”（差异）改造而来，只是将原词中的一个字符“e”更换为“a”。这个改动使得“a”摆脱了拼音的束缚，仅仅作为一个视觉标识符起到空间性分辨作用（德里达，2000，p. 68），就像汉字助词“的、地、得”，在汉语口语中它们同音而且近义，但汉字用三个不同形体区分了它们语法意义的微妙差异，或者说，汉字通过字形的视觉标识性介入了口语中“de”这个助词的分类。标识符是图像符号中的一种，如物体上的标签、公共指示符号、方位识别符号等。标识符有两个特点：一是单符性，它只与在场物或特定概念相连，而与线性叙事链条无关；二是指物性，它不代表某个形式化、结构化的音素，而标识自身之外的某个实体——在场物、现实物或观念物。如国际音标（外文词典中每个单词后面的注音符号）就是标识符：它只孤立地用于分辨特定音素，而不具有连缀性；国际音标指示的音素是实物——物理形态的语音。形式化的字母文字则相反，它记录的音素是形式而非实体，即进入某个语音系统中的结构单位，每个字母表达的音值不来自它的物理性质而来自系统的分配关系，所以字母的表音单位更准确地叫作音位。相对而言，国际音标符号是实体性的标识符，具有离心的图符性质；字母文字符号是形式化的结构性记号，具有向心的语符性质。

因此，真正的标识符附着于物体之上，随着人们的指指点点引导着现代游牧者的各种现场辨识活动。随着德里达在“différence”（差异）这个词中强行抹去记音符“e”，而插入一个标识符“a”，人们不得不中断对“différance”（异延）的线性阅读而滞留于对“a”的空间性凝视中，或者说，单符性、非线性的标识符一旦进入记音符结构，便对线性语音串具有解构力量，引出一种非线性的视觉解读，这是一种口治和目治的双重经验。当一个

① 现在我们往往用“文字”来表示这些东西：不仅表示书写铭文、象形文字或表意文字的物质形态，而且表示使它成为可能的东西的总体；并且，它超越了能指方面而表示所指方面本身。因此，我们用“文字”来表示所有产生一般铭文的东西，不管它是否是书面的东西，即使它在空间上的分布外在于言语顺序，也是如此：它不仅包括电影、舞蹈，而且包括绘画、音乐、雕塑等“文字”。（德里达，1999，p. 11）

标识符进入记音符的组合（如 I♥you 中的 ♥），或者一个记音符兼有了标识符的功能（如上述“différance”中的“a”），这时标识符就失去了它单纯标识的功能，而具有语象双重编码性：既是一个显示视觉差异的离心化的图像标识符号，又是一个跟着语音线性序列走的表音符号。由此，德里达揭露了拼音文字离心性的另一面，即它与空间性图像符号相关的特性，从而说明拼音文字并不忠实于语音，它在表音或言说的同时，又把视觉性的空间力量强加给语言。索绪尔举了法语单词“oiseau”（鸟）的例子，实际上该词应读[wazo]，字母读音与该词的实际读音完全不通。据此他指出，“文字遮掩了语言的面貌，文字不是一件衣服，而是一种假装”（索绪尔，1980，p. 56），人们常常把书写形式误作读音规则，结果产生了文字对语言的歪曲。

③文字中图像元素的三种类型。

但是，德里达并不满足于仅在字母串中发现图像性标识元素，或者在西方文本的线性阅读中发现空间凝视，他更感兴趣的是汉字以及各种象形字的图像性或离心性。他斥责了那些贬低汉字或象形字的“偏见”（德里达，1999，p. 117），并认为这些文字才符合他理想的书写或文字形态，并在此基础上建构了一种全新的符号学体系，即语图融汇的书写学。

笔者认为，人类文字体系中的图像性符号元素主要包括三类：

第一，标识符。拉丁字母兼具记音符和标识符双重性质。纯粹的标识符是贴在物体上的标签，是不具有连缀性的单符，而标识功能的字母一旦出现于线性字符串时，便切断了字符串的语音连续性而成为无声的图形辨识单位。如英语中的“often”（常常）和“soften”（使柔和），通常它们的“t”是不发音的，只起到形体视觉辨识的作用。字母标识符是拼音文字内部的图像或离心要素，它引发了人们对字母的语象双重关系意识。

第二，相似符。指文字形体主要通过相似性、类比性的形象理据来标识所指物。包括（a）单符性相似符。如汉字独体象形字𠆢，画一个羊头，转喻“羊”这个概念；大画一个成人身体，隐喻“大”这个概念。它们共同的表达机制是修辞的、类比的，就是一个单纯的符号“含蓄意指”① 着某个概念，我们统称其为单符性相似符。（b）组合性相似符。主要指汉字中多个义符构成的会意字。如“伐”，从人持戈；“炙”，从肉在火上；“囚”，从人在口中。这些会意字通过对两个字符概念的联想而产生的画面感，来表达背后的

① “含蓄意指”或称“内涵意指”的概念借自罗兰·巴尔特（1999，p. 83），意为符号的能指或表达面本身就是携带某种理据性的符号，它成了所指内容面的表达层。含蓄意指是一种符号的双重意指现象，如汉字的字形义和字义、字面义和词义，就是含蓄意指。

词义。组合性相似符也是一种含蓄意指，与前者区别在于，这种充满蒙太奇画面感的含蓄意指效果产生于字符之间的组合。(c) 混合相似符。即声符和义符的混合体，以汉字形声字为代表。如“啤”，其声符“卑”指涉“啤”的具体意义和读音，具有表音、向心的特点；形旁则从“口”的转喻角度提供一个关于啤酒的联想形象，是义符，具有相似理据、离心的特点。所以，在符号学看来，形声字的混合性就是指一个组合性语象结构：义符以转喻形象参与了对声符的补充、说明，声符作为语言符号又参与了形声字的组合并对义符进行限定和解释。① 关于混合相似符我们在下文中还有讨论。

第三，像似符。建立在视觉性像似基础上的符号就是像似符，典型的如绘画、照片等。文字中的像似符主要指象形字，如（山）、（人），所见即所得。唐兰（2001，pp. 75－80）将甲骨文象形字分为“象形”和“象意”两类，前者就是独体的像似符，后者则是独体的相似符（如前述的象形字“羊”和“大”）。撇开象形字向心的一面即表语言的功能不谈，象形字或初文还具有离心的一极，即像似符的性质。下面分析象形字即像似符和独体字即相似符的两个主要特征——单符性和指物性。

(a) 单符性。“独体为文，合体为字”，在汉字发展初期以单符或独体的象形字即“文”为主。象形字单符性的第一层意思是说它的外部非连缀性，一般只作为一个孤立的符号与指物对象相结合。如古埃及早期的标签性象形字，以及被认为是象形字直接来源的某些史前孤立的陶符、印章符号，等等（陈永生，2013，p. 26）。单符性的第二层含义是，进入成熟期的象形字在外部可以进行线性连缀，如，是一个偏正性词组结构（大鹿），而不是两个画面的非连缀并置（人和鹿）②。但是，即使在外部可以进行语法性连缀的象形字，一般在内部仍具有结构上的整体性或不可分析性。如甲骨文（鹿）一般不认为是由两个字符组合而成，其内部结构是单一的、独体的符号，也是如此。外部的非连缀性和内部的整体不可分解性，是单符性图像符号的主要区别性特征。但是成熟的象形字已非纯粹的单符，虽然组合能力有限但

① 徐通锵将汉字的形声结构区分为义类和义象：“‘形’表义类，‘声’表义象。为什么？因为义类属于‘辨类属’的范畴，是对某一类现实现象的概括反映，而义象是从不同的义类中抽象出来的，是深一层的概括。”（2015，p. 108），但是笔者认为，徐通锵是站在向心的立场上，即站在文字的语义或语言分析的角度来观察形声结构的。本文则是站在离心或语象融汇的立场上对形声字进行重新分析。当然，本文并不否认向心立场的理论价值。

② 裘锡圭区分了这两个象形符号的双重性：作为图画的非连缀性和作为象形字的连缀性（1988，p. 3）。

已可以连缀，许多被认为是独体的象形字实际上已经具备有限的二合能力或结构的二元性。如（鹿）、（兔）、（犬）、（象），一般认为这四个象形字都是独体字，但它们其实共用了同一个模件——程式化的、简约为两条腿的躯干。这四个字就是在同一模件基础上加不同动物的头部组合而成。也就是说这些被认为是独体的象形字，其内部结构仍保留某种有限的二分性。再如（果），由一个字符和描摹果的图符合成。由此可见，象形字的单符性是相对而言的。有限的连缀性和有限的二合性又使得象形字区别于图画，后者的单符性更纯粹：图画一般有个画框，使其保持了自己的边界和单符性。单符性是一个“差异关系”的概念，即德里达所谓的“痕迹”(trace)[①]：自身与他者的差异关系运动，即一个要素的性质取决于同另一要素的差异关系，借助与他者的差异关系来显示或隐藏自身（或他者）。比如我们说今天的方块汉字外部连缀性、内部合体性更强时，是为了显示象形字这个他者的单符性和离心性，并隐藏了象形字的向心（记录语言）属性；当说象形字较之图画具有更多的连缀性和二合性的时候，是为了显示他者——图画的单符性和目治性，并隐藏了图像的写意（言说）性。

（b）指物性，即符号在近处显示或指示在场物的效能。图像性标识符的指物性最强，如贴在商品上的图像性或文字性商标，胸牌、台签、名片、招牌、印章、物品标签、货物名单、交通符号、公共场所符号……这些符号总是关联着一个在场物。符号指物性可从表达面和内容面两个方面分析（一个现实中可以吃的苹果和一个画面中只能看的苹果，后者是符号的表达面，前者是符号的内容面）。从符号表达面看，指物性意谓以物象的方式或有理据的方式显示所指内容的能力。如用表示爱意，以玫瑰花的物象含蓄意指一种抽象精神情感。另如“仙人掌”这个词，它的所指对象是一种植物，但它的字面义却隐喻“像仙人的手掌”，抽象的概念获得一种物质性、具象性呈现方式。相对而言，的指物性高于“仙人掌”，因为前者诉诸视知觉经验，后者则要靠对词语的形象联想。从符号内容面看，指物性意谓在近处标出、关联一个在场物的能力。如这个标识符可以唤起我们对某款耐克鞋的形象联想，尽管鞋子并不在现场出现。当然，显示可见对象最强的指物方式还是贴在实际产品上的：标识符与标识对象共同在场。可见，内容

① “不想保留指称结构内的差别，我们就不能设想人为的痕迹，正是在指称结构中，差别才如此显示出来，并使各项之间的自由变动成为可能。……痕迹的运动必然是隐秘的，它将自身变成自我遮蔽。当它物如此显示自身时，它却在自我隐蔽中呈现出来。”（德里达，1999，p. 64）

面的指物性是符号关联物的能力，关联性最强的是在场物和图像，其次是在心理联想中产生的关于物的形象。

象形字的指物性远远高于表意的方块汉字。首先，在表达面“以物象的方式显示所指内容的能力”方面，象形字是以图像的方式，而方块表意字则图像性或象形理据逐渐减弱，如“马”字的演变：

甲骨文　金文　战国文字　篆文　隶书　楷书(繁体)　楷书(简体)

汉字“马”的演变

其次，在内容面“标出、关联一个在场物的能力”方面，象形字时代还没有完全脱离它与在场物的关联。如古埃及的标签性象形字，每个标签上都有一个小穿孔，以方便将标签系在所标识的物品上，形成在场性关联。当然更多情况下，这种关联在场物的能力指的是一种“索引词”（陈嘉映，2013，p. 25）的功能：一个像似符的意义主要不来自与其他符号的组合关系，而来自它与特定时间、空间、表达者和表达对象等在场现象的关联。如甲骨文的意义更多的不是来自文本的线性叙事，而是来自甲骨卜辞与在场性占卜情景相关的整个仪式事件；甲骨文的破译更多依赖的不是训诂学或语言文字学而是考古学，更多的不是用于阅读而是观看。

综上所述，人类文字不同体系中的图像性主要包括三类：标识符（以拉丁字母为代表）、相似符（以方块汉字为代表）、像似符（以象形字为代表）。其共同特征是指物性、单符性，这体现了文字符号系统内部隐藏的离心性、目治性一面。长期以来，语音中心主义文字观将向心看作文字的本质特征，而忽略或隐藏了其离心即图像的属性。汉字符号学的主要任务之一，就是通过汉字分析来揭示文字中被隐藏了的离心性，还原文字所存在的语象双重编码性质。此外，这三类文字之间也存在着向心和离心的差异关系（“痕迹”——自身与他者的差异关系运动）：象形字一方面在与纯粹图像的差异关系中获得了自己的向心性（表语言性），另一方面又在与方块表意字的差异关系中获得了自己的离心性（图像性）；表意汉字在与象形字的差异关系中获得了自己的向心性或口治性，另一方面又在与字母文字的差异关系中获得了自己的离心性或目治性。

三、汉字形声字中的向心和离心

（一）超符号

根据差异关系符号观，所有符号都是不自主的：口语符号需要文字的锚固，文字符号产生于语言的无能，图像符号需要语言灵魂附体，语言符号需要图像“立象尽意”……符号的这种不自主性决定了其他符号进行补充的需要，决定了任何符号都具有异质性的双重或多重编码性质，都是超越自身而内部隐含、外部关联了一个异己的他者，并在这种异质关联中实现自己的价值。这种差异符号观我们也称之为超符号观。超符号（trans-sign）即一个超越自身而内部隐含、外部关联了其他异质符号的符号。超符号的最主要表现为符号的语象融汇性：如图像符号自身包含了趋就语言的向心要素，或者语言、文字符号自身包含了趋就图像的离心要素。巴尔特对这种超符号的语象关系综合体总结道：

> 物品、图象、动作可以表达意义，并且它们实际在大量表达着意义，但是，这种表达从来不是以自主的方式进行的，所有的符号系统都与语言纠缠不清。（巴尔特，1999，p. 2）

汉字是典型的超符号，“汉字是在与汉语、汉民族的视觉符号的关联中定义自身的”（孟华，2014，p. 15）。画家徐冰就是从汉字的语象交织的超符号性中获得启发，创作了他的《天书》和《地书》作品系列（伯利塞维兹，2014，p. 23，p. 27）。《天书》中徐冰自创了一些没有任何表意或记言功能、谁也看不懂的“假汉字”，而把观众的视线由对汉字的向心性阅读转向离心性观看，引向一个语言尚未抵达之处：对方块汉字图像美学的纯粹注视，进而将汉字的离心化推向极致。《地书》则把一些图像性公共标识符号改造成能够记言和连缀叙事的“象形字”，人们凭借这些图像、图标和商标就可以得到一篇故事：图像被向心化、语符化、文字化了。徐冰向我们展示了两种语图融汇的超符号：《天书》是离心化超符号，《地书》是向心化超符号。

（二）汉字形声字的向心和离心

超符号向心和离心的差异关系运动也深深地隐藏于汉字形声字中。传统文字观将形声字的义符和声符看作表意和表音的两类语符（或字符），而汉字符号学将它们转换为异质的语象关系：义符以相似性视觉理据行使离心的图符功能，声符以任意性编码行使向心的语符功能。

下面是以形为纲和以声为纲的两类形声字字族的例子①。先看以形（义符）为纲的离心性形声字族（例字引自许慎《说文解字》）：

狗：孔子曰："狗，叩也。叩气吠以守。"从犬句声。

狡：少狗也。从犬交声。

猝：犬暂逐人也。从犬卒声。

默：犬暂逐人也。从犬黑声。读若墨。

犯：侵也。从犬巳声。

狠：犬斗声。从犬艮声。

獲：猎所获也。从犬蒦声。

狼：似犬……从犬良声。

上述字族中的不同声符围绕同一可视性、理据性义符"犬"（犭）的不同意义网络进行区分、注音、限定：当形旁或义符的意义负荷超载，或可视理据模糊时，语言性声符服从于可视性义符的限定。因此这类形声字体现了离心、以言定象的方式。

再看以声为纲的向心性形声字族，典型的是宋王圣美的"右文说"（义符表类、声符表义说）中的例字（沈兼士，1986，p. 83）：

浅：水之小者曰浅。

钱：金之小者曰钱。

残：歹之小者曰残。

贱：贝之小者曰贱。

从造字的角度分析，右文说中的声符同时也是义符："浅、钱、残、贱"中的"戋"做声符的同时也有"小"义，具有义符和声符双重特征。此类结构在造字之初本质上也是一个会意结构，只不过其中一个义符同时兼声符或者说它不是纯任意性的声符。但是倘若未经专业训练，多数人无法理解声符中的意义理据，而仅仅把浅之"戋"、坑之"亢"、瞳之"童"、婢之"卑"、增之"曾"、拱之"共"等声符看作无意义的表音符号或任意性记号，需要

① 徐通锵首先提出了形声字的向心和离心问题，尽管他不是从符号学的语象关系立场出发："以声为基础而生成字族的方法是向心造字法，而以形为基础……则可以总结出离心造字法。""向心和离心，这是汉语字法结构的两种最重要的规则。"（2005，p. 120）

不同的视觉理据（义符）对其解释。以声为纲的形声字体现了以义符注声符、以象定言的向心化方式。

在汉字形声字的上述两种语象关系方式中，起主导作用的还是离心的“以象定言”，它与周易符号“立象尽意”传统一脉相承，其价值远远超越文字学本身而成为具有普遍意义的视觉文化语法。美国意象派诗人庞德编选的美国汉学家费诺罗萨的论文，将汉字中这种“以象定言”的方式叫作“意符诗法”（徐平，2006）：“思维并不处理苍白的概念，而是察看在显微镜下事物的运动。”（费诺罗萨，1994）所谓概念在“显微镜下事物的运动”，就是指汉字“以象定言”——视觉优先于语言概念的指物性传统：在可视性物象中显示抽象的语言概念。美国学者徐平分析了这种意符诗法在诗学文本中的表现：

> 唐代孟棨在《本事诗》中写道：“白尚书姬人樊素，善歌，妓人小蛮，善舞，尝为诗曰：‘樱桃樊素口，杨柳小蛮腰。’”此处，诗人在形容樊素的口（或者更准确地说，她的唇）非常红艳，而小蛮之腰十分纤细。但他并没有使用“红”和“细”这类字眼，而是用“樱”比喻“樊素口”，以“杨柳”比喻“小蛮腰”。（徐平，2006）

显然，“樱桃”“杨柳”这些意象性的符号代替了直白的概念“红”“细”，相当于形声字的义符；而“樊素口”“小蛮腰”则是直接表达有声语言的概念单位，相当于“声符”。它们“以象定言”的结构式为：

> 樱桃（义符，象）+樊素口（声符，言）
>
> 杨柳（义符，象）+小蛮腰（声符，言）

汉语中的“雪白、碧绿、天大、海量、樱口、鼠窜、蛙跳、猫步、菜色、仙逝、奶白、油滑、（一）捧水、（一）把米、（一）包书、鬼哭狼嚎、枪林弹雨……”也属“义符+声符”的意符诗法结构：画线的语素相当于义符（视觉意象），其余的则相当于声符（听觉的语言概念单位）。

可见，意符诗法既是造字法，也是“以象定言”的超符号文化语法，即在向心和离心的双重运动中，坚持以可视性、有理据、离心为主导的方式去表达汉语、表达世界。

四、结语

汉字符号学的主要任务之一，就是通过汉字分析来揭示文字中被隐藏的离心性，还原文字所存在的语象双重编码性质。我们用向心和离心取代文字的表意和表音，体现了由文字学向符号学的转变：文字外部关联和内部隐含了一个语象间差异关系的运动——从文字的外部看，文字是向心的，图像是离心的；就文字内部而言，象形字是离心的，表意字是向心的；汉字是离心的，拉丁字母是向心的。同时，汉字又是典型的向心和离心异质结合的中性化符号系统，它一手抓着图像，一手抓着语言，隐藏着今天读图时代深层的超符号语法：语言与非语言符号之间向心和离心的双重运动法则。

“读图时代”这个说法容易导致“进入图像符号时代”的错觉。应准确地描述为对文字的观看性阅读和对图像的阅读性观看二者之间的游移；或者说，图像具有阅读性（向心），文字具有可视性（离心）。所以，读图时代应该称为“超符号”时代——语象并重、语言符号与非语言符号融汇的时代。

汉字符号学的核心是超符号问题，超符号主要研究语言符号和非语言符号（文字、图像、实物、音乐、建筑、服装、踪迹等）的关系问题。这种关系包括两种基本范畴：向心（以语言为中心）和离心（以非语言符号为中心），最集中地表现在语象关系和言文关系中。语象关系还包括了词与物的关系：如“实指”——手指一个熊猫用口语指称它；“标指”——不用口语而用图像或文字性标签指称和说明在场的熊猫。“实指”过程中人们重感知物而忽略口语的存在，是“先物后名”的离心方式；“标指”过程中人们首先以标签（词、名）为认知在场物的前理解，是“先名后物”（孟华，2014，p. 353）的向心方式。当然，向心和离心这对范畴也可用来分析其他超符号，比如标题音乐就是一种向心模式，其文字和标题阐述了作品的内容或情节，音乐向文学（语言）靠拢，语言标题规定了作品内容理解的方向。而无标题音乐则是离心的，它没有向语言靠拢的意图，它着重于音乐本身的音响美、形式美或抽象的情感意味，尽管不同听众可能会给无标题作品以不同的私语性阐释，但这种语言阐释后于纯音乐感知而发生，语言理解服从于纯音乐感知，而不是相反。

引用文献：

鲍诗度（1993）. 西方现代派美术 . 北京：中国青年出版社 .

巴尔特，罗兰（1999）. 符号学原理（王东亮，等译）. 北京：生活·读书·新知三联书店.
伯利塞维兹，马修（编）（2014）. 徐冰的《地书》之书. 桂林：广西师范大学出版社.
陈嘉映（2013）. 简明语言哲学. 北京：中国人民大学出版社.
陈永生（2013）. 汉字与圣书字表词方式比较研究. 北京：人民出版社.
德里达，雅克（1999）. 论文字学（汪堂家，译）. 上海：上海译文出版社.
德里达，雅克（2000）. 后现代性的哲学话语（汪民安，等主编）. 杭州：浙江人民出版社.
费诺罗萨，厄内斯特（著），庞德，埃兹拉（编）（1994）. 作为诗歌手段的中国文字（赵毅衡，译）. 诗探索，3，151－172.
福柯（2012）. 这不是一只烟斗（邢克超，译）. 桂林：漓江出版社.
黄亚平，白瑞斯，王霄冰（主编）（2009）. 广义文字研究. 济南：齐鲁书社.
莱辛（2006）. 拉奥孔（朱光潜，译）. 合肥：安徽教育出版社.
卢梭，让－雅克（2003）. 论语言的起源（洪涛，译）. 上海：上海人民出版社.
孟华（2008）. 文字论. 济南：山东教育出版社.
孟华（2014）. 汉字主导的文化符号谱系. 济南：山东教育出版社.
米歇尔，W. J. T.（2006）. 图像理论（陈永国，胡文征，译）. 北京：北京大学出版社.
裘锡圭（1988）. 文字学概要. 北京：商务印书馆.
沈兼士（1986）. 沈兼士学术论文集. 北京：中华书局.
索绪尔，费尔迪南（1980）. 普通语言学教程（高名凯，译）. 北京：商务印书馆.
萨克斯，大卫（2008）. 伟大的字母（康慨，译）. 广州：花城出版社.
唐兰（2001）. 中国文字学. 上海：上海古籍出版社.
肖锦龙（2004）. 德里达的解构理论思想性质论. 北京：中国社会科学出版社.
徐平（2006）. “物”与“意符诗法”（涂险峰，译）. 长江学术，2，50－60.
徐通锵（2015）. 汉语结构的基本原理. 青岛：中国海洋大学出版社.
伊斯特林（1987）. 文字的产生和发展（左少兴，译）. 北京：北京大学出版社.
赵毅衡（编选）（2004）. 符号学文学论文集. 天津：百花文艺出版社.

作者简介：

孟华，中国海洋大学教授，研究方向为汉字符号学。

Author:

Hua Meng, professor of Ocean University of China. His research field is semiotics of Chinese characters.

Email: menghua. 54@ 163. com

谈古埃及象形文字内外的语象关系*

陈永生

摘　要：象形文字是图像与语言双重编码的符号系统，衔接了视觉和听觉两种知觉，融观看和阅读于一身。古埃及象形文字是人类四大象形文字（还有汉字、苏美尔文字和玛雅文字）中图像特征最为突出的一种，最典型地体现着图像与语言的互动关系。这种互动关系既体现在象形文字与所处图像场景的关系上，也体现在象形文字内部意符和音符的关系上。本文通过一个图文并茂的古埃及浅浮雕分析这两方面的语象关系。充满了语图平面设计感的古埃及象形文字，为语象合治的现代符号学研究提供了无尽的宝藏和灵感。

关键词：古埃及象形文字，语象关系，汉字符号学

On the Image-Language Relationship Inside and Outside Egyptian Hieroglyphs

Chen Yongsheng

Abstract: A pictographic writing system is formed by double codes: code of image and code of language. It connects both visual and auditory perceptions, and blends the process of viewing and reading. The Egyptian hieroglyphic writing system is of the most prominent imagery feature among the four ancient pictographic writing systems

---

* 本文为国家社科基金青年项目“汉字与古埃及文字比较研究”（13CYY047）的中期成果。写作过程中，孟华先生曾提出极为宝贵的建议，笔者在此表示诚挚的谢意。同时，高善铭博士（Sam Goldstein）为摘要做了准确的英译，孙梦雪同学协助整理分析了相关德文资料，王梦雅同学在行文上给出了很好的修改建议，也一并致谢。

(Sumerian, Egyptian, Chinese, and Mayan), so it most typically reflects the interactive relationship between image and language. That interaction lies not only between the texts and the surrounding scene, but also between the ideograms and the phonograms inside the writing system. The article analyzes those two aspects through an ancient Egyptian bas-relief containing both scenes and texts. The Egyptian hieroglyphic writing, which is full of graphic design, provide perennial inspiration for the research of modern semiotics.

Keywords: ancient Egyptian hieroglyphs, language-image relationship, semiotics of Chinese characters

DOI: 10. 13760/b. cnki. sam. 202002006

人类历史上创造的成熟象形文字并不多，主要的有四种：汉字、古埃及文字、苏美尔文字和玛雅文字。[①] 说它们“象形”，是因为它们以描绘物像或事像的图符为元符号；说它们“成熟”，是因为它们能够逐词记录语言。这些象形文字最显著的符号学特征，在于它们是图像与语言双重编码的符号系统，衔接了视觉和听觉两种知觉，融观看和阅读于一身。

四种象形文字中，埃及圣书字（Hieroglyphic）的图像性特征最为突出，它使用的图符像似度较高，所绘物像也较易辨识。尤其与众不同的是，这种最象形的书体在古埃及3500余年的历史中始终未退出历史舞台。它与在其基础上草化而成的僧书字（Hieratic）和民书字（Demotic）[②] 分工，专门使用于神圣庄重的场合，作为其他艺术形式（浮雕、塑像、壁画、建筑等）的必要组成部分，发挥着美学价值和信息价值。相反，汉字甲骨文和苏美尔原始楔文（Proto-cuneiform）[③] 在衍生出其他简便书体后，便完全退出了历史舞台。如果借用王力先生的比喻，前一种书体演进关系可以称为“牛生犊式”，后一种可称为“蚕化蛾式”[④]。

埃及象形文字对图像属性的坚守，使它最典型地体现着图像与语言、视觉与听觉的互动关系。这种互动关系既体现在象形文字与所处图像场景的关

① 赫梯象形文字（即安纳托利亚象形文字）也是已破译的成熟象形文字，但是其使用地域和影响较小。印度河谷文字（哈拉帕文字）很可能也是成熟的象形文字，但至今尚未破译。

② 民书体产生较晚，是对僧书体的进一步草化。

③ 原始楔文是尚未变成楔形笔画的象形体阶段。

④ “牛生犊”和“蚕化蛾”都是王力先生在谈词义引申时发明的比喻。（王力，1980，p. 572）

系上，也体现在象形文字内部意符和音符的关系上。本文将通过一个图文并茂的古埃及浅浮雕（下图），分析这两方面的语象关系。

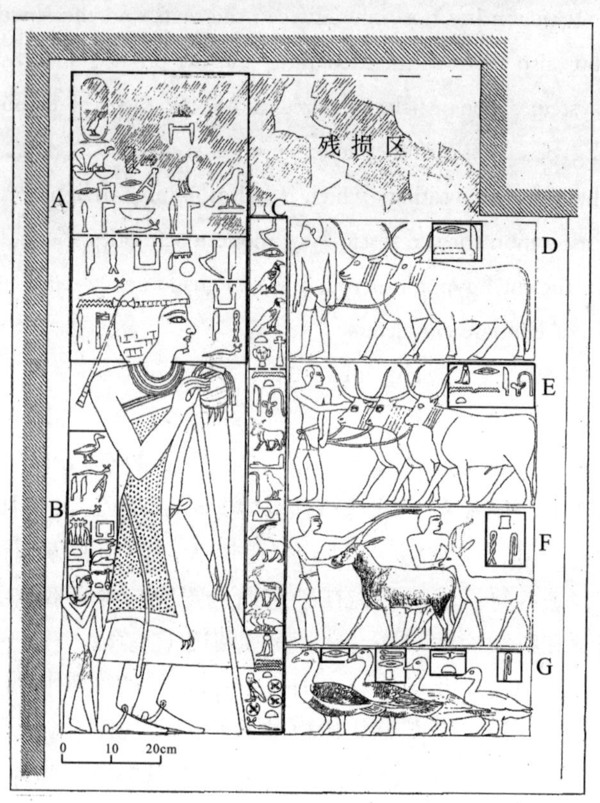

卡海夫祭拜堂北墙浮雕上的图像和铭文

（采自 Junker，1943，p. 127，笔者稍做了改动）

一、象形文字对场景的补充

我们要讨论的浅浮雕来自古埃及第六王朝（约公元前 2345—前 2181 年）官员卡海夫的马斯塔巴墓①（参考 Junker，1943，pp. 94 - 155）。浮雕场景描绘的是墓主人领着他的儿子观看献礼，场景空隙中插入了说明性的象形文字。原浮雕和象形文字都是彩色的，上图是埃及学家制作的黑白摹本。为了分析

① “马斯塔巴”是埃及古王国时期贵族常用的一种墓葬样式，分为地上部分和地下部分，因为地上部分是平顶且四壁向上内收，外观像阿拉伯人所用的“石凳”（mastaba），故有此名。卡海夫的马斯塔巴位于吉萨金字塔群近旁，该浅浮雕来自地上部分的祭拜堂的北墙。

的方便，笔者用黑框对几组象形文字分别做了标记，并冠以字母序号 A、B、C、D、E、F、G。

（一）整体场景与核心标题

整体场景

整体场景可分彼此相对的左右两大部分：左侧是墓主人和他的儿子观看献礼，右侧是献礼者带着礼物向墓主人走来。为了突显墓主人的形象，他被描绘得极为高大，而其他人物则明显较为矮小。右侧场景又被横线隔为四栏，是献礼者和他们带来的牛、羊、雁。

核心标题 C

位置：核心标题 C 呈纵列排布，置于左右两部分场景中间。

文字内容（语言内容）：“观看（从他的村子带来的）礼物：牛、野羊、雁。”①

字符朝向：这组文字的字符朝向是经过创作者精心安排的。以笔者标出的虚线为界，上下两部分的字符朝向正好相反。上部分表达的是“观看礼物”，字符统一朝向右侧的礼物场景，与墓主人朝向一致（其中动物的朝向极为明显，如两个埃及秃鹫字符）；下部分表达的是“牛、野羊和雁，从他的村子带来的”，字符统一朝向左侧墓主人，与右侧场景中的礼物的朝向一致。（参 Fischer，1977，p. 73）这种巧妙安排，应该说是人类早期文明中“版式设计”的一个高峰。

行文方向：虚线之上部分是从上到下，从右往左，字符顺序依次为：。虚线之下部分是从上往下，从左往右，字符顺序依次为。

字符特点：四个字符与右侧场景中的牛、羊、雁的形象高度一致，体现出埃及象形文字基本符号的图像来源。但是，象形文字内部图符之间的大小比例不以现实为准则，而以节省空间和组合美观为准则，例如，大羚羊的图符与埃及秃鹫和猫头鹰大小相仿，人的手臂与牛的长短相同，猫头鹰图符竟然大于村落的图符，丘陵图符竟然

---

① 注意：“从他的村子带来的”这个短语是修饰“礼物”的，在原埃及语中处于“牛、野羊、雁”之后。这段文字的字词详解可参考文后附录。

小于大羚羊图符。

（二）场景元素与标签文字

1. 墓主人与标签 A

墓主人的形象

墓主人神情喜悦、姿态舒展地观望着送来的丰盛礼物。他的着装尽显贵族雍容：头佩饰带，颈戴宽项圈，内着长而宽松的下身围裙，外披豹皮斗篷（豹尾从臀后垂到两小腿中间，两个豹爪在左膝和左肩），足履凉鞋。他的姿态悠闲舒适：上半身稍微前倾，倚靠着手杖（右手握手杖顶端，左手自然下垂搭到手杖中下端），重心放在右腿，左腿稍弯而踮脚。

标签 A

位置：墓主人头上方及两侧的场景空白处。

文字内容（语言内容）：墓主人的头衔和名字。笔者标出的长虚线上方，本是墓主人的四个头衔，从右往左呈四个纵列排布，现在残泐严重。① 长、短虚线之间，有一行文字，末尾延伸至墓主人头后方，表达的是“尊者：先王的卡海夫”。短虚线以下，墓主人面前又一次标出了墓主人名字“卡海夫”。

字符朝向：统一朝右，与墓主人共同面向献礼者和礼物。

行文方向：从上到下、从右往左，长短虚线之间的字符顺序依次为。

2. 儿子与标签 B

儿子的形象

站在墓主人身后，赤身露体，颈佩项圈，左手抱着父亲的腿，右手伸向嘴巴。

标签 B

位置：儿子（名为“杰德奈弗利特”）头上方的场景空白处

文字内容（语言内容）：儿子的身份和名字——“他（按：指墓主人）的儿子，他喜爱的人，王室土地的承租户②，杰德奈弗利特。”

字符朝向：统一朝右，与儿子朝向一致。

---

① 这里不再详释，有兴趣的读者可参考 Junker（1943，p. 96）。

② “王室土地的承租户”这一翻译尚不确定。

行文方向：总体上也是从上往下、从右往左，但是有一点混乱（以笔者标出的虚线为界，第二纵列在第一纵列的右边，未完全贯彻从右往左的顺序）。整组文字的字符顺序依次为。

3. 礼物与标签D、E、F、G

礼物场景

第一栏的牵牛人左手牵着两头肥牛，身体略朝墓主人前倾。第二栏的牵牛人是一个秃发的长者，他用力牵拽着三头牛，但似乎牛不是很顺从，于是他转身用右手去拽一头牛的耳朵。第三栏的两位献羊人分别拖拽着一只肥壮的大羚羊和一只轻健的瞪羚（都是野味），二人姿势相似，都是左手握一只羊角，右手攥着羊的口鼻。第四栏是向墓主人走来的四只不同种类的雁（此栏省略了献礼者，是因为没有足够的纵向空间来容纳与上面几栏一样高度的人）。

标签D、E、F、G

位置：动物的身体上方的空白处。

字符朝向：统一朝左，与动物共同面向墓主人。

行文方向：从上到下、从左往右，例如标签E的字符顺序依次为。

文字内容（语言内容）：标签D表达牛的种类（后方有一个字符残损）是“幼牛”；标签E表达的是“带来幼牛”；标签F表达的是“瞪羚”这一名称，这里没有标出前面一只大羚羊的名称（“大羚羊”），可能是遗漏或是出于空间和美学考虑；标签G表达的是四只雁的种类：，其中第三种雁是“针尾鸭”，而另外三种具体雁种尚未确知。

（三）小结

通过以上分析，我们把埃及象形文字补充场景的特点总结为以下两个方面。

第一，从分离和区别的角度看，象形文字以异质于图像的语言补充场景图像在信息准确性上的局限。通过这种异质性补充，场景的主题与人物得以明确。作为语言的象形文字虽然使用的也是图符，但明显有别于场景图像：首先，大小有别，场景图像大，而文字图符小；其次，规则有别，场景图像的大小、位置基本遵循现实规则，模仿非线性的现实空间[1]，而象形文字图符的大小和位置则遵循语言的线性规则进行铺排。

第二，从统一和互补的角度看，象形文字以其所兼有的图像性质，实现与场景图像的协调统一。首先，在位置上，象形文字填充于场景的空白处；其次，在形象上，象形文字图符与场景图像遵循同样的艺术法则，当所描绘的是同一事物时，形象完全一致；[2] 最后，在方向上，象形文字图符与所说明的对象朝向一致，行文的头尾与所述物像的前后相应。可以说，象形文字并非纯然的语言替代物，它通过与场景的协调统一实现某些信息功能和美感功能。

二、象形文字内部的意音互补

古埃及历史的后期经历了希腊和罗马的相继统治（公元前 332 年—公元 641 年），后被阿拉伯帝国征服（公元 641 年），成为阿拉伯帝国的一部分。在外族统治下，埃及的传统文化和宗教受到巨大的冲击，象形文字的使用变得越来越少。公元 391 年，罗马将基督教定为国教，极力排斥一切异教，与埃及传统宗教密切关联的象形文字最终被完全抛弃，成为无人能识的死文字。[3] 此后至商博良重新破译这种文字（1822 年）的 1400 多年里，无数的好奇者与智者曾揣度这种文字的含义与原理，但都未能成功。其中一个最重要的原因是人们被它的图像性吸引和迷惑，认为各个图符都是充满神谕的神秘符号，或认为这些图符都是记录思想理念的超语言符号，而没有真正意识到这些符号本质上是记录古埃及语言成分的符号。

与其他几种成熟象形文字一样，古埃及文字为了实现准确表达语言的目标，对图符进行了语言化操作，创造了“意符”和“音符”两种基本字符。商博良成功破译的关键一步，就在于他意识到埃及象形文字中除了意符还有音符的存在。

（一）意符（Ideogram）

例如，核心标题 C 中，“雁”这个词是通过雁的形象来表示的。因为在

---

① 当然，并非绝对模仿现实，如墓主人被故意夸大，又为了节省空间而把献礼分为上下四栏。

② 更多例子可参威尔努斯（2019，p. 91）。

③ 今天所能见到的古埃及人书写的最晚圣书体文字，是公元 394 年在菲莱岛一所神庙墙壁上的涂鸦。

句子中它是复数，所以重复了三次以喻其多：

Apdw“雁”（复数）[①]

这种通过描绘形象来表现词语的图符就是“意符”。

再如，标签 B 中，表示“王宫”的固定短语 pr-aA（字面义是“伟大的房子”），是用两个意符共同表示的。前者是用房子的形象直接表示“房子”pr，后者则是用柱子的形象喻指“伟大”aA。（注意：在古埃及语中，修饰语在中心语之后。）

又如，标签 A 中，表示“先王”的固定短语 nTr-aA（字面义是“伟大的神”），是用两个意符共同表示的。前者是用神旗的形象转指（借助邻近关系）“神”nTr，后者还是用柱子表示词语“伟大”aA。

也就是说，利用图符的形象表词的时候，有时是直接的，有时是间接的。下面我们再列举一些埃及文中常见的直接意符和间接意符。直接意符，如 r“口”、 ra“太阳”、 mw“水”、 s“男人”、 msi“生子”、 sSn“荷花”、 st“座位”、 abA“权杖”。间接意符，如 （牛头之形）表示 kA“公牛”， （麦穗之形）表示 bty“二粒小麦”， （啤酒罐之形）表示 Hnqt“啤酒”， （否定的手势）表示 n“不”， （风帆之形）表示 TAw“气息、风”。

（二）音符（Phonogram）

例如，在标签 B 的开头，“儿子”一词是用针尾鸭的图符 表示的。因为，在埃及语里“儿子”的读音 zA 与“针尾鸭”的读音 zAt 很相近。这种利用谐音关系来表词的图符就是“音符”。西方学者常常称这种方法为“画谜法”（Rebus Principle），中国文字学里则称之为“假借”。

再如，标签 B 中，在“儿子”一词后面有一个表示物主的代词 f“他”，是用角蝰的图符 表示的，也是基于“他”f 与“角蝰”ft 的音近关系。

---

① 为了表示古埃及文字的读音，研究者们使用小写拉丁字母（辅以少量特殊字母和标号）对古埃及文字进行了转写，如将“雁（复数）”一词转写为 *ꜣpdw*（参马克·科利尔，2015，pp. 3－6）。本文为了排版方便，采用了大小写结合的电脑转写系统（参 Allen，2014，p. 17），将一些特殊字母和带标号字母进行了如下转换：ꜣ-A，ꜥ-a，ḥ-H，ḫ-x，ẖ-X，š-S，ḳ-q，ṯ-T，ḏ-D。

除了使用单个谐音图符表词的方法，埃及文字还使用多个谐音图符相拼合的表词方法，尤其是对于多辅音结构的词[①]。例如，标签 F 中，gHs“瞪羚”是一个三辅音结构的词，拼合了三个谐音符：（g，水罐架）、（H，绞拧的灯芯）、（s，折叠的布）。标签 G 中，第二个雁的名称是 Trp，也拼合了三个谐音符：（T，栓动物双腿的绊脚）、（r，嘴）、（p，芦苇凳）；第三个雁是（zAt，“针尾鸭”），拼合了两个谐音符：（z，门闩）、（t，面包）[②]。

象形文字使用谐音符主要有两方面原因：一是语言里有许多词语的意义较为抽象，不易直接画出；二是有些词语虽可以画出但容易误读。前一种情形，如前文提及的 f“他”。再如 xt“东西”中，（胎盘［存疑］）表示 x，（面包）表示 t；xpr“变成”，借用了蜣螂图符；Hna“连同……”（介词）中，（灯芯）表示 H，（水波纹）表示 n，（手臂）表示 a；xA“一千”（数词），借用了藕荷图符。后一种情形，如前文讲过的 zA“儿子”，画出一个男孩儿的形象不难，但是让读者认出表示的是“儿子”而不是“男孩”就很难。

（三）意符兼音符

象形文字中的图符往往可以兼有意符和音符两种功能，如既可以用作意符表示“嘴”r，也可以用作音符表示单辅音 r；既可以用作意符表示“房子”pr，也可以用作音符表示双辅音 pr。

（四）意音结构

除了单纯用意符表词和单纯用音符表词，埃及象形文字还用意符和音符合成的意音结构表词（类似于汉字中的“形声字”）。意音结构从生成上看有两种基本模式：在意符上补充音符和在音符上补充意符。[③]

在意符上补充音符。例如，核心标题 C 中的第一个词 mAA

① 古埃及词语所含辅音有一到四个不等，其中三辅音结构最为常见，四辅音结构极少。

② A 并未得到记录。

③ 孟华先生曾使用“以象定言”和“以言定象”两个说法（参“智慧树”网站的国家精品开放课程“意象的艺术：汉字符号学” http://coursehome.zhihuishu.com/courseHome/2028301#teachTeam）。

"看"，本来可以用意符表示，但为了进一步说明要表示的是"看"而不是"眼睛"，就加了三个音符补充提示"看"的读音：（mA，镰刀）、（A，埃及秃鹫）、（A，埃及秃鹫）。这种起补充说明作用的音符叫作"音补"（phonetic complement）。

音补除了用来提示意符的读音，也常用来提示音符的读音，尤其是语音结构较复杂的音符。例如，标签A中的 imAxw "尊者"一词，含有一个四辅音音符（imAx，流髓脊柱），以及另外三个对其进行提示的音补：（i，芦苇花）、（mA，镰刀）、（x，胎盘［存疑］）。

在音符上补充意符。例如，核心标题C中有一个固定短语 aw. t -xAst "野羊"，由[1] aw. t "羊"（集合名词）和[2] xAst "野外、沙漠"两个词复合而成，有趣的是，后面又加了两个意符（大羚羊）和（瞪羚）来补充说明野羊的具体种类。这种起补充说明作用的意符可以叫"意补"（semantic complement）。

埃及文字中的意补可以分为具体型（specific semantic complement）和类别型（generic semantic complement）两种。（参 Gardiner，1957，p. 31）具体型只用于个别词语，如上面所讲的两个羚羊的意补，再如 znHm "蝗虫"中的（参 Gardiner，1957，p. 477）。类别型则用于批量词语，表示类属意义，如（树枝）常用在木制器具的名称中提示质料，如 wxA "柱"、 afdt "箱"、 iAAt "杖"、 wsr "桨"，等等[3]。

（五）小结

如果强调象形文字内部两种符号的异质性，可以说意符是图像性的符号，音符是语言性的符号。音符通过对语词读音的体现，缓解了图像直接表现语词（尤其是抽象语词）的困难，而优化了的意音结构从图像和语音两个方面出发，使词语的记录更加简便而明确。从上述内容来看，意音互补的象形文

---

① 含一个音符（awt，农民用的曲柄杖）和三个音补：（a，手臂）、（w，小鹌鹑）、（t，面包）。

② 用作意符，描绘的是丘陵地带。

③ 这些例子中，之前的字符都是音符。

字系统实际上也是一个语象互补的符号系统。

结　语

综上，不论是从埃及象形文字和场景的关系，还是从埃及象形文字内部意符和音符的关系，我们都可以明显地看出象形文字的“语言－图像”双重编码性质，或者说“视觉－听觉”双重编码性质。视觉和听觉是人类认知世界的最重要的两种知觉，埃及象形文字向我们展示了这两种知觉是如何地交织在一起，难以截然分开。这同时启示我们，象形文字的研究必须在语言和图像的关系中进行，忽视其中的哪一个都容易出现偏差。孟华先生从符号学角度提出“合治文字观”，认为：“文字的性质，是在文字与‘听’的语言、文字与‘看’的象符号的双重互动关系中被定义的。”（2008，p. 11）这种语象“合治”是现代符号学研究的核心领域之一，充满了语图平面设计感的古埃及象形文字，为现代符号学研究提供了无尽的宝藏和灵感。

附录：卡海夫浮雕中的象形文字详解

（一）核心标题 C

mAA nDt-Hr　nt　iwAw　aw.t　xAs.t　Apdw　innt　m　niwt.f

（画线部分行文方向是从右往左）

观看（来自他村子的）礼物：牛、野羊和雁。

（Seeing the gifts of cattle, wild goats and geese, which are brought from his village.）

（1） mAA “看”，含有一个意符（眼睛）和三个音补：（mA，镰刀）、（A，埃及秃鹫）、（A，埃及秃鹫）。

（2） nDt-Hr “礼物”，这是一个固定短语，字面义尚不清楚。（Faulkner，1962，p. 144）

（3） nt，是所有格形容词“n”的阴性形式，与前面的 nDt 保持一致，都含阴性词尾 t，语法意义类似于英语里的“of”。

（4） iwAw “牛”（复数），是 iwA “牛”的复数形式，含一个复写三次的意符①和两个音补：（i，芦苇花）、（wA，捕套）。

（5）aw. t xAst“野羊”（参 Faulkner，1962，p. 39），这实际上是一个短语，其中 aw. t 是集合名词“羊”，含一个音符（awt，农民用的曲柄杖）和三个音补：（a，手臂）、（w，小鹌鹑）、（t，面包）；xAst“野外、沙漠”含一个意符（丘陵地带）；这个短语之后加了两意补：（大羚羊）、（瞪羚），以形象补出了野羊的具体种类。

（6）Apdw“雁”（复数），含一个复写三次的意符（雁）。

（7）innt“带来的（东西）”，是动词 ini“带来”的现在分词形式（科利尔，2015，pp. 140－142），修饰前面的名词短语 nDt-Hr“礼物”，并与其保持一致（都有阴性词尾 t）。此文字形式含有一个合体意符（碗＋行走的双腿，双腿带来了一只盛食物的碗）和一个音补（n），两个音符（n）、（t，面包）。这里双腿的方向与右侧献礼者的腿的方向一致。

（8）m“从……”（介词），含一个音符（m，猫头鹰）。

（9）niwt“村子”（复数），含有复写三次的意符（有交叉道路的村子）和一个音补（t，面包）。

（10）f“他的”（后缀代词表物主），含一个音符（f，带角的蝰蛇）。

（二）标签 A

（从右往左）

aAnTr n kA Hif imAxw

尊者，先王的卡海夫。（The revered one，Kaihif of the King.）

（1）imAxw“尊者”，含有一个四辅音音符（imAx，流髓脊柱）和三个音补：（i，芦苇花）、（mA，镰刀）、（x，胎盘?）。

（2）kA Hif“卡海夫”，含有四个音符：（kA，举起的双臂）、（H，绞拧的灯芯）、（i，芦苇花）、（f，带角的蝰蛇）。注意：此名

① 因空间有限，只表露出重复的痕迹。

字在墓主人面前又出现了一次。

（3）n，所有格形容词，意义相当于英语里的“of”，含有一个音符：（n，水波纹）。

（4）nTr“神”，含有一个意符（神旗的形象代指“神”）。

（5）aA“伟大”，含有一个意符（柱子的形象比喻“伟大”）。

（三）标签 B

（从右往左）

Dd-nfrt pr-aA xnty-S mry.f zA.f

他的儿子，他喜爱的人，王室土地的承租户，杰德奈弗利特

（His son，his beloved，the leaseholder of the court，Dednefret）

（1）zA“儿子”，含一个音符（针尾鸭，zA）。

（2）f“他的”，是一个用作物主的后缀代词，含一个音符（f，带角的蝰蛇）。

（3）mry“喜爱的人”，含两个音符：（mr，锄头）、（y，两朵芦苇花）。

（4）f“他的”（同第 2 条，后缀代词用作物主）。

（5）xnty-S，“王室土地的承租户”（此解释存疑），这是一个固定短语，其字面义尚不确定。

（6）pr-aA，“王宫”，这是一个固定短语，字面义是“伟大的房子”，含两个意符：（pr，房子）和（aA，伟大）。

（7）Dd-nfrt，“杰德奈弗利特”，这是墓主儿子的名字。含五个音符：（D，眼镜蛇）、（d，手）、（nfr，心脏和气管）、（r，嘴）、（t，面包）。

（四）标签 D

rn iwAw

幼牛（复数）（young cattles）

（1）rn“幼小”，含有两个音符：（r，嘴）、（n）。

（2）iwAw“牛”（复数），含有两个音符：（i，芦苇花）、（wA，捕套）。

（五）标签 E

int　rniwAw

带来幼牛（bringing young cattle）

（1）int“带来”，它是动词 ini“带来”的不定式形式，语法意义大致类似于英语里的 *v.* -ing 形式（科利尔，2015，p. 75）。含有一个合体意符（碗 + 行走的双腿，双腿带来了一只盛食物的碗）和两个音符（n）、（t，面包）。

（2）rn iwAw“幼牛”，参标签 D 的解释。

（六）标签 F

瞪羚（ghs）

（1）此词含有三个音符：（g，水罐架）、（H，绞拧的灯芯）、（s，折叠的布）。

（七）标签 G

r	Trp	zAt	s
雁名	雁名	针尾鸭	雁名

（1）r 表示某种尚不清楚的雁名，含一个音符：（r，嘴）。

（2）Trp，表示某种尚不清楚的雁名，含有三个音符：（T，拴动物双腿的绊脚）、（r，嘴）、（p，芦苇凳）。

（3）zAt“针尾鸭”，含有两个音符：（z，门闩）、（t，面包）。

（4）𓋴s，表示某种尚不清楚的雁名，含一个音符：𓋴（s，折叠的布）。

引用文献：

科利尔，马克（2015）．古埃及圣书字导读（陈永生，译）．北京：商务印书馆．

孟华（2008）．文字论（汉语字本位研究丛书）．济南：山东教育出版社．

王力（1980）．汉语史稿（下册）．北京：中华书局．

威尔努斯，帕斯卡尔（2019）．古埃及象形文字的基本原理．载于克里斯坦（主编）．文字的历史：从表意文字到多媒体，73－93．北京：商务印书馆．

Allen, J. p. (2014). *Middle Egyptian: An introduction to the language and culture of Hieroglyphs*. 3rd ed. Cambridge: Cambridge University Press.

Faulkner, R. O. (1962). *A concise dictionary of middle egyptian*. Oxford: Griffith Institute: Ashmolean Museum.

Fishcher, H. G. (1977). *The orientation of Hieroglyphs: Part 1. Reversals*. New York: Metropolitan Museum of Art.

Gardiner, A. (1957). *Egyptian grammar: Being an introduction to the study of Hieroglyph*. 3rd ed. London: Oxford University Press.

Junker, H. (1943). *Gîza VI: Bericht über die von der Akademie der Wissenschaften in Wien auf gemeinsame Kosten mit Dr. Wilhelm Pelizaeus unternommenen Grabungen auf dem Friedhofdes Alten Reiches bei den Pyramiden von Gîza*. Wien, Leipzig: Hölder-Pichler-Tempsky A. G.

作者简介：

陈永生，汉语言文字学博士、埃及学博士后。现为中国海洋大学文学与新闻传播学院中文系副教授，研究方向为古代象形文字之间的比较研究（包括古汉字、古埃及文字、苏美尔文字、玛雅文字等）。

Author:

Chen Yongsheng, Ph. D. of Chinese Philology and Post-doc of Egyptology, associate professor at the College of Liberal Arts, Communication and Journalism, Ocean University of China. Field of research is the comparative study between ancient pictographic writing systems (Chinese, Egyptian, Sumerian, Mayan, etc.).

Email: yongshengch163@163. com

文人画中的汉字性：以苏轼的《潇湘竹石图》为例*

匡景鹏

摘　要：“何谓文人画”一直是艺术史上非常有争议的一个问题。画家和学者们大都在历史框架内考察文人画的内涵与外延，然而却很难达成共识，这主要是因为它作为一种理想形态与历史真实存有差异。因此，我们需要换个角度来重新认识这个富有争议的话题，那就是不再关注其本体论特征，而是用汉字符号学的方法考掘其构意法则。汉字是中国文化的根元素，汉字性是生成文人画的重要机制。汉字性根本特征就是语图融汇，文人画内容面的意符性特征和表达面的笔墨性特征都具有汉字性的本质特征。

关键词：文人画，汉字符号学，汉字性，语图融汇

The Attribute of Chinese Characters in Literati Painting: With *Xiaoxiang Zhu-Shi Painting* by Su Shi as Case

Kuang Jingpeng

Abstract: The question of “What is literati painting?” has always been disputed in the Chinese art history. Painters or scholars tried to research the connotation and extension of the literati painting; however, there was no consensus. So we need re-recognize this question by other perspective—the literati painting dose not focus on the essential

* 本文为2018年度重庆市社会科学规划项目“福柯的画论与20世纪艺术史学范式的转换”（2018p. Y92）中期成果；四川美术学院重大博士培育项目“福柯的画论与20世纪艺术史学范式的转换”（18BSp. Y005）中期成果。

feature, but describe its rule of means with semiotics of Chinese characters. The attribute of Chinese characters is an important mechanism for becoming the literati painting. The fusion of language and image is the basic feature of attribute of Chinese characters, which is reflected in the content side of ideograph and expression of surface on brushstroke in literati painting.

Keywords: literati painting, semiotics of Chinese characters, attribute of Chinese characters, the fusion of word and image.

DOI: 10. 13760/b. cnki. sam. 202002007

在20世纪中国社会激荡与变迁的时代背景下，文人画一度成为画家或学者们热议的对象。这主要是因为他们都把文人画看作极具中国文化属性的一种艺术形态，甚至以此引出对国运和传统文化危机的隐忧。在当今“全球化艺术”① 的大背景下，我们该如何充分发掘中国艺术的独特性，“何谓文人画”的问题又被重新提了出来。前辈学者们在讨论这个问题时，大都试图厘清文人画的边界，进而界定到底哪种绘画类型属于文人画，但是他们各自的讨论路径却不相同，大致可归纳为以下几类：陈衡恪、俞剑华等学者试图从画家所属的社会阶层（文人、士大夫身份）的角度来界定；滕固受西方艺术史写作传统的影响，试图从艺术风格学的角度来界定文人画；石守谦指出了上述两类研究在界定何谓文人画方面的不足，并给出了相应的解决方案，那就是不再把“文人画”理解为线性历史中一个有着固定内涵和外延的概念，而是在具体的历史语境中确定它（2010，pp. 53 – 66）。

在相关研究基础上，笔者进一步质疑了文人画的概念及其历史连续性，并试图从汉字符号学的角度重新界定文人画。一般而言，语言文字属于规约性符号，是阅读的对象；图像属于像似性符号，是观看的对象。可是，汉字并非是汉语的透明载体，这使它同时具有图像符号与语言符号的双重属性。② 以此反观文人画，我们会发现它同样具有汉字所特有的双重属性，并且规约性占主导。本文把上述汉字性特征视为文人画的构意法则。为什么汉字性会

---

① 巫鸿先生在接受《东方早报·艺术评论》采访时，提到“全球化艺术”的概念，并认为其有意思的地方就是它的丰富性（2017，p. 275）。

② 孟华先生曾提出汉字以谐音的方式记录汉语，它并非汉语的透明载体；他对汉字的这种属性的解释是“汉字一手抓着汉语，一手抓着图像”。相对于汉语，汉字具有汉字性特征；相对于图像，汉字具有语言特征。

成为文人画的构意法则？一方面是由于画与文字异体而同源，张彦远在《历代名画记》中曾记载过颜光禄的话，云："图载之意有三：一曰图理，卦象是也；二曰图识，字学是也；三曰图形，绘画是也。"（2014，p. 2）宋代郑樵言："书与画同出。画取形，书取象；画取多，书取少。"（《通志·六书略·象形第一》，转引自周积寅，2013，p. 174）另一方面是由于以汉字为核心的书写文化在汉文化中占绝对优势，成为其他文化的存在形式。高友工认为，字的创造在华夏文化中被认作一件石破天惊的伟业。[①] 孟华把汉字视为中国文化诸多元素中的根元素[②]，并认为中国文化符号的存在方式为汉字化存在，非书写性符号被汉字书写，或者典籍文化精神投射到这些非书写符号中，成为其意义的来源（2015，p. 12）。在这种强大作用力的推动下出现了绘画被典籍化的现象，宋代韩拙道："山者有主客尊卑之序，阴阳逆顺之仪。其山布置各有形体，亦各有名。习乎山水之士，好学之流，切要知之也。主者，乃众山中高而大者是也。有雄气而敦厚，旁有辅峰聚围者岳也。大者要尊，小者要卑也。"（《山水纯全集》，转引自俞剑华，1986，pp. 662－663）这意味着经学典籍文化对山水画的投射，儒家的尊卑观念成为绘画构图的原则。另外，关于绘画被汉字化，方闻在讲范宽的《溪山行旅图》时认为："全图为中央的巨仞立壁占据，两侧山峰与之共同构成象形文字'山'的图示。"（2016，p. 133）我们甚至可以说，文人画呈现出的汉字性特征的深层原因是以汉字为中心的书写文化。

汉字性在文人画中的具体表现特征是什么呢？简言之，它表现为以形表意、语象融汇，包括两个方面：在内容面上，它具有意符性[③]特征，即用形象表达观念；在表达面上，它具有书法性特征，表现为相对固定的书写规则

---

① 高友工认为后人企图从庖牺作八卦、神农结绳直迄仓颉造书契拟构出一个文字滋生的源流。这种传说在战国时已屡见，而《系辞》和《说文叙》就已很系统化，明确肯定了它与文明社会的关系。（2008，p. 187）

② "根元素"指一个文化符号系统中起主导作用的符号单位，它的性质决定了该符号系统的性质。

③ "意符性 "是指从图像性、象形性较强的文字符号演变为高度概念化、意象化的文字符号特征（孟华，2014，p. 60）。

和冲破规则的墨戏之间的张力运动。比如说，苏轼的《潇湘竹石图》[①]（绢本，纵 28 厘米，横 105.6 厘米，现藏于中国美术馆），与宋代早期山水画相比，其画面显得简单，仅为一块石和几支带叶的竹枝，而且石竹皆以简笔画成，但画意不减，如其所言“谁言一点红，解寄无边春”（《书鄢陵王主簿所画折枝二首》，转引自李福顺，2008，p. 49）。画面中的竹石物象好像一个由不同偏旁部首构成的大写象形字，具有表情言志的功能。此外，画面呈现出的简、淡、孤寂的视觉风格特征，主要来自书法用笔，即文人们以写代画，在遵从运笔运墨规则的前提下，实现任运自然、自由挥洒的艺术效果。接下来，本文将结合《潇湘竹石图》来展开讨论文人画中的汉字性问题。

一、画为有形诗

汉字的意符性的特点是字典义和字用义的融合，它是一个程式化的、被普遍理解的概念（字典义），与用字者个人所赋予的特殊意涵（字用义）的统一体，我们也把这种特性称为汉字的意符思维。这一思维模式在绘画中表现为绘画的典籍化（字典义表达模式）和个体性“托物言志”（字用义表达模式）二者的融合。

当我们打开《潇湘竹石图》时，映入眼帘的画面以潇湘为背景，墨竹、枯石位于前景中，竹石以书法笔法画成，无论是画法还是图式都有很强的程式化特征，缺乏相应的逼真。此外，前景中的竹石与淡墨晕染出的背景缺乏必然的关系，给人一种空灵、失真之感，如同一个梦幻空间。显然，苏轼的画的主旨不是再现，而是表情达意，如他所言：“文以达吾心，画以适吾意。”其中，情动是绘画创作的诱因，以苏轼为核心的元祐文人们开始借绘画创作抒情。据记载，1088 年，苏轼知贡举，阅卷之余，常与门人黄庭坚、张耒、晁补之及李公麟一起画马、画竹解闷，还依次为所绘之图赋诗。（艾朗诺，2013，p. 171）在元祐年间，苏轼心情不好时亦作墨竹之类的绘画。黄庭坚曾评论过苏轼的竹石题材的绘画，道：“东坡老人翰林公，醉时吐出胸

---

① 《潇湘竹石图》由邓拓命名，可能跟“应写潇湘雨后枝”的题诗有关。此作的真伪存有争议，吴湖帆最早质疑该作非苏轼原作，其《丑簃日记》1937 年 5 月 16 日有记：“孙伯渊携来苏东坡《竹石》绢本卷，画系元人作，非真迹，但元明人题者二十六家，均真而精，洵奇事也。”（吴湖帆，2004，p. 47）但认定此画为真品者居多，认为该作在题材、艺术构思以及笔墨技巧等方面与苏轼的艺术特质很符合，邓拓先生撰文言：“苏东坡所作《潇湘竹石图》卷，可谓古画中杰出作品之一。……总观二十六家题跋，都非泛泛应酬之作，而是针对东坡之《潇湘竹石图》立论。”后来黄胄、杨仁凯等人在《光明日报》上的联名文章也从这几个方面确定此作为真品。本文倾向于此作为真迹。

中墨。”（《题子瞻画竹石》，转引自李福顺，2008，p. 183）

表情达意为其主旨，苏轼等文人借所画物象的典籍化意义来言个体之志。所谓典籍化就是某个物象被诗文典籍反复书写，形成了相对固定且被熟知的文本义。这些被典籍化的物象成为文人画的创作题材，这个过程就是文人画的典籍化现象，其结果是文人画成为一个意符，像象形字那样负载某种意义。如“潇湘”“竹石”就是一些典籍化的物象：“潇湘”在唐代中期，就已衍化为诗歌创作中的地域名称，具有抒情特征，李白、刘禹锡、柳宗元、杜甫等文豪笔下都有以潇湘为题的精美诗文。自唐五代之始，潇湘题材的绘画出现了，董源作《潇湘图卷》（现藏于北京故宫博物院）；在宋代，潇湘题材受到了画家和文人们的广泛欢迎，画家李迪曾创作《潇湘八景图》[①]，苏轼为其赋诗，云“西征忆南国，堂上画潇湘。照眼云山出，浮空野水长。旧游心自省，心手笔都忘。会有衡阳客，来看意渺茫”（《宋复古画潇湘晚景图》，转引自李福顺，2008，p. 69）。此外，他还曾为惠崇的潇湘题材绘画题过诗，云“惠崇烟雨芦雁，坐我潇湘洞庭”。可见，潇湘由于其文化意涵而受到苏轼等文人的喜爱，他们以此为题进行诗画创作。竹文化历史悠久，早在春秋战国时期，人们就以竹喻人格了：“瞻彼淇奥，绿竹猗猗。有匪君子，如切如蹉，如琢如磨。”（高亨，1980，p. 79）晋代江逌著有《竹赋》，唐代大诗人白居易在《养竹记》中以竹比贤士们本固、性直、心空、节贞的品性。宋代文人画兴起后，竹子更是文人们喜爱的题材，被用以比德和表情达意。苏轼生平爱竹，因为在他看来，竹石皆有美好的品质和寓意：竹子的品质是“萧然风雪意，可折不可辱”；怪石品质如玉，“嵌空翠润，有圭璋之质”，从中可以看到君子之德。

苏轼把典籍化了的潇湘、竹、石等物象在诗文典籍中形成的美好寓意转移到了绘画中，从而使“画外意”成了绘画所要追求的主旨，由此文人画被意符化。在评文同的墨竹时，他曾言：“与可之文，其德之糟粕。与可之诗，其文之毫末。诗不能尽，溢而为书，变而为画，皆诗之余。其诗与文，好者益寡。有好其德如好其画者乎？悲夫。”（《文与可画墨竹屏风赞》，转引自李福顺，2008，p. 106）在此，他对于德、文、诗、书、画五者间的关系及其次序有了明确定位，并且也进一步明确了绘画的主旨就是借物寓兴，即寄寓画者的品德、节操、怀抱和际遇。《潇湘竹石图》卷末有“轼为莘老作”五字

① 据沈括《梦溪笔谈》：“度支员外郎宋迪工画，尤善为平远山水。其得意者有平沙雁落、远浦归帆、山市晴岚、江天暮雪、洞庭秋月、潇湘夜雨、烟寺晚钟、渔村落照，为之八景。”

题款，据明代吴勤考证该作乃苏轼被贬黄州期间所作。结合这一创作背景，我们可知所图母题凝聚着他某种复杂的人生境遇的表达。南宋朱熹也曾道："东坡老人，英秀后凋之操，坚确不移之姿，竹君石友庶几似之。百世之下观此画，尚可想见也。"（《跋陈光泽家藏东坡竹石》，转引自李福顺，2008，p. 244）

在《潇湘竹石图》中，苏轼到底要借潇湘、竹、石等意象表达何意？首先，所画物象间的组合不是以再现而是以"意"为原则的。为了表意甚至可以主观臆造，这最早可能源自王维，他的《袁安卧雪图》有雪中芭蕉之景①。苏轼推崇王维的诗和画并以他为楷模，因此，苏轼也在画中有反常态的做法。据说，苏轼在试院时，兴至无墨，遂用朱笔画竹。米芾在《画史》中也曾记载过一则苏轼绘画反常态的做法，道："作墨竹，从地一直起到顶，或问何不逐节分，曰：竹生时何尝逐节分耶?"（《子瞻画墨竹》，转引自李福顺，2008，p. 204）米芾对这种反常态的解释是"合于天造，厌于人意"（《净因院画记》，转引自李福顺，2008，p. 58）。也就是说，绘画要"依乎天理"，任运自然，而不被外物限制，因为画为心声。

再来看《潇湘竹石图》，画中的墨竹枝干虬屈，石头造型奇特，而且竹子绕石而生，这都显得不合常态。竹子绕石而生的物象组合有何寓意，苏轼并没有留下相关文献对此解释。不过，他在《〈柏石图〉并叙》中描述过松柏与石头组合的寓意，道："柏生两石间，天命本如此。虽云生之难，与石两终始……君看此槎牙，岂有可移理？苍龙转玉骨，黑虎抱金柅。"（转引自李顺福，2008，p. 51）此诗言明，松柏生于两石间，是其天命，但它已与石相伴长久，也已习惯了如此艰难的环境，并重获新生。《潇湘竹石图》中的竹石组合与柏石组合类似，竹子和松柏的文化意象也非常接近，都象征着君子的美好品质。再结合此作为苏轼被贬黄州之后所作，我们可推断，苏轼可能是想借竹石物象的组合来表达他已习惯了流放黄州的艰难生活，并表达他"风霜锻炼愈坚重，怒浪喷激不可没"的高洁品格。

综上所述，在文人画系统里，"形似"并不那么重要，如苏轼言："论画以形似，见于儿童邻"（《净因院画记》，转引自李福顺，2008，p. 58），而

① 沈括在《梦溪笔谈》中记载："予家所藏摩诘画袁安卧雪图，有雪中芭蕉。"（俞剑华，1986，p. 43）

“有常理”[①] 才是画之主旨。文人们因情作画，情由实景与虚景相互触发而生，借被典籍化的物象及其它们之间的组合来言个人之志。文人画成了一个携带诗情的、带有阅读性的意符，而非纯观看性的像似符号。

二、书法亦画法

文人画的意符性是从符号内容的角度分析的，从符号表达面看则体现为书写与描绘的融合：书法即画法。以文房四宝为物质载体的传统汉字书写与字母的线性快速画写不同，前者形成了独特的、介于线性书写和非线性描绘之间的、语象融汇的书法艺术。汉字书法艺术包括笔法、字法、构法、章法、墨法、笔势等内容，书写过程中受两种力量制约：一是模仿、记录语言的倾向，比如汉字的笔顺、间架结构首先要服从便捷表达语言的需求，并遵循线性语言结构规则，这些结构规则与语言语法一样，是社会约定俗成的既定规范；二是走向非线性视觉表达的倾向，将笔顺、笔画的既定规范变成自由变化的线条，以利于书写者抒发个人性情。因此，在书法的笔法、墨法、章法、笔势等中最核心的是笔法和字法，即线性、规范的笔画、笔顺与非线性、自由变化的线条之间的协调艺术。简言之，书法的精髓可概括为规范的笔画和自由的线条之间的张力运动。在这两种力量中，笔画化是汉字书法向语言靠拢的要素，线条化则是书法向绘画艺术靠拢的要素。

以书入画是文人画的重要创作方法，就是将以字法、笔法为核心的汉字书法诸原则投射到文人画的创作中。笔画化和线条化两种书法要素在文人画的创作中表现为，一方面需要按照经长期训练的书法笔法和字法作画，是为笔画化倾向；另一方面，笔法、字法在绘画中具有抒发个人情意的功能，在具体的创作过程中，要超乎技，以“墨戏”的态度为之，是为线条化倾向。

首先看笔画化倾向。为了达到自由表情达意的目的，苏轼要求绘画“出新意与法度之中，寄妙理于豪放之外”（《书吴道子画后》，转引自李福顺，2008，p. 19）。其中“法度”接近书写规则，以约定俗成的、程式化的笔法作画，而这种笔法主要通过书法习得，即书法的笔画化要素。书法的笔画化是文人教育的基本部分，与苏轼非常重视的书法基本功的训练有关，他对此

---

① 苏轼在《净因院画记》道：“余尝论画，以为人禽宫室器用，皆有常形，至于山石竹木、水波烟云，虽无常形，而有常理。常形质失，人皆知之。常理之不当，虽晓画者有不知。故凡可以欺世而取名者，必托于无常形者也。虽然，常形之失，止于所失而不能病其全。若常理之不当，则举废之矣。以其形之无常，是以其理不可不谨也。”（王世襄，2010，p. 171）

多有论述：

> 真生行，行生操，真如立，行如行，草如走，未有未能行立而能走者也。（《书唐氏六家书后》）
>
> 书法当自小楷出。（《跋君谟书赋》）（李福顺，2008，p. 32，p. 27）

这表明他主张学习书法先从楷书开始，练习转腕用力。这对绘画同样至关重要，郭熙认为，世人多谓善书者往往善画，盖由其转腕用笔之不滞也。（《林泉高致·画诀》，转引自周积寅，2013，p. 126）绘画中的书法用笔就是画者经过长期书法练习而形成的握笔、落笔、运笔，以及徐急转折的动作规范，从而形成了简古、奇幻、韵秀、苍老、淋漓、雄厚、清逸、味外味等不同笔意。这既是文人们长期书法训练所要达到的目标，也是相对固定的、被行家们公认的用笔用墨规则呈现出的视觉风格。

以书入画之“书”的线条化要素即文人们作画时遵照“意在笔先”的创作原则，由画者个人意向和情感所驱动的对笔画性现成规范和套路的突破，体现为在程式化的笔画和自由的线条之间的摆渡，即所谓以“墨戏”态度作画。苏轼在《题文与可墨竹并叙》中云：“斯人定何人，游戏得自在。诗以草圣余，兼入竹三昧。”（转引自李福顺，2008，p. 105）他又在《石苍舒醉墨堂》中写道：“我书意造本无法，点画信手烦推求。”（转引自李福顺，2008，p. 54）也就是说，在书画创作过程中，画家必须超越笔墨法度的限制，以墨戏的态度，自由畅快地抒情言志，如其言：“读书作乐以自娱，戏翰弄墨，自适其志，正所谓‘丹青弄笔卿尔耳，意在万里谁知之’。”

透过《潇湘竹石图》，我们能感受到苏轼在作画时心如止水、波澜不惊，笔受制于手，手受制于心，笔蘸满浓墨在纸上缓缓展开，物象随之生成。笔法婉转、自然、流畅，无做作之感，简、淡、孤寂的空灵之感扑面而来。可是，画中的每一笔都是那么的有章可循，石用草书笔法，画竹则用楷书和行书的笔意，画云烟、山及远树则用淡墨晕染，而张弛有度的笔法恰恰也反映了其平和的心态。结合所画竹石物象，我们可推知他对功名、荣辱、成败已释然，如获新生。因此，我们可以说，文人画中“写意”与“墨戏”同义。

三、文人画与汉字性

通过上述对《潇湘竹石图》的描述，我们可知文人画中的汉字性表明它融汇了图像符号的像似性特征和语言符号的规约性特征，因此也可把文人画中的汉字性的本质归结为语图融汇。其在内容面与表达面皆有表现：在内容面上，文人画首先以图像符号呈现在我们眼前，画面具体可感的形象是观看的对象；可是它又以诗题为主，且画面中的物象也是被典籍化了的物象，这使图像符号又具有了规约性特征，画由“状外物”转向了“写我意”，即以形表意、立象尽意，以托物言志、表情达意为主旨，成了阅读的对象。在表达面上，文人画中线条书法性特征具有双重功能：一重是用于造型，是构成画面图形的主要手段，即线条化，具有一定的自由度；另一重是表意，书法线条以笔法、字法和墨法为核心，其不仅具有书写的时序感，而且还因被程式化而具有了表意功能，即笔画化，具有规约特征。文人画呈现出语中有图、图中有语的融汇状态。

西方后现代语境中的语图融合关系是以反思彼此的边界为前提的，即使语图在同一媒介中出现，如图形诗、马格利特的绘画作品《这不是一只烟斗》以及芭芭拉·克鲁格的图文融合的摄影作品，等等；二者在相互确证对方存在的同时，又彰显各自清晰的边界，语言与图像仍保持着很强的界限感和张力感。然而，文人画中的语图融汇是以消弭二者的边界为前提的，文字与图像的关系既趋同又自我异化为彼此。文字与图像可自由地相互僭越，以汉字为核心的诗学原则和典籍化可成为文人画的成像法则，二者的张力感消失了。孟华先生把中国文化中的这类特有的符号称为“类文字”。[①] 总之，文人画兼具了相似性与规约性的双重符号编码规则，并且由于它依汉字化而存在，规约性在其双重编码规则中占据主导地位。以规约性编码规则为主导的文人画为符号学研究提供了极具中国文化特性的超符号编码方式，本文根据它的这种符号特性重新界定了文人画的内涵。

引用文献：

艾朗诺（2013）. 美的焦虑——北宋士大夫的审美思想与追求（杜斐然，等译）. 上海：上海古籍出版社 .

卜寿珊（2017）. 心画：中国文人画五百年（皮佳佳，译）. 北京：北京大学出版社 .

方闻（2016）. 中国艺术史九讲（谈晟广，编译）. 上海：上海书画出版社 .

高亨（1980）. 诗经今注 . 上海：上海古籍出版社 .

高友工（2008）. 美典：中国文学研究论集 . 北京：生活 · 读书 · 新知三联书店 .

① 文字与图像之间既否定又肯定，既趋同又自我异化的性质，称为“第三空间”，也称为“类文字”。（孟华，2014，p. 68）

李福顺（2008）. 苏轼与书画文献集. 北京：荣宝斋出版社.
卢辅圣（2009）. 中国书画全书（第一卷）. 上海：上海书画出版社.
李霖灿（2014）. 中国名画研究. 杭州：浙江大学出版社.
孟华（2014）. 汉字主导的文化符号谱系. 济南：山东教育出版社.
石守谦（2010）. 风格与画意. 台北：石头出版公司.
巫鸿（2017）. 全球景观中的中国古代艺术. 北京：生活·读书·新知三联书店.
吴湖帆（2004）. 吴湖帆文稿（梁颖，编校）. 杭州：中国美术学院出版社.
王世襄（2010）. 中国画论研究. 桂林：广西师范大学出版社.
徐复观（2014）. 中国文学论集. 北京：九州出版社.
俞剑华（1986）. 中国古代画论类编（下）. 北京：人民美术出版社.
张彦远（2014）. 历代名画记. 杭州：浙江人民美术出版社.
周积寅（编著）（2013）. 中国历代画论（上）. 南京：江苏美术出版社.

作者简介：

匡景鹏，艺术史博士，四川美术学院通识学院讲师，主要研究方向为现代艺术理论与艺术哲学。

Author:

Kuang Jingpeng, Ph. D. of art history, lecture in teaching department of common course, Sichuan Fine Arts Institute. His research interest is modern art theory & art philosophy.

E-mail: kuangjingpeng2009@ qq. com

传播符号学

波德里亚符号政治经济学视域下的奥运会*

魏 伟

摘　要：波德里亚是后现代理论的核心学者之一。运用他的符号政治经济学理论中的商品系统和消费社会理论，可以清晰地发现奥运会的明星崇拜和“失败者凝视”；他的“他者”理论和去符号化观点可以让人们理解和洞察西方体育中心化的思潮；他的“致命策略”和对暴力的观点是考察奥运会球场软暴力的重要理论基础；受他的理论影响推导出的“伴随文本”诸概念和“伴随文本执着”可以用来解释奥运会的许多伴随文本现象；他的“超真实”理论在奥运会的电视和新媒体传播领域依然适用。

关键词：波德里亚，奥运会，符号政治经济学，后现代

Examining the Olympics through Baudrillard's Political Economy of the Sign

Wei Wei

Abstract: Jean Baudrillard is one of the core theorists of postmodernism. This paper focuses on his theories of the commodity system and consumer

* 本文为中央高校基本科研业务费专项资金项目“2022 年北京冬奥会的国际传播”（2020JJ003）的中期成果。

society in the political economy of the sign, the cult of the celebrity and the gaze on the losers at Olympics. His theory of "l'autre" and opinion on desemiotisation have provided insight into the Zeitgeist of centralisation in Western sports. His "fatal strategies" and standpoints on violence are the fundamental theoretical basis for investigating soft violence in the Olympic arena. Concepts created under the influence of his theories, such as the co-text and co-textual obsession, could be used to illustrate many co-texts of the Olympics. Moreover, his theory of the "hyperreality" can also be applied to television and new media communications at the Olympics.

Keywords: Baudrillard, Olympics, political economy of the sign, postmodernism

DOI: 10.13760/b.cnki.sam.202002008

让·波德里亚被誉为后现代主义左翼学者中“具有领袖地位的”（Best & Kellner, 2002, p.111）、“学术界的吉米·亨德里克斯”（Levin, 1996, p.25）、“高级牧师”（Willis, 1990, p.152）和“变装皇后”（Ashley, 1997, p.49）。他还被称为“过去20年里可能是最具挑衅性和最富争议的社会理论家”（Giulianotti, 2004, pp.225-239）。他提出的“致命策略”“符号交换”“仿像”“超真实”和“内爆”等理论深刻影响着人文与社会科学领域诸多层面。美国学者克里斯托弗·诺里斯认为“过去30多年时间里他游历在结构主义和后结构主义中，等待着这条路的尽头”（Norris 1992, pp.11-31）。美国学者道格拉斯·凯尔纳认为他是“终结现代性和将其带入后现代性的社会与历史新阶段的先驱”（Kellner, 1989, p.94）。

波德里亚的早期理论深受卡尔·马克思、罗兰·巴尔特和让·保罗·萨特的影响。从《忘记福柯》一书开始，波德里亚逐渐形成了自己独立的、颇富法国批判精神的思想体系。波德里亚的诸理论为学者们厘清后现代社会中的诸多“怪现状”提供了理论依据，但也因观点偏激布下了不少理论迷局。本文尝试运用波德里亚的诸理论对奥运会的诸多文化现象展开符号政治经济学批判，冀望获得相对明晰的结果。

一、消费社会语境下的奥运明星崇拜和“失败者凝视”

商品社会语境下的奥运会跟过往相比有较大的变化。早在1984年洛杉矶奥运会后，波德里亚就指出，“奥运会不过是一场彻头彻尾的行为艺术，对国家的自我庆典的集体参与……奥运会的一切都离不开广告，所有都情绪高涨，所有都很纯粹，百分之百的广告活动”（Baudrillard，1986，p. 58）。随着时间的推移，30 多年过去了，当前的体育资本市场较之以往更加活跃，奥运会的商业化气息有增无减。按照波德里亚的“消费社会”理论，“要成为消费客体，物品必须符号化……物品转化为系统中的符号，这种变化也涵盖人与人之间关系的转变，即为消费关系”（Baudrillard，1968，p. 277）。这种系统形成之后，大家就“处于‘消费’统治整个生活的局面”（Baudrillard，1970，p. 23）。消费结构中的消费品系列，是一整套消费品之间存在的必然的有序性关联，在其中起决定性作用的是符号话语制造出来的暗示性的结构性意义和符号价值。“消费是用某种编码及某种与该编码相适应的竞合的、无意识的纪律来规训他们……让他们进入游戏规则。”（Baudrillard，1970，p. 137）

在强大的资本利益驱使下，已经被过度商业化的奥林匹克运动会不得不做出各种妥协。美国 NBC 购买里约奥运会电视转播权的费用高达 12 亿美元，几乎占到总转播权费用的一半，因此热门赛事便“自然而然”地服务于主转播商所在的国家。在 2016 年里约奥运会期间，田径、游泳、体操等受到美国观众青睐的项目决赛被安排在美国电视的晚间黄金时段播出（魏伟，2015a）。为了确保收视率和广告效益最大化，与里约只有一个小时时差的美国依然选择延播奥运会开幕式。欧洲电视观众抱怨只能在午夜时分收看沙滩排球比赛，因为比赛被安排在美国西部时间 20：00 进行。羽毛球、乒乓球等中国运动员擅长的比赛项目被安排在中国的晚间黄金时段进行，因此羽毛球男单决赛以 7. 08% 的收视率成为中央电视台里约奥运会收视率最高的单场比赛。进入淘汰赛阶段的中国女排的比赛在国内连续创造收视率新高，也与成功地避开了夜场比赛有较大关系。在 2018 年平昌冬奥会期间，国内电视的收视量超过 6. 5 亿人次。由于东道主韩国与中国只有一个小时的时差，因此被放置在黄金时段播出的短道速滑各项比赛囊获了冬奥收视率的前 12 名，最高收视点出现在短道速滑男子 500 米决赛。尽管与中央广播电视总台央视《新闻联播》同时段播出，但收视率仍然高达 1. 53%，收视人群超过 2500 万。

奥运会期间，超级明星们自然得到了媒体的超级关注，媒介神话中的明星凝视几乎是约定俗成的（魏伟，2011）。迈克尔·菲尔普斯的奥运“二十三金传奇”，尤赛恩·博尔特的连续三届奥运“三金王”，游泳新王者莱德茨基和体操小将西蒙娜·拜尔斯的四金表现，内马尔率领巴西男足夺冠和内村航平卫冕体操全能王等突出表现获得了广泛的关注，他们的一举一动都被无限放大。在里约奥运会期间，菲尔普斯身上的拔罐印激起世界范围内的关注，于是拔火罐开始引领西方民众消费新时尚。菲尔普斯 1.93 米的身高却有 2.03 米的臂展，使他可以完成普通人难以想象的双手向后抱住自己后背的“菲鱼抱”，这在里约奥运会期间成为热门话题，继“反手摸肚脐”和“A4 腰”之后被各国民众消费。显然，这一系列消费行为已经属于波德里亚的仿象三等级中的第三层级“仿真”（la simulation）（Baudrillard, 1976, p. 77）。体育迷热衷于消费自己崇拜的体育明星喜爱的商品和生活方式，这种消费的“超一致性”所呈现出的是他们对体育明星的戏仿。因此，即便是如球王马拉多纳、丹尼斯·罗德曼、保罗·加斯科因等“坏小子”明星的消费方式也被拥趸们一并戏仿。这是当代消费社会的一个典型特征。菲尔普斯在比赛中的“英雄”表现让体育迷彻底忘却了那个因吸食大麻而成为反面典型的青少年。

有趣的是，在里约奥运会上，新加坡泳坛新秀斯库林在比赛中击败了他昔日的偶像菲尔普斯，于是他于比赛 8 年前在新加坡与偶像合影的照片广为流传。这在一定程度上激励年轻人接近偶像，勇敢追梦，无疑更加迎合普通民众的消费观。

奥运会追求“更高，更快，更强”的目标让体育英雄和名流在商业大潮下应运而生。波德里亚在《符号政治经济学批判》中指出，“在比赛中获得胜利，运动员就激活了完整的价值体系，由此也换来个人的名誉地位”（Baudrillard, 1972, p. 262. 1）。但这种崇高化导致在过往奥运会绝大多数报道中普通运动员和失利运动员的集体缺席。波德里亚指出：

> 在现实的符号世界中，欲望是无法通过幽灵般的构造来满足的，反而可能会引来由欲望带来的可耻的失败。失利的运动员通过自己的方法质疑了价值交换系统，这一价值体系的形式已经不再局限于对工薪阶层以及消费者的控制……这里存在的剥削与出卖劳动力一样严重，正是这种伪造的交换机制使得失利在无意识中迸发了。在这一意义上，每一个与那些“正常性”（这种正常性不过就是一种资本主义法则所构筑的氛围）相对立的“心理障碍”都可以进行政治性的解读。（Baudrillard, 1972, p. 262. 1）

因此，波德里亚得出的结论是，体育运动的意识形态是潜在规则以及强者规则的混合物（Baudrillard, 1972, p. 265. 1）。

在这种意识形态的掌控下，“失败者”也开始得到媒体和民众的“凝视”，尤其是那些堪称经典的“失败者”。里约奥运会前夕，媒体消费的对象是美国射击运动员马修·埃蒙斯，他曾经连续三届奥运会在最后一枪将到手的金牌拱手相让，人们为他寻觅到的对应者是中国乒乓球运动员王皓，他曾连获三届奥运会男单亚军。在里约奥运会期间加入这个叙事序列的是马来西亚羽毛球运动员李宗伟。他曾连续两届奥运会决赛不敌林丹，里约奥运会上虽亲手挫败林丹，却在决赛中不敌另一名中国选手谌龙，从而“三连亚”。这一叙事延续了奥运会悲壮的“失败者”叙事模式。

事实上，在2016年里约奥运会期间，这类叙事的对象经常翻转成为主角。第七次参加奥运会的跳马女王丘索维金娜，里约奥运会难民代表团里的多名成员，无法代表祖国参赛，夺冠后无国旗、国歌相伴的科威特射击运动员，都属于这一个叙事组。默默无闻，从英雄的神坛跌落，或是本该成为英雄却失之交臂，这类叙事有着较为清晰的叙事框架，甚至有类似的情节和视角。这是里约奥运会叙事区别于北京奥运会和伦敦奥运会的一大差异，这类被叙述者的领军人物是奥运开幕式点燃主火炬的巴西马拉松运动员范德莱·德利马，这位获得雅典奥运会铜牌的选手曾完美地诠释了遭遇意外痛失金牌却泰然处之的奥运精神。波德里亚的消费社会理论能够比较精准地观照奥运“失败者”叙事，这在同类型理论中是不多见的。

二、西方体育中心化语境下的奥运去符号化

奥林匹克运动会源自西方文明中的古希腊，现代奥林匹克运动会也是以西方体育为起点，因此西方体育中心化的格局由来已久。不仅在项目设置上，西方优势体育项目占据压倒性多数，在单项国际体育组织中，西方人也占有压倒性的优势。从2010年之后的国际体育传播研究来考察，西方体育项目主导的趋向也比较明显（魏伟，2016）。那么，在东西方文化发生激烈碰撞的奥运会上，东西方对于体育的认知和理解也存在不可小觑的差异。波德里亚在《邪恶的透明性》中提出的“他者”（l'autre）理论被一些文化学者运用于分析以英美为代表的西方体育文化与非西方体育文化的碰撞，这事实上是另一种层面的符号交换行为。“在英美等帝国主义的殖民时期，西方殖民者把西方体育放置于殖民地并谆谆教诲非西方国家。在今天，非西方文化看上去更像是在消费西方体育，尤其是来自非西方的运动员在西方人公认的‘主流项目’中击败西方运动员的时候。”（Blain & O'Donnell，2000，pp. 1 – 22）因此，无论是姚明、刘翔、李娜，还是马拉多纳、梅西、韩国女子高尔夫球群

体以及来自印度的顶尖板球运动员，总能够引起西方体育社会的高度重视，这实际上仍然是以西方为中心的体育传统理念造成的。“这些西方体育文化的‘他者’，无论他们的运动技巧多么高超，抑或是他们拥有无与伦比的欺骗技巧，无非是在消除东西方的差异，实质上仍然是在巩固西方体育文化的核心地位。”（Blain & O'Donnell，2000，pp. 1 – 22）

在西方体育中心化的语境下，由体育引申出的符号现象层出不穷，对此，波德里亚给出了一个近乎完美的实例。1992 年巴塞罗那奥运会开幕式上，世界级男高音歌唱家卡雷拉斯与现场 12 万观众就现场超大屏幕影像间的互动，像极了西班牙画家委拉斯凯兹的名画《宫娥》。此时，“古典时期的目光游戏已经变成了电视视觉时代的目光越位”（波德里亚，2009a，pp. 69 – 70）。这种“越位”其实投射出的是符号的元语言冲突。当歌唱家面对自己在超大屏幕上的影像唱歌时，现场观众反而只能看到侧影，于是又将目光投向远到几乎无法辨认的歌手本人。体育的符号意义在于它能够将赛场上的暴力与现实中的纷争隔离开来。因此，在马岛战争中落败的阿根廷人能够通过 1986 年墨西哥世界杯比赛中对英格兰的胜利获得异乎寻常的快感，甚至通过“上帝之手”这样的额外幸运提升这种快感消费。从符号学的视角来考察，奥运会各国和各地区奖牌榜的排名是想象暴力与消除冲突的符号隐喻，彰显着国家体育硬实力和软实力，乃至国家硬实力和软实力（魏伟，2014a）。符号学家赵毅衡提出，软实力的实质就是符号实力。近年来，随着一些西方国家开始重新重视奥运会奖牌榜的排名，奥运会奖牌榜日益成为展现国力的场域。里约奥运会奖牌榜排名前五位的美国、英国、中国、俄罗斯和德国恰好是国际政治和经济影响力较大的五个国家，因此这层符号隐喻已经相当明显。这也许就是各国民众重新开始看重金牌和奖牌榜的深层原因。值得注意的是，里约奥运会期间，多家媒体注意到中国民众不再只关注金牌，更多是在享受奥运带来的快乐。境外媒体纷纷指出，中国“去金牌化”的舆论趋势开始挑战“唯金牌论”，这是一种新境界。“令人失望的奖牌榜可能会刺激政府重新思考其奥运梦想。”

在 2016 年里约奥运会期间，中国民众格外重视裁判的判罚和一些“非正常现象”。例如，女子 4×100 米半决赛中，美国队依靠申诉挤掉中国队而进入决赛，这一前所未见的实例被国内许多民众甚至不少专家解读为国家体育硬实力和软实力方面较量的挫败。此外还有：拥有最高动作难度、具有夺金实力的女子高低杠选手范忆琳因为预赛早场被故意压低分数而无缘单项决赛，男子举重运动员吕晓军因为哈萨克选手疑似不成功的试举被判成功而痛失金牌，女子举重选手黎雅君因为没能及时获知裁判改判而丢掉金牌，拳击选手吕斌在大家普遍认为应当获胜的比赛中被意外判负。在2018年平昌冬奥会上，中国短道速滑队遭遇多次不利判罚，让时任主教练李琰泪洒赛场。事实上，随着许多奥运比赛项目规则的日益透明化，对于比赛结果的解读已经不再单纯由以往小范围的仲裁组专家决定，而是会接受媒体和各国民众的“细读”，加上社交媒体的强势介入，这种每届奥运会上都普遍存在的争议判罚被人为放大，导致奥运“去符号化”现象一再上演。

奥运会是青年人的聚会，但在这场盛会中还是有许多不和谐的“去符号化”现象发生。2016年里约奥运会期间，黎巴嫩代表团拒绝与以色列代表团同车前往开幕式现场，埃及柔道选手谢哈比失利后拒绝与以色列选手萨松握手。与之形成鲜明对比的是，朝鲜女子体操运动员洪恩珍接受韩国选手李恩珠的邀请完成合影自拍，这可能是众多不和谐元素中的一个反例。

波德里亚有关体育符号功能的阐述，在他的《赛车手与他的双重角色》一文中较为完整。这篇写就于1995年3月的文章集中论述了F－1车手的角色符号。在F－1这项“烧钱”的游戏中，车手和赛车都被推至极限，而二者是通过速度来协调的（Baudrillard，2002，p. 166）。一辆赛车的好坏（所指）是由包括研发人员、技师、各种工作人员在内数以千计的人决定的，但最终的胜负（能指）只在车手一个人身上，因此，这是一种高度压缩的能指与所指之间的关系。

波德里亚的这一论述很容易让人想起罗兰·巴尔特在《什么是体育》中有关赛车比赛的“多重悖论说”（任文，魏伟，2011）。但波德里亚与巴尔特的观察视点不尽相同。波德里亚认为，“一级方程式赛车手扮演双重角色：一方面他是精密仪器的自动终端，是一个机械师；另一方面他同时是观众热情和死亡冒险的符号操控者”（Baudrillard，2002，p. 169）。对于F－1车迷而言，他们也时刻处于矛盾之中，一方面他们希望比赛顺利进行，另一方面他们也希望不断看到各种意外和车手与死亡之间的博弈。“对于车队来说，他们也时刻处在投资与赠送礼品的矛盾之中。”这种符号意义的多重矛盾导致波德里亚得出了最后的结论：“F－1赛车比赛就是一个怪物，这种聚焦于技术、金钱、雄心和威信的东西是个十足的怪物。”（Baudrillard，2002，p. 169）这个在技术上不断追求完美的怪物最终会毁掉这项运动，而且它还将在一定程度上“污染日常生活中的驾驶技术”（Smith，2010，pp. 209－210）。

波德里亚对于商业意味浓重的当代奥运会的反讽是持之以恒的。为了与法国大革命两百年纪念相吻合，他故意将洛杉矶奥运会说成是在1989年举行。“奥运会是一个完全的行为艺术，对国家的自我庆典的集体参与……（洛杉矶奥运会）一切都受赞助，一切都情绪高涨，一切都很干净，百分之百的广告活动。”（Baudrillard，1986，p. 58）这显然是对作为商业奥运会开端的洛杉矶奥运会的极端戏讽。不仅如此，波德里亚还用反讽的方式讥笑了12年后再度在美国举行的奥运会和稍后进行的残奥会。“剩下的只有把性也变成奥林匹克的一个竞技项目：奥林匹克性运动会。如同在亚特兰大那样，还有与之平行的残疾人性运动会。”（波德里亚，2009b，p. 47）显然，在这里，波德里亚并不是为了讥讽参加残奥会的残疾人运动员，而是针对夏季奥运会和残疾人奥运会相继在一个商业气息浓郁的地方举行这种劳民伤财的形式。

三、致命策略语境下的当代体育暴力

波德里亚在《致命的策略》中的《沉默的大多数的阴影》一文中批判了马克思主义中有关大众的论述。他认为当代社会不是由“社会王国”构成，而是由沉默的大多数组成的“大众”构成的。“群众退到沉默中之后，就不再充当主体，它不再被人们谈论、言说和代表，也不能经历政治的‘镜像阶段’和想象辨认的循环。人们看到其中的威力有多大。一旦不再充当主体，群众就不再被异化——既不能在它自身语言中，也不能在任何其他语言中。”（波德里亚，2015，p. 135）大众并非主体的社会叠加，他们“是一群权力来自于沉默和看似被惯性所宰制的‘狡诈客体’”（Baudrillard，1997a，p. 45）。“包括民意调查人、宣传工作者、政论家和社会学者都在试图解读大众，但大众却用‘致命的策略’——谋略、技巧和模棱两可的话语来搪塞这些主体，并保持一步的领先。”也就是说，在大众与政治力量的博弈中，大众处于小幅领先地位（Baudrillard，1990a，pp. 82－88）。因此，政治的剧本被改写为：大众不再被政治力量唤醒，而是大众在决定政治的走向。当代资本主义精英阶层认为自己仍然控制着社会权力和影响，但那在波德里亚看来不过是“权力的幻觉……就像在镜中起舞（danser devant un miroir）”（Baudrillard，1990b，p. 48）。“高层权力不是来源于领袖与现代解放，而是来源于让其他人永远处于怀疑的致命策略中。”（Baudrillard，2007，pp. 116－118）波德里亚的大众理论深刻揭示了当代社会中大众可能起到的重要作用。

在此基础上，波德里亚尝试探讨体育以及体育可能给社会带来的问题。在《沉默的大多数的阴影》一文中，他列举了1978年同时发生的两件事：从法国引渡回德国律师克劳斯·科洛桑特，引起几百人抗议；一场世界杯足球赛的资格赛，引起两千多万人关注。多数法国知识分子谴责足球被来自大众的力量神秘地操控了。波德里亚认为，“大众对于足球的忠诚和痴狂是被给定的理想主义的，也是启蒙的，他们既没有被误导，也没有被魅惑”（Baudrillard，1982，pp. 12－14）。因此，大众对体育的痴迷是社会现实造成的，并非孤立的社会现象。

波德里亚把体育场内的暴力称为“恐怖主义之镜，是潜在暴力的瞬间结晶”（Baudrillard，1990a，pp. 82－88）。这一观点得到了不少学者的认同。英国学者理查德·朱利安诺蒂认为“足球流氓抓住了公众的想象力，看上去威胁到了政府对暴力的垄断，敢于通过在球场上制造令人瞩目的暴力景观来颠覆场上的比赛。与当代恐怖主义者一样，足球流氓的‘致命策略’意在诱使国家陷入对深层权力资源的揭露”（Giulianotti，2004，pp. 225－239）。2012年2月1日发生在埃及塞得港的足球暴力事件，被专家和学者普遍解读为这个国家之前一年多时间内发生的一系列政治事件在足球场内的激化呈现。自波德里亚的《恐怖主义之镜》问世，几乎所有后来的有关足球流氓和体育暴力的研究都无法绕开他的这一研究。波德里亚将“海瑟尔惨案”界定为“安全的灾难性反讽”（Baudrillard，1990b，p. 64）。98名球迷在赛场内所谓“安全”的护栏下遭到致命的伤害（“海瑟尔惨案”的实际死亡人数为39人），警察为了避免球迷冲入场内对赛事造成影响，竟然拒绝球迷冲出护栏逃生。这种所谓的“超保护”系统只会失去正常的防护功能而使事件滑向“恐怖的可逆性”（Baudrillard，1990a，pp. 82－88）。

当然，波德里亚对“海瑟尔惨案”的定性也不可避免地受到了当时舆论的影响。他将观众（尤其是英国球迷）指涉为“尝试角色翻转”的“另一种逻辑”，因为“他们把自己变成了演员，在媒介的凝视下篡夺了球员的主角地位，他们制造了自己的奇观”（Baudrillard，1990a，pp. 82－88）。但后来的事实证明，现场的英国（利物浦）球迷其实也是受害者，警方的不作为是事件的重要诱发因素。在2016年里约奥运会期间，巴西体育迷的嘘声和喝倒彩似乎是要尝试角色翻转，不啻为里约奥运会的一道风景线。这与风靡2014年南非世界杯的“呜呜祖拉”有很大的差异。在东道主现场观众山呼海啸般的嘘声中，法国撑竿跳高选手雷诺·拉维莱尼痛失金牌，在领奖台上失声痛哭。部分俄罗斯游泳运动员因曾服用兴奋剂而被喝倒彩，美国女足队员霍普·索洛因在赛前公开担忧寨卡病毒而被现场观众高呼“寨卡寨卡”。巴西观众嘘声和喝倒彩的对象主要是美国、俄罗斯和中国这三个“体育大国”，以及巴西在南美洲的主要体育对手阿根廷。此外，巴西体育迷还在球场内对美国女足队员高喊“同性恋”。在巴西队与阿根廷队的男篮比赛中，现场球迷用极其恶毒的语言和下流的手势“问候”阿根廷人。德国网球选手达斯丁·布朗在与东道主选手的网球比赛中不慎摔倒扭伤脚踝，竟然激起了现场球迷的一片叫好声。捷克队与巴西队的沙滩排球比赛中，现场的巴西观众不顾现场官员“不要发出嘘声”的请求，满场嘘声一片。在击剑这个要求相对安静的比赛中，巴西观众仍然用疯狂的嘘声来应和。当然，嘘声和喝倒彩声未必都能产生作用。中国女排便在现场观众贯穿始终的声浪中击溃两届奥运会冠军，巴西女排主帅吉马雷斯的孙子痛哭的画面成为里约奥运会的经典影像之一。

波德里亚还探讨过由足球暴力事件引发的“足球比赛魅影”现象。由于球迷闹事，1987 年 9 月在马德里进行的皇家马德里队与那不勒斯队的欧洲冠军杯比赛被安排在一个没有球迷的空球场进行，但这场比赛仍然因为电视直播而让全球的观众目睹。这可能是后现代体育的一个显著的特征：“几乎没有多少人能够亲历比赛，但每个人都可以看到画面。体育成为了一项纯粹的赛事……事实上缺乏任何依据，很容易被合成的图像所取代。”（Baudrillard, 2008, p. 8）这在很大程度上证实了竞赛型演示叙述中观众的强大力量（魏伟，2015b）。由于新冠肺炎疫情的影响，2020 年举行的绝大多数体育赛事都是空场进行，波德里亚的“足球比赛魅影”现象成为常态。赛场赛事和媒介赛事叠合的当代体育赛事成了纯媒介赛事，凸显出鲜明的后现代特征。今天，类似奥运会和世界杯这样的“奇观”赛事能够吸引到几十乃至上百亿人次的观赏，但真正能够到现场观看比赛的人是极其有限的。“足球比赛魅影”现象更多涉及的是后文将谈及的超真实理论。

四、伴随文本执着语境下的文本翻转

波德里亚在晚年开始提出一系列令人匪夷所思的理论。例如他在《波湾战争不曾发生》中提出“我们看到的海湾战争不过是媒介呈现的一场虚拟战争，真正的战争根本不曾发生”（布希亚，2003，p. 24）的惊人观点，饱受争议。他指出，“当战争进入新闻，已经不再是一场实在的战争，而变成一场虚拟的战争，也就是症候般的战争。就像一切经过心理机制的，都成为无止尽镜映的对象，所有透过新闻运作过的，都成为无止尽炒作的对象，一种全然不具确定性的场域”（布希亚，2003，p. 49）。这一观点在当时遭到了令人难以置信的反驳，不少学者甚至以此来攻击后现代主义。克里斯托弗·诺里斯认为，这一系列荒谬的观点“暴露了后现代主义思想在智力与政治上的破产”，见证了“西方知识分子因为极端反现实主义与非理性主义而陷入道德与政治上的危机”（Norris，1992，pp. 11 －31）。但美国语言学家诺阿·乔姆斯基等却公开表达了对波德里亚观点的认同。

根据波德里亚的观点，法国学者让－菲利普·杜桑就2006年德国世界杯决赛中令人震惊的“齐达内头顶马特拉齐事件”进行了阐释：“齐达内的行为，很难察觉，令人费解，更像是没有发生过的奇观现象。如果一个人在体育场内限制了自己的行为，让其他人没有察觉到，观众和裁判也没有当场目睹，那么这个行为根本就没有发生过。”（Toussaint，2007）杜桑的观点当然是“海湾战争不曾发生”理论的实际运用。波德里亚甚至还提道，“在媒介时代，事件如果没有经过电视和广播的‘实时直播’就等于没有发生”（Baudrillard，1995a）。但杜桑并不知道，波德里亚本人就“齐达内头顶马特拉齐事件”有过较为详尽的评论，载于其逝世三年后出版的《嘉年华与食人族》一书中。波德里亚对这位同胞球星没有为法兰西带来第二座大力神杯的行为毫不宽容，他指出：

> 齐达内的举动是对世俗身份认同仪式的毁灭……他让整个决赛从表演的高潮达到功能障碍的高潮，他以华丽的举动来反对美好的事物，瞬间在全球化的中心突出地证明了虚无。这个简单的举动在任何意义上投射出的都不是一种反抗的态度。有人会说这个举动超出了个人主体意识的范畴，是来源于身体之外。这是导致整个系统被瞬间愚弄的高潮部分……齐达内的这一举动就是恐怖主义行为。（Baudrillard，2010，pp. 76 －84）

显然，波德里亚并不认为齐达内头顶马特拉齐的动作从来没有发生过。这个举动虽然逃过了当值主裁判和绝大多数现场观众的视线，甚至没有被转播机构 HBS 的常规镜头捕捉到。但转播机构用于制作纪录片的“明星机位”全程捕捉到这一时刻，因此这组镜头立即被激活并在转播中反复播放。于是，全世界都看到了这个本来“应该没有发生过”的瞬间。更有不少新闻媒体赛后请到唇语专家，通过齐达内和马特拉齐的嘴型来解读当时可能发生的对话。一个细节改变了一届世界杯冠军的归属，甚至在一定程度上改变了全世界对一位传奇足球明星生平的认知。这看上去既是一个提喻，又像是一个有趣的反讽。

为了更好地考察文本与文本外的意义流变，在克里斯蒂娃和热奈特的理论的基础上，赵毅衡提出了全套“伴随文本”的概念。伴随文本可以分为副文本、型文本、先后文本、前文本、评论文本和链文本等。在当今社会中，伴随文本越来越去边缘化，成为主导文本形式和内容的决定性力量。“我们忍受不了某一种伴随文本过分明显地控制解释，我们也摆脱不了伴随文本的普遍控制。”（赵毅衡，2016，p. 154）“伴随文本执着”成为当代文化产业发展的助推器。随着社交媒体影响力的日益扩大，伴随文本的作用益发彰显。傅园慧的意外走红即源自在赛场边接受的采访，“洪荒之力”成为深刻影响2016年中国流行文化的重要词汇。跳水运动员秦凯对何姿的求婚仪式成为轰动世界的头条新闻，冠军选手施廷懋反而在场边成为陪衬。有趣的是，这场“现场直播”的求婚仪式中的单膝跪地、送求婚戒指的元素都是西式的。被求婚的还有马术赛场上的英国选手夏洛特·杜雅尔丹，她的未婚夫用T恤上“现在你愿意嫁给我吗？”的方式实现了求婚。赵帅、郑姝音情侣搭档双双夺冠，“赵帅是郑姝音的搭档”“身高不及女友”等文本评论压倒了赛事本身的相关报道。与此类似的还有羽毛球运动员谌龙与女友王适娴夺冠后的高调示爱，射击运动员庞伟与妻子杜丽这对“神枪侠侣”，跳水奥运五金得主吴敏霞与男友的互动等。这些评论文本深度满足了受众对于彼时热点人物信息缺失的遗憾，不仅主导了社交媒体的议程设置，甚至还深刻影响了传统主流媒体的报道方式和议程设置。

事实上，伴随文本的影响力经常被提升至国家层面。澳大利亚游泳选手马克·霍顿在击败孙杨后，指责孙杨是“服用兴奋剂的小人”，随后又解释称这是一种战术。这一套伴随文本涉及副文本、评论文本和链文本等环节，引发了两国民众在社交媒体上的冲突。随后法国游泳选手卡米尔·拉库尔也在采访时抨击“孙杨的尿是紫色的”，与霍顿的言论形成“组合拳”，这甚至引起了国际奥委会和国际泳联的高度关注。2020年孙杨被国际仲裁法庭CAS宣布禁赛8年竟然成了这一事件伴随文本翻转的注脚。郎平带领中国女排夺冠激发了排球迷的群体记忆。她以运动员的身份率领中国队在1984年洛杉矶奥运会夺冠，又在2004年雅典奥运会以排球解说员身份解说中国女排夺冠，在2008年北京奥运会上带领美国女排击败中国队，这些前文本渊源都被挖出。美国游泳名将、12枚奥运奖牌得主瑞安·罗切特因为报假案使“整个国家蒙羞”。这些伴随文本不再是奥运会的“佐料”，有的甚至直接影响了文本——比赛的结果。这可能是波德里亚没有预料到的。

五、超真实语境下的媒介奇观赛事

类似奥运会和世界杯能够吸引全世界目光和媒介高关注度的赛事被称为

“媒介奇观赛事”。媒介化转向是体育传播学近年来最显著的转向之一，它集中体现在“体育重大事件”这一概念的引入（魏伟，尚希萌，2020）。学者马丁·穆勒根据一系列指数，把体育赛事分为巨型事件（giga-event）、重大事件（mega-event）和主要事件（major-event）（Müller，2015，p. 636）。奥运会属于巨型事件。美国学者史蒂夫·雷德海德就是运用波德里亚的理论，对1994年美国足球世界杯进行了考察，得出了世界杯“就是一届全球媒介赛事：一个没有真正参考的仿像和超真实的奇观”（Redhead，1994，pp. 291－309）的结论。媒介奇观赛事的叙述框架是多元的，这与普通的竞赛型演示叙述有根本的区别（魏伟，2015b）。根据报道，2016年里约奥运会期间，传统电视频道转播了125000小时的比赛，比2012年伦敦奥运会提高25%，全世界有近50亿人观看了里约奥运会的比赛，创下纪录。

波德里亚关于拟像和超真实的观点，在传播研究领域，尤其是电视体育赛事转播的研究中运用得十分广泛。他认为，西方社会业已进入超真实时代，超真实包含了对现实的集约化。整个世界被看作一个拟仿物，超真实让现实看上去“比真实更真实”。用波德里亚的“内爆”观点来看，“传播与意义所产生的拟像与超现实的过程，比真实更加逼真。因此，真实被内爆掉了……在真实中，媒介自身也内爆了。在某种超真实的星云中，媒介与真实都内爆了”（Baudrillard，1981，pp. 119－124）。波德里亚指出，“影像不再能让人想象现实，因为它就是现实。影像也不再能让人幻想实在的东西，因为它就是其虚拟的实在。就好像这些东西都已贪婪地照过镜子，自认为已变成了透明的，全体在自己体内就位，在充足的光线下，被实时地、毫不留情地复制”（Baudrillard，1995b，pp. 18－19）。他曾经列举过的情色产品、迪士尼乐园和高保真音响等都是超真实的现实呈现。具体到电视体育转播领域，“真实场景模型的生产都是以（NBC对奥运会）过往制造模型的拟仿作为参考的。因此，NBC对奥运会的模式化生产就是媒介文本被内爆、再模式化的生动事例，是对现实的‘混账’阐释”（Andrews，1998，pp. 5－18）。在今天的奥运会转播中，虚拟现实的现场广告板、模拟世界纪录的实时动态线、VR转播带来的360度视角的沉浸式图像一一验证了波德里亚的预言。

波德里亚曾经准确地预言了作为声画结合的电视在传播中的统治地位：“我们将持续寻找比传播更为迅捷的东西：挑战它，与它决斗。传播的速度过慢，它通过接触和言语来达成，是慢的代名词。目睹当然更快，它是媒介的渠道，是最快速的一种。所有事物都在瞬间呈现。”（Baudrillard，2008，p. 8）作为仿像的当代体育赛事转播给受众带来的超真实感，已经远远超越了在赛场边现场观众的感受。各种视角、各种速度、各种高清的画面满足了人们的各种需求；埋在沙坑里和别在裁判员腰间的麦克风让受众有身临其境的感觉。正如波德里亚所言，“电视的扩散进入了生活，生活的扩散进入了电视”（Baudrillard，1983，p. 21）。为此，他感叹，“我们可能永远也无法再知道历史从新闻中的恶化到技术上的完美都历经了什么，我们可能永远也无法再知道模具从消失到完成中都发生了什么”（Baudrillard，1987，p. 26）。超真实的再现覆盖了真实事件，以至于人们无从知晓现实究竟发生了什么。2010年温哥华冬奥会成为历史上首届“第二屏幕”奥运会；2012年伦敦奥运会实现了3D转播，被称为“数字”奥运会；2014年索契冬奥会成为“社交媒体”奥运会；2016年里约奥运会首次用VR技术进行赛事直播；2018年平昌冬奥会实现了5G传输；为了准备东京奥运会，日本NHK电视台提前开始试用8K转播技术；2022年北京冬奥会将使用云端转播技术。新技术的规范化和转播媒体的连贯性让媒体中的奥运呈现出标准化的样态。画面中的里约奥运赛事与北京奥运和伦敦奥运似乎没有太大的差异。新技术甚至可以让空场的比赛充满假观众和仿真度极高的观众喝彩声。但事实上，除了满场的嘘声和喝倒彩声，奥运会的独特性并没有充分展现出来，这是由拟仿先在的媒介技术决定的。

波德里亚认为，“电视传媒通过其技术组织所承载的，是一个可以任意显像、任意剪辑并可用画面解读的世界的思想（意识形态）。它承载着的意识形态是，那个对已变成符号系统的世界进行解读的系统是万能的”（Baudrillard，1970，pp. 189 - 190）。电视体育转播带来的超真实感经常给人虚幻的感觉，正如我们在看3D、4K和VR转播时常常会有目睹电子游戏的错觉。媒介体育赛事可能是对体育人物和事件的误读，也可能是对体育文化内涵的曲解（魏伟，2019）。奥运会游泳和田径比赛转播中由计算机模拟出的世界纪录线和运动员代表的国旗或队旗时常被部分受众认为是赛场里客观存在的。美式橄榄球比赛场内五彩斑斓的线条和特技虚拟出的线条交织在一起，有时连较为专业的体育迷也无法辨认。由GPS技术主导的F - 1和纳斯卡赛车比赛转播几乎成了统计学领域的恶斗，千分之一秒的差距和从一档到七档的变化被肆意放大。对此，波德里亚告诉我们，“虚拟现实是真实世界的对极。高清晰度是现实高度稀释的代名词。媒介的高清晰度往往对应着信息的最低精度。信息的最高精度对应着事件的最低精度”（Baudrillard，1997b，p. 26）。奥运会上媒介技术的不断提升，不过是为波德里亚的超真实感理论增添一个又一个注脚。人机结合的“赛博人”是否会主宰今后的职业赛事甚至是奇观赛事？体育比赛还需要人类的具身判罚吗？人本主义是否应当从体育赛事中退场？这些都在短时间内成为可以探讨的话题（Wei & Shang，2020）。

六、结语

波德里亚对于当代社会的发展趋向具有前瞻性。他曾指出，“我们时代的歇斯底里性格的根源在于，真实的生产与再生产的歇斯底里”（Baudrillard，1981，p. 41）。波德里亚对于虚拟现实和高清晰度的发展研判是基本准确的，但社交媒体的迅猛发展却使他有关电视将长时间主宰体育媒介市场的预言产生偏误。根据国际奥委会发布的媒介报告，早在2010年温哥华冬奥会时，使用双屏收看奥运会的人数就已经两倍于单纯收看电视的人数。根据NBC发布的数据，里约奥运会期间，2.27亿脸书用户发表15亿条帖子，推特用户发表1.87亿推文，吸引了750亿次浏览量。反观美国日平均电视观众人数，却从伦敦奥运会的3300万人跌到2790万人。这似乎证明了社交媒体的影响力已经在逐渐超越电视。但NBC表示，这场社交媒体的胜利有一部分功劳要归功于自己。脸书上奥运视频6亿多的浏览量，最初的来源就是NBC。德国Statista公司的研究表明，91%的年轻人会一边看电视，一边使用手机和平板电脑等第二屏幕。尼尔森的报告显示，电视媒体是中国受众观看奥运会的主流渠道，83%的中国人通过电视观看奥运会，67%使用手机观看，其中有大量的用户是双屏同时观看。因此，电视在奥运会期间的主导地位实际上并没有受到真正意义上的挑战。

波德里亚的诸理论是后现代主义研究的重要文本。美国体育社会学者劳伦斯·文内尔运用波德里亚的理论，通过对超媒介、超商品化和超现实的后现代体育酒吧的空间地理学考察（Wenner，1998，pp. 301－332），奠定了之后“脏言”理论的基础。英国学者加里·万内尔利用波德里亚的符号政治经济学原理，探讨了媒介体育明星制造过程中电视转播权、赞助商和娱乐市场的关系（Whannel，2002）。学者罗布·范文斯伯格和伊安·里奇也将波德里亚的理论作为基础，对奥运五环标志进行了后现代符号学研究，认为五环标志成了一个超商品化的能指（Van Wynsberghe & Ritchie，1998，pp. 367－384）。美国学者约翰·贝尔在研究了波德里亚的大量理论后，认为这些理论能够“成为今后环球流行文化大部分机器的引擎”（Bale，1994）。法国学者热内维埃夫·雷勒可能是把波德里亚的理论最多运用到体育社会学研究的学者之一，他认为“后现代体育是后现代社会文化的生产者和再生产者，是过度消费的特权客体”（Rail，1998，pp. 143 - 161）。英国学者朱里亚诺蒂和瑞士学者克劳泽在对体育重大赛事和恐怖主义的梳理中运用了波德里亚的恐怖主义之镜的观点（Giulianotti & Klauser，2012，pp. 1 - 17）。加拿大学者阿特金森和凯文·杨对波德里亚的十本著作进行了系统分析，在对体育奇观和体育恐怖主义的研究中将波德里亚的超真实和非事件理论作为核心加以论述（Atkingson & Young，2012，pp. 1 - 21）。澳大利亚学者大卫·洛弗在对“齐达内头顶马特拉齐事件”引发的媒介、体育与种族化的探讨中也使用了波德里亚的非事件理论（Rowe，2010，pp. 355 - 371）。笔者在梳理了波德里亚有关符号的理论体系以后，将其列为影响体育符号理论发展的四位先驱之一（魏伟，2012）。在西方体育文化研究这一维度，波德里亚的体育思想也是三大学派中法国后现代主义的代表理论（魏伟，2014b）。波德里亚是一个充满争议的学者，不同于其他法国学者理论的晦涩，他的理论相对清晰，但也充满偏激的观点。正如雷德海德所言，运用波德里亚的理论进行体育社会学研究，“需要相当小心和慎重”（Redhead，1994，pp. 291 - 309）。但近十余年的相关研究中，能够完全摆脱波德里亚理论的并不多。

引用文献：

波德里亚，J.（2009a）. 冷记忆 3：断片集（张新木，陈旻乐，李露露，译）. 南京：南京大学出版社.

波德里亚，J.（2009b）. 冷记忆 4（张新木，陈凌娟，译）. 南京：南京大学出版社.

波德里亚，J.（2015）. 艺术的共谋（张新木，杨全强，戴阿宝，译）. 南京：译林出版社.

布希亚，J.（2003）. 波湾战争不曾发生（邱德亮，黄建宏，译）. 台北：麦田出版公司.

任文，魏伟（2011）. 奇观体育与体育奇观：罗兰·巴尔特的符号学体育赛事观. 体育科学，11，85 - 93.

魏伟（2011）. 解读神话：南非世界杯电视转播的符号学研究. 中国体育科技，2，47 - 51.

魏伟（2012）. 体育符号研究的发展述评. 成都体育学院学报，8，1 - 6.

魏伟（2014a）. 符号学视角下体育与软实力的关系. 上海体育学院学报，6，69 - 74.

魏伟（2014b）. 西方体育文化研究的流派辨析. 成都体育学院学报，1，12 - 14.

魏伟（2015a）. 重访电视与体育的“天作之合”：从布尔迪厄说起. 成都体育学院学报，2，33 - 39.

魏伟（2015b）. 叙述公正与叙述惊喜：竞赛型演示叙事研究. 符号与传媒，1，91 - 103.

魏伟（2016）. 近年来国际体育传播的转向和趋向. 体育科学，5，10 - 17.

魏伟（2019）. 解构当代体育媒介赛事的权力迷思：基于约翰·费斯克的视角．上海体育学院学报，1，72－79.

魏伟，尚希萌（2020）. 体育传播学的媒介化转向：从媒介体育到体育重大事件．未发表论文．

赵毅衡（2016）. 符号学：原理与推演．南京：南京大学出版社．

Andrews, D. (1998). Feminizing Olympic reality: Preliminary dispatches from Baudrillard's Atlanta, *International review for the sociology of sport.* 1, 5－18.

Ashley, D. (1997). *History without a Subject: The postmodern condition.* Boulder: Westview Press.

Atkingson, M., Young, K. (2012). Shadowed by the corpse of war: Sport spectacles and the spirit of terrorism, *International review for the sociology of sport*, 3, 1－21.

Bale, J. (1994). *Landscapes of modern sport*, London: Leicester University Press.

Baudrillard, J. (1968). *Le système des objets.* Paris: Gallimard.

Baudrillard, J. (1970). *La société de consommation: Ses mythes ses structures.* Paris: Denoël.

Baudrillard, J. (1972). *Pour une critique de l'économie politique du signe.* Paris: Gallimard.

Baudrillard, J. (1976). *L'échange symbolique et la mort.* Paris: Gallimard.

Baudrillard, J. (1981). *Simulacres et simulation.* Paris: Galilée.

Baudrillard, J. (1982). *A l'ombre des majotités silencieuses ou la fin du social.* Paris: Denoël.

Baudrillard, J. (1983). *Simulations* (Paul Foss, Trans.). New York: Columbia University Press.

Baudrillard, J. (1986). *Amérique.* Paris: Grasset.

Baudrillard, J. (1990a). *La transparence du mal: Essai sur les phénomènes extrêmes.* Paris: Galilée.

Baudrillard, J. (1990b). *Cool memories II (1987－1990).* Paris: Galilée.

Baudrillard, J. (1995a). The virtual illusion: Or the automatic writing of the world. *Theory, culture & society.* 4, 97－107.

Baudrillard, J. (1995b). *Le crime parfait.* Paris: Galilée.

Baudrillard, J. (1997a). *Le paroxyste indifférent.* Paris: Bernard Grasset.

Baudrillard, J. (1997b). Aesthetic illution and virtual reality. In Nicholas, Z. (Ed.). *Jean Baudrilllard: Art and artefact* (Nicholas, Z., Trans.). London: Sage.

Baudrillard, J. (2002). The racing driver and his double. In *Screened out* (Turner, C., Trans.). London: Verso.

Baudrillard, J. (2007). *Forget Foucault* (Dufresne, N., Trans.). Cambridge: MIT Press.

Baudrillard, J. (2008). *Fatal strategies* (Beitchman, P., Trans.). New York: Semiotext(e).

Baudrillard, J. (2010). *Carnival and cannibal, or the play of global antagonism* (Turner, C., Trans.). London: Seagull Books.

Best, S. & Kellner, D. (1991). *Postmodern theory: Critical interrogations.* Basingstoke: Guilford Press.

Blain, N., & O'Donnell, H. (2000). Current developments in media sport, and the politics of local identities: A "Postmodern" debate? *Culture, sport, society*, 2, 1 - 22.

Giulianotti, R. (2004). The fate of hyperreality: Jean Baudrillard and the sociology of sport. In Giulianotti, R. (Ed.). *Sport and modern social theorists.* New York: Palgrave Macmillan.

Giulianotti, R., & Klauser, F. (2012). Sport Mega-event and "Terrorism": A critical analysis, *International review for the sociology of sport*, 3, 1 - 17.

Kellner, D. (1989). *Jean Baudrillard: From Marxism to postmodernism and beyond.* Stanford, CA: Stanford University Press.

Levin, C. (1996). *Jean Baudrillard: A study of cultural metaphysics.* Hertz: Harvester Wheatsheaf.

Müller, M. (2015). What makes an event a mega-event? Definitions and sizes. *Leisure studies*, 6, 627 - 642.

Norris, C. (1992). *Uncritical theory: Postmodernism, intellectuals & the Gulf War.* Anherst: University of Massachusetts Press.

Rail, G. (1998). Seismography of the postmodern condition: Three theses on the implosion of sport. In Rail, G. (Ed.). *Sport and postmodern times.* New York, NY: State University of New York Press.

Redhead, S. (1994). Media culture and the World Cup: The last World Cup. In Sudgen, J. & Tomlinson, A. (Eds.). *Hosts and champions: Soccer cultures, national identities and the USA World Cup.* Aldershot: Arena.

Rowe, D. (2010). Stages of the global: Media, sport, racialization and the last temptation of Zinedine Zidane, *International review for the sociology of sport*, 3, 355 - 371.

Smith, R. (2010). *The Baudrillard dictionary.* Edinburgh: Edinburgh University Press.

Toussaint, J. - p. (2007). Zidane's melancholy, *New formations*, 1.

Wei, W., & Ximeng, S. (2020). Illusion or reality?—A semiotic phenomenology analysis of the "electronic justice" of contemporary sports events, *IAMCR Annual*, Helsinki.

Wenner, L. (1998). In search of the sports bars: Masculinity, alcohol, sports and the mediation of public space. In Rail, G. (Ed.). *Sport and postmodern times.* New York, NY: State University of New York Press.

Whannel, G. (2002). *Media sport stars: Masculinities and moralities.* London: Routledge.

Willis, p. (1990). *Common culture: Symbolic work at play in the everyday cultures of the young.* Milton Keynes: Open University Press.

Van Wynsberghe, R., Ritchie, I. (1998). (Ir) relevant ring: The symbolic consumption of the Olympic logo in postmodern media culture. In Rail, G. (Ed.). *Sport and postmodern times*, New

York, NY: State University of New York Press.

作者简介：

魏伟，博士，北京外国语大学国际新闻与传播学院教授，博士生导师，研究方向为体育文化传播、符号学等。

Author:

Wei Wei, Ph. D., professor of School of International Journalism and Communication, Beijing Foreign Studies University. His research focuses on sports and culture communication, semiotics, etc.

Email: wwei@ bfsu. edu. cn

游戏符号学的意义与价值

宗　争

摘　要： 游戏漫长的发展史与游戏研究极不相称的短暂历史形成了鲜明的对照。作为重要的文化现象，同时也作为学术研究中的冷门，学界尚未有对中西方游戏研究历程和脉络的系统梳理。本文系统梳理了游戏研究在中西方的发展，指出了游戏研究在“专门性/非专门性”研究上的区别和联系，并详细讨论了以电子游戏研究为基础的“游戏学”研究的近况以及发展方向。从而，在总体上对中西方游戏研究发展做出了比较全面和细致的观察与评述。以此为基础，文章详细论证了符号学作为游戏研究的学理化基础的原因，指出了游戏符号学在现阶段的游戏研究中存在的意义和价值，提出了坚持和发展游戏研究需要符号学方法的观点。

关键词： 游戏研究，游戏学，符号学，电子游戏，体育游戏

The Significance and Value of the Semiotics of Games

Zong Zheng

Abstract: The long history of games stands in contrast to the short history of game studies. Games are both an important cultural phenomenon and a rarity in academic research, and scholars have not yet systematically examined the course and context of Chinese and Western game studies. This paper systematically summarises the development of game studies in China and the West, pointing out the differences and connections between "specialised/non-specialised" studies in Western game studies, and discussing in detail the recent situation and development direction of ludology based on video game studies. Therefore, this paper offers relatively comprehensive and detailed observations and comments on the development of Chinese and Western game studies in general. Based on this, this paper demonstrates in detail why semiotics is the academic and theoretical basis for game research, points out the significance and value of semiotics of games in current game studies, and finally argues that a method based on semiotics is needed to develop game studies.

Keywords: game studies, ludology, semiotics, video game, sports games

DOI: 10. 13760/b. cnki. sam. 202002009

游戏的历史可以追溯至人类文明产生之前——在人类学会使用文字表达之前，关于游戏的图画就被刻绘在岩壁上，昭示着游戏的历史。而在动物性与人性的模糊地带，游戏亦穿插其中，并且从来不令人感到突兀——动物在觅食、求偶等本能行为之外做出的那些莫名其妙的行为，通常也被称为游戏。历史叙述当然也没有忘记游戏，中外的史书都不约而同地为游戏留下了篇幅。

然而，尽管关于游戏的论述散见于诸多学者的专著，专门性游戏研究的历史却不足百年，而游戏研究在学术界占有一席之地只是近20年的事。似乎不难体会其间的矛盾：游戏很重要，但似乎又不太重要；“玩”是在观念中最容易被抛弃的，但似乎在实际生活中又最难割舍。在以意义为最终目标之一的人文社会科学研究中，通常被视为“无意义”的游戏显得格格不入。

1933年前后，赫伊津哈（Johan Huizinga）在苏黎世、维也纳和伦敦等地做了多次关于游戏的演讲，演讲的主题围绕着“文化的游戏成分”，他执拗地多次拒绝了东道主将主题改为“文化中的游戏成分”的建议。赫伊津哈认为，“游戏先于文化；在某种意义上，它也优于，至少是超乎文化”（1996, p. 21）。游戏（或多或少地）造就和影响了人类文化，它不应当仅仅被视为文化的一个子项。这些演讲的内容后来汇总为他的专著《游戏的人——关于文化的游戏成分的研究》，亦成就了他“游戏学之父”的美誉。

以游戏学的开创者赫伊津哈的研究为界，游戏研究的历史可以被分为两个部分：在时间维度上划分为游戏研究的“史前时代”和“文明时代”。或者更准确地说，这里包含着两个维度：“本体论/非本体论”意义上的游戏研究，或“专门性/非专门性”的游戏研究。

一、游戏的非专门性研究

西方游戏研究的“史前史”，可追溯至古希腊，柏拉图（尤其是《理想国》《法律篇》）、亚里士多德等都对游戏进行过专门论述。18 世纪，游戏的意义被重新发掘，康德和席勒都从美学的意义上讨论游戏。康德视“诗”为“想象力的自由游戏”，席勒则称“人应该仅仅同美进行游戏”，将游戏视为人类实现感性与理性和谐，完成自身完善和超越的最重要途径之一。席勒的观点启发了德国美学家谷鲁斯和英国哲学家斯宾塞。前者于 1898 年和 1901 年分别发表了《动物的游戏》和《人类的游戏》，提出游戏可以分为低级和高级两类，分别侧重“外模仿”和“内模仿”。后者则提出了游戏是高等动物用于发泄生存活动之外的多余精力的自由模仿活动，或称为“过剩精力说”。

这些研究共同的特点是，仅讨论“观念上的游戏”，而非“事实上的游戏”，无法将游戏研究发展为一种独立的学说，游戏只是其各自理论构建中的一个有机组成部分。

在这条脉络上最具成就者是哲学家路德维希·维特根斯坦，他的“语言游戏论”，是其语言哲学中占据关键地位的重要理论。他使用“下棋”作为例证，指出了语言与下棋、词语与棋子、语法与规则、语境与棋势的对应关系。（1992，pp. 24 –60）

在这条路上走得最远也最接近专门性游戏研究的是哲学家伽达默尔，虽然最终他也只是借助游戏来阐明艺术理论。作为哲学家，伽达默尔享有得天独厚的优势，一方面他对此前的哲学著作非常熟稔，另一方面，他显然也非常熟悉赫伊津哈的专著《游戏的人》，在《真理与方法》中对其多有引证。

游戏在伽达默尔的阐释学理论中占有举足轻重的地位，在《真理与方法》中，有整整一个章节来讨论“作为（艺术）本体论阐释主线的游戏”。作为阐释学的领军人物，他更为关注的不仅是游戏活动本身，而是游戏之交互性和阐释性，并以此来对应艺术活动。他的观点的独特之处在于：第一，游戏是一种“自我表现”，游戏的主体并非游戏者，游戏仅仅通过游戏者表现出来，游戏真正的主人是游戏自身，他吸引游戏者入内，并赋予游戏者游戏的精神；第二，游戏的意义只有借由观赏者的阐释才能够得到彰显，但取悦观赏者并不是游戏的真正目的。（1999，pp. 137 –140）游戏的表意的开放性如艺术一样，这也保证了对其阐释的多样性。

伽达默尔的艺术游戏论可以说是最系统、最完整的游戏衍生理论。然而，对于游戏研究而言，很遗憾的是，他的目的不在于研究游戏，而是利用对游戏的分析来说明艺术阐释之理。因而，为了阐明理论，他最终构建了理想的游戏模型——“艺术游戏”，并以此为旨归，而“艺术游戏”并不是典型意义上的游戏活动，只是伽达默尔借用游戏模式来指称的“审美活动”。

二、游戏的专门性研究

从时间线索上，维特根斯坦与赫伊津哈几乎处在同一时代，因此，我们仍要再次强调，游戏研究真正的分割并不完全是时间维度上的，而是两种学术源流及其对待作为研究对象的游戏的方式与态度的差异。

游戏的专门性研究，肇始于赫伊津哈。作为一位文化史学家和语言学家，赫伊津哈旁征博引，系统检视了诸种文化形态（如法律、诗歌、哲学、艺术、文明等）之中游戏的地位和作用，他是第一位正视游戏事实而非仅讨论游戏形式的学者，也因其历史与考古的学术能力，这种特殊的理论视角成为可能；他也是第一位试图界定游戏的学者，他称：“游戏是在某一固定时空中进行的自愿活动或事业，依照自觉接受并完全遵从的规则，有其自身的目标，并伴以紧张、愉悦的感受和‘有别于’‘平常生活’的意识。”（1996，p. 30）在此基础上，他又相继讨论了游戏之自由性、虚拟性、目的性、封闭性等问题，提出了与“理性的人”形成对照的“游戏的人”，“游戏乃是人类文化的基础”等观点。在此意义上，赫伊津哈的研究与其他学者隔靴搔痒、借艇割禾的思路形成了鲜明的对照，他是学术史上第一位开展专门性的游戏研究，并且构建了本体论意义上的游戏研究的学者。

赫伊津哈游戏研究脉络的继承者，是法国学者罗杰·卡约瓦（Roger Caillois），他于1958年出版了专著《人、玩乐与游戏》（*Man，Play and Games*）。卡约瓦怀着对赫伊津哈的悼念和崇敬来撰写这本书，因此其理论充满了对赫伊津哈的理论进行回应、商榷与论战的意味。他更加直白地表述了“把游戏作为游戏本身”（Caillois，2001，p. 167）来进行研究的理论思路。

当然，我们也不要忽略了卡约瓦自身的学术背景。他在法国巴黎高等师范学校读书时，师从马赛尔·莫斯，而莫斯则是法国结构主义社会学的代表人物埃米尔·涂尔干的学生，而且是他的外甥。因此，卡约瓦的理论，显现出强烈的结构主义和人文主义倾向。譬如，他关于游戏的类型划分——赌（agon）、斗（alea）、仿（mimicry）、晕（ilinx），以及将玩乐方式区分为嬉玩（paidia）与竞玩（ludus）的方式，都带有鲜明的结构主义特征。后结构主义的先驱，法国哲学家乔治·巴塔耶，亦是卡约瓦过从甚密的同学兼朋友，他们年轻时曾一同建立过一个名为“社会学学院”的秘密学术团体，有过相当密切的交流。据此也就不难解释，为什么我们会在罗兰·巴尔特、皮埃尔·布尔迪厄、让·波德里亚、德里达等学者那里，看到关于游戏或体育现象的专论。他们为什么会对此产生兴趣？这来自巴黎高师的学术承继关系，也与巴塔耶等人的学术影响力有莫大的关联。

据《理论诠释：体育与社会》一书描述，卡约瓦积极推进体育社会学的建立，通过教学和主持出版刊物，培养、扶持了后世一批体育社会学的研究者，学界誉其为“体育社会学之父”（马奎尔，2012，p. 35）。十分有趣的是，在这本书的中文译本中，译者将我们前文中提到的卡约瓦的著作《人、玩乐与游戏》译为了《男人，运动和比赛》，并且将卡约瓦构建一门“根植于游戏的社会学（sociology derived from games）”（Caillois，2001，p. 67）的愿景译为了“为从体育中发展社会学打下了基础”（马奎尔，2012，p. 36）。这或许不完全是误译，其深层次的原因是游戏与体育之间复杂的纠葛。

卡约瓦当时的意图十分明确，就是构建“游戏社会学”，当然，如同赫伊津哈，体育也在他的讨论范围之内。体育社会学有不少学者继承了卡约瓦的研究思路，如洛伊（J. W. Loy）对游戏类型、社会结构和社会反常状态的分析，就将卡约瓦的游戏类型学和默顿（R. K. Merton）的个人对制度化目标的五种适应模式——一致、创新、形式主义、逃跑主义和反抗——进行了深度融合。在体育社会学领域，结构主义思潮至今仍然具有深远影响。

三、游戏研究的中国境遇

中国的游戏研究面临着与西方迥异的历史境遇，但是在结果上，具有高度的相似性。在中国传统文化体系中，游戏并不是一个值得被讨论的课题，关于游戏的记述散见于史书艺文部、文人札记等，且尽管古代汉语中有“游戏”之说，但其用法灵活，多指一种自由散漫的生活状态或心境，没有明确的游戏概念，杂技、表演、歌舞、说唱等与游戏杂糅，其外延极其宽泛。

晚清、民国时期，中国知识分子“开眼看世界”，向西方学习，吸纳西方学术研究的理论与范式，探索现代学术体系的建立。而在当时，率先传入的现代体育观念接管了游戏。

1864 年，在美国人创办的山东登州文会馆教会学校中，出现了最早的体育（体操）课程。而在维新派人士开办的新式学堂中，还出现了将中国古代游戏移植到教学中的情况。如 1878 年张焕纶开办的正蒙书院在课程设置上就有击球、投沙囊、投壶、习射、蹴鞠、超距、八段锦诸课，分日轮流演习。1897 年，"体育"一词经日语转译到中国，其最初的意义比较单纯，即"身体的教育"，体育、体操、卫生、保育等概念相互杂糅，无明显的界限。

1906 年的《学部奏请宣示教育宗旨折》中，更明确提出："体操一科，幼稚者以游戏体操发育其身体，稍长则以兵式体操严整其纪律。"在这里，体操活动对应青少年，而游戏活动对应婴幼儿，其目的都在于促进身体发育，培养健康的生活方式以及心理。显然，游戏，最初是作为体育活动的补充，针对低龄儿童所开展的一种体育教学活动而被重新认识的。

据此而开展的关于游戏的引介、推广及应用性研究，则带有强烈的教育意味。1933 年吴蕴瑞、袁敦礼合著的《体育原理》中称，"故体育之意义，乃以身体活动为方式之教育"（1933，p. 10）。

20 世纪八九十年代，在体育学科领域，出现了专门的"体育游戏"研究，有些学者开始尝试从哲学、社会学等宏观视野对"体育游戏"进行重新定位与思考，展开宏观、系统性、本体论意义上的研究，极大地扩展了原本在体育学科框架之内被窄化的游戏研究外延，如孟刚《体育游戏与人的社会化》、司马容《体育游戏：人类生存的辩证法——现代哲学家对体育本体的多维反思》等。游戏显然与体育是两个概念，刻意融合实际上是忽略了游戏自身的丰富样态，一部分体育研究者们本能地意识到了这个基本问题，故而在"体育游戏"意义上的讨论，实际上已经产生了溢出体育学科范畴的实际效果。然而，进入 21 世纪，"体育游戏"研究再次转入对象性研究，回归原有的体育学框架之内，游戏本体论上的讨论几乎难见。

中国的游戏研究则携带着历史的烙印。与西方游戏研究的发展脉络不同，中国的现代学术体系沿自西方，因此不存在一个可以和体育学比肩的游戏研究传统。游戏甚至还没来得及为自己正名，得到一个恰如其分的概念，就被体育接管了。现代体育观念甫一登陆中国，就接管并改造了游戏活动，尽管这种改造的实际效果是窄化了游戏的外延。其结果是，对游戏的研究仅限于体育教育的路径，并且被限定在婴幼儿活动中，游戏被视为一种低幼化的体育现象，无法得到正确的对待。直到今天，这种刻板印象依旧未能被清除。在体育学和教育学学科压制下的游戏研究，处处掣肘，且受限于论文发表制度的影响，缺乏母学科支撑的游戏研究还需要很长一段时间才能被中国学界渐渐接受。

四、“游戏学”的重启

在体育科学建立、发展、壮大、成熟的近50年间，游戏研究式微，并逐渐被体育科学接管，除了一些针对个别游戏活动的专门性论著，系统性的游戏研究几乎消失。同时，一些与身体没有直接关联的游戏活动（如棋牌游戏、益智游戏等）也被纳入体育领域，从而扩展了原有体育研究的外延。

1971年，麻省理工学院的学生诺兰·布什内尔（Nolan Bushnell）设计了世界上第一个电子游戏《电脑空间》（Computer Space）。伴随着计算机硬件、编程、图像等软件以及网络技术的进步与发展，电子游戏在数量和质量上得到了迅速发展，成为新的、独立的专门性行业。

在今天看来，游戏学的重启完全是个偶然事件，它的契机，毋庸置疑，就是电子游戏的出现，电子游戏悄然登上了历史舞台，并迅速成长为不容忽视的产业力量。

经过20多年时间的积蓄和准备，电子游戏界决定另起炉灶，开创属于自己的独立研究。1999年，乌拉圭籍电子游戏研究者恭扎罗·弗拉斯卡（Gonzalo Frasca）在其论文《当游戏学遭遇叙述学：（电子）游戏与叙事的异同》中提出，希望电子游戏研究能够自立门户，形成一门独立的学科，并将其命名为“游戏学”（Ludology）。

2001年，作为主持人，阿瑟斯（Espen Aarseth）在“电子游戏研究元年”的网络大会上发表檄文，表示出强烈的建立独立的游戏研究的愿望：“诚然，游戏可以由现存的各学科和部门来进行研究，例如媒介研究、社会学、英语文学等，还能说上一堆。但游戏的重要性使之不能归属于其中任何一门学科（这些学科在30年的时间内什么都没干）。”（Aarseth，2001）这一年被称为“电子游戏研究元年”，很重要的原因在于“学者和专家们第一次将电子游戏作为一个难以忽视其价值的文化领域来严肃对待”（Aarseth，2001）。这一年，美国高校正式为“电子游戏研究”提供正规的课程和独立学位，这标志着游戏研究不再依附于“新媒体与数字研究”，其独立性得到了高等教育和学术界的认可。3月，在丹麦哥本哈根大学举行了第一个关于电子游戏的国际性学术会议。7月，阿瑟斯主持建立了游戏研究学术性期刊网站“游戏研究网”（www.gamestudies.org），并发表了该网站的第一篇文章，这一网站也成为电子游戏研究的重要学术支撑阵地。有趣的是，也许是为了与传统学术界“划清界限”，这本刊物一直以“网络期刊”的形式在

“游戏研究网”上发行。

20年过去了，今天，我们有机会从更加微观的角度，来重新审视西方游戏研究的发展及其内在变化与趋势。在一篇重要的综述文章《游戏研究近况——2000—2014年学术景观分析》中，梅尔瑟（Melcer，2015）等学者特别关注了欧美国家21个游戏研究核心刊物以及27个游戏研究核心会议，锚定了游戏研究48个“核心论域”。

据此，电子游戏研究大致可以分为两类：一是关注技术手段的研究，目的在于更好地理解和开发游戏，涉及如人工智能、计算机建模、可视化、图像研究等方面；另一个则是探索游戏的非技术方面的论题，研究方法涉及人文、艺术、设计和社会科学等多个领域，比较常见的论题包括叙述问题、用户体验、虚拟世界、角色扮演、游戏设计、游戏哲学等。然而，没有证据显示，这两类研究方向之间存在着明显的协同关系和作用，它们所构成的学术景观依然非常模糊。

欧美电子游戏研究的发展，也为中国的游戏研究带来一股新风。电子游戏独特的游戏特征令它从直观上即无法被体育科学所容纳，从而为独立的游戏研究提供了可能性。然而，由于中外学术生态与学术共同体上的巨大差异，国内学界没有能力构建相对独立的游戏研究。最初的游戏研究者（包括西方游戏研究著作的译者等），基本上都是游戏行业的从业或准从业人员，他们的诉求并不是进行系统化的游戏学术研究，而是为个人进入游戏行业寻求一些理论上的帮助。

从一种被动和潜在的效果来看，异军突起的电子游戏似乎在某种意义上恢复了游戏的本来面目，它既不像赌博一样带有明显的盈利意图，也不像字面意义上的“体育”一样，具有内在的教育意图。虽然电子游戏产业本身是营利性的，但游戏的过程本身却是无明确指向性的。也正因如此，对电子游戏的“电子鸦片”“游戏成瘾”等污名化的指责，实际上也可以看作对游戏自身意义的一种反向还原。

五、符号学：游戏学的学理化基础

纵观中西方游戏研究短暂的发展历程，即便是电子游戏研究建立后，游戏研究实际上仍未构建出具有清晰脉络的学理化基础。

游戏研究被其他学科分割的情况明显，传统的游戏研究的研究路径主要包括：

文化学：从游戏实存状况的历史出发，探讨游戏对人类文化构建的作用和意义，以赫伊津哈为代表。社会学：对作为社会现象的游戏进行总体性研究，具有较强的结构主义特征，以卡约瓦为代表。教育学（体育学）：截取部分游戏作为研究对象，强调游戏的教育意义，目的在于设计具有可控诉求的游戏活动。

电子游戏出现之后，游戏研究又增加了几个新的维度：

文学：试图将电子游戏所带来的新的叙述方式囊括进经典叙述学框架；或强调电子游戏跨媒介叙述与传统叙述的差异，将其作为新的课题。传播学：关注电子游戏所构建的新的传播方式，强调游戏所带来的视觉效果和情感体验。文化研究：以游戏细节及其引发的效果为研究对象，涉及“游戏暴力”“性别歧视”等文化研究基本课题。计算机技术：试图构建游戏程序设计的标准结构模型，来操控游戏性。

在此，文化学与社会学的路径面临着后继无人的状况，教育学的路径则携带着预设观念，而文学、传播学、计算机技术等路径上的讨论则通常仅涉及游戏的个别方面。并且，电子游戏研究者通常将电子游戏视为一种极其特殊的游戏活动，对非电子游戏问题避而不谈。以电子游戏为基的“游戏学”或曰“新游戏研究”，难以直面游戏全域，不能说是名副其实。

是否存在一种覆盖游戏全域，具有清晰的理论框架，能够兼容既有的游戏研究课题，又能够契合未来游戏发展的游戏研究方式呢？在理论的丛林中，我们谨慎地选择了符号学，并用近10年的时间，构建了游戏符号学理论。而在此要强调的是，符号学是游戏研究的一种，也是至今最优的一种理论选择。

第一，游戏是符号文本，游戏的核心是由游戏规则构建的符号系统。

游戏的规则和框架是由人为预先设计的规则体系决定的，规则设定本身的要求就是内在逻辑的自洽性。在规则中，不允许出现模棱两可或语义矛盾的情况，且不包含任何赘余无用的表达，意义的圆融自洽是系统性的最直接标志，而这与计算机逻辑语言具有内在的共通性。因此，单就规则系统而言，任何游戏都可以被“计算机化”。

实际上，在赫伊津哈和卡约瓦试图给出游戏的定义（与维特根斯坦等人一样，他们本人其实都反对游戏的概念化，认为这并不可能）后的很长一段时间，寻找游戏概念的工作一度停滞，直到电子游戏研究重启后，才有诸多学者从电子游戏的计算机程序编写的角度，给出游戏的定义。

克里斯·克劳福德（Chris Crawford）在认为：游戏“有四个共同的要素：再现（在一个封闭系统内，主观呈现一系列真实），互动，冲突和安全

（游戏的模式较游戏结果更为残酷）”（Crawford，1982）。《玩之规：游戏设计基础》一书中则称：“游戏是一个系统，玩家参与系统内的一次人为冲突中，该冲突受到规则的限定，会导致一个可计量的结果。”（Salen，Zimmerman，2004，p. 96）英国游戏学家杰斯伯·尤尔（Jesper Juul）在梳理了10余种游戏定义后，仍然认为：“游戏是建基于规则的形式系统，具有多样且可计算的结果，不同的结果被赋予了不同的价值，玩者看重结果，而为了影响结果，他们会付出努力，并且游戏的影响具有可协商性和非强制性。”（Juul，2011，p. 30）

强调规则所构建的系统性，切中了游戏设计的基本原理，而规则之内核，则是一个标明了施用范围的，由命题组成的语义系统，也就是由一系列语义符号（它可以直接转化为计算机语言）构成的符号系统。因此，在《游戏学：符号叙述学研究》中，笔者将游戏定义为：“游戏是受规则制约，拥有不确定结局，具有竞争性，虚而非伪的人类活动。”（宗争，2014，p. 38）在游戏研究中，这已经是一种有意义的尝试，试图在传统游戏与电子游戏研究之间找到具有通约性的游戏概念。

第二，游戏的实际进程决定了它必须被视为一个符号文本。

由规则系统决定赋义玩者的实际游戏行为，生成了具体的游戏符号文本。以“文本”一词的“编织物”的本意，在游戏文本中，玩者的任何行为都被符号化，都具有意义，或都应被解释为具有意义，但却并非都遵循游戏设计者所倾向和规定的意向性。这些意义行为，在更高的层次上得到阐释和解读，正如球迷在观看球赛时，不仅仅关注比赛（游戏）进程，其他的伴随性信息也同样被囊括进对该游戏符号文本的整合和解读中。

系统论与控制论如同孪生兄弟，电子游戏的研究者们在特别关注游戏程序的符号系统性时，往往忽略了实际的游戏行为，认为电子游戏的“输入/输出”机制完全决定了玩者的行为方式。事实上，如同伽达默尔指出的，游戏者不是游戏的主体，游戏设计者也无法担当此任，玩者的具体游戏行为往往逃逸出设计者预先构建出的意义框架。游戏文本呈现出的从来都不是一个简单的线性结构，它是包含着各种表意符号及庞大意义滑动空间的复杂文本。为此，“游戏符号学”提出了“游戏文本的双重互动传播结构”（宗争，2014，p. 80）来解释游戏文本表意和传播的特殊模式，后又提出“游戏文化机制”（p. 39）的“四次赋义”来解释游戏文化形成的意义生成机制。如此，就弥合了赫伊津哈式的游戏研究对文化阐释的关注与电子游戏研究明显的系统-控制论倾向之间的矛盾。

第三，游戏总体形成了与其他社会活动相对应的意义活动。

自亚里士多德做出劳动与闲暇的区分，关于玩乐行为和游戏活动的意义构建就无法逃脱这一对二元对立关系。教育学（体育学）对游戏的阉割和改造，恰恰是令其服膺于一个更高层次的诉求，携带着具体而显明的教育目的。电子游戏研究者则专注于电子游戏设计所可能营造的游戏感和拟态环境。美学、哲学、文化学意义上的讨论，则视游戏为主体性自由高扬的明证，但社会学的路径反而提示我们，游戏已经成为意识形态的一种公开的麻醉剂和当代神话。而游戏符号学，恰恰能够提供一种更为开放的理论环境，它可以微观地观照具体的游戏符号的细节，亦可以更为开放的态度看待游戏活动及游戏文化在社会生活中的意义构建。

第四，坚持和发展游戏研究，需要符号学与叙述学的方法。

符号学家曾广泛使用游戏作为例证，游戏的规则体系是符号学恰如其分的对应物。索绪尔也不止一次地使用“棋局”来例证语言内部的指涉法则，以说明语言系统共时性/历时性的内在二重性：“在我们所能设想的一切比拟中，最能说明问题的莫过于把语言的运行比之于下棋。两者都使我们面临价值的系统，亲自看到它们的变化。语言以自然的形式呈现于我们眼前的情况，下棋仿佛用人工把它体现出来。”（1999，p. 128）法国人类学家列维－斯特劳斯则钟情于用扑克牌作例子。符号学家罗兰·巴尔特则在各种体育与游戏活动（美式摔跤、环法自行车赛）中找到了“现代神话”的最有力证明。

而当代游戏研究中最为前沿的问题，也就是游戏设计与游戏叙述问题，皆直接关涉游戏符号学的论域。游戏设计本身就是个符号学问题，游戏规则与框架的搭建，就是对具体符号进行强制性赋义的过程。而当弗拉斯卡（Frasca，2011）试图在电子游戏的拟真与叙述之间做出判断时，他所面对的，是以文学叙述为代表的经典叙述学。倘若他能够关注叙述学由经典叙述学向广义叙述学的发展，这一论题将在叙述学内部得到消解，不攻自破。从实际样态来看，既有的游戏研究与符号学存在着广泛的交集。

游戏的符号叙述学已经在游戏研究中率先完成了理论构建。复杂的历史境遇，令中国学者有机会从学科源流、理论脉络、研究侧重等方面对游戏研究进行更为全面的观照。如张新军的专著《可能世界叙事学》（2010）、关萍萍的博士学位论文《互动媒介论——电子游戏多重叙事模式》（2010）、刘研的博士学位论文《电子游戏的情感传播研究》（2014）等一系列研究，恰恰都沿用了符号学或叙述学理论，这是中国学者紧密跟进西方电子游戏发展，开展游戏系统性研究的证明。而宗争的《游戏学：符号叙述学研究》（2014）

试图构建游戏全域研究的理论框架，是国内第一本具有本体论意义的游戏学专著，可以视为中国游戏符号学发展的端点。

六、结语

从 1933 年赫伊津哈在莱顿大学做演讲开始，真正的游戏研究的历史尚不足百年，尽管游戏活动的样态不断推陈出新——从希罗多德笔下的吕底亚人的骰子游戏到各种现代体育竞技活动，再到电子游戏，游戏无时无刻不显示出它巨大的影响力。我们很难想象，在人类历史中如此重要的一项文化活动，竟然遭受如此冷遇。

毫无疑问，游戏是绝好的例证，康德、席勒、伽达默尔、德里达、索绪尔、维特根斯坦、罗兰·巴尔特、哈贝马斯等一大批影响后世的学者，都从游戏那里获得了灵感，来构建他们宏大的理论体系和学术事业。然而，在他们那里，游戏甚至不是作为研究对象，而只是作为某种辅助性的证据出现的。

赫伊津哈是当之无愧的“游戏学之父”，但是，我们也需要承认，仅仅凭借一部著作、一人之力，很难支撑起一个独立的学科。游戏研究需要更多的投入和关注，但显然，它的运气差了些。如同没有罪孽的维吉尔却无法随同但丁游览天堂，赫伊津哈、卡约瓦并没有机会看到更为复杂的电子游戏。他们的后继者也没能接续他们的工作，或是将游戏导向了体育，或是将目光紧盯在了更具特殊性的电子游戏上。而在电子游戏研究极有可能拓展出关于游戏的总体研究时，由于现有的游戏研究者自身学缘结构的局限，以及不想过早独树一帜的温和气质，独立、系统的游戏学的发展进程被拖延了。

游戏符号学的创立，是中国学者审时度势后的自主选择，符号学天然的“人文社会科学公分母”的属性，令它既能够继承游戏相关研究的理论成果，也能够从容涉足新的电子游戏研究的诸多论域，亦能够扩展更大的研究空间。它无疑是现阶段我们能够认识、掌握并推广的最为优化的研究方案。

与能够带来巨大经济利益的游戏产业不同，游戏的学术研究是极其艰辛的事业，它需要的是踽踽独行的研究者，而不是沽名钓誉的弄潮儿。

引用文献：

弗拉斯卡，恭扎罗（2011）. 拟真还是叙述——游戏学导论（宗争，译）. 符号与传媒，2，247 - 261.

关萍萍（2010）. 互动媒介论——电子游戏多重叙事模式. 浙江大学博士学位论文.

赫伊津哈（1996）. 游戏的人（多人，译）. 杭州：中国美术学院出版社.

伽达默尔（1999）. 真理与方法（洪汉鼎，译）. 上海：上海译文出版社.

刘研（2014）. 电子游戏的情感传播研究. 浙江大学博士学位论文.

马奎尔，扬（编）.（2012）. 理论诠释：体育与社会（陆小聪，译）. 重庆：重庆大学出版社.

索绪尔（1999）. 普通语言学教程（高名凯，译）. 北京：商务印书馆.

维特根斯坦（1992）. 哲学研究（汤潮，范光棣，译）. 北京：生活·读书·新知三联书店.

吴蕴瑞，袁敦礼（1933）. 体育原理. 上海：勤奋书局.

张新军（2010）. 可能世界叙事学. 苏州：苏州大学出版社.

宗争（2014）. 游戏学：符号叙述学研究. 成都：四川大学出版社.

宗争（2017）. 射何以成道——游戏文化机制的符号学研究. 成都体育学院学报，2，37 -41.

Aarseth, E. (2001). Computer game studies, Year One. Retrieved from http://www.gamestudies.org/0101/.

Aarseth, E. (2015). Meta-game studies. *Game studies*, 15, 1. Retrieved from http://gamestudies.org/1501/articles/editorial.

Caillois, R. (2001). *Man, play and games* (Meyer Barash, Trans.). Chicago, IL: University of Illinois Press.

Crawford, C. (1982). The art of computer game design. Retrieved from http://www.vancouver.wsu.edu/facpeabody/game - book/Coverpage.html.

Frasca, G. (1999). Ludology meets narratlolgy: Similitude and differences between (video) games and narrative. Retrieved from: http://www.ludology.org/articles/ludology.htm.

Juul, J. (2011). *Half real: Video games between real rules and fictional worlds.* Cambridge: MIT Press.

Melcer, E. et al. (2015). Games research today: Analyzing the academic landscape 2000 - 2014. Proceedings of the 10th International Conference on the Foundations of Digital Games. Retrieved from http://www.fdg2015.org/papers/fdg2015_ paper_ 41.pdf.

Salen, K., & Zimmerman, E. (2004). *Rules of play-game design fundamentals.* Cambridge: MIT Press.

作者简介：

宗争，成都体育学院新闻与传播学院副教授，主要研究领域为游戏符号学、体育文化传播、符号哲学。

Author:

Zong Zheng, associate professor of School of Journalism and Communication, Chengdu Sport University. His research interests include semiotics of game, sports culture communication and philosophy of semiotics.

Email: zongzheng2012@126.com

论“国潮”品牌跨界的符号双轴关系*

蒋诗萍　周诗诗

摘　要：近年来，“国潮”成为炙手可热的社会文化现象，于中国品牌的发展以及中国文化的弘扬有着重大意义。品牌“国潮”化的具体实践是品牌跨界，其实质是两个符号并置形成一个新文本的过程，这是双轴操作的结果。“国潮”品牌跨界的聚合轴是宽幅的，而这个幅度的不断疯长正在促成品牌跨界的“选择悖论”，这不利于品牌的长远建设和“国潮”的长期且大范围存在。

关键词：国潮，品牌跨界，符号双轴，宽幅

The Biaxial Relationship of Signs in the *Guochao* Brand Crossover

Jiang Shiping　Zhou Shishi

Abstract: In recent years, *guochao* has become a hot social and cultural phenomenon that is of great significance to the development of Chinese brands and the promotion of Chinese culture. The specific practice of *guochao* is brand crossover, and its essence is the process of collocating two signs to form a new text, which is the result of a biaxial operation. *Guochao* has a wide convergence axis. The continuous and rapid increase of its range contributes to the "paradox of choice" of brand crossover, which is not conducive to the long-

* 本文系国家社科基金青年项目“中国品牌国际传播中的文化符号生产与认同机制研究”（17CXW023）的阶段性成果之一，上海财经大学青年教师预研究项目（2020110198）成果之一。

term development of the brand or to the long-term and large-scale existence of *guochao.*

Keywords: *guochao,* brand crossover, biaxial relations of signs, broad width
DOI: 10. 13760/b. cnki. sam. 202002010

近年来，“国潮”悄然兴起，成为炙手可热的社会文化现象。在线导购平台返利网发布的一组数据显示，2019 年 1 月到 7 月，“国潮”关键词搜索量同比增长 392. 66% 。“国潮”是以品牌为载体，以文化为语言的一种现象，在这一现象中，品牌作为具象和意象的中国文化精神的承载体，是中国文化的具体形式。

一方面，中国传统文化融入品牌创意，形成了独特的品牌风格，不断推出热销产品，实现了品牌重塑和品牌价值的提升，促进品牌产业的发展。从联名唇膏到快闪店的冰激淋、奶茶，大白兔等“中华老字号”成功破除圈层，传承文化和基因的力量绽放新生；从回力帆布鞋、太平鸟到巴黎时装周上的李宁潮款设计，越来越多的消费者迷恋上了略带潮牌风范的国货；从故宫口红到稻香村的故宫联名礼盒，百年故宫成为超级 IP，小小物件就能掀起购买狂潮。在阿里巴巴平台上，2018 年与中国元素相关的关键词累计搜索量超过 126 亿次。2019 年“双 11”当天，天猫平台上 237 个成交额破亿元品牌中，国货品牌占比过半。

另一方面，中国文化元素附着于品牌，是中国传统文化的一种新的表现形式，是传统文化的现代展示。每一个品牌所代表的内涵和价值就是品牌背后的民族和国家文化，品牌的生产、传播与消费也就是中国文化符号的再生产、表达与认同。年轻人成为“国潮”的主要追逐者，数据显示，“90 后”和“00 后”已成为拉动国潮消费的主力群体，在 2019 年 1 月至 7 月，他们为“国潮”贡献了超过 57. 73% 的购买力，其中“95 后”以 25. 8% 的占比成为“国潮”第一大消费群体。这反映了当下主流消费者对中华文化的积极心态，反映了国民对“国潮”品牌以及中华文化的共鸣和认同感，更反映了中华文化自信的提升。

“国潮”的迅速兴起与发展，于建设品牌与弘扬中国文化二者来说，重要性是不言而喻的。我们应该让“国潮”成为一种稳定而普遍的社会常态，而非短暂的昙花一现的潮流，让中国文化、中国元素成为永远的市场热点。然而，潮流是一种流行，它作为一种动态的存在，往往会成为时尚而暂时得到人们的推崇，随后迅速消失。如 20 世纪 90 年代，以韩国电视剧、流行音乐等时尚元素为代表的“韩流”席卷整个中国，韩国明星与韩式打扮成为年轻人疯狂追逐的对象，他们争相去韩国旅游以体验电视剧中的浪漫场景，去韩国整容以模仿韩星的妆容。到了2005年，“韩流”逐露颓势，日渐萧条。时至今日，其大势已去，不可挽回。

同时，当前的具体“国潮”品牌实践也问题重重，各类相关的品牌营销失败案例也层出不穷。仅从2019年来看，前有杜蕾斯跨界喜茶的闹剧，后有小杨生煎联合稚优泉推出小龙虾生煎面膜的无厘头事件，其间还有旺旺开起了酒店并卖上了家具，马应龙推出口红，“万物皆可故宫”等一系列大众反映褒贬不一，但的的确确带来一定的不适感的营销活动。这都反映出在利益驱动与商业化运作的背景下，“国潮”的大部分表现形式在某种程度上只是带有新鲜感的营销举动：同质化的营销策略、机械复制般的创意模式开始让消费者失去新鲜感；纷繁复杂的品牌符号的解构与重组，造成受众对品牌理解的混乱。于是，对于“国潮”，大众也有了越来越多的怀疑和争议。

上述关于“国潮”的两大问题都促使我们思考以下问题：“国潮”品牌应如何“国潮”化？“国潮”如何能规避潮流易逝的特点而成为一种社会文化常态？回答这两个问题的关键在于厘清“国潮”品牌的符号文本结构以及符号表意方式。因此，本文将以此议题为中心，展开对“国潮”品牌的符号学审视，从双轴关系理论出发，以品牌“国潮”化的具体实践为具象文本，对“国潮”品牌的符号文本结构、“国潮”品牌的表意特征做出剖析。

一、品牌“国潮”化的具体实践：品牌跨界

从营销学来看，“国潮”化是品牌的一种有效增值与营销模式，它能点燃新的消费需求，提升品牌价值感，其主要的品牌实践活动为品牌多领域跨界。

第一种跨界是品牌间的跨界产品联合，即两种分属不同产品领域的品牌联合推出产品，如生产奶糖的大白兔与护肤品牌郁美净推出联合款唇膏。

第二种跨界是国货跨界时尚潮流，主要体现在国货产品潮流化，如食品品牌旺旺推出带有街头时尚风格的卫衣；国货设计上的潮流化，如电视品牌创维援引中国古籍《山海经》中精卫填海、共工触山、嫦娥奔月、夸父追日四大经典神话故事，推出一款结合中华传统刺绣工艺而研发的刺绣电视；国货登上秀场，进军时尚圈，如中国潮流先行者李宁品牌服装，分别于2018年、2019年两次现身纽约时装周，成功跻身于运动时尚界。

第三种是借助 IP 联名跨界营销，最为经典的案例莫过于百年故宫，它已成为超级 IP。2019 年，故宫新推出一款“古风神兽”雪糕，迅速上了热搜，成了名副其实的新“网红”，深受年轻人追捧。不只是美食，故宫 IP 席卷了消费的方方面面，打造出一款又一款的潮品。

从符号表意过程来看，“国潮”形成一个新文本的符号运作过程，是两个原先携带着不同意义的符号组合在一起的结果。老字号品牌之间的联姻、现代品牌与传统文化的结合，抑或是国货品牌潮流化，都是通过两个符号的并置形成一个陌生的符号文本。德国著名戏剧家布莱希特曾经说过：“对一个事件或人物进行陌生化，首先很简单，把事件或人物那些不言自明的，为人熟知的和一目了然的东西删去，使人对之产生惊讶和好奇心。”（杨向荣，肖萍，2010）

消费社会中由于符号更新迭代的速度加快，社会大众在符号层面的认知与实践不断积累，因此想要在一定时间内寻找到完全新颖的符号形式并不容易。而符号陌生化这样一种将原有的符号解构重组、重新排列的方式，成为编码者符号创新的捷径之一，因为它可以让社会大众对过去接触到的符号及其意义产生陌生感，从而再次收获大众的注意力资源。

二、“国潮”品牌的符号双轴关系

两个品牌或品牌与文化的结合实现文本陌生化，这实际上包含了一个选择机制，而任何符号文本的构建都是符号双轴的操作，品牌跨界形成的“国潮”符号文本亦是如此。双轴操作即符号的横组合与纵聚合关系，是符号学中的一对经典概念，最早由语言学家索绪尔提出。横组合又称为句段关系，指的是符号的线性组合，解决的是符号链的结构问题。在横组合中，我们考虑的是每个句段之间的相互关系和整体与部分之间的关系。纵聚合又被称作联想关系，即“在话语之外，彼此具有某些共同性的词会在人的记忆中联想起来，并形成了由各种关系支配的集合”（索绪尔，1980，p. 147）。由于联想关系是基于人的联想而构建起来的关系，因此它是潜在的、无序的。

“国潮”品牌符号文本的选取和意义的解释，便是符号双轴操作的结果。“国潮”品牌文本是已完成编码的陌生化文本，“在已编码的文本层面上，人们需要应对的既有明显的内容，又有各种看不见的、并被想当然的意义”（斯蒂文森，2003，p. 127）。“明显的内容”即符号文本的横组合，“看不见的意义”则是符号纵聚合传达出的意义感知。

在品牌“国潮”化的传播过程中，品牌方从潮流环境中提取符号素材，通过对所选取内容的重新组合，演绎出品牌的潮流意义。这个横组合的产生，是品牌方为了能够准确表达自身所要传达的意义而加以遴选和编织的，遴选和编织的标准便是品牌商关于品牌一系列意义的想象，这是一个从纵聚合探知横组合的过程。

而消费者对“国潮”品牌符号进行解释，是一个解码活动。他们感知符号文本的包括颜色、文案、画面构成、纹样、故事情节等在内的一切信息，即关于品牌符号文本的横组合，再结合自身社会生活经验与解释能力，触发了纵聚合层面上的联想与延展，从而解释出文本的独特意义。这一过程是由横组合引发的纵聚合探知，与编码过程恰好相反。

可见，“国潮”品牌符号的完整表意过程中，品牌商对符号元素的选取组成了横组合，实现了对品牌意义的编码；消费者通过对横组合的感知，触发了纵聚合层面上的联想与延展，形成了对品牌意义的解释与延伸。比如大白兔和郁美净推出联合款唇膏。大白兔的主营产品是醇香奶糖，之前从未涉足日化领域，多年来人们只要一想起童年记忆中的奶糖味，就会想起大白兔这个品牌，但随着市场竞争的加剧和日本悠哈等国外奶糖品牌对市场的抢夺，大白兔逐渐淡出市场，成为一种记忆。品牌编码者将奶糖与唇膏这两个毫不相关的事物结合起来，显现的横组合是“奶糖味儿的唇膏”。但在创造这一符号文本时，必须在各大品牌间进行聚合挑选，可以是其他生产糖果的品牌，也可以是生产其他食品的品牌，甚至可以是非食品品牌，但最后大白兔品牌被选择，这样的挑选组合是按照怀旧、童年记忆等意义标准进行的符号活动。

“国潮”品牌的形成还是一个转喻过程，在这个符号的解构和重组过程中，原有意义转移，新意义产生。朱迪思·威廉森在《解码广告》中也曾表示：“广告讯息意义建构的方式之一，就是将一个符号的意义转移到另一个符号。”（杨晓强，2008）比如，旺旺推出卫衣产品，就是要将卫衣所携带的意义转移到旺旺品牌中来，以重塑旺旺的品牌形象与品牌价值。首先，卫衣本身就是随性街头风的潮流代表，它已经成为潮款服饰的代名词，旺旺推出卫衣，则将这种潮流气息转移到旺旺品牌上来，使旺旺俨然成为食品界的“潮哥”。不仅如此，旺旺作为老字号品牌与时尚的结合，还获得了复古意味，于是，旺旺又成了复古时尚潮流的典范。

三、宽幅的“国潮”品牌聚合轴

不同文本背后的聚合轴宽窄并不一致，有宽幅与窄幅之分，宽窄的不一致，会直接影响文本的风格。“一旦文本组合形成，聚合轴就退出操作隐藏起来，但并不是说它没有留下痕迹。聚合轴的影响始终存在，而且始终影响着文本的各种品质。”（赵毅衡，2011，p. 163）比如，雅典和斯巴达同为古希腊城邦，文化差异却很大，雅典十分注重开放和自由，因此对个人的职业选择的限制不严格。人们可以学习不同的知识，成为政治家、商人、诗人、哲学家，因此职业选择的聚合轴是宽幅的。而斯巴达则崇尚武力，不重视文化，想要把每一个人培养为武士，斯巴达人职业选择的聚合轴就是窄幅的。这种聚合轴的宽窄差异造成文本差异：雅典的文化十分繁荣，更崇尚自由，更加开放进取；斯巴达则是封闭的、保守的、崇尚武力的。

就品牌跨界来说，“国潮”品牌跨界是宽幅的，因为它有很多的选择。首先，不同领域的品牌可以联合，就大白兔来说，可以与郁美净联合推出唇膏，与气味图书馆联合推出香氛系列，与乐町联合推出服饰，与快乐柠檬推出奶茶，与光明牛奶推出大白兔奶糖味牛奶，等等。其次，任一品牌都能搭上时尚潮流顺风车，如旺旺推出卫衣后，老干妈、卫龙也相继推出卫衣；李宁走过国际时装周秀台后，太平鸟、海澜之家也走了起来；大白兔有了香水以后，泸州老窖也推出酱香型香水。最后，同一 IP 也可以与任何品牌联合，如故宫 IP，自百雀羚出了故宫款，就有了润百颜故宫口红、稻香村故宫联名款、农夫山泉故宫联名款，甚至国外美妆品牌欧莱雅、圣罗兰（YSL）、魅可（MAC）都要来蹭一波故宫热。

而且这个宽度还在不断扩展，原因主要有两个。

其一是在互联网时代能指与所指的断裂与重组造成大量新兴符号的涌入。在大众传播的过程中，能指的多样化为表意渠道的多样化创造了条件，使得话语符号的传播表征更加具有多元性、创造性和趣味性，社会大众间的交流也大多借助“能指的解构和重新排列组合”这一条捷径来处理和传达信息。这一点在网络语言的使用上表现得尤为明显，比如用“666”来表达很厉害的称赞；“红红火火恍恍惚惚”“hhhhhh”和“哈哈哈哈哈哈”实则为一个意思；“蓝瘦香菇”原是源于一则短视频中广西男子的不标准发音，而后发展成为“难受想哭”的代名词；再如“对你笔芯”“是个杯具”实则是把“比心”“悲剧”的同音词这一能指当作了它们自身所指的替代。

这样的例子不胜枚举。不得不承认的是，在这一时代背景下，能指与所指的断裂、解构与重组正在以前所未有的速度进行着，并迅速在传播与解读中获得理据性，进而进入大众传播的话语体系，其生命周期或长或短。这一过程所带来的能指的极大丰富以及表意的多元化，为“国潮”品牌跨界提供了聚合轴幅度加宽的可能性。

其二是符号在使用过程中必然会获得理据性，并且理据性与符号文本使用频率与范围呈正相关。当一个社群坚持使用一个符号时，一个没有理据性的符号也能很快获得理据性，甚至成为高理据化的象征。相反，已经获得理据性的符号在使用过程中也可能意义磨损，从而产生去理据化现象。理据性的上升与滑落是符号使用过程中的一种常态。

在后互联网时代，信息的快速流动和碎片化的呈现方式使得符号意义的生成与滑落的周期大大缩短，理据性的滑动也变得更为普遍。正是有了符号理据性的滑动，国货品牌潮化的表意行为才有了更为丰富的表达与呈现。“国潮”品牌间的跨界联合、设计潮牌化以及依托 IP 推出限定款等营销行为，使得“国潮”化成为一场充满新奇感、创造力的活动，使得之前在社会大众心中固化、无趣、陈旧的国货品牌符号的意义生成与传达方式变得活跃起来，从而为社会大众提供了充满趣味性和颠覆感的“国潮”化的认知体验。

四、“国潮”品牌跨界的选择悖论

语言的发展中有个规律叫作“词义弱化”，指的是我们的用词大多都会随着时间的推移和使用频次的增加，而内涵减弱。后互联网时代“短平快”的特点加速了这种弱化，比如现在的“美女”已经不足以称赞一个姑娘的美丽，“美女”的升级版本——“女神”也在遭遇一轮语言界的“通货膨胀”后，迅速迭代成“仙女”。在当下社交网络上，人们大量使用“顶格表达”来发言，痛苦的要极致痛苦，美丽的要如神仙一般，网上经常能见到“秒杀”“完爆”“千年一遇”此类形容程度的词。

词语的刺激使得大众表达的阈值不断提高，于是一旦新词被提出，人们就争先恐后地使用。这种短时间的频繁使用，会导致这个词更快贬值，继而被归为陈词滥调，随后更多的话语符号被创造出来。商业社会的语境下，我们的话语符号变得很矛盾——既丰富又贫乏，因此，我们已经很难找到一个合适的词来描述处于极美与极丑之间的女性的样貌了。

同理，这种高速的词汇迭代，也迫使品牌在具体的“国潮”化实践中不得不不断突破之前的固定文本样式，为创意绞尽脑汁。对于部分“国潮”品牌来说，它们能在这场跨界运动中成为创新的佼佼者，与“国潮”品牌跨界的幅度过宽有关，但对于大部分品牌来说，它们自由到无法找到自己的风格，因为可供选择跨界的品牌和时尚太多了，在令人眼花缭乱的选择中，大部分品牌只能依从其他品牌跨界时所选取的标准。这就出现了选择悖论：表面上的跨界创意时实际上并无选择可言，“一切皆故宫”便是有力证明。

所以，在“国潮”品牌的实践操作中，这种宽幅实际上是一种假性宽幅，尽管看上去充满了无限的选择，但大部分品牌都没有自己的标准，只能跟着已获成功的“国潮”品牌走，跟着超级IP走。这种机械的复制粘贴，虽然能为品牌制造一定的热度，带来一定的流量，但都是暂时的，这种热度和流量会迅速消失在下一波跨界联名中，而且会稀释品牌自己原有的形象，造成品牌形象的纷杂化，于品牌长远的发展来说，这无异于饮鸩止渴。

再者，如此“国潮”化，会形成“国潮”刻板化、模式化的印象，没有灵魂的“潮”也会使得社会大众对“国潮”产生误解和反感，导致“国潮”不再流行，反而被打上“没有创意”的标签，最后将会使得“国潮”与其他潮流一样，快速流行，却又快速衰退，这有悖于“国潮”化的初衷。

结　语

本文以“国潮”为考察对象，对“国潮”品牌的具体实践活动——品牌跨界做了文本的符号学分析，通过运用双轴关系理论，剖析了“国潮”品牌的符号文本结构与表意机制，认为“国潮”品牌跨界实质是两个符号并置形成一个新文本的过程，这是一个双轴操作的结果。“国潮”品牌跨界的聚合轴是宽幅的，但是这个幅度的不断扩展正在促成品牌跨界的选择悖论，并真实反映在了具体的品牌跨界实际操作过程中，使得“国潮”品牌面临重重问题与质疑。这不利于品牌的长期建设，不利于“国潮”长期且大范围存在，不利于保持中国文化、中国元素在市场上的热度，也不利于吸引人们对中国文化的关注。

因此，我们应对此保持足够的警惕。正视“国潮”品牌聚合轴的宽幅性并不意味着放弃品牌跨界，相反，在品牌跨界实践中，应冷静对自身品牌进行定位，避免盲目跟风，鼓励突破与创新，如此方能推动中国品牌的发展，亦能推动“国潮”成为社会文化常态，这也是本文讨论“国潮”品牌跨界的意义之所在。

参考文献：

索绪尔，弗迪南（1980）．普通语言学教程（高名凯，译）．北京：商务印书馆．

斯蒂文森，尼克（2003）．认识媒介文化（王文斌，译）．北京：商务印书馆．

杨晓强（2008）. 从符号的双轴关系看广告传播中意义的增值. 当代传播, 2, 88－89.
杨向荣, 肖萍（2010）. 布莱希特"陌生化"的批判解读. 陇东学院学报, 2010, 6, 54－57.
赵毅衡（2011）. 符号学：原理与推演. 南京：南京大学出版社.

作者简介：

蒋诗萍，博士，上海财经大学人文学院讲师、硕士生导师，研究方向为品牌文化的符号叙述学研究。

周诗诗，上海财经大学人文学院硕士研究生，研究方向为广告与品牌传播。

Authors:

Jiang Shiping, Ph. D., lecturer of College of Humanities, Shanghai University of Finance & Economics. Her research field is semiotics of brand communication.

Email: jiangshiping2016@163. com

Zhou Shishi, Master Degree candidate of College of Humanities, Shanghai University of Finance & Economics. Her research field is advertising and brand communication.

Email: zsszoes@163. com

重复：电影改编的艺术基底*

赵禹平

摘　要：重复是恒常的电影现象。由根据新闻事件改编的电影，到根据真人真事改编的电影，根据小说、自传等改编的电影，再到根据旧版电影翻拍的电影，都是重复运动的结果。重复是不断深化意义的符号活动。电影改编作为重复的方式之一，使电影不断以改编的方式，将过去的经验或影像反复重现于观众面前。电影改编是寻找差异、展开重述行为的运动，电影改编在使文本成为崭新之物的同时，又不失对同属同类事物的思考。通过重复来理解电影改编，意在说明电影改编的目的、形式及文化意义。

关键词：重复，电影改编，象征符号

Repetition: The Artistic Basis of Film Adaptation

Zhao Yuping

Abstract: Repetition is a frequent phenomenon in the film industry. Films adapted based on news, true stories, novels, autobiographies and old films are all the result of repetition. Repetition is an activity involving signs that constantly deepens meaning. As one mode of repetition, film adaptation enables a film to reproduce past experience or images for the audience. To adapt a film is to seek differences and carry out restatements; it makes the text a new thing while

---

* 本文为江苏省研究生科研创新计划项目“真人真事改编电影的符号述真研究”（KYCX20_1198）的阶段性成果。

considering the same kinds of things. To understand film adaptation in terms of repetition is to explain the purpose, form and cultural significance of film adaptation.

Keywords: repetition, film adaptation, symbols

DOI: 10.13760/b.cnki.sam.202002011

重复是不断深化意义的符号活动。电影改编作为重复的方式之一，使电影不断以改编的方式，将过去的经验或影像反复重现于观众面前。电影改编，包括根据新闻事件改编的电影，根据真人真事改编的电影，根据小说、自传等改编的电影，根据旧版电影翻拍的电影，都是重复运动的结果，是寻找差异、展开重述行为的运动。它们在使文本成为崭新之物的同时，又不失对同属同类事物的思考。这一恒常的电影现象，充盈着独特的文化意义。

一、重复：从根据到存在

人类处在一个整体重复的集合中，过去是现在的基础，而现在又保持着不断衍生的状态。人类生活，就是经验不断累积的结果。重复，是最常见的意义活动。人类对同一语言文字的重复使用，使得语言文字得以传承。正如约翰·雷德蒙所说："我们思考的方式是至关重要的：我们通过重复来学习——语言本身可能就是从重复中产生的。"（Redmond，2006，p. 56）普拉东对重复的理解，扎根于他的"回忆"（recollection）理论当中。他认为每一种知识都存在于人们灵魂之中，但人们却忘记了它们，因此他强调学习的作用是记住（remembering），是去回忆那些人们已经忘记的知识。因而他断定，追求和学习只不过是回忆罢了，学习取决于坚定的外部资源。也就是说，既有一个完整的外部，又有一个回忆的行动依赖它，回忆便是重复行动。

弗洛伊德在《超越快乐原则》中，几乎总是将重复称为强迫行为，并将其描述为一种"驱力"（drive），由此形成一个简单的因果关系：驱力导致行为。"当行为变得重复时，这种重复就构成了驱动行为存在的证据。这是一种超越快乐原则的本能。"（Rogers，1987）弗洛伊德还从控制论－系统－符号学的角度将神经症看作一个循环的符号，认为重复就是问题的表现方式。尼采的"永恒回归"学说，对他那个时代的能量学抱有浓烈的兴趣。尼采的"永恒回归"在时间上基本是无限的，事件会无限重复它们自己。海德格尔受尼采"永恒回归"理论的影响，提出了"新起点"（Woodward，2014，

p. 18）理论。克尔凯郭尔则把重复放在高于回忆的位置。他解释道：“重复和回忆是同一种运动，只是方向相反；因为被回忆的东西是被回忆过去的，而真正的重复是被回忆起来的。”（Kierkegaard, 2009, p. 3）

吉勒·德勒兹对尼采“永恒回归”理论的探讨更具有本体论意义。永恒的回归是德勒兹差异理论的核心。在尼采的《永恒的回归》中，一切都在重复，但他坚信回归的不是相同而是不同。换言之，在每一次重复中，返回的不是相同，而是相似，同时又有差异。德勒兹专注于重复之中存在的变化，他认为：没有存在，只有变化。德勒兹强调，“重复不改变重复对象中的一切，但是却使得静观着它的心灵中的一些东西发生了变化”（德勒兹，2019，p. 70）。“生产过程的差异，在每次重复中产生变化。”（Parr，2010，p. 225）。每一次重复都会带来新的东西

（一）重复与艺术

重复，对艺术表现而言至关重要。康定斯基认为：“重复是一种强化内在情感的有力手段，同时也创造出一种原始的节奏，而这种节奏反过来又在每一种艺术形式中达到一种原始的和谐。”（Kandinsky，1994；转引自 Akyel，2015，p. 11）这种和谐还可由节奏统一带来，所以拉米雷斯说：“重复创造了一种统一的感觉，通过使用共同的因素，产生了一种节奏，和谐、一致的状态。在你的脑海里想象一个红黑相间的棋盘，从红色到黑色的重复变化建立了一种节奏感，其形状的相似性产生了和谐一致的感觉。”（Ramírez，2013，p. 16）

史密斯－奥塔尔（Smith-Autard）谈舞蹈与重复：“必须把重复作为一种主要方式装置于舞蹈创作中”，通过重复，“一系列主题的发展和变化将不可避免地出现”，“这应该确保内容是有趣的，而且作为重复材料可以识别”，另外，“每一种舞蹈都有自己的主题”。（Smith-Autard，2004，p. 39）“没有重复的主题就会被遗忘。”（2004，p. 66）舞蹈中的变化和对比确保了主题的重复拥有观众，这就是重复在舞蹈艺术中的作用。雷德蒙德认为在诗歌中，重复创造了一种期待的感觉，“当这种期待在一段时间内得不到满足时，就会产生紧张感”（Redmond，2006，p. 56），可见，重复在艺术表现中可以具有多样功能。

重复本就是电影产生的原因之一。电影产生的目的，是对人类生活经验的记录与再现。电影从来都不是避开表象不谈，反而是重现表象、挖掘表象的重要手段。电影创作就是在重复的过程中满足各种叙述的安排，如时空、

人物、对话等的规则。电影重复走向极端，要么是完全的记录，要么就是抽象的表达。不管是对生命的缩合，还是对生命的夸张表现，重复从来都不会在电影发展的进程中停止、停滞。“各种改写、改编、挪用、拼贴都是利用互文作艺术表现，且重复可以用多媒介的方式”（陆正兰，2015），改编电影亦是典型的重复行动。

重复重要的是对“崭新之物”的塑造，“重要的事情反而是行动，是使重复本身成为一种革新，也就是成为自由和自由的任务”（德勒兹，2019，p. 16）；“不但用重复来反对习惯的一般性，而且还要用它来反对技艺的特殊性。这也许是因为只有习惯才能从一种从外部被静观的重复那里‘抽取出’某种新的东西”（2019，p. 19）。电影改编实际就是利用重复的艺术方式将其他媒介所表现的事件重新演绎，使其成为崭新事物。这是一种替代性的解放任务。人们在生活中难免会有这样的印象，两个人无论多么的不一样或者行为多么的对立，却都在前赴后继地上演着一个个“相同的生命”，“这便是人们常说的命运”。（2019，p. 151）普雷瑟和桑德伯格却说，“我们没有一劳永逸的人生故事”（Presser，2015，p. 3），因为故事是为特定的场合而创作和改写的，它们受到特定的背景的影响。如果没有重复的访谈、特定的方法，以及任何其他的设计，就无法整合出上下文如何影响叙述变化或叙述如何构成行动，就没有在特定时间点对评价和自我评价的重复探查。电影改编就是要在重复之中去探查看似相同的人生，寻找差异。

（二）重复是恒常的电影现象

波德维尔和汤普森讨论电影内部的重复现象，认为“电影形式是一种系统——是一组统一的、相关的、相互依赖的元素，必须有一些原则来帮助创建各部分之间的关系”（Bordwell & Thompson，2010，p. 67）。重复是使各组成单元之间产生联系的重要方式和原则，波德维尔进而提出了一个注重叙述的重复理论。他更关注文本内的重复叙述现象，在他关于米尔德丽德·皮尔斯·大卫·博德威尔小说的文章中介绍了“重播”（replay）的用法，即“闪回”（flashback）：“重现我们已经见过的场景。”（Bordwell，2013）这是电影文本内部的重复叙述，而放置电影全文本语境下，电影改编作品则是对改编对象的一次“重播”。

重复使各部分结合在一起，以使观众参与电影，促成恒常的交流方式。特别是在电影叙述的问题上，重复基本上构成了电影与观众之间的交流。重复系统以最清晰和最和谐的形式运作，就意味着电影具有统一性。重复是

“让我们意识到电影形式中相似性和差异性是如何运作的一种方法”（Bordwell & Thompson，2010，p. 72）。

对观众而言，他们关心的是改编的电影“出自哪里”，“根据”什么而来，或期待能够从这个电影改编作品的蛛丝马迹之中探寻事件、人物的源头。文本的开放性和恒常性就在于此，它可以通过观众和创作者的不断发问和不断回应，围绕某一思想而激活更多的艺术作品。毕竟，感知的东西是需要借助外力来固定的，媒介表现所有思想幻象中的可能，又通过屏幕来确定那些想象中的可能。原初作品如果引发思考，就不单单是一种短暂而偶然的激情。有了老舍的《骆驼祥子》，才有了经典电影《骆驼祥子》；有了胡金铨执导的《龙门客栈》，才引出经典的《新龙门客栈》，因而又有了《龙门飞甲》；有了李翰祥的《倩女幽魂》，才有了1987年张国荣和王祖贤版的《倩女幽魂》，进而产生了刘亦菲版的《倩女幽魂》。重复就是在认知、再生和类似之中被把握。

另外，影视改编作品是包含了个体主观性的修改和移置，这是认识前文本的恒常方式。人们在面对一个新事物时候，总是会反复唠叨或机械替代、重复。尤其在面对艺术作品时候，外部对作品的理解甚至会超过自在的艺术作品，那些依托各自审美感官的变形就会不断产生。（滕锐，2018）《嫌疑人X的献身》从东野圭吾的悬疑小说，到日本改编的电影，再到中国改编翻拍的同名电影，其文本反复被提起和再创造，这就是一个重复运动的过程。但是观众并不会因为后文本而忽略前文本，有时候甚至会因为后文本的出色，去重新温习最初的艺术作品。

基于此，重复就是典型的文本生成方式，所以对电影创作而言，重复是一个恒常的现象。文本与文本之间的亲和性不需要通过真、假来区分，因为对源头的改编不是单纯的利用，而是电影人思考的结果，至于优劣，则又走向另一条公议之路。波德维尔重视电影系统中重复对观众的作用，在改编及改编重拍的电影叙述系统中，有一些相互关联的元素使观众参与电影并对其产生反应。在获得受众期望回应的过程中，意义和情感是最基本的问题，它们是正式的、战略性的结构，与重复有着密切的联系。

海德格尔认为重复就是在问题与重复的联系之中不断地展开自身，他认为“保有一个问题就意味着：将问题自由地和惊醒地保存在种种内在力量中，而这种内在力量就使得作为在其本质基础上的问题得以可能。可能之物的重复，说的绝不是再回头抓住那些‘常见而流逝’的东西”（海德格尔，2011，p. 194）。对表象的挖掘是潜入可能世界的深层次体验，重复不应是对所有表象的复制、延续，而是要抓住具有展示力量的具有标出性的事物。当一个平平无奇的作品展现在眼前时，它不足以引起后续的夸耀；只有可能充盈奇异点的作品，才会被把握，由此有了新的开端。所以德勒兹会说："重复只有对不能被替代的东西来说才是一种必然的、有根有据的行为。作为行为与观点，重复所涉及的是一种不可交换、不可替换的奇异性。"（2019，p. 8）

（三）重复引起前后文本的共存

改编电影，如根据真人真事改编的电影、根据小说改编的电影、根据新闻事件改编的电影、根据传记改编的电影、由某一旧电影翻拍的新电影等，都是由"根据"而来，以新文本的形式存在。"'重复'内含'重新拿走'到'再次给出'在同一个瞬间里的运动转变：所有曾在又不在了的东西现在正在（或将要）进入存在。"（克伦凯郭尔，2019，p. 8）笔者认为重复便是电影文本存在的艺术基底，没有对过去的重复，没有对"记忆"的翻新，就不可能有另外的媒介形式的产生。跨媒介的艺术表达，说到底就是重复的艺术再现。一个符号文本就可以产生一个确定的、连续的、多样的繁复体，这样"一对多"的事实本质即是原型理念潜在地可以使众多可能成为显现因素，并从附庸关系中解放出来。这种理想性的邻接关系，是一种内在的延续，可能在延续过程中还保留中着某种内在性和差异性。

重复在电影创作中必不可少，人无法消解对过去的剖析，因为过去无论成功还是失败都会以较为客观的形象成为人研究的对象，而改编则可以注入主观的解释，使对象有再生的效果，从而使得观众在重复的经验中得到快感和满足。电影改编后的文本，就是将"根据"转为"存在"，这是重复运动的结果。现实与文本是无穷尽的对象关系，而改编文本对文本本身而言又是超越的，或者是维度外延的。

毫无疑问，重复使得前文本与后文本共存，曾经的现实并不会因为文本的重复性而消失，反而通过当下现实形成了前后相继的存在一定时空距离的共存系列。比起文本的派生，笔者更愿意将其理解为同在的包含主体构想的再生文本。电影改编是一个强制性的重复，但是又是现实现象的一种自动性再生，这是过去与现在的共振现象。笔者认为，这也是创作主体的有意识创作与集体的无意识重复的呼应。"每一个生命都是一个流逝的当前，每一个生命都可以在另一个层面上重演另一个生命。"（德勒兹，2019，p. 151）

重复的延伸并不只是在空间维度上，这种横向的发展是个体重新被塑造的结果，充满了个体化因素。但同时，本源的挖掘也是一种深度上的拓展，深度上的追踪不是向外展，而是一种向内的力量，即先前所存在的事物总是需要以一个新的深度去进入立体的维度塑造。所以，改编后的电影作品并不只是与前文本相关联的影子，而是一个实际存在的关系对象，关系对象从影子中脱身成为一个显现了过去和当前的综合体。这个综合体就是以记忆和过去为基础的复杂存在，是容积扩大的结果。

当重复不断地发生，一个恒定的对象就被构成，从根本上提高了原作品的知名度，而观众便是见证者和重复使用者。一旦作品不断被改编翻拍，作品的广度便得到扩散，深度也不断被挖掘。同时，所有作品都会存在于语境之中，成为观众讨论的参照项。因此，笔者认为改编电影作品是有界限但无限量的重复，作品彼此观照，存在着特定的关系。观众对作品的感觉是有界限的，且因改编作品的超越性而肯定或反对改编作品所覆盖或挖掘的东西，毕竟观众是有先验知觉和感性体会的。

电影创作者们就是用改编剧本的方式来重述过去的经典，又通过荧幕呈现它们，这是重复的运动。创作者通过这些运动，去寻找“一种直抵灵魂的运动、归属于灵魂的运动的问题”（德勒兹，2019，p. 22），这是重复存在的意义。重复本身就充满可能性，这项运动让有价值的东西充满更多的可能性，由此便可容纳更多的思想和价值，而思想是电影作品能够长久不衰的法宝之一。所以运动着的重复对电影作品尤其是经典作品而言是必然的，这种前后文本的共存现象激发着更多的艺术批评，由此构成了漫长的批评史和比较史。

二、两类重复：同一与对立

电影形式的重复方法，在电影文本内部的研究中多有分析。蒙太奇的“诗意的重复”（poetic repetition），或里蒙－凯南（Rimmon-Kenan）提出的“建设性重复”（constructive repetition），都是对内部叙述形式的考察。在谈电影改编时候，学者们所面对的就不只是文本内部，而应当注意电影文本的外部环境。改编可以是刻板复制，也可以另立新起点，重新建构。笔者认为电影改编还会涉及两类带来不同效果的重复：同一或对立。

（一）同一

如前所述，电影形式的统一是最重要的形式问题之一。电影的各个部分、电影与电影之间，应该严格地相互依赖。构建这样一个强有力的统一结构的目的是要在电影和观众之间建立一种联系。在统一的体系之中，建立与前文本的强联系，亦有助于先文本与观众建立强联系。同一，更注重的便是这种强烈的统一式联系。文本与改编文本，走的是一条“相似”的道路。

沙汉姆（Shaham）认为，电影形式的重复通过提醒来提供信息，从而提供电影和观众之间的交流。改编电影中所展现的信息，对观众参与电影起到了至关重要的作用。信息重复是由对我们的回忆、对人物的回忆和对故事的回忆组成的。例如观众印象中的人物描述，被不同创作者的作品表现出来，却呈现出连贯性的特征。这些连贯又同一的信息特征就以重复的方式提醒着观众，吸引着观众参与前后文本大链条之中。笔者认为同一性的重复改编，更多强调的是重复之覆盖作用，它体现的是一种包含、内含和扩展的关系。此类作品并不标榜与源头的差异，而是寻求与源头的共鸣，例如《新白娘子传奇》无论如何改编，白素贞和小青在外形与性格上都符合原传奇的人物设定。

同一性重复就拍摄理由而言，是原著、原事件或原作品受到社会各界的关注，而此类的电影改编较多体现“忠实”的元素，以确保不为“忠实”的观众所排斥。张皓导演的电影《命中注定》改编自《我心属于你》，基本保留《我心属于你》的故事线，延续了浪漫兼喜剧的风格。连导演、故事叙述手段都未曾变化的《我是证人》，则完全忠实于安相勋导演 2011 年的作品《盲证》。好莱坞电影《无间行者》由马丁·斯科塞斯操刀，改编香港经典电影《无间道》，导演将前文本中的故事叙述策略糅合其中，恰到好处地融入了好莱坞的文化内涵，撇去温情、诗意，改为直抒胸臆，顺利得到了奥斯卡金像奖。

中、日、韩、泰各自拍摄的《奇怪的她》（或《重返二十岁》）则直接采用同一剧本。另一部经由中、日、韩三方分别拍摄的《嫌疑人 X 的献身》，均改编自东野圭吾同名小说，虽然在各自改编中，有的还原原著含蓄压抑风格，有的大刀阔斧改变原著风格，但剧情的发展则忠实于原著。中国的《误杀》借泰国之地，还原印度《误杀满天记》的悬疑情节。经典电影作品《十二公民》便是由美国电视剧改编而来，且出现了各种电影版本，如俄国的《十二怒汉：大审判》、日本的《十二个温柔的日本人》以及中国的《十二公民》，都根据各自国家的制度设定相应的内容，但主旨仍然是还原法律与人性的较量。

同一，就是指无论作品如何被改编，最终都是接近同样的结果：主体的理解都处在原初环节上，无论对主题的表现是削弱还是增强，它们都自动选择忽略较多的差异性，选择更多的同一性。另外，所有作品虽然皆属同类，是在同类范畴之内的具有同一性的作品，但改编有好坏之分，或者说每一个艺术创作者都有自己的见解、观点，他们的改编作品不可能是简单的复制，而是修补，同时也会涉及对立的问题。

（二）对立

重复意味着某种事物被改变，而被改变后的事物则成为当前的存在。当一部电影作品被改编，就意味着有另外的解读方式来构成另一部具有相似性的作品。所以，改编也不是单纯的记忆性重复活动，而是记忆与反思共存的认知性活动。既然是认知，那就有重新解释的权利，改编作品作为重述，可能同一性居多，但必然也会存在差异。

同一性重复的作用是填补缺失的信息或提醒观众不要留下缺失点，让观众在不分散注意力的情况下跟踪电影及其改编。而里蒙－凯南的早期论文《重复的矛盾状态》（The Paradox Status of Repetition，1980）中提出的“建设性的重复”（constructive repetition）则强调差异，要给观众以空间，而不是通过讲述和放映来让观众停留在电影里。这种重复会鼓励观众走出电影，从电影外部来看待问题。里蒙－克南“建设性的重复”基本上是通过比较来实现的，通过这种方式，一步一步地揭示重复中的变化，呈现不同的开端，并将它们联系起来。在改编的电影之中，重复的作用是通过相同带来相似和不同。重复通过介入同质性而改变同质性，并通过同质性揭示相似与不同。

对立是这样一种重复，它强调重复之中的变化，重新建构电影叙述，更追求“通过内化自身而颠覆自身”（2019，p. 8）。即使创作主体意在“忠实”于原作品，但这并不代表大多数的改编作品都是一成不变的。实际上，“从一个事物逐步过渡到另一个事物并不能消除这两个事物之间的本性差异”（德勒兹，2019，p. 9），在面对电影创作时，很多创作者想要更大的叙述空间，通过多种叙述策略来体现事件情节的跌宕起伏，表现出和原初事件、原作品构造的迥异之处。笔者认为，通过重复体现差异，质疑被重复对象，就是塑造对立面或寻找对立角度，提出疑问。这也是重复的特征之一：“它质疑法则，它揭露了法则的唯名性特征或一般性特征，而这是为了一种更为深刻、更具艺术性的实在。”（2019，p. 11）改编的电影作品可以是从重复中稀释出某种崭新之物，也就是从习惯性的理解中激活新的思维，构成新的符号，即更多地包含与原作品对立的元素。反讽、幽默是最常见的对立方式，创作者们通过反讽和幽默的方式来颠覆重复对象，试图在重复中更新自我。所以德勒兹认为重复“从本性上说是僭越，是例外”（2019，p. 15）。对立是极为重要的重复方式，如果没有对固定范式思维的突破和原则的反讽，就不会有更多的艺术内质得到更深入的挖掘，那么重复就仅仅是重复，毫无新意。

由此，对立性重复的电影作品可能存在三种形式：第一种，保留原作品的主干情节，却在此基础上增加或减少某一人物角色，突出或弱化某一人物性格；第二种，对原作品进行更大程度的改动，不按照原来的范型和规则进行建构；第三种，戏谑、嘲讽式作品，对原作品进行完全对立的解读，如《大话西游》就是在《西游记》的基础上进行夸张式改编的作品，从而又衍生出《西游降魔篇》等更多与原著相违背的作品。就对立的结果来看，这样的电影作品体现的是一种重复和被重复者之间的冲突关系。对立的作品往往是套着源头作品的外衣，融入更多值得批判的现实，即通过伪装经典表现现实。这种看似游戏的伪装，也是常见的重复形式，很大程度上也具有补充的作用，如《青蛇》这部作品在某种程度上就是对源头作品的翻转，颠覆了固定思维。

在尼采和克伦凯郭尔那里，“重复恰恰被设定为对习惯和记忆的双重谴责，重复所以才成为未来的思想：它既与古代的回忆范畴对立，又与现代的习性范畴对立”（德勒兹，2019，p. 19）。对立性重复实际就是挣脱了“根据”。虽然改编电影作品以过去和记忆的综合为基础，但和源头关联程度的强弱是可以改变的。一部对立作品的真正意义不在于多大程度上“反对”“背叛”原作品，而是要重新界定观众感觉的界限，把握住教育和换位思考的角度和强度，不至于既无法构成典型，又无法颠覆经典。这可以从很多跨国改编翻拍的电影中寻找到蛛丝马迹。韩国导演朴赞郁执导的《老男孩》，2013 年被美国导演斯派克·李翻拍。斯派克·李一改原作品中的情感、意境路线，将故事叙述的重点放在电影逻辑之上。张艺谋的《三枪拍案惊奇》是对科恩兄弟的处女作《血迷宫》的改编，张艺谋一改原作品的惊悚感，反而以戏谑和幽默的方式来展现疑案。

无论是同一的电影改编还是对立的电影改编，都可能会引起对立的结果。即作品会呈现优劣之分。重复的过程是困难的，因为创作者们需要将过去的表现为当前的，或者将远距离的记忆表现为现实的。改编本身就是一个难度颇大的工程——变形既不能太过夸张又不能毫无根据。正如赵毅衡的分析，“历史的进步不仅仅是重复中包含了正向延伸，进步的重复更可能充满了危险，因为不管如何防范，多半会引向与原意图完全相反的结果”（赵毅衡，2015）。毕竟，改编失败的例子也不胜枚举。由安相勋导演的影片《我是证人》，便是由他自己于2011年导演的电影作品《盲证》翻拍而来，两部电影不仅故事叙述如出一辙，导演、叙述方式等都未改变。虽然最后呈现的电影作品不能算完全失败，但这样的重复带来的价值也仅仅停留在商业利润上，看似无改编痕迹，却失去了重复的意义。还有些改编，把原作品中的精髓丢掉之后融入的反讽幽默，反而成了哗众取宠的廉价笑料。电影改编应当是通过重复来获得意义，无论是通过重复赢得还是失去某些东西，重复都应该有它必须追求的价值。

三、符号象征：朝向普遍性的重复

所有的符号化过程都使用符号来表示意义。皮尔斯说，符号是代替其他事物的事物，“符号，或表征物，是在某种方面代替某人的事物”（1955，p. 99；转引自Rogers，1987，pp. 579－590），代替（represent）的意思是重复、复制、替代或再现。重复的过程就是意义被制造的过程，皮尔斯说符号“传达信息”（convey information），信息则告诉接收者重复意味着意义不断的派生。重复便是意义。“当符号重复使用累积达到一定程度，其意义就越来越富厚，最后就会出现质的飞跃。如果这种累积是正向的，社会性地一再重复使用，会不断增加该符号的理据性，理据性增加到一定程度，我们就称之为一个象征。”（赵毅衡，2015）

（一）象征意义的延续

英语单词“symbol”来源于古希腊语单词“symbolon”，字面意思是“拼凑在一起”，“它最初用来描述两件事，一件是整体的一部分，是分裂的；另一件是重新组合而成整体。因此，从同一张纸上撕下的两块或两块陶器碎片重新结合在一起，对于持有它们的人来说，可能是一种‘誓言’（pledge）或象征。从更广泛的意义上来说，象征意味着任何涉及不止一方的协议——这是一种‘传统的’安排，有别于自然产生的一种安排。象征意义作为比喻的、非文字的、隐藏的或神秘的意义是后来的、派生的意义”（Barnett，2015）。

“象征原是一般的比喻，经由重复而累积意义才形成：文化对某个比喻集体地重复使用，或是个人对某个比喻重复使用，都可能达到意义积累变成象征的效果。”（赵毅衡，2019）如《红楼梦》《西游记》成为文化象征，正是因为被反复传播。根据《红楼梦》改编的影视作品有1936年的有声故事片《黛玉葬花》、1939 年的《王熙凤大闹宁国府》、1944 年的电影《红楼梦》；根据《西游记》改编的动画、电影更是不胜枚举，如 1995 年的《大话西游》、2013 年的《西游降魔篇》、2014 年的《西游记之大闹天宫》、2015 年的《西游记之大圣归来》、2016 年的《西游记之孙悟空三打白骨精》等，在改编与不断重新呈现的符号活动中，将历史文化演进成人类社群的文明。很多作品被不断地改编、翻拍，本质上是因为它们具有象征意义，代表着某一文化的精神内核。文化的意义正依靠形式的重复来奠定基础的。

克利福德·格尔茨认为，艺术行为和艺术现象是由一套完整的符号系统构成的，他在《地方知识》中写道："艺术与集体生活的核心关联，不在于这样一种工具性的层面，而在于一个符号学的层面。"（格尔茨，2014，p. 116）格尔茨从符号学出发研究艺术，既强调符号的象征作用，又观照符号媒介在特定语境中对人情感层的作用。艺术相对于其他非艺术媒介而言，能更紧密地联系社会环境，融进文化元素，从而传达它所承载的特别的情感、历史等意义。这在不断改编的电影艺术作品中显得尤为突出。《唐顿庄园》因连续剧大受欢迎而被重新改编为电影版《唐顿庄园》，但其中所影射的都是英国革命时期的工业文化，第一次世界大战对英国庄园经济的影响及其前后英国上层社会生活状态的变化，英国典型庄园的生活文化等内容。对于一个历史悠久的国度而言，记忆的重拾正是通过一次又一次重述、一部又一部作品来实现的。《了不起的盖茨比》《战争与和平》《飘》这些本已经是经典的文学作品，通过一次次的电影媒介又再现为荧幕经典。

罗伯特·罗杰斯认为，"重复总是有意义的。弗洛伊德所说的'强迫性重复'的真正意义不在于它的驱力属性，而在于它的象征方面的实际力量：作为意义的力量，而不是作为力量的意义。作为意义，重复总是形式（Informational）的，因为它是非随机的。重复总是重新呈现，而重新呈现总是再现"（Rogers，1987）。重复的象征性力量，就是重复可以在多次运动之后成为一个路标，提供新的认知。基里·维罗妮卡·沙利文通过关注重复的模式，"研究早期电影中的特定群体是如何正式地、自我反射地标记他们的特定时刻的"（Sullivan，2017，p. 802）。考虑到像电影这样的文化作品可以承载他们自己的历史，他认为"这些电影（以及他们的制片人）实际上是在预测未来，而且不一定喜欢他们所看到的"（2017，p. 802）。

对象征的追求，实际上是实在世界中欲望、期待的投射。实在世界无法被符号分割开，而象征界却可以借象征符号来构建一个理念化、观念化的世界。从包裹着实在世界元素的象征界出发，这些象征符号就是文化的内核。

所以，有学者提出，“这种重复的符号活动形成的记忆是意识与意义世界发生关联的最基本方式”（张骋，2019）。

（二）文化号召力的呈现

重复受文化号召力的影响，与象征有关，重复的运动不断在提示经典，提示社会需要再现的问题。作品被改编源于文化号召力，其一在于经典文化本身所具有的意蕴。对传统文化而言，它们的电影改编是文化精髓直接再现的绝佳方式。当某一意象被反复提起，人们甚至将其作为某一事物的替代品时，其传播便成功了。

人类经验离不开重复，“无论是以文本为基础，还是以读者为基础，就像当前的时尚一样，绝大多数试图描述文学事件的批评性尝试都依赖于对重复文本特征的感知，以作为其认识论基础”（Metzidakis，1986，p. 159）。电影艺术亦离不开重复。重复是电影改编的艺术基底，有价值的作品才被反复提起，正是因为被反复提起，才成为永远被讨论的对象，这即经典之所以成为经典的原因。改编自《疤面人》的《疤面煞星》，作为一部隐含厚重暴力美学的电影，仍然是以对美国梦的追求为起点，又以美国梦的幻灭为终点。电影的改编以诉说时代特征的方式重新地温习着一代人的集体记忆。在历史长河之中，重复就是这样不断地呼吁文化内核的觉醒，例如文艺复兴时期，“文艺复兴”所指向的重生，就是古代精神的复苏。象征事物的形成与人的心理追求是不容分割的，人们在不知不觉中随处可以体会重复对事物的整合。因此，笔者认为，重复是象征形成的基础，而文化潜意识的号召又是重复的基础。

作品被改编源于文化号召力，其二在于不自觉重复的驱动作用。对于善于探索的艺术心灵来说，重复的对象明显是吸引人的。符号学家不可避免地要对重复的符号序列进行协调：“接收者受到嵌在文本中的路标（signposts）的指引，他们受到那些无论行为举止如何都参与重复出现的网络中的人的指引。重复的含义或意义因此派生，至少在很大程度上，从相互作用的行为中，铭刻再现，重新浮现变体，重新建立预先建立的系统，或者传播和促进它们的存在，或者经斗争而成为其他的，不同于它们表面上模仿性复制的先例。”（Barnett，1988）重复使得符号对象在相互作用之中斗争并产生变体，接收者总是会受到重复力量的影响，无意识地加入派生意义的传播行列当中。

重复关涉人类集体情感，人类正是通过情感来感知外物的生命力。在德勒兹那里，电影非但不与各个艺术门类相并列，还是世界影像、生命影像之外第三种宇宙影像，或者第三种宇宙感知。朗西埃将影像拆分为视源本身、影像再现及影像伦理三个层次，或分出做、看和说的三重界面。“朗兹曼（Claude Lanzman）等人的集中营电影和集中营照片最能解释朗西埃的美学政治理论，因为集中营的影像构成和再现都涉及了一个伦理的问题，而集中营照片更不单是一种影像伦理的象征，它的影像本身负载着生与死的实存问题……他们的存在从影像传递并获得受众的感性分享，但这种感性经验的本质也是其自身存在的毁灭。”（洪席耶，2001，p. 3）遗忘的东西被重复唤起，丢失的记忆被重复召回，遗忘与影像的关系正通过重复的驱动力联系起来，由此才会有“精神不死”之说。

因此，改编作品虽然散见于各国家、各时代，但它们通过联合的形式汇合。若一部作品的内容应被大众和时代铭记，那么主体便有意识地改编，从而又达成无意识的重复。对电影的改编是在整合的立场上书写智性和情感的结合。当表象被数次重复之后，表象就不再是个体化的，而是普遍的。一部改编作品可能是社会规约的结果，也可能是主流意识需要的效果，社会文化催生了统一性和同一性。并且这种永久的聚合是无定形的，它以交流的方式被敞开。在重复带来的广延的场域里，观众在“我们”的世界里感受聚合的重复，又促使电影结构形成。

总之，通过重复来理解电影改编，既是对电影形式的一次观照，也是对这一常见的艺术现象的一次考察。文化的现实意义通过电影的改编得以恒常在场，并且在不断的重复运动中，改编的作品本身又成为被重复的对象而持续存在于物理空间之中。同时，重复又可分为同一和对立两种转换形式，这既表明，电影改编可以是统一而延广的电影解读，也可以是否定性的意义解释；另外也表明重复改编的电影作品面对着肯定和否定的接受群体，观众可能会因为纯粹机械的重复而产生共鸣，也可能因叙述角度、程度上对原作的差异性解读而产生反感。然而，无论改编内容如何改进、转换，创作主体及接收者们对文本的重视和再解读，都体现某些精神的不衰不朽。终极的重复和终极的电影大概是既可以以某种方式聚集一切，也可以以某种方式毁灭一切，一种重复导致的另一种重复就是凭借艺术作品内在的精神力量才被不断重复又不断颠覆着。

引用文献：

德勒兹，吉尔（2019）. 差异与重复（安靖，张子岳，译）. 上海：华东师范大学出版社.

格尔茨，克利福德（2014）. 地方知识（杨德睿，译）. 北京：商务印书馆.

克伦凯郭尔（2019）. 重复（京不特，译）. 北京：商务印书馆.

海德格尔（2011）. 康德与形而上学疑难（王庆节，译）. 上海：上海译文出版社.

洪席耶，贾克（2001）. 影像的宿命（黄建宏，译）. 台北：编译馆.

陆正兰（2015）. 重复：艺术的基本构建方式. 中外文化与文论，3，285-292.

滕锐，李志宏（2018）. 认知美学视域下新媒体艺术的“亚审美性”. 福建师范大学学报（哲学社会科学版），209（2），159-165+173+177.

张骋（2019）. 从共现到重复：从符号现象学论“电影影像生成性”. 符号与传媒，1，28-38.

赵毅衡（2015）. 论重复：意义世界的符号构成方式. 河南师范大学学报（哲学社会科学版），1，120-127.

赵毅衡（2019）. 论艺术的“自身再现”. 文艺争鸣，9，77-85.

Barnett, R. L. (1988). Review on repetition and Semiotics. *South Atlantic review*, 53, 4, 103-105.

Bordwell, D. (2013, June 26). Twice-told tales: Mildred pierce. Retrieved from http://www.davidbordwell.net/blog/2013/06/26/twice-told-tales-mildred-pierce.

Bordwell, D., & Thompson, K. (2010). *Film art: An introduction.* New York, NY: McGraw-Hill.

Kierkegaard, S. (2009). *Repetition and philosophical crumbs* (M. G. Piety, Trans.). New York, NY: Oxford.

Lindsay, K. C., & Vergo, p. (1994). *Kandinsky: Complete writings on art.* New York: Da Capo Press.

Metzidakis, S. (1986). *Repetition and semiotics.* Birmingham: Summa Publications.

Parmentier, R. J. (2015). Representation, symbol, and semiosis: Signs of a scholarly collaboration. *Signs and society*, 3, 1, 1-7.

Parr, A. (2010). *The Deleuze dictionary revised edition.* Edinburgh: Edinburgh University Press.

Presser, L., & Sandberg, S. (2015). *Narrative criminology: Understanding stories of crime.* New York, NY: New York University Press.

Ramírez, L. R. (2013). *Design principles and methods for composing artwork.* Bloomington: iUniverse.

Redmond, J. (2006). *How to write a poem.* Malden, MA: Blackwell Publishing.

Rimmon-Kenan, S. (1980). The paradoxical status of repetition. *Poetics today*, 1, 4, 151-159.

Rogers, R. (1987). Freud and the semiotics of repetition. *Poetics today*, 8, 3/4, 579-590.

Smith-Autard, J. (2004). *Dance composition: A practical guide to creative success in dance making.* New York, NY: Routledge.

Sullivan, K. V. (2017). *Repetition and the temporal double in cinema: A theory of critical cinematic time-travel*. Melbourne: The University of Melbourne.

Woodward, A. (2014). *Understanding Nieztcheanism*. Oxon: Routledge.

作者简介：

赵禹平，南京师范大学文学院戏剧与影视学专业博士研究生，四川大学符号学－传媒学研究所成员，研究方向为影视符号学、叙述学。

Author:

Zhao Yuping, Ph. D. candidate of drama, film and television, Nanjing Normal University, member of the ISMS Research Team. Her research fields are semiotics of cinema and narrative.

Email: yupingzhao@ qq. com

人设：作为一种风格的想象

刘　娜

摘　要：人设是符号消费时代的一个普遍现象。接收者寄托于人设的表面形象，在人设中寻求和确立自我，从而满足精神上的愉悦，形成与发送者共同狂欢的局面。为迎合接收者的意义期待和情感期待，发送者采取类型化的表意模式，由此编织人设的意义网络。因此，本文基于符号学的相关理论，以明星人设为切入口，从风格的界定、风格的编码、风格的解码三个方面进行详细阐述，指出明星人设实际上是风格化意义的再现与传播，所谓人设不过是接收者的想象。

关键词：人设，风格，想象

Public Persona: Imagination as a Style

Liu Na

Abstract: The public persona is a common phenomenon in the era of semiotic consumption. The receiver relies on the superficial image of a public persona to seek and establish the self, so as to attain spiritual pleasure and form a carnival situation with the sender. In order to cater to the spiritual and emotional expectations of the receiver, the sender adopts a typed mode of signification, thus weaving a network of meanings for its public persona. Based on semiotic theory, this paper looks at the public persona of celebrities and makes a detailed exposition of the definition, encoding and decoding of style. It points out that the public persona of celebrities is actually the reproduction and dissemination of the meaning of style, and that the image of the so-called "public persona" is nothing more than the imagination of the receiver.

Keywords: public persona, style, imagination

DOI: 10.13760/b.cnki.sam.202002012

引　言

"人设"通常被解释为人物设定，来自日本动漫小说、漫画，原意是指对虚拟角色的外貌特征、性格特点的塑造。从 2016 年开始，"人设"一词被引入娱乐圈，成为明星对自身形象定位的代名词。人设的出现成为沟通明星与粉丝的桥梁，诸如"学霸"人设、"老干部"人设、"真性情"人设、"吃货"人设等正面的、接地气的人设纷纷出现，形成娱乐圈一道独特的风景线。人设对于明星而言，具有很重要的意义，甚至从某种意义上讲，没有人设就意味着没有人气。人设的制定已成为娱乐产业链中一个重要环节，直接带动娱乐经济的发展。

娱乐圈的人设之风也吸引了学界的广泛关注，形成传播学、社会学、心理学三条路径，分别聚焦于人设的表意和传播、人设崩塌、人设对受众尤其是青少年受众的影响等重要问题。这些研究都对人设现象进行了不同程度的剖析，有利于对人设有更清晰的认识。但是需要注意的是，所有的衍生问题，例如人设表意、人设崩塌等，都与人设的本质有关，明确人设的内在特征才是解决其他问题的前提。

一直以来，人设一直被等同于形象，明星人设便是明星的形象。这样的分析仅看到人设与形象之间表面的像似性，缺乏对人设表意模式共性的深层次分析。人设不是个别现象，更不单单是明星的个人活动。尽管人设依附于明星的身体和行为，但人设并不能直接等同于明星本人。人设已然成为娱乐界打造明星的基本模式，在维系明星和受众的关系中起到了不可小觑的作用，其类型化的构建手段使人设逐渐形成固有的表意风格。不同的人设在表达层面呈现出各种不同的形式，表面看似风格多样化，实则并无根本区别，都沿用了同一种编码模式，即在明星文本上附加各种人设符码。笔者认为人设并非明星的形象，而是风格的编码投射到接收者心中的一种想象。为说清楚此问题，笔者将以符号学的相关理论为基础，从风格的编码与解码深入剖析人设的表征与本质，力图厘清人设与形象之间的联系与区别，从而对人设有更准确、更深入的认识。

一、风格

风格遍及各种人类行为，无处不在。一种风格有别于另一种风格正是由于其区别性特征，当有了人设后，明星之间便区别开来，形成各自独有的标签。显然，正是风格的使用，即意义行为的植入，促使人设文本具有一定的区别性特征。作为文化符号系统中的一个突出意义行为，风格自然需要从意义的角度解释。因此，笔者将对风格重新做一解读：风格是一种附加在核心文本之上的符码组合，是核心文本在形式上的附加要素的集合。

在这个概念中，符码是风格的构成要素，也是风格形成的主体；核心文本是风格依附的载体，是风格作用的客体；将主体和客体联结在一起的正是附加的方式。人设就是在明星文本的基础上进行的附加编码，也就是说，人设是形式层面，表达的是形式意义，与表达内容意义的核心文本分属于全文本的两个不同层面。风格意义与文本指称意义并不一定完全一致。常态下，二者可以保持一致，但两种意义不一致的情况并不少见，其在人设的表意中体现得更为明显，可以细分为以下两种情况：

其一，风格大于实指。当风格成为表意的主导因素，指称意义被淡化，营造一种风格成为文本表意的基本需求。人设崩塌就是典型的例子，刻意打造出来的人格无法与自身的行为相契合，二者发生冲突，导致人设崩塌。

其二，风格有意脱离实指，甚至意义完全相反。这种表意行为相对来说稍显复杂，风格并非表意文本的实指。风格表意的真伪需要解释者根据具体的语境进行判断。在某些语境，例如综艺节目、广告宣传等特定场合中，明星有意表现出人设之外的某些品质，其真假难以辨别，但会吸引受众的注意力，加深受众对该明星的认识。

风格意义与指称意义是否一致取决于表意机制是以形式还是以对象为主导因素。对接收者而言，风格的强度与指称的清晰度成反比。风格意义越强烈，指称意义越模糊；风格意义越微弱，指称意义越清晰。这与形象的表意有区别，形象追求清晰的意义表达。胡易容将形象分为自我形象（ego）与社会形象（social）两种向度：“自我形象是镜像的演变，而社会形象是一套社会评价元语言的结果。”（2015，p. 25）自我形象强调主体对自己的认知，而社会形象则是形象接收者对形象主体的理解和接受。两种向度都需要形象主体有意识地对自身形象进行定位，在不同的社会语境中积极建构并清晰地展示出完整、丰富、立体的形象。

明星本身就是通过舞台或银幕展示出的一种符号，这种符号表现为理想的人格，具有极强的不可靠性。费斯克（John Fiske）深刻地洞察到这种特殊性，他认为明星是“公众从其舞台与银幕之上——与之外——的虚构外貌与表演种产生的种种理想与价值的化身”（2004，p. 270）。被展示的明星与明星本人完全有可能相差甚远。例如，美国著名影星加里·格兰特（Cary Grant）的名言“人人都想成为加里·格兰特，就连我自己都想”，无奈地道出：媒介中的明星形象只是他者即受众对明星的想象而已。当从明星转向人设的表意模式后，原本的明星表意被附加上了新的意义，要使新的表意广泛被受众接受且被认为具有较强的可靠性，就需要在明星身上附加某种类型化的符码，并要求明星根据相应的人设随时做出调整。在人设时代，人设早已超越明星原有的指称意义，成为一种书写明星风格的工具。

二、人设风格的类型化编码

“人设”这个词中包含了两个概念：“人”与“设”，这两个概念表明了作为风格的人设的核心内容。这里所说的“人”是风格的对象，并非明星本人。为了使风格显得真实，对原有文本进行再度编码，使其表面接近人设所指称的意义。“设”是风格的形成策略，即根据市场的需求充分利用附加符码对明星进行设定。

（一）风格的再现式呈现：形象的像似性

在动漫中，“人”指人物，“人设”主要是对人物的外在形象和性格的设定，如对人物的高矮胖瘦、服饰穿戴的设计。对明星的人设而言，“人”自然包括明星的外在形象，但外在形象仅仅是人设呈现的载体。换句话说，明星的外貌、言行举止等外在特征由人设的表意决定，人设是外在形象的先决条件，有了人设才有相应的外在形象与之匹配。例如有着“暖男”人设的张艺兴受到不少观众的喜爱。“暖男”是指温柔体贴，能很好理解和体谅别人的男性。每当张艺兴出现在公众的面前时，他的表情、声音和举止，无一不透露出他是一个温暖而有耐心的人。而被誉为“娱乐圈清流”的“老干部”人设在纷繁的娱乐圈中格外标出，其之所以受到观众的一致好评，是因为有这类人设的明星往往自律、有涵养、淡泊名利，在生活中处处透露出文化气息，迥异于急功近利的娱乐圈人物。人设充分展示出明星人格中积极的一面，有了人设的明星，如同身上贴上了标签，一旦被提及，受众首先想到的就是他们的人设而不是外在形象。可见，人设中的“人”，并不是人物，更不是明星本人，而是“人格”（persona），确切地说是标签化的人格。

根据荣格（Carl Gustav Jung）的集体无意识理论，戴上人格的面具可以达到“给人一个很好的印象以便得到社会的承认”的目的（霍尔，诺德贝，1987，p. 48）。其实这也是打造明星人设的目的，即给观众留下美好的印象从而收获更多的“粉丝”。因此，人设不单单是明星人格特征，更重要的是通过这些特征凸显明星人格中具有标志性的一面，形成明星表达自我的风格，凸显明星的辨识度。人设俨然表意行为，而任何表意行为都离不开符号，“符号是被认为携带意义的感知”（赵毅衡，2016，p. 1）。这个概念提到了符号的两个重要特征：一个是携带意义，另一个是感知。作为符号的人设，以可感知的方式将隐藏的意义凸显出来。明星人设正是通过其言谈举止对人设的表意，如努力学习、积极向上、热爱公益等潜在意义进行再现。在再现的过程中，受众会对人设进行再度认知、理解和阐释。在这个意义下，人设的对象是明星，解释项是人设的内涵，再现体即作为符号的人设。

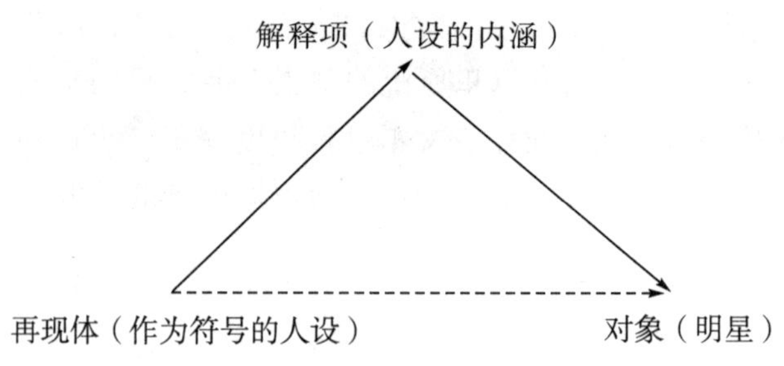

人设意义三分示意图

人设与对象的联系不是任意的，而是基于符号的理据性。皮尔斯（Charles Sanders Peirce）指出，理解事物要从三个方面进行分析：“首先，对于事物本身我们会有一个基本的理解；第二，我们会考虑到这个事物与其他任何事物之间的联系；第三，我们会将第一项与第二项联系起来理解，如此，它就能够给我们的思想传递某个事物的意义。这样，它就是一个符号，或者表征。”（1998，p. 5）据此观点，符号之为符号，其中重要的一点就是事物与事物之间的联系，即理据性。在理据性中，符号之间的像似性（iconicity）是一个重要的特征。皮尔斯（CP 3. 362）认为“一个符号代替另一个事物，因为与之像似”。例如照片、绘画之类的符号就与对象之间有明显的像似性。为了详细说明这一问题，皮尔斯把像似性分成了三个级别：形象式（imaginal）像似、图表式（diagrammic）像似及比喻式（metaphorical）像似。

三个级别的划分是按照像似的程度进行的，其中形象式像似是程度最高的像似，而比喻式象征是程度最低的像似。但恰好是像似程度最低的比喻式像似最能唤起接受者的想象，表意功能反而最强。

人设正是利用了符号的像似性，将展示出的形象与人格通过像似联系起来，属于比喻式像似符号表意。比喻式像似的表意主要通过解释社群对符号的认知和理解得到阐释，反过来，解释社群的阐释又会进一步巩固符号的像似性，以达成粉丝对明星的“真知”为目的（赵毅衡，2018）形成双向阐发的互动链条。例如，“吃货”人设中对美食的热爱不容易由明星外貌来展示，但可以通过其他途径表达，充分展现明星生活中接地气的一面，以赢得观众的喜爱。在综艺节目《奔跑吧兄弟》中迪丽热巴就是“吃货”人设，她的行李箱中装了不少的家乡特产。整个节目中迪丽热巴总是表现出对吃的极大热情，不仅热衷于介绍家乡特产，而且特写镜头中的她似乎就没有停止过品尝美食。迪丽热巴在节目中的表现显然出乎观众的意料，他们甚至推测迪丽热巴在日常生活中也是如此。观众在迪丽热巴的人设中仿佛看到了生活中的自己，与明星的距离一下子近了许多。解释社群的认知和接纳再次稳定了明星的人设。为了维护人设，明星必须保持一言一行与人设表意之间的像似关系。例如 TF Boys 的人设表意是青春阳光、充满活力，他们在任何公共场合都必须展示出青春飞扬、积极努力的形象。这样的人设使其成为青少年受众的偶像，也成为许多中老年受众心中的“乖孩子”的代表。

对人设的维护当然有利于明星的发展，但是作为独立的人，明星的人格本来应该是丰富且多样的。为保证与人设的一致，并使人设表意能得以较好地实施，像似性就只能聚焦于一点，从而符号与事物之间的像似性容易被类型化。无论是“吃货”人设、“暖男”人设还是其他人设，都只是人格的一种类型，明星人格本来的丰富性被淹没于其中。在这种情况下，明星的主体性下滑，明星形象意义的整体性消失，取而代之的是碎片化的存在，人设成为单一、平面的风格符号，约束和裹挟了明星的全面发展。

（二）风格的附加编码：表演的文本

前面谈到人设中的“人”指的是人格，而人格类型的完成离不开“设”，即对人格的设定。这种设定并不是人设主体对自我的认知和定位，也就是说人设的人格并不是自我镜像演变的结果，而是由他人设定。人设主体只需要接受设定的人格，并将该人格演示出来。这与形象的塑造有所区别，形象离不开主体的自我认知，是主体的自我建构，而人设是被动的接受和表演，具有很强的演示性。明星的人设是预先给明星设定的模式，明星在预设好的场域中按照既定模式进行表演。如何表演、表演什么都是预先设定好的。尽管人设类型不同，但明星都会选择类似的表演方式，进行类型化的表演。

在前人设时代，对艺术的追求是成为明星的内驱动力，支撑起明星整体形象的是其代表作品，如歌星的演唱、钢琴家的弹奏、画家的画作、演员的影视作品等。而在人设时代，明星的人格的设定必须符合市场需求，准确说来是迎合观众对该人格类型的喜好。市场需要什么，就会产生出什么样的明星人格。被赋予的人设不是新的存在，而是日常生活中可以成为范本的人格类型。“这些范本变化丰富却处于固定类型之中，范本间的差别细微以便于观众选择……就像一个顾客在各式各样、质优价廉的商品中进行挑选一样。”（理查德，2011，p. 131）人设中的明星只是被动地展示由团队打造的人设，向观众兜售设定好的人格。人格意义的突出消解了明星本来的意义，观众无法记住他的作品，只能想起来他的人设。当明星拥有了人设后，不再具有整体的人格，而是仅仅依附于人设。人设一旦崩塌，明星的形象也与之俱毁，相关的产业链也会大受重创。因此，在人设时代，明星的核心任务就是通过各种途径再现和表演人设的内涵，使其与设定高度重合。

组合轴和聚合轴的双轴是符号文本展开的两个向度，双轴操作暗含了选择的关系。在对符号文本进行建构时，组合轴形成框架，聚合轴通过比较与选择，从而筛选出最符合文本特征的成分并将其放置于组合轴上进行文本填充。在人设的建构过程中，明星努力迎合受众，力求接近受众的期待，最终迎来受众对人设文本更疯狂的消费。为了实现这一目的，明星必须有意识地对附加符码进行筛选和再编码，从而形成各种不同风格的人设。约翰·埃利斯（John Ellis）曾谈及：“任何表现的意义都来自对那种表现的选择。”（Elli，1974，p. 122）也就是说，无论是明星的小清新风格、学院风格，还是甜美风格等，归根结底都是明星团队根据预期的设定进行双轴操作的结果。

双轴操作需谨慎，一旦操作不当，就容易导致人设受损甚至人设崩塌。例如，靳东作为拥有“老干部”人设之一的男明星，外貌儒雅，爱使用繁体字，微博内容几乎都是对节气的介绍，散发出浓浓的文化气息。在媒体曝光的日常生活镜头中，他也经常是埋首书卷之中。这些文本组合在一起，凸显了靳东有文化修养的人设内涵。尽管微博中时不时出现用词错误，但受众尚能接受，直到靳东说“在这个薄情的世界上深情地活着”是凡·高的名言，并提到最近在阅读“诺贝尔数学奖得主的文章”，受众一下子从人设的幻象中清醒过来，意识到之前的种种不过是明星为了人设所进行的文本表演罢了。

理查·戴尔（Richard Dyer）曾认为“明星是这样一种映像，公众从中揣摩以调整自己的形象”（戴尔，2010，p. 7）。在人设时代，不妨将这句话改写成“人设是这样一种映像，明星从中揣摩以调整自己的人格表演”。

三、人设的风格解码：投射与想象

人设的意义只有在接收者进行解释后才能实现。影响接收者解码的重要因素就是情感。皮尔斯（1935）意识到情感在符号意义生成过程中的重要作用，提出了“情绪解释项”（emotional interpretant）。他认为情感具有强烈的意动性，可以促使接收者对符号文本进行分析和阐释。根据这个解释，可以发现在符号意义的生成过程中文本、情感、对象、文本接收者四个因素相互作用的结果：在文本内部，情感与符号过程中的对象直接关联；在文本外部，情感影响接收者的情绪；情感由符号文本产生，从而促使接收者对其进行解释；接收者在解释的过程中会对文本内容产生感觉，并将这种感觉投射到符号过程中的对象上。

人设是按照特定人群的需求进行打造的，明星人设瞄准的就是受众群体。情感如同纽带般联结了受众和人设，受众对人设的狂热正是基于情感。克罗斯伯格（Lawrence Grossberg）的“情感感受力”可以进一步证实这一点，他认为“受众对于某些实践与文本的投入使得他们能够对自己的情感生活获得某种程度的支配权，这又进一步使它们对新的意义形式、快感及身份进行投入以应对新的痛苦、悲观主义、挫败感、异化、恐惧及厌倦”（克罗斯伯格，2009，p. 146）。人设是个动态化的符号过程，在这个过程中，受众的情感起了主导作用。人设对其内涵进行再现的主要途径是文本的表演，主要目的就是为了与受众在情感上达到共鸣。

人设的出现解构了传统的明星形成模式，建构了自下而上的新模式。在前人设时代，明星与受众之间有着不可逾越的鸿沟。受众对电视或电影节目的接受属于被动的接受，对明星的印象停留在银幕中的人物形象。人设出现后，受众拥有了主动权，可以自主地筛选自己喜欢的明星；与此同时，明星不再是高高在上，而是要根据受众的心理需求进行定位，形成特定的属性，瞄准受众群兜售人设。人设越接近受众所期待的形象，就越受到受众的关注和喜爱。

网络是人设展示的重要场域，尤其在微博出现后，受众可以和明星直接联系和沟通。“演艺明星在多重虚拟场景和空间中的符号互动与日常呈现，又形成虚拟实境（virtual reality）之间的杂糅”（曼纽尔，2006，p. 461），从而为人设的呈现增添了可靠性。受众在“虚拟网络社区里获得了符号狂欢的快感”（王燕，2006，p. 102），这种快感来源于受众对虚拟实境中人设的感知和接受，以及心理和情感期待的满足。如果说形象的建立是印象的叠加，那么人设的成熟就是明星与受众磨合的结果。明星一次次努力迎合受众，力图最大限度地贴近受众所期盼的形象设定，这种设定与其说是对明星的建构，不如说是受众自己的情感与想象在明星身上的投射。（付森会，2020）冯·弗兰茨（Von Franz）将荣格的“投射”概念概括为：“一种在他人身上所看到的行为的独特性和行为方式的倾向性”，“是把我们自身的某些潜意识的东西不自觉地转移到一个外部物体上去”。（转引自杨韶刚，2002，p. 72）受众将自己的情感转移到明星身上，寄托于人设的表面形象，试图从人设身上寻求心中理想形象的影子，寻求和确立自我，找到自我的归属，从而满足精神上的愉悦，形成与发送者共同狂欢的局面，这是现代消费的特征。“现代消费的本质就在于追求一种自我的梦想。人们消费的核心不是在于对商品的使用价值的实际选择、购买和应用，而是对各种想象性愉悦的追求。”（柯林，2006，p. 1）

受众对明星人设的想象源于对生活中某种欲望的幻想与追求。比如“好男人”人设通常是指已婚男明星不仅事业有成，而且还是好丈夫、好父亲，满足众多女性受众对另一半的所有幻想。张丹峰曾经被誉为“好男人”，和比自己大十岁的妻子结婚，对继子视如己出，迅速立下“好男人”人设，收获了不少“粉丝”。不管是被媒体曝光还是微博中的自我展示，都是围绕家庭的温馨时光，在满足受众窥视明星隐私的欲望的同时，更重要的是强化了受众对张丹峰“好男人”人设的认知。但这种认知只是片面化的认知。要维持人设就必须保持真我被架空，处于人设框架之外，一旦真我进入人设框架，就会出现真我与人设的冲突，导致人设崩塌。当张丹峰被媒体曝光生活中真实的一面时，受众也从之前的“集体欢腾”转变为“想象的颠覆”，毕竟人设只是受众自己的欲望和情感的投射，而欲望往往“通过实际上都是替代品的真实客体追逐着对它而言最真实的一个想象客体”（克里斯蒂安，2005，p. 47）。想象客体的失败意味着受众对该人设情感阐释力的丧失，而缺乏了阐释意动性的人设，难以再唤起受众的共鸣。

结　语

当下文化的发展不能脱离市场经济的语境，符号消费的突显使得大众文化中的种种现象不再只是个人喜好或需求的体现，而逐渐发展为群体共有的文化行为，无论是文化的发送还是接收都是群体之间的互动。因此，直接将人设等同于个人形象的观点看到了人设的外在表现，却把接收者感知到的印象等同于形象，缺乏对形象主体的深入认识，忽视了人设的形成过程，这种看法流于表象，未免过于简单和片面化。人设背后是明星碎片化的主体，人设所依附的并不是明星本人，而只是人格。人格以风格化表意为主导，追逐人设表面形式的风格多样化，缺乏对明星应有的内涵的反思。

在这种情况下，艺术的内驱力已被对商业价值的追求取代，明星强大的符号影响力成为获得商业价值的法宝。人设的出现充分利用了明星的符号价值，受众对人设的消费其实是对符号价值的消费。有学者对此不无担心地指出，“不仅制造者逐渐丧失理性，连同这种文化下培养出的受众也丧失理性，集体沦落成毫无审美情趣和判断标准的纯消费动物”（王小峰，2015，序言）。显然，大众文化已成为受众、市场和明星团队的共谋。受众主导着人设的生产和消费，大众将想象安置于人设框架下，满足内心的情感需要。人设在本质上是符号意义的再现和分享，明星所进行的不过是一场表象与本质分离的文本表演，受众沉醉于其中，难以分清真实与幻象、形象与想象。

引用文献：

戴尔，理查德（2010）. 明星（严敏，译）. 北京：北京大学出版社.

费斯克，约翰，等（编）（2004）. 关键概念：传播与文化研究词典（李彬，译）. 北京：新华出版社.

付森会（2020）. 社交媒体中的友谊：相似性机制与情感传播逻辑. 福建师范大学学报（哲学社会科学版），2，131－139＋171.

霍尔，C. S.；诺德贝，V. J.（1987）. 荣格心理学入门（冯川，译）. 北京：生活·读书·新知三联书店.

胡易容（2015）. 符号学方法论与普适形象学. 中国人民大学学报，29（1），19－26.

坎贝尔，柯林（2006）. 浪漫伦理与现代消费主义精神（章戈浩，译）. 西北师大学报（社会科学版），43（4），1－7.

克罗斯伯格，劳伦斯（2009）. 这屋里有粉丝吗?：粉都的情感感受力. 粉丝文化读本（陶东风，编）. 北京：北京大学出版社.

卡斯特，曼纽尔（2006）. 网络社会的崛起（夏铸九，等译）. 北京：社会科学文献出版社.

麦茨，克里斯蒂安（2005）. 想象的能指. 载于吴琼（编）. 凝视的快感. 北京：中国人民大学出版社.

麦特白，理查德（2011）. 好莱坞电影：美国电影工业发展史（吴菁，等译）. 北京：华夏出版社.

王燕（2008）. 百度贴吧“粉丝文化”解读. 青年记者，20（7），102.

王小峰（2015）. 只有大众，没有文化：反抗一个平庸时代. 桂林：广西师范大学出版社.

转引自杨韶刚（2002）. 精神的追求：神秘的荣格. 哈尔滨：黑龙江人民出版社.

赵毅衡（2016）. 符号学：原理与推演. 南京：南京大学出版社.

赵毅衡（2018）. 皮尔斯“真知目的论”与维纳“反馈目的论”. 福建师范大学学报（哲学社会科学版），2，145－153.

The Peirce Edition Project (1998). *The essential Peirce: Selected philosophical writings, Vol.* 2, 1893－1913. Bloomington, IN: Indiana University Press.

Ellis, J. (1974). *The theory of literary Criticism: A logical analysis.* Berkeley, CA: University of California Press.

Peirce, C. S. (1931－1958). *Collected papers of Charles Sanders Peirce, Vol.* 5 (C. Hartshorne, p. Weiss, Eds.). Cambridge, MA: Harvard University Press.

作者简介：

刘娜，四川大学符号学－传媒学研究所成员，重庆三峡学院外国语学院副教授，研究方向为符号学、叙述学、比较文学。

Author:

Liu Na, member of the ISMS research team, associate professor of School of Foreign Languages, Chongqing Three Gorges College. Her research field is semiotics, narratology and comparative literature.

Email: 13353794@ qq. com

广义叙述学

创伤记忆的叙事判断、情感特征和叙述类型

王　欣

摘　要：本文从创伤叙述中出现的错误感知出发，讨论了创伤叙述判断中历史真实和感知真实的区别，认为强烈的情感是创伤叙述的重要特点。创伤记忆中的情感具有无时性、传染性，每一次创伤记忆被唤起，都会重复造成身体和情感的重击。创伤叙述因而常常伴随着强烈的个体的情感反应；该情感具有打破受害者意识和影响他人的能量，对于同一集体中无创伤经历的听众具有传染性，创伤回应也具有病理性。从创伤信息的传递和交流来看，创伤叙述可以分为三种类型：独白式创伤叙述、见证式创伤叙述和回顾式创伤叙述。独白式创伤叙述着重“我”的故事；见证式创伤叙述传递创伤心理，塑造了“他或她”的故事；回顾式创伤叙述重构了“每个人”的故事。当创伤记忆在集体、家庭、代际传递时，情感强度递减，叙事性加强，逐渐象征化和原型化，成为集体中个人自我和身份塑造的依据。

关键词：创伤，错误感知，情感特征，叙述类型，代际传递

Narrative Judgements, Affective Features and Narrative Modes in Memories of Trauma

Wang Xin

Abstract: This paper stems from false perceptions in trauma narratives, discusses the differences between historical truth and the perception of authenticity in trauma narrative judgements, and points out that strong affective features are important characteristics of trauma narratives. Affect in memories of trauma encompasses such features as timelessness and infectiveness; therefore, once the memory of trauma is aroused, the body and the emotions are repeatedly wounded. Accordingly, trauma narratives are accompanied by a strong personal affective response. Such affect also has the power to reach beyond the consciousness of the victim and influence others in the same community, thus infecting listeners who have no experience of trauma to such an extent that their responses represent the same pathology. Through the transference and communication of information about trauma, trauma narratives can be divided into three modes: monologues, testimonies and retrospections. Monologues of trauma narratives focus on "I" stories; testimonies pass on the affect of trauma by narrating "he or she" stories; and retrospections reconstruct "everybody" stories. When memories of trauma are transmitted within the community or family and between generations, the intensity of affect decreases while the narrative is processed until the memory is symbolised and the characters are stereotyped as reference points for the construction of the self and of identity in the community.

Keywords: trauma, false perception, affective features, narrative modes, inter-generational transmission

DOI: 10. 13760/b. cnki. sam. 202002013

创伤是指“在突然的，或灾难性的事件面前，一种压倒性的经验，对这些事件的反应通常是延迟的，以幻觉和其他侵入的现象而重复出现的无法控制的表现”（Caruth，1996，p. 11）。通常来说，个人创伤是指“对心理的一次打击，这种打击如此突然，并伴随着如此野蛮的力量，它撕裂了一个人的抵御机制，以至于个人不可能有效地回应”（Erikson，1995，p. 187）。由于创伤经验无法吸收，创伤患者通常出现内疚、焦虑、回避、解离等多种应激反应，感觉个人和世界的联系被割裂，并常常被过去的噩梦困扰。创伤叙述成为治疗创伤、修复认知的方式。目前国内外的研究对创伤的心理机制、创伤叙事以及临床治疗多有涉及，并结合历史、文学、医学、社会学、媒介传播等学科，对创伤再现、创伤记忆和创伤叙事等进行跨学科探索，成果颇丰。创伤叙述时的错误感知和叙事判断、情感特征、叙事记忆和创伤叙述的类型方面，还存在继续讨论的地方。

一、创伤回忆的错误感知和叙事判断

创伤诉说提供了对创伤的理解、对创伤事件的回应和阐释，但我们如何判断创伤回忆的真实性呢？创伤回忆中的沉默、错误认知是否构成了创伤回忆的不可靠性？心理分析家劳卜（Dori Laub）和费尔曼（Shoshanna Felman）在合著的《证言：文学、精神分析和历史中的见证危机》中，提供了一例著名的案列。劳卜在耶鲁大学进行犹太人大屠杀证词的口述实录工作，一名奥斯维辛集中营幸存者回忆起1944年集中营起义的事件时说道："【1】我们看见四个烟囱着了火，爆炸了。火焰冲上天空，人们四散奔逃。"（为便于后文论述，编号为笔者所加，后同）（Laub，1992，p. 59）然而，几个月后在一次历史学家的会议上，专家们却不认可这位女士的证词，因为据考证，当时在奥斯维辛被炸掉的烟囱并不是四个，而是只有一个。这份创伤叙事被认为不具备证据的价值，因为这个回忆不正确。但劳卜认为："这位女士证明的，并不是爆炸的烟囱的数量，而是一些完全不同的东西，一些更为极端的、更为核心的东西，即一个不可想象的事件的真实。"但劳卜并没有明确他所指的真实是什么，原文这样说道：

> 【2】房间里出现了一篇宁静，一片死一般的宁静，在这片宁静中刚才听到的话语回响着，好像它们携带着胜利的回声，这歌声里的声音在铁丝网后面爆发出来，尝试着逃脱的人们的脚步声、喊声、枪声、战争的呼喊声、爆炸声。奥斯维辛那死气沉沉的无时间性消失得无影无踪，过去那炫目的闪光时刻呼啸着穿透了沉默的、像坟墓一样的风景般冻结的寂静，带着流行一样飞快的速度，在它撞击的时刻飞溅出一片图像和声音。但是来自过去的流星飞走了。【3】这位女士再次沉默了……她又恢复了她的颓唐的态度，她的声音再次沉入了一种毫无生气的、几乎是单调的控诉音调。奥斯维辛的大门被关上了，遗忘和沉默的面纱既压抑又让人窒息，又重新降了下来。（p. 59）

作为一名专职的医生和历史记录者，劳卜在采访这位女士时事实上是充当了一名受述者；之后，在转述这位女士的口述时，劳卜变为了一名叙述者，补充了他听到、接受这个证人证词时的见证。可以看出，第一层见证【1】和第二层见证【2】之间存在着情感的交流，第二层见证人对创伤幸存者的痛苦、激动、恐惧和沉默的亲身经历抱有同情。第三层见证【3】是对见证过程本身的见证。正如阿莱达·阿斯曼（Aleida Assmann）对劳卜的记录进行研究后所指出的："多里·劳卜在他的描述中强化了报告的效果，这给人留下了深刻的印象。回忆的隐喻使用的一方面是流星、彗星、爆炸、反抗等图像，另外一方面是冷冻的寂静、毫无生气和死亡般的寂静，这些都和被报告的事件即这一起义相似，并且把集中营中的事件和在访谈情况下的事件叠印在一起。"（阿斯曼，2016，p. 314）可见，在创伤内叙事中，存在叙述者和受述者之间的移情现象，劳卜所提到的"真实"即着眼于此。但从叙事学的角度看，这位女士的叙述是否属于不可靠叙述呢？对第一层见证【1】的叙事判断存在几种维度，我们可以用叙事学中的不可靠叙述理论来研究。

韦恩·布斯（Wayne Booth）在《小说修辞学》中衡量不可靠叙述的标准是作品的规范，这种规范是指作品中的事件、人物、问题、语气、技巧等各种成分体现出来的作品的伦理、信念、情感、艺术等各方面的标准。倘若叙述者的叙述与隐含作者的规范保持一致，那么叙述者就是可靠的。布斯在这里对叙述的判断一方面涉及故事事实，另一方面涉及价值判断。之后，布斯的学生詹姆斯·费伦（James Phelan）把不可靠叙述从事实/事件轴和价值/判断轴这两大类型，发展到了三大类型，增加了知识/感知轴。（申丹，2009，p. 60）如果运用费伦的判断轴，可以看到，劳卜叙事中这位女士的证言，从事实/事件轴来看，是不可靠的，或用历史学家的话来说，是不真实的；从价值/判断轴来说，是不充分判断；但从知识/感知轴来说，这位女士的证词提供了"回忆的撞击，它带着流星般的自然强力穿透这位女士的身体，使她再次经历了那一时刻"（阿斯曼，2016，p. 314）。从情感的角度来看，这位女士的证词唤起了身体和感觉的记忆，不仅让叙述者自身再次经历创伤事件，也同时感染了受述者，成为叙述者和受述者分享的共同经历，成为第二层见证【2】的记忆原始证词，具有特殊的价值。

在创伤叙事中，由于创伤事件超越了人的心理、生理承受程度，意识和自我受到损害，所以知识/感知轴可能出现意义错位，这可能构成事实/事件轴的不可靠叙述。同时，历史学家会以所掌握的历史事实，对叙述者的叙述做出一个预期判断：符合事实（包括档案、数据、文件等细节）或不符合事实（错误记忆、偶然事件或情绪化叙述）。詹姆斯·杨（James Young）对劳卜这段材料进行研究后指出，历史学家们在叙事判断上有时是拙劣的访谈者，原因是："他们太坚信自己的知识了，所以他们总是促使被访谈的见证人去证实人们反正已经知道的东西。他们不让见证人作史实不确切的陈诉，因而就轻率地放弃了那些错误感知对理解历史事件所具有的价值。"（杨，2007，p. 29）历史学家的判断注重考据，但从叙事判断的角度来看，叙述者叙述时所出现的情感，或者说回忆时选择的叙述方式，也是一种经验性历史事实。因此，在事实/事件轴上，我们可以说，第一见证人提供的是历史体验；在知识/感知轴上，提供的则是一种回忆体验，这种体验更为情感化、私人化。回忆体验虽然不符合历史事实，但也是一种真实的回忆方式，其真实性在于：虽然历史事件被留在了过去，但情感却成为过去仍然萦绕着现在的证据，证明了创伤事件的现在性。这段对口述实录真实性的讨论，说明了在创伤叙述中创伤记忆情感特征研究的重要性。

二、创伤记忆的情感特征和语言特征

"情感"这一术语可以追溯到14世纪，而其现代概念来源于17世纪英国经验主义。约翰·洛克（John Locke）发表的《有关人类理解的论文》（Essays Concerning Human Understanding）提出，人类所有的知识都来源于情感经验，人脑在获得经验之前是一块白板。感觉能力（the capacity for sensation）被看作"情感"（sensibility），以区别于大脑的认知（perception）能力。（Wickberg，2007，p. 665）从经验主义哲学出发，法国心理学家倾向于用感觉或感觉经验解释心理过程，认为感觉是心理的唯一来源和基础，肯定感觉的绝对可靠性，并将心理现象视为感觉的堆积、压缩和变形。"同情"（sympathy）的概念经历了一系列转变。它最早是医学用语，18世纪爱丁堡的医学家开始用这个词指示"人体器官之间情感的交流"，这些器官可以是眼睛和耳朵，所以目睹和耳闻是情感交流的重要方式，同情的效果就是感伤，是"一种情感的特殊案例"。（Wickberg，2007，p. 665）18世纪的伦理修辞研究借用了这种成果，认为情感和身体之间存在相通关系。拉奎尔（Thomas W. Laqueur）指出，18、19世纪发展出的"人文性叙事"（humanitarian narrative）就是对"个人身体"（personal body）感受的再现，如他所说，"肉体会言说"（the flesh speaks）。（Laqueur，1989，pp. 177－179）在记忆过程中，身体感受和情感伴随着回忆发生，却往往被忽视。史学家科泽勒克曾提供了一段对自己回忆的真实性的批判性反思：

> 有这样一些经历，它们像炙热的岩浆一样灌进你的身体并在里面凝结。自此，它们一动不动地呆在里面，随时而且毫无改变地听候你的调遣。在这些经历当中，有许多都不能转换成真实可信的回忆；可是一旦转换了，那它们就是基于自己的感性存在的。气味、味道、声响、感觉和周围可见的环境，总之，不管是快乐还是痛苦，所有感官都重新醒来了，它们不需要你做任何记忆工作就是真实的，而且永远都是真实的。（2007，p. 59）

科泽勒克的反思提出了创伤回忆中感性真实存在的观点。创伤记忆造成受创者自我认知的破坏，带来心理负罪感、内疚、怀疑等情感障碍，并伴随着强烈的身体感受，包括疼痛、恶心、痉挛等身体反应，身体成为一种记忆的存储器或者“记忆之场”（借用诺拉的术语），上面铭刻着创伤记忆的强度和冲击力。正如尼采所说：“痛苦是记忆术最为有力的辅助工具……人们要让一些东西留下烙印，才能把它们留在记忆中。只有不停地疼痛的东西，才能保留在记忆里。”（尼采《道德的谱系》第五卷，转引自阿斯曼，2016，p. 279）创伤记忆如同埋在过去的痛苦的楔子，每一次触发，都引起现在的创伤幸存者的疼痛。因此，创伤记忆的情感特征首先在于其无时性（timeless）。一般来说，记忆保存过去的事件，提供了过去和现在之间的历史连续性，但创伤记忆却具有无时性，这意味着每一次创伤记忆被唤起，都会重复造成身体和情感的重击，让受创者再度痛苦，再度受到伤害，创伤叙述因而常常伴随着强烈的个体的情感反应。在个人生活中，创伤回忆和强烈情感会融合成一个不可分割的复合体，值得注意的是，情感在这里不仅是记忆的激发基础，而且创伤回忆的重要维度。

情感包含观点、情绪、认知和经验，这种结构涉及对一种思想的直接的感性理解。凯鲁斯（Cathy Caruth）认为，“创伤的历史力量不仅仅是经验在遗忘之后又被重复，而正是在内在的遗忘之中和通过遗忘，创伤才被第一次经历”（Caruth，1996，p. 17）。创伤经历被理解为一种固定的无时性图像式记忆，存储于大脑的某个地方，却具有打破意识和影响他人的能量。创伤记忆的情感特征其次在于“传染性”（infectious），即创伤情感具有传染无创伤个体或集体的能力。这意味着创伤概念视创伤回应同样为病理性的，换句话说，创伤叙述的伤痛和病理性使所有对创伤经历的回应都生产出解离的意识。劳卜认为，“创伤故事的听众不自觉地参与故事，和故事的主人公一起成为创伤事件的主角……故事中创伤受害者和创伤事件一起影响着读者和故事事件之间的关系，读者逐渐和故事中的受害者共同体会着困惑、伤痛、迷茫、恐惧、冲突。……听众和受害者一同与他（或她）的惨痛经历留下的伤痕累累的回忆和刻骨铭心的‘伤疤’进行斗争”（Laub，1992，pp. 230 - 232）。讲述或叙述的行为是治疗创伤的重要方式。拥有情感被视为道德价值观的来源，讲述之中产生的情感交流对于减轻创伤痛苦有帮助作用，分担创伤经历则创造了一种集体交流，可以缓解创伤幸存者的孤独感和内疚感。其中，“同情”对交流起着感知、认同和交换的作用。史密斯（Adam Smith）分析人类同情中的心理和情感因素，指出同情是两个个体的、内部的状态中的片段式联系，“因为我们没有其他人感受到的即时的经历……只有通过我们自己在类似场合下感受到的来感受……通过想象我们把自己置于他的境地，我们感受到我们自己正在经受同样的折磨，我们进入他的［身体］，在某种程度上成为和他同样的人，于是形成他感觉到的一些念头，甚至感受到一些他的感受，尽管强度上不及”（Smith，2000，pp. 3 - 4）。可以看出，情感是叙述交流的一种媒介，和认知类型、情绪状态、集体或文化定位都有联系。

这里还要注意的是，创伤叙述中也会重复出现对创伤事件的相同描述，叙述者倾向于选择用同样的词语来建构过去，而这些重复在一次次的叙述中使认识得到巩固，这就形成了叙事回忆。哈布瓦赫（Maurice Halbwachs）曾指明，回忆是在同他人和他人回忆的语言交流中构建的。“有许多事情，我们对它们有多少回忆，取决于我们有多少机会对别人叙述它们。有些事情，我们叙述它们的次数越多，就越是不怎么记得起自己对这些事情本身的体验，倒是越能记得起此前叙述它们时所使用的那些话语。”（韦尔策，2007，p. 61）这意味着回忆通过重复得到巩固，而得不到重复的回忆，就逐渐消失，进入遗忘的区域。因此，在创伤记忆转换为叙事记忆的过程中，情感强度会不断降低，而叙事性会不断加强，人物形象逐渐清晰并开始具有某种典型意义。

三、创伤叙述的三种类型

尽管创伤经历被封闭在头脑中，但创伤携带破坏性情感并具有影响他人的能量，通过叙述，通过共同的祖先、种族、集体等得到传播。因此，凯鲁斯认为创伤经历的传染性意味着创伤“从来不是某个人独有的……而恰恰在于我们根植于彼此的创伤之中”（Caruth，1996，p. 17）。这种关于创伤虽然是不可分辨但仍然具有感染性的观点，使凯鲁斯等将创伤经历视为“跨历史性”（transhistorical）的，可以跨越代际鸿沟，通过口头和读写的记忆工作来得到传递。

从创伤信息的传递和交流来看，创伤叙述存在三种类型：独白式创伤叙述、见证式创伤叙述、回顾式创伤叙述。独白式创伤叙述的叙述者为创伤幸存者，受述者可能是自己或不确定的单个或多个对象，叙述的目的在于对创伤事件的自我反思或重塑受到损害的自我认知。独白式创伤叙述中，创伤情感的体验对创伤叙述和语言都形成了一定的影响。贝克尔（Huston Baker）认为，“只有当身体舒适的时候，当它停止作为观念和关心的客体的时候，意识才能发展出其他的客体［语言］”（Baker，1993，pp. 38 – 50）。痛苦摧毁了受害者的语言和文字表达能力，同样也摧毁了受害者的自我意识和“意识内容”（the contents of the consciousness）。朗格尔（Lawrence Langer）发现，在大屠杀幸存者的语言中存在着“一大批概念的意义错位，这些概念本来应该巩固整合的自我，比如：选择、意志、思维能力、满怀期待”（Langer，1991，p. 177）。创伤事件对幸存者而言是独一无二的，很难用日常词汇来表述，甚至某些词汇会直接引起创伤应激反应。叙述者试图通过语言重新整理记忆，认知往事，却在叙述中遭遇表述障碍。在独白式创伤叙述中，“我”的出现率非常高，但却由支离破碎的感受、印象、记忆和痛苦的体验构成，这也是创伤幸存者讲述中出现错误感知的原因之一。

创伤事件造成了时间的断裂，个人生活似乎被创伤划分为前后两个阶段，因而在独白式创伤叙述中，叙述时间的连续性被打断，创伤经验无法被认知，也就无法融入叙述者的经验之中。廓尔克（Bessel van der Kolk）认为，当创伤经历如此让人震惊，以至“它们无法被整合进存在的头脑结构中时，［这些经历］就被解离了，之后作为片段感官或行动的经历而侵入性地返回——醒着的时候是闪回，睡眠的时候是噩梦”（Van der Kolk，1996，p. 168）。解离意味着个人无法支配意识，因而在叙述中常常出现时间错乱或闪回，这也是独白式创伤叙述的特有方式。同时，独白式创伤叙述中，由于回忆和遗忘互相介入，叙述者的记忆常常表现为两种极端：一方面似乎患有创伤遗忘症，以至于不能讲述一个完整的故事，叙述缺乏开始、发展、结束的结构；另一方面，记忆似乎可以准确地再现创伤事件发生时的每一个细节，似乎往事不自觉地浮现并不断上演。创伤叙述者讲述了什么、讲述了多少，是由叙述方式决定的。叙述方式透露了创伤的绝大多数信息。对于独白式创伤叙述者而言，活着的意义就是追问创伤事件的真实含义，而追问的历史构成了创伤的全部。

见证式创伤叙述指两个主体之间的叙述交流活动，包括讲述和倾听、叙述和受述的叙述行为。见证式创伤叙述可以分为多种层次，如第一节中劳卜采访奥斯维辛集中营幸存者的记录：第一层见证【1】是这名女士关于自身经验和经历的见证，受述者是劳卜；第二层见证【2】是劳卜对倾听第一层见证的证词，这对第一层见证起到补充和丰富的作用，其中劳卜是叙述者，读者为受述者；第三层见证【3】是对叙事过程或见证过程的观察，叙述者劳卜观察叙述者（这名女士）和自身（作为受述者和叙述者的劳卜）怎样在靠近经验或退后观察中做出叙述交流。见证式创伤叙述重视叙述交流，叙述者作为创伤的见证者，为受述者提供了关于创伤事件或创伤历史的知识；受述者通过倾听，深入之前不了解，或拒绝被了解，或情况和信息被隐藏的创伤历史中。在这个意义上，见证式创伤叙述涉及公共领域，因为创伤证言（testimony）不仅是对个人创伤的证词，也“涉及一种有公共意义或重要性的姿态，超越了个人移情或遭遇，生产出集体感”（Kaplan，2005，p. 23）。见证因此毫无疑问的是一种公共形式（public form）。在这个叙述交流的过程中，形成了记忆传递过程中的共识，强烈的情感往往凝结成象征，使关于过去的知识和信息被了解，被传递，并得到解释，帮助公众矫正一种错误的认识或改正一种不公正的看法。

见证的公共形式意味着叙述者脱离了孤独的状态，创伤记忆逐渐转化为叙事记忆。廓尔克指出，“人和动物都拥有行为记忆，而叙事记忆属于人类能力……叙事记忆包括思想建构，人们用它来理解经验”（Van der Kolk，1996，p. 168）。叙事记忆具有社会成分，服务于社会功能。见证的过程就是将个人的创伤记忆集体化的过程。保罗·利科（Paul Ricour）认为，集体记忆让每个家庭成员的自我回忆都拥有一个文化和历史的框架。（Ricour，2004，p. 437）记忆传递过程中的讲述和接受形成了集体记忆的框架，关于集体中某个人的故事也成为该集体独特的回忆，成为仅仅对其成员才揭示的秘密。这增加了该集体成员之间情感上的亲密感，同时也成为集体历史的一部分，成为外来者或新加入者需要习得以获取认可的标记。见证式创伤叙述可以发生在同代人之间，也可以发生在不同代之间，而后者对于家庭或家族而言，是塑造赖以流传的家庭记忆的传输环节。费内尔（Lee Anne Fennell）指出，“这种家庭和集体的记忆不仅通过语言来传递，而且通过无意识或潜意识来吸收、接受”（Fennell，1999，pp. 35 - 47）。家庭内部的见证，不仅通过话语讲述，也通过行为重演、习惯、禁忌等传递。家庭记忆代际传递中，第二代对创伤记忆的讲述删减了第一代创伤记忆造成的混乱语言，增加了这个家庭或集体所崇尚的价值和规范。创伤情感强度减弱，创伤记忆原型化，成为集体记忆中“他或她”的故事，这个故事伴随着第二代的成长历程，对于第二代的自我塑造和认知有重要意义。

创伤具有一种双重的时间结构，也就是说，创伤经历开始时并没有被意识感知，因为主体缺乏理解力，不能给予创伤一个有意义的语境并加以解释。但“创伤一直潜伏，直到它和另一件似乎不相关的事情发生了联系。在这个过程中，主体已经得到了必要的知识，才能抓住原初的经验，创伤才被经历”（Batra，2007，p. 40）。同一个年龄段的群体，可能因为共同经历的历史事件，而在说话和思维方式、精神创伤等方面都具有共同性。但这种同代人记忆的载体是和同一个经历和回忆的时代证人相联系的，延续时间通常不超过 80 年。

回顾式创伤叙述指代际传递中第三代对前辈创伤记忆的延续。独白式创伤叙述中，叙述自我是且一直是“正在经历的自我”（experiencing self）；回顾式创伤叙述中，叙述者的创伤记忆来自家庭、家族、种族等集体创伤记忆，叙述自我是经验自我（experienced self）。由于和创伤事件之间的时间距离，回顾式创伤叙述者已经预知创伤事件并了解创伤的后果。过去和现在之间是一种类比关系，过去成为现在的一种象征资源（symbolic source），沉淀在家族、地区或者历史中的集体记忆已经成为第三代个人历史的一部分，并决定了他或她的自我认知。

佛特尔（Greg Forter）认为，“历史自身也是一段从来没有停止的创伤，历史事件会侵扰那些即便在地理上、时间上都不在现场的人”（Forter，2007，p. 292）。作为幸存者的第三代，创伤叙述者自己没有创伤的直接经历，而只能通过集体记忆了解自己和过去的联系。正如怀特（Geoffrey M. White）所说，“在各种语境和媒介中某些故事的重新生产是制造集体记忆的一个必要因素”（White，2000，p. 504）。在记忆的强迫性重复下，讲述过去的创伤成为一种道德责任。独白式创伤叙述讲述的是一种失去（loss），即创伤对生活的破坏造成的原有人际关系、安全感、家庭等的失落。回顾式创伤叙述讲述的是先辈历史传承中的某件事物或意义的缺席（absence），如美国历史中，非裔美国人的祖先几乎都遭受过奴隶制的剥削，丧失了公民权和人权。奴隶制和历史上白种人的种族政策造成创伤的代际传递中第一代的创伤经历，对后代非裔美国人的身份附加一种固有的品质，奎特（J. Brooks Bouson's Quiet）认为这种品质是一种“习得性的文化羞耻”（learned cultural shame）

(Bouson, 2000, p. 4)。所以，在莫里森等作家的回顾式创伤叙述中，祖先记忆的历史缺席构成了非裔集体自我身份的本体性的缺失。回顾式创伤叙述讲述上一代的故事，通过记忆重演反思创伤带来的延续性破坏，这种回顾同时也塑造了集体和种族等的身份认同和历史意识。

结 论

正如杜克（Leigh Anne Duck）所指出的，“和过去拥有这种创伤关系的个人……都在遭遇了某个特别时刻后被孤立，这个遭遇在他们的生活中具有毁灭性和私密性，他们不能理解这种遭遇”（Duck, 2003, p. 94）。创伤的毁灭性打击对创伤患者造成认知障碍和表述障碍，也常常造成听众对创伤叙述的质疑。然而，从叙事角度感知轴进行叙事判断，可以看出，创伤叙述中的情感具有特殊的历史价值。创伤记忆中的情感具有无时性、传染性，这意味着创伤不仅发生在过去，也发生在现在，每一次创伤回忆过程中被唤起的个体情感反应，都是创伤的复现。同时，创伤情感还具有打破意识和影响他人的能量，在创伤交流中的听众和同一集体中造成同情或移情现象。从创伤信息的传递和交流来看，创伤记忆的形成、保持和延续分别对应着三种创伤叙述类型，即独白式创伤叙述、见证式创伤叙述和回顾式创伤叙述。独白式创伤叙述着重“我”的故事；见证式创伤叙述传递创伤心理，塑造了“他或她”的故事；回顾式创伤叙述重构了“每个人”的故事。创伤记忆通过代际传递，提供了对过去的见证，塑造了具有记忆传递价值的典型人物和创伤文化意象。

参考文献：

阿斯曼，阿莱达（2016）. 回忆空间：文化记忆的形势和变迁（潘璐，译）. 北京：北京大学出版社.

科泽勒克，赖因哈特（2007）. 炙热的岩浆凝成回忆——对战争的种种告别：无法交流的经历. 载于哈拉德尔，韦尔策（编）. 社会记忆：历史、回忆、传承（季斌，王立君，译）. 北京：北京大学出版社.

申丹（2009）. 叙事、文体与潜文本. 北京：北京大学出版社.

韦尔策，哈拉尔德（编）（2007）. 社会记忆：历史、回忆、传承（季斌，王立君，译）. 北京：北京大学出版社.

杨，詹姆斯（2007）. 在历史与回忆之间——论将回忆之声重新纳入历史叙述. 载于哈拉德尔，韦尔策（编）. 社会记忆：历史、回忆、传承（季斌，王立君，译）. 北京：北京大学出版社.

Baker, H. (1993). Scene... not heard. In Robert Gooding-Williams (Ed.). *Reading Rodney King: Reading urban uprising*. New York: Routledge.

Bouson, J. B. (2000). *Quiet as it's kept: Shame, trauma, and race in the novels of Toni Morrison*. New York: State University of New York Press.

Caruth, C. (1996). *Unclaimed experience: Trauma, narrative, and history*. Baltimore and London: The Johns Hopkins University Press.

Duck, L. A. (2003). Faulkner and traumatic memory. In Hamblin, R. W. & Jackson, M. S. et al. (Eds.) *Faulkner in the twenty-first century*. Jackson: University Press of Mississippi.

Erikson, K. (1995). Notes on trauma and community. In Caruth, C. (Ed.). *Trauma: Explorations in memory*. Baltimore and London: The Johns Hopkins University Press.

Felman, S. & Laub, D. (1992) *Testimony: The crisis of witnessing in literature, psychoanalysis and history*. New York and London: Routledge.

Fennell, L. A. (1999). Unquiet ghosts: Memory and determinism in Faulkner. *Southern Literary Journal*, 31, 35-47.

Forter, G. (2007). Freud, Faulkner, Caruth: Trauma and the politics of literary form. *Narrative*, 15.

Kaplan, E. A. (2005). *Trauma culture: The politics of terror and loss in media and literature*. New Brunswick, New Jersey and London: Rutgers University Press.

Van der Kolk, B. A. & Van Der Hart, O. (1995). The intrusive past: The flexibility of memory and the engraving of trauma. In Cathy Caruth (Ed.). *Trauma: Explorations in memory*. Baltimore: The Johns Hopkins University Press.

Langer, L. (1991). *Holocaust testimonies: The ruins of memory*. New Haven: Yale University Press.

Laqueur, T. W. (1989). Bodies, details, and the humanitarian narrative. In Lynn Hunt (Ed.). *The new cultural history*. Berkeley: University of California Press.

Laub, D. (1992). Bearing witness or the vicissituds of listening. In Shoshana Felman & Dori Laub. *Testimony: Crises of Witnessing in Literature, Psychoanalysis, and History*. New York: Routledge.

Nandita B. et al (Eds.) (2007). *Narrating the past: (Re) constructing memory, (re) negotiating history*. Newcastle: Cambridge Scholars Publishing.

Ricoer, p. (2004). *Memory, forgetting, and history*. Chicago, IL: The University of Chicago Press.

Smith, A. (2000). *The theory of moral sentiments*. New York: Prometheus Books.

White, G. M. (2000). Histories and subjectivities. *Ethos*, 28.

Wickberg, D. (2007). What is the history of sensibilities? On cultural histories: Old and new.

American historical review, 112(3), 665.

作者简介：

王欣，文学博士，四川大学外国语学院教授，研究方向为西方文论与英美文学。

Author:

Wang Xin, Ph. D., professor of College of Foreign Languages and Cultures, Sichuan University. Her researches include Western literary theories, British and American Literature.

Email: joywang2002@163. com

试论陶瓷图像图与事的叙述类型——兼论图像叙事*

倪爱珍

摘　要： 图像叙事有广义和狭义之分，本文所研究的陶瓷图像叙事，取其广义，即关涉一个故事的图像，并据此将图像叙事中图与事的叙述类型分为三种：以图概事——类型事件——象征；以图指事——特定事象——抒情说理；以图演事——具体事态——审美娱乐，梳理出它们在中国古代陶瓷上的流变及其对图像叙事传统形成的影响。同时，将其与文学叙事中图与事的叙述类型进行比较，以管窥语图叙事的异同。这三种叙事类型反映了图像关涉事件的三种不同的方式和功能，但是这种分类不是绝对的，只能说偏重哪一种。对图像叙事类型的不同判断会带来图像意义的不同阐释，所以，作者进行图像叙事时，要根据不同目的选择图像叙事类型，接收者也只有在图像叙事类型认知上与作者达成一致，才能更好地领会作者意图，实现图像的社会价值和文化价值。

关键词： 陶瓷，图像叙事，以图概事，以图指事，以图演事

The Narrative Genre of the Image and Events on Ceramics and Image Narrative

Ni Aizhen

Abstract: Image narrative can be classified into two: general narrative and specific narrative. This article deals with image narrative generally, i. e. concerning the image of a story, and thereby classifies the

* 本文为国家社科基金重点项目“陶瓷图像的文学叙事研究”（18AZW004）的阶段性成果。

narration of an image and an event within image narrative into three genres: summarizing the event via the image—stereotype events—symbol; representing events by the image—specific events and phenomenon—expressing emotions and presenting reasons; performing events on the image—concrete events—aesthetic entertainment. And it sorts out their changes in Chinese ancient ceramic and the influence they exert on the tradition of the image narrative. Meanwhile, it compares them with the narrative genres on image and events in the literature narrative to detect the differences and similarities between text narrative and image narrative. These three genres reflect three different ways in which images relates events and its function. Whereas this classification is not categorical, but a kind of weighting. Different judgement on the genre of the image narrative brings about different interpretation of the significance of the image. Therefore, when an author narrates a story via image, he/she chooses the different genre of the image narrative, while receivers, only who agree with the author on the cognition of the image narrative genre, can better grasp the author's intention, realizing the image's social value and cultural value.

Keywords: ceramic, image narrative, summarizing the event via the image, representing events by the image, performing events on the image

DOI: 10. 13760/b. cnki. sam. 202002014

叙事，简单地说就是讲故事，同人类的历史一样久远，是人类作为群居动物在地球上得以生存的一个必要条件，罗宾·邓巴等人类学家对此已有详细论述。人类最早采用声音、动作、实物以及图像等符号来记录事件、传递信息，之后发明了文字。在人类历史的早期，图亦文，文亦图，文图无法截然分开，都服务于记事这一目的。这从现今留存下来的新石器时代的彩陶和岩画中可窥一斑，比如仰韶文化遗物鹳鱼石斧彩陶缸，据专家考证，可能是为了记录以鹳为图腾的氏族战胜以鱼为图腾的氏族这个重大事件。人类学家弗朗兹·博厄斯研究早期北美印第安人的绘画时认为：“严格地说，他们的表现艺术不过是粗糙的象形文字。这些人没有高超的绘画技巧，他们所画的马、人、水牛和帐篷等仅是为了记录生活中的某些事件。”（博厄斯，1980，pp. 59 – 60）以图叙事是图像最原始的功能，随着当今社会成像技术的发达又再次兴盛，“读图时代”早已来临。

图像叙事，就是用图像来叙述一个故事，常被称为“叙事画”“故事画”“故实画”。综观前人研究，对这一概念的理解有广义和狭义之分，前者指关涉一个故事的图像，后者指描绘故事具体场景的图像。本文所研究的陶瓷图像叙事，取其广义。关于叙事，赵毅衡有个底线性质的定义：“1. 某个主体把有人物参与的事件组织进一个符号文本；2. 此文本可以被接受者理解为具有时间和意义向度。”（2013，p. 7）也就是说，叙事有三个基本要素，即卷入人物、时间向度、意义向度。对叙事性图像（尤其是单幅图）而言，接收者直接看到的只有人物，故事的时间向度和意义向度需要经过二次叙述才能感知。所以，本文所研究的陶瓷上的叙事性图像要满足一个必要条件，就是图像中有人物，或是人格化的物。

图像如何关涉故事，也即图像叙事中图与事的叙述类型有哪些？董乃斌在《中国古典小说的文体独立》一书中认为任何文学作品都是以某种“事”为内容或至少是为背景而创作的，但是对事的表达方式多种多样，可以直叙其事，可以变形加工，甚至掺入虚构，总体来说，文学与事的关系可以概括为四种：含事、咏事、述事和演事。（1994，pp. 12－53）图像作为符号，和语言一样具有叙事功能，但图像是空间艺术，无法像语言叙事那样直接展现时间变化、故事进程，只能展现特定场景，所以图像叙事中的图与事的关系和文学叙事中的文学与事的关系既有相同点，也有不同点。对此，艺术学界已有研究。巫鸿在研究汉画像石上的人物图像时，将对称构图和正面主神的构图称作“偶像型”，将非对称、人物总是被描绘成全侧面或四分之三侧面的构图称作“情节型”①，并且强调这样的人物“总是处于行动的状态中”。（2015，pp. 149－150）他是从艺术学构图的角度研究人物图的，但他指出了叙事的核心要素——人物的行动。经典叙事学研究的一个重要范式就是对行动进行分类。若从叙事学角度来看，他所说的这两类都属于图像叙事，因为都关涉故事，只是关涉方式不同。孟久丽（Julia K. Murray）认为叙事的视觉表现涉及三个主要要素，即概念性方法、作品结构、作品形式，其中最难以解释清楚的是图画与相关故事之间的概念性关系，她列举了两类，但没有详细论述。（2014，p. 26）本文以陶瓷上的叙事性图像为例来探讨这一话题，并且将其与文学叙事中图与事的叙述类型进行比较，以管窥语图叙事的异同。

① 这种类型专指那些以叙事文学为基础的作品。

一、以图概事——类型事件——象征

以图概事，即图像是对某一类事件的高度概括化表现，其因长期的文化积累而形成，最终成为一种象征型符号，其中的人物身份不明确，只是作为行动的主体，如陶瓷上大量的仕女图、婴戏图、高士图、社会风情图（如渔樵耕读、琴棋书画、书生赶考、状元荣归）。这种图像，无论是人物行动、图像模式还是思想内涵，都具有相对的稳定性，对其意义的解释需要较多地借助社会文化规约。

比如陶瓷上的携琴访友图，最早出现在宋代磁州窑瓷枕上，其后在元明清瓷器上大量出现。在这个图像中，谁访友、去哪里、访什么朋友、为什么访友等都不清楚，观者能看到的就是高士执杖、童子抱琴，行走于深山小桥上。这是最典型的携琴访友图像模式。中国历史上关于琴的故事很多，最著名的是出自《列子》的“高山流水”和汉牟融《理惑论》的“对牛弹琴”，表达的都是寻觅知音的主题。四库全书收录的元明清诗人作的“携琴访友”题画诗（或题跋）有9首，其中元1首、明7首、清1首；古代也流传下来一些携琴访友图，如宋范宽，明戴进、文徵明、清陈卓、王翚等人的作品。这些历史故事、诗文绘画共同创造了“携琴访友”这个类型化故事和经典图像模式，表达了知音难觅、归隐山林等意义，在中国文化传统中已经成为一种象征性符号。

再如陶瓷上的仕女图，最早见于唐代长沙窑瓷器，宋元时期较为少见；明代早期由于受青花原料表现人物的限制而不多见，明中期为数也还不多，明晚期时则大量出现，这与当时商品经济繁荣、市民文化发达有关；清代仕女图尤为盛行，而且不同时期风格各不相同。就题材来讲，以游园、扑蝶、弄花、赏画、煎茶、焚香、弹琴、弈棋、吹箫、乐舞、对镜试妆、金盆弄月及戏婴、课子居多。这些图像是对中国古代封建社会中上层女性生活中具有普遍性的事件的概括化反映，表征着女性在封建社会中“被看”的命运、贤妻良母的身份认同等。她们是谁并不重要，她们行动的表征才是最重要的。研究明代视觉文化的英国学者柯律格（Craig Clunas）认为：“艺术作品能产生政治和社会以及文化的意义，而非仅仅是对这些意义的表现。”（2011，p. 9）中国古代大量的仕女图不仅是对女性生活的表现，更参与建构了“女性”这一身份以及相应的社会规范。陶瓷器物多为日用品，遍布于日常生活的各个地方，其上的图像对人们思想的影响更直接、强烈，如钱德拉·慕克吉所说：“物为观念的载体……它们被生产出来之后长期存在于物质世界，从而有助于形成外在于观念的自主力量……正是这种物质的和象征的双重限制，赋予物质文化以一种影响人类行动的特殊力量。” （柯律格，2019，p. 16）

概事型图像具有事件类型化、图像程式化特征，是图像叙事传统中的一支重要力量，深刻影响着人们的思维方式和表意方式。仍以陶瓷上的仕女图为例。仕女图表现的是具有象征功能的美人而非具体的美人，而对何为美人又有明确的标准。明末清初时期，徐震的《美人谱》从容、韵、技、事、居、候、饰、助、馔、趣10个方面界定什么是美人，卫咏的《悦容编》从随缘、葺居、缘饰、选侍、雅供、博古、寻真、及时、晤对、钟情、借资、招隐、达观13个方面对女性美进行描述。仕女图中人物的行动类型化，形象也常常是千人一面，成为一种图像叙事传统，影响着后世比如晚清画报的插图。画报的第一要义是新闻性、时事性，但许多画报编者喜欢在其中插入古代的仕女图，陈平原认为这既是一种用以吸引读者的销售策略，也不无借此提高艺术品位的意图。（2008，p. 221）比如李菊侪在《醒世画报》上刊登启事时称：“北京画师报界同人中，能绘人物好手，除家兄李翰园及刘君炳堂早有心得外，能为社会普遍欢迎者，实为寥寥”；而“绘事中，莫难于时派美人，仕女图又为妇孺注释之集线”，于是决定在画报上“添绘时装仕女图百幅，与各报同人互相研究，使绘图同臻善境”。（陈平原，2017）插入仕女图，能吸引大众视线，能切磋技艺同臻善境，可见这一传统的影响力之大。这影响，不仅在绘画构图上，还在图像思维上，比如不重视原创，不重视人物外貌的个性化，从陈平原所举的两个例子可以管窥。一是《日新画报》上《举案齐眉》的故事，作者虽然提醒大家“孟光长得很丑”，但画面上依旧是美女一个；二是《醒世画报》上《实在难看》的例子，嘲笑两个女人在胡同里没有教养地聊天，但画面采用的却是李菊侪绘的“时派美人”模式，观者丝毫感觉不到嘲讽刺意味。所以陈平原感叹：“强大的仕女画传统，抹平了所有中国女性的面孔。”（2008，p. 222）

二、以图指事——特定事象——抒情说理

以图指事，即用图像来指示特定事件，人物身份是明确的，但图像所展现的不是故事中的具体情节，而是故事中的一些标志物，即事件之“象”，如人物的衣着、配饰、动作、工具、场景，从而引发接收者对故事的联想，

以达到抒情说理的目的。巫鸿所说的“偶像式”图像、孟久丽所说的“通过描绘一个或多个主角、故事的背景、重要的道具等来暗示或者象征一个故事，而不用表现任何特定的叙事瞬间”（2014，p. 26）都属此类。

柯律格谈论过一只螺钿镶嵌漆盒上的图像——有“梅妻鹤子”之称的隐士林逋（图1），这个图像并不是为了再现隐士林逋植梅养鹤的故事本身，而是借一个有梅有鹤的画面来“使人联想到一整套与品行高洁、避世隐居有关的典故”（2011，p. 47），歌咏他的隐逸情操。如何惠鉴所说：“一旦这些图像的权威性通过‘约定俗成’这一社会文化过程得到确立，通过巧妙地操作，有效地实行，仅仅提到某人或某地就会立刻唤起一种难以抗拒的抒情性共鸣，指向所示空间和时间，并通过人事结合起来。”（2011，p. 47）

图1　螺钿镶嵌漆盒（转引自柯律格，2011，p. 44）

指事型图像和含事型、咏事型文学在符号与对象的关系和符号功能上都有相通之处，两者都用符号指示具体事件，都借事抒情说理。含事型文学和咏事型文学都包含着具体事件，只是前者不直接描述想说的事，而是采用暗指、隐喻等手法转弯抹角地说，从文字表面看不到所写何事，只能看到一些模糊的线索，后者则通过标题、小序、注释或正文等多种形式明确地指出歌咏的事件。（董乃斌，1991，p. 17，p. 24）语言符号表意非常清晰，图像表意则具有模糊性的特点，所以以图指事如果不借助文字提示，就只能采用故事中的标志物。陶瓷图像的主要功能是装饰，绝大多数图像都没有文字提示，因此更需要借助标志物来提高故事的辨识度，也因此陶瓷图像构图的程式化色彩要浓一些。

陶瓷上典型的指事型图像，如由故事演变而来的吉祥寓意图（如八仙祝寿、麻姑献寿、郭子仪拜寿、海屋添筹、蟾宫折桂、吹箫引凤、钟馗捉鬼）、历史人物图、小说戏曲人物图，目的都是引发观者对故事的联想，借事抒情说理，常常有很强的实用功能，比如祈愿、送礼、教化、仪式、身份建构等，这从明文震亨《长物志》中的《悬画月令》可以管窥。古人对何时何地悬何种题材的画甚是讲究："岁朝宜宋画福神及古名贤像；元宵前后宜看灯、傀儡；正、二月宜春游、仕女、梅、杏、山茶、玉兰、桃、李之属……至如移家则有葛仙移居等图；称寿则有院画寿星、王母等图；祈晴则有东君；祈雨则有古画风雨神龙、春雷起蛰等图；立春则有东皇太乙等图。皆随时悬挂，以见岁时节序。"（文震亨，1936，p. 39）陶瓷上还有很多小说戏曲人物绣像图，著名的如"水浒叶子"图[1]，大多源于小说戏曲版画插图，其目的是引起读者对故事的联想，引发思想情感上的共鸣。

再如陶瓷上的"四爱图"，属于高士图。高士，即志行高洁之士，多指隐士。最早的"四爱图"出现在两只元青花梅瓶上（图2），器形和纹饰相似度都非常高，都采用"开光"[2] 的方式画了四幅图，即黄庭坚爱兰、周敦颐爱莲、林和靖爱鹤梅、陶渊明爱菊[3]。元中后期孙存吾编辑的元诗总集《元风雅后集卷七》中收录有《四爱题咏》，为19位元代著名文人和宗教大师吟咏叶成辅居所"四爱堂"的诗文总集，其中有7人在作品中解释了"四爱"的含义。他们在爱菊、爱梅鹤、爱莲的主人公上意见一致，但在爱兰的主人公上有分歧，一些人认为是黄庭坚，一些人认为是屈原，后人又认为是王羲之。接收者总是要为这个故事确定一个主人公，这是指事型图像的一个鲜明特征。"四爱图"在后来的发展中逐渐成为一种题材类型，不再仅仅局限于这四爱，而是扩展到米芾爱石、孟浩然爱梅、俞伯牙爱琴、王子猷爱竹等。这些图像虽然包含着故事，但绘图的目的都不是为了再现故事中的某个场景，而只是提取故事中的一些标志性符号，唤起观者对人物超然于世、悠然自得的高洁品行的感知。

---

① 《水浒叶子》是明末清初画家陈洪绶在传统民间马吊牌基础上的创新之作，以小说《水浒传》中的人物作为牌面图像主体，塑造了40名梁山泊英雄形象，歌颂他们的英雄气概和反抗精神，陶瓷画工将其搬到了陶瓷上。

② "开光"指在器物平面上以线条勾勒出圆形、菱形、扇面形等多种多样栏框，框内绘上图案，因为像古建筑上开窗见光而得名。

③ 有两幅早期被解读为王羲之爱兰、孟浩然爱梅，后有些学者认为它更可能是黄庭坚爱兰、陶渊明爱菊，也有学者认为是屈原爱兰。

图2　元青花“四爱图”

（分别由湖北省博物馆、湖北省武汉市博物馆藏，见徐华峰，2016，p. 16）

指事型图像的故事是明确的，也唯有明确，才能借事抒情说理，表达特定意义。有些图像会因标志物不明显、缺乏文字提示、传播过程中信息损耗等而显得故事题材不明确，接受者在解释过程中总是试图将其明确化，这样就会出现“箭垛效应”，即将类似图像都归到同一个故事上。这一概念源自胡适的《〈三侠五义〉序》：

> 历史上有许多有福之人。一个是黄帝，一个是周公，一个是包龙图。上古有许多重要的发明，后人不知道是谁发明的，只好都归到黄帝的身上，于是黄帝成了上古的大圣人。中古有许多制作，后人也不知道究竟是谁创始的，也就都归到周公的身上，于是周公成了中古的大圣人，忙的不得了，忙的他“一沐三握发，一饭三吐哺”！这种有福的人物，我曾替他们取了个名字，叫“箭垛式的人物”；就同小说上说的诸葛亮借箭时用的草人一样，本来只是一扎干草，身上刺猬也似的插着许多箭，不但不伤皮肉，反可以立大功，得大名。（2013，p. 965）

比如陶瓷上的“李白醉酒”图，有一些配了诗文，点名人物是李白（图3）；有一些没有文字提示，但根据图像的信息，如儒生装扮、酒杯或酒罐、书籍或童子读书，接收者还是把它解释为“李白醉酒”（图4、5、6）。这种现象在以陶瓷图像为代表的民间器物图像解释中非常普遍，因为这些器物上的图像多是摹写其他媒材上的图像或者其他人的作品，绘图者不注重图像信息的完整性。反过来看，接收者如何解释这些图像，能反映特定历史时期的社会文化。

图 3　清光绪粉彩“李白醉酒”圆花盆
（汪庆正，1999，p. 213）

图 4　明崇祯青花人物故事瓶
（北京保利 2008 年金秋拍卖会第 1231 号拍品）

图 5　清光绪五彩人物笔筒
（北京保利 2017 年第 39 期古董精品
拍卖会第 59 号拍品）

图 6　清光绪五彩人物笔筒
（北京保利 2015 年第 32 期精品
拍卖会第 134 号拍品）

三、以图演事——具体事态——审美娱乐

以图演事，即用图像演示故事中的具体情节，详细地描画故事场景、人物动作、事态进程，目的是让接受者感知故事本身，获得审美愉悦，而不再仅仅是借事抒情说理。以图演事的图可以是单幅图，也可以是连续图；事可

以是文学作品中的事，也可以是现实发生的事。巫鸿所说的“情节型”图像、孟久丽所说的“通过描绘一个能够令人回忆起整个故事的单一情节或场景来概述整个故事”（2014，p. 26），都属于此类。

文学作品详细地叙述故事，可以采用两种方式：一是述事，即“对所述之事尽可能作具体可感、原原本本、细致周到的描述，需将事件的原委过程、来龙去脉、前因后果尽可能地交代清楚”，比如小说；一是演事，对应的文体是剧本，即主要通过人物的行动和对话，尤其是对话，来叙述事情。（董乃斌，1994，p. 38，p. 48）图像叙述故事，无法完整地展现故事的时间进程，即使是多幅图，也同样面临如何选择特定情节来表现故事以及如何构图来表现情节这些重要问题。这一过程，既与作者意图有关，也与文化传统有关。

就中国古代陶瓷而言，唐以前的器物上没有典型的演事型图像，到宋金元时期的河北磁州窑瓷枕才开始大量出现演事型图像。磁州窑是中国北方最大的民窑体系，窑址在今河北省邯郸市峰峰矿区的彭城镇和磁县的观台镇一带，古有“南有景德，北有彭城”之说。磁州窑在五代末至北宋早期开始生产化妆白瓷，北宋中期达到鼎盛，南宋、元明清有延续。瓷枕的大量生产是在宋金元时期，元末明初时，很多窑场停烧，瓷枕的数量也就越来越少了。现存有纪年的瓷枕有 30 多个，涉及宋、金、南宋、元，明代的两个存疑。（张子英，2000，p. 12）

磁州窑瓷枕的装饰内容非常丰富，首次将大量的山水、花鸟、诗词、警句以及人物故事搬上瓷器。从现存实物来看，元代瓷枕最多。磁州窑为故事图的诞生提供了先决性的物质条件：枕的面积大、平整，易于绘画；装饰技术要求不高，在制作好的花纹上罩上一层透明釉即可。此外，还有一个重要条件，那就是磁州窑的民窑性质使向来不能登大雅之堂的小说戏曲故事有机会广泛传播。从北宋开始，注重表现自我的文人画占据中国美术主导地位，叙事画退居为一种“功能性艺术”，“用于实现记录、呈现、说明、教育、证实或声明主张等需求”（孟久丽，2014，p. 15）。而且，宋代主流审美崇尚平淡，体现在陶瓷艺术上，就是追求质地细腻、造型简洁、色泽淡雅、纹饰清新、意境悠远，简单地说就是“似玉”。所以，宋瓷以高度发达的单色釉著称，以青瓷、白瓷、影青瓷最为著名。磁州窑则与之不同，瓷枕上的人物故事图代表了民间的审美风尚，诞生于北方的元杂剧的繁荣更是激发了磁州窑工匠的创作热情和灵感，推动了萧何月下追韩信、三顾茅庐、李逵负荆、西游记、司马仲才梦苏小小、尉迟恭单鞭夺槊、相如题桥、秋胡戏妻、柳毅传书等故事图在瓷枕上的大量出现。

如果说演事型图像在北方的磁州窑瓷枕上是登堂入室，那么在南方的景德镇窑元青花上则是大放异彩。它构图丰满、工艺精湛，颜色上改含蓄内敛的黑与白为优雅明快的蓝与白，创造了不朽的视觉经典。元青花是蒙古帝国时期世界文化大交流的产物，如日本学者杉山正明所说："伊朗有钴蓝和彩绘技法，中国有高超的瓷器生产技术，蒙古令两者合而为一。深蓝与白的调和色彩，是蒙古自身的品位，青花就这样地成为权力与财富的象征而在欧亚普及。这毫无疑问地融合东西方的精华。"（2016，p. 141）

元青花生产总量不大，现存器物国内外总计只有300件左右，绝大部分在国外，尤其是中东地区，可见当时它主要是为外销而生产的。从器形来看，除了东南亚地区多见小型器外，其余多是胎体厚重，器形硕大，以大盘最多，口径多是四五十厘米，这是为适应中东地区的生活习俗而设计的。元青花大件器形的特征为复杂的人物故事图的出现提供了前提。现存元青花上绘有人物故事图的有20余件，从故事类型来看，有历史故事，如鬼谷子下山、昭君出塞、三顾茅庐、周亚夫屯兵细柳营、萧何月下追韩信、尉迟恭单鞭救主；有爱情故事，如百花亭、锦香亭、江州司马青衫湿；有高士故事，如四爱故事。前两类故事都有相应的元杂剧文本基础。（徐华烽，2016）可见景德镇元青花故事图的出现与元杂剧从北向南的传播、繁荣紧密相关。这些人物故事图多见于大罐、梅瓶、玉壶春瓶等器物上。元朝的海外市场主要是伊斯兰国家，这些国家由于宗教教义而反对偶像崇拜，因此器物上很少有人物纹饰，据此推测这些人物故事纹元青花器物应该是供应国内市场，而且是上层阶级的，不是为了实用，而是为了欣赏，由此可见元杂剧在上层阶级中也深受喜爱。

元青花故事图的题材源于元杂剧，构图又多与平话插图有关，如元青花上的"鬼谷子下山"（图7、8）与现藏日本国立公文书馆《新刊全相平话乐毅图齐七国春秋后集》中《鬼谷下山》插图（图9）相似，"三顾茅庐"（图10）则与《新刊全相三国志》中的《孔明下山》插图（图11）相似，尤其是主要人物鬼谷子、诸葛亮的形象。其他故事虽然没有同名的平话插图，但是在空间布局、人物造型、景物装饰等方面借鉴了其他题材的平话插图，所以很多人物造型甚是相似。元青花上面这些人物故事图属于典型的演事型图像，着重刻画故事中的某一情节，人物形象生动，动作鲜明，叙事性、视觉审美功能都很突出。

图 7　元青花“鬼谷子下山”图罐

（英国私人藏品，见陈燮君，陈克伦，2012，p. 63）

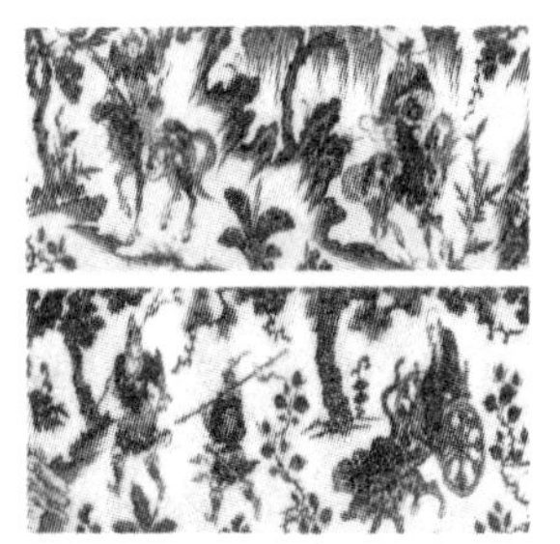

图 8　元青花“鬼谷子下山”图罐展开图

（徐华峰，2016，p. 15）

图 9　《新刊全相平话乐毅图齐七国春秋后集》中《鬼谷下山》插图

（日本国立公文书馆藏）

图 10　元青花“三顾茅庐”图带盖梅瓶

（美国波士顿艺术博物馆藏，见陈燮君，陈克伦，2012，p. 81，p. 80）

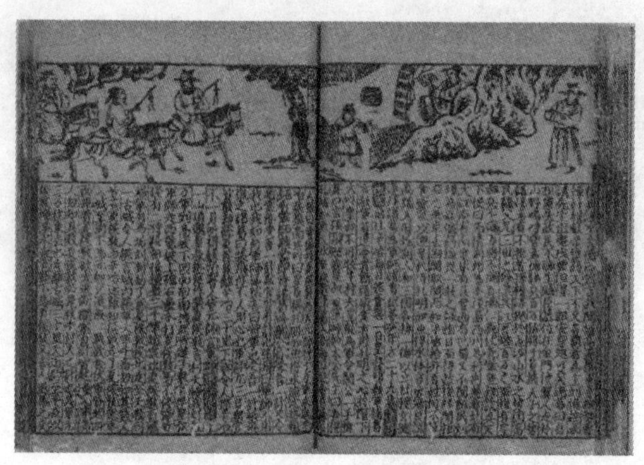

图 11 《新刊全相三国志》中《孔明下山》插图
（日本国立公文书馆藏）

演事型图像在明代陶瓷上的运用是非常广泛的，其中一个重要来源即是小说、戏曲的版画插图。明清两代曾有四次对通俗小说的大规模禁毁，分别是明初、明末、清初和清末，《水浒传》《金瓶梅》《红楼梦》都曾位列其中，导致一些版画插图艺人转入年画、陶瓷等民间绘画行业，不仅提高了民间绘画的水平，而且为民间绘画带来大量的戏曲小说故事。柯律格建议用卡洛·金斯伯格（Carlo Ginzburg）提出的概念——“图像环路”，来描述具象艺术体系中“某种特定图像在涉及图绘的不同媒介之间的流通”（柯律格，2011，p. 32）。他认为在 1400—1700 年（即明代）的中国存在两条环路，“可以假定为它们分别由指示性图像和自我指示性图像所代表，由于后者——现在所谓‘文人画’——在上层文化中取得霸权地位，两者因此渐行渐远。这样前者就被剥夺了话语权，直至叙事性图像成为不能想象、不能书写的对象”（2011，pp. 50 - 52）。明代时，叙事型图像地位低下。明文震亨在《长物志》卷七《器具编·香筒》中说：“旧者有李文甫所制，中雕花鸟竹石，略以古简为贵；若太涉脂粉或雕镂故事人物，便称俗品，亦不必置怀袖间。”（1936，p. 255）香筒上雕镂人物故事画，被视为俗品，可见文人对叙事画的贬抑态度。但喜欢故事是人之天性，远古即然，“故事在远古时代就已经出现，可以追溯到新石器时代以至旧石器时代。从当时尼安得塔尔人的头骨形状，便可判断他已听讲故事了”（傅修延，2018）。明藏书家郎瑛《七修类稿》卷五十《奇谑类·不知画》讽刺了两个不懂得赏画的太守要求画家在画面空白处增加三战吕布、官员出行的故事，若换个角度看，这正反映出人们对故事的喜爱和对故事画的需求。所以，叙事画从文人圈里退出后并没有消失，而是转移到民间器物上。

清代陶瓷上演事型图像继续着明代的繁荣，尤其是刀马人题材，这一方面是受小说戏曲繁荣的影响，如清陈浏在《匋雅》中说："成化万历五彩皆画戏剧之习战斗者，洋商所谓刀马人者也。波谲云诡、牛鬼蛇神，又似宋代法画，一一有故实可指。"又说清代陶瓷"踵事增华，精仿宋元绢画人物故事，几于笔有来源。后之客货推波助澜，圆绘小说、演义，泛滥及于戏剧。虽曰荒唐不经，要其态度俶诡，足以发扬蹈厉，使人忘倦。盖自朱明以来而已然矣"。(2011，p. 35，p. 125) 民国许之衡在《饮流斋说瓷》中说康熙窑"人物故实标新领异，波澜推衍，穷极诙诡，大抵皆导源于小说稗官，然皆与历代丹青画法相结合也。至雍正小品始有绘剧场装者，其须必为挂须，或作小丑状，盘辫于顶"。又说乾隆窑"人物工致绝伦，故事则举汉晋以来暨唐人小说，几于应有尽有。下至《西厢》《三国》《水浒》之伦，亦穷秀极妍，并称佳妙。至末叶乃益曼衍，如水浸金山等不经之事，实亦入绘事。盖争奇斗巧，踵事增华，势必至也。然明末清初已有采取《封神演义》绘千里眼、顺风耳者，则又不自乾隆始矣"。(2005，p. 85，p. 92) 另一方面，受外销瓷的影响。西方人对人物故事极为嗜好，如许之衡所言："绘战争故事者谓之'刀马人'，无论明清瓷器皆极为西人所嗜。至挂刀骑马而非战争者，亦准于刀马人之列也。"(2005，p. 85)。晚明时期，英国曾向中国订购一批青花瓷器，并且对瓷器上的绘画提出了明确要求，希望以人物仕女为主，有故事情节者为佳。景德镇根据这一要求烧制了一批以《西厢记》为题材的瓷器，也因此《西厢记》成为外销瓷上数量最多的故事图题材。《西厢记》故事就此通过瓷器传入西方，而《西厢记》的第一个英译本至 1898 年才出现，且仅有其中一折而已，晚了将近 300 年，如蒋星煜所说："早在明刊本《西厢记》流传到欧洲之前，早在《会真记》、《董西厢》、元杂剧《西厢记》诸书被英译、德译、法译之前，欧洲人早已从青花瓷器的图案上接受并欣赏《西厢记》的故事情节和人物形象了。不言而喻，这一大批青花瓷器为《西厢记》的刊本传入欧洲以及英译、德译、法译起了媒介作用和诱导作用。而这一点，过去无论给中国戏曲史或中外文化交流史上的专家是完全忽略掉的。"(1997，p. 582)

陶瓷上的演事型图像，除了单幅图外，还有连幅图。这与陶瓷图像的独特构图方式"开光"有关。陶瓷图像可以利用多个开光，按时间顺序讲述一个故事，类似于连环画。开光式陶瓷图以《西厢记》故事图最为典型，其构图、工艺之精美令人惊叹（图 12、13[①]）。

图 12 清康熙五彩《西厢记》故事图纹鱼缸

（德国德累斯顿国立瓷器博物馆藏图，见 Liebeskunst，2002）

图 13 清康熙青花《西厢记》故事图纹棒槌瓶

（英国国立维多利亚与艾伯特博物馆藏，见吕申章，2012，p. 365）

日本学者古原宏伸（Kohara Hironobu）将中国手卷和日本手卷进行比较研究，用故事情节来分类，提出了一些关于中国叙事画的观点。孟久丽认为其有些观点存在争议，与他发现的中国例子不充分有关。古原宏伸认为，

① 图 12、13 由倪亦斌先生提供。

"中国的手卷显示了很少的'叙述兴趣'，而且很少一幅接一幅地描绘一个故事的发展，中国画家反而更喜欢（有时候是很长的）单幅画面中以象征手法来表现一个故事，而这是他在日本手卷中没有见过的一种概念性手法"。古原宏伸认为这种根本的差异源于中国人看重儒家道德并且轻视虚构故事以及幻想作品，"因而那些提供情节和娱乐的图画被极大地限制了"。（孟久丽，2014，p. 15）古原宏伸的这些话很适合概括中国文人画的特征。文人画追求的是自我表现，而非再现事件，所以很少绘演事型图像。但是，如果将研究的视野拓展至文人画以外的民间艺术天地，则并非如此，汉画像石、敦煌壁画、小说戏曲版画以及上文所述的陶瓷图像均是另一番风景。

四、结语

以图概型、以图指事与以图演事，反映了图像关涉事件的三种不同的方式和功能，但是这种分类不是绝对的，只能说有所偏重。第一，概事型与指事型、演事型的区别在于所指涉事件是类型事件还是个别事件，但叙事图像作为一种符号，是个别符还是类型符，从根本上说，并不取决于符号本身，而是取决于解释者，如赵毅衡所言："符号本身不可能决定对象是个别符或类型符，符号只可能被解释出'个别性'或'类型性'，取决于接收者个人以及语境。"（2012，p. 117）比如前述漆盒上的林逋故事，对于了解这个故事的接收者来说，它是个别符，但对于不了解这个故事的来说，则可能认为是类型符——表现高士、隐士的图像，如英国博物馆出版的书籍上对它的介绍即是："一位智者及其仆从，坐在亭子外的平台看鸟飞过。"（柯律格，2011，p. 43）第二，指事型与演事型所关涉的事件都是具体的，区别在于图像所表现出的事件信息的多寡、场景的逼真程度，但这种区别也是相对的，是在比较中实现的，本身并没有客观标准，比如以下这四幅"昭君出塞"故事图（图 14—17），第一幅比较详细地展现了出塞场景，人物形象、送别氛围更真实，图像本身即具有较高的审美价值；另外三幅场景简化，只用一些标志物，比如骑马抱琵琶、关于明妃的诗文等表明这是《昭君出塞》的故事；其中有一幅风格戏谑化，借事抒怀的意图很明显。

图 14　元青花《昭君出塞》图纹罐（安徽博物馆，2009）

图 15　元青花人物纹高足杯
（钟健华，陈雨前，2016，p. 225）

图 16　清青花人物纹瓷砖
（中国嘉德四季 2007 年第 12 期拍卖会第 2850 号拍品）

图 17　清雍正“昭君和亲”图纹碟（铁源，2001，p. 177）

因此，图像叙事类型的判断会出现见仁见智的现象，而不同的判断又会带来对图像的社会历史文化意义不同的阐释。比如中国美术史上的著名绘画题材“袁安卧雪”。据史载，宋代进士丁谓去金陵上任之前到宫中向宋真宗辞别，宋真宗赏赐给他一幅题为《袁安卧雪》的画。（1986，p. 334）宋真宗是将其看作指事型图像，借卧雪之事抒发对袁安高风亮节的赞赏，同时也借此激励丁谓。这个意图的实现，是建立在宋真宗和丁谓对这幅画的类型和功能的相同判断上。这幅画在一些博物馆收藏中多被题为“冬季山水”[①]，如此，则它的意义就完全不同了。所以，作者进行图像叙事时，要根据不同目的选择图像叙事类型，接收者也只有在图像叙事类型认知上与作者达成一致，才能更好地领会作者意图，实现图像的社会价值和文化价值。

引用文献：

安徽博物馆编（2009）. 元瓷之珍. 北京：文物出版社.

陈浏（2011）. 匋雅. 北京：金城出版社.

博厄斯，弗朗兹（1980）. 原始艺术（金辉，译）. 上海：上海文艺出版社.

陈平原（2008）. 左图右史与西学东渐——晚清画报研究. 香港：三联书店.

陈平原（2017）. 追摹、混搭与超越：晚晴画报中的古今对话. 岭南学报，2，19－44.

陈燮君，陈克伦（2012）. 幽蓝神采：元代青花瓷器特集. 上海：上海书画出版社.

邓巴，罗宾（2016）. 人类的演化（余彬，译）. 上海：上海文艺出版社.

邓巴，罗宾（2017）. 梳毛、八卦及语言的进化（张杰，区沛仪，译）. 北京：现代出版社.

董乃斌（1991）. 中国古典小说的文体独立. 北京：中国社会科学出版社.

傅修延（2018）. 人类为什么要讲故事——从群体维系角度看叙事的功能与本质，天津社会科学，4，114－127.

蒋星煜（1997）. 西厢记的文献学研究. 上海：上海古籍出版社.

胡适（2013）. 胡适古典文学研究论集（下）. 上海：上海古籍出版社.

柯律格（2011）. 明代的图像与视觉性（黄晓鹃，译）. 北京：北京大学出版社.

柯律格（2019）. 长物：早期现代中国的物质文化与社会状况（高昕丹，陈恒，译）. 北京：生活·读书·新知三联书店.

吕申章（2012）. 瓷之韵：大英博物馆、英国国立维多利亚与艾伯特博物馆藏瓷精品. 北京：中华书局.

孟久丽（2014）. 道德镜鉴：中国叙述性图画与儒家意识形态. 北京：生活·读书·新知

① 研究中国艺术史的美国学者班宗华（Richard Barnhart）及其合作者抢救恢复了一大批非文人画作品，其中有一批相当数量的“袁安卧雪”图，但在博物馆收藏中多被题为“冬季山水”。（柯律格，2011，p. 52）

三联书店．
杉山正明（2016）．蒙古颠覆世界史（周俊宇，译）．北京：生活·读书·新知三联书店．
铁源（2001）．明清瓷器纹饰鉴定（人物纹饰卷）．北京：华龄出版社．
文震亨（1936）．《长物志》（卷五）．北京：商务印书馆．
汪庆正（1999）．中国陶瓷全集（清，下册）．上海：上海人民美术出版社．
巫鸿（2015）．武梁祠——中国古代艺术的思想性．北京：生活·读书·新知三联书店．
许之衡（2005）．《饮流斋说瓷》译注（叶喆民，译注）．北京：紫禁城出版社．
徐华烽（2016）．元青花人物故事器物的艺术渊源及相关问题．故宫学刊，1，8－20.
张子英（2000）．磁州窑瓷枕．北京：人民美术出版社．
赵毅衡（2012）．符号学：原理与推演．南京：南京大学出版社．
赵毅衡（2013）．广义叙述学．成都：四川大学出版社．
钟健华，陈雨前（2016）．景德镇陶瓷史（卷二）．南昌：江西人民出版社，
Cheney, D. L., Seyfarth, R. M., Silk, J. B. (1995). The role of grunts in reconciling opponents and facilitating interactions among adult female baboons. *Animal behaviour*, 50, 249－257.
Liebeskunst (2002). Liebeskunst und Liebesleid in the Weltkunsk. Museum Rietberg Zurichu.

作者简介：

倪爱珍，文学博士，研究员，江西省社会科学院文学研究所所长，重点学科“中国叙事学”带头人，博士后科研工作站导师，主要研究方向为叙事学、符号学。

Author:

Ni Aizhen, Ph. D., researcher, director of Literature Research Institute of Jiangxi Academy of Social Sciences, leader of key subject “Chinese narratology”, instructor of postdoctoral research station, majoring in narratologies & semiotics.

Email: niaizhen1976@163.com

再论“双层区隔”：虚构、纪实的性质与判断困境[*]

王长才

摘　要：本文对于由赵毅衡先生提出、谭光辉教授进一步阐发的“双层区隔”论，从“双层区隔”作为辨识标准还是性质规定、二度区隔的“进一步再现”的性质、二度区隔是否虚构所独有、虚构区隔框架与人格－框架二元叙述者是否合一、虚构框架是客观存在还是主观认定等方面进行了再讨论，并认为建立在模仿叙述基础之上的“双层区隔”论在处理非自然叙述（反模仿的虚构叙述）时可能会遇到挑战。本文建议从修辞交流的理想情况及非理想情况的不同层面讨论虚构、纪实问题，进而以影射作品、戏拟文本、戏剧表演等较复杂情况讨论了虚构、纪实的判断困境。

关键词：双层区隔，虚构，纪实，非自然叙述，阐释漩涡

Revisiting the “Double Framing” Principle: The Nature of Fictional and Factual Narrative and the Judgemental Dilemma

Wang Changcai

Abstract: This paper revisits the “double framing” principle, a theory proposed by Mr Zhao Yiheng and further developed by Tan Guanghui, and discusses the following questions: Is the “double framing” principle an identifying criterion or a kind of characterisation? What is the

* 本文为国家社科基金项目“非自然叙述学研究”（16BZW013）的阶段性成果。

nature of secondary segregation? Is secondary segregation peculiar to fictional narrative? Is the fictional separation in the same frame as the personality-frame binary narrator? Is the fictional frame objective or subjective? This paper holds that the "double framing" principle, based on mimetic narratives, seems to face challenges when dealing with unnatural narratives (anti-mimetic fictional narratives). Therefore, this paper suggests that fictional and factual issues should be examined at different levels of ideal and non-ideal rhetorical communication situations, and discusses the dilemma of judging fictional and factual narratives in more complex situations, such as insinuative texts, parody texts and performances.

Keywords: the "double framing" principle, fictional narrative, factual narrative, unnatural narrative, interpretive vortex

DOI: 10. 13760/b. cnki. sam. 202002015

“双层区隔”（二度区隔、双区隔）是赵毅衡先生提出的区分纪实叙述和虚构叙述的理论，认为一度区隔用媒介化把再现与经验分开，二度区隔把虚构叙述与纪实再现区分开来。一旦因某种原因忽视区隔，虚构世界就会被当作“真实”。这种别开生面的解释在学界引起了较大反响，笔者在对《广义叙述学》的书评中对此进行了讨论，认为“双层区隔”理论将虚构解释为“叙述者与接收者都遵循的表意－解释模式”“一种体裁规范”（2015），引入作者与读者相互作用的两极，相对于以作者意图、指称或者风格作为衡量虚构与否的根据，具有了动态性及更多的包容性；另外，也可以很好地解释为何读者会将虚构作品视为纪实性的：读者只要搁置了二度区隔的框架，就到了一度区隔的再现区隔框架之中。但笔者对再度媒介化（二度区隔）和一度媒介化（一度区隔）是否有质的不同，为何经过二度区隔后纪实叙述就变成了虚构叙述，以及作为虚构的区隔框架和叙述者框架是否能够同一等问题提出了疑问。谭光辉教授《论虚构叙述的“双层区隔”原则》《再论虚构叙述的“双层区隔”原理》等文章也对“双层区隔”原则进行了进一步讨论，尤其后者是一篇厚重的长文，对笔者的一些疑问做出了有力的回应，在很多方面都加深了笔者对“双层区隔”原则的理解。但虚构与纪实的问题仍未能穷尽，因而本文继续探讨这一话题，希望得到赵毅衡先生和谭光辉教授的指正。

一

“双层区隔”原则引起的最大困惑，或许就在于如何在具体情境中作为标准对于虚构和纪实做出准确的判断。

在赵毅衡先生最初的表述中，此框架为“可能比较抽象、但可能更合理的判别标准”（2014，p. 140），观众或读者对程式化的虚构叙述区隔的识辨，可靠得多（p. 143）。但笔者认为观众或读者可能是先有了对文化程式的认定，才去寻找双层区隔（王长才，2015，pp. 154－156）。谭光辉教授也产生了和笔者同样的困惑，对其可操作性提出了疑问（谭光辉，2015，p. 110），而在《再论虚构叙述的“双层区隔”原理》中解决了这一疑问。从题目上的微妙变化也可以看出来：将原来表述中应用于实践判断的双层区隔“原则”改为“原理”，从具体情境中抽离出来，成为对虚构与纪实区分的一种抽象的描述：

> 基础学科主要回答的问题是“是什么”和“为什么”，应用学科要回答的问题是“怎么办”，如何区分纪实与虚构，是“怎么办”的问题。而《广义叙述学》的核心任务是回答虚构是什么，为什么虚构需要区隔。怎么区分纪实与虚构，是一个应用型问题。（谭光辉，2017，p. 102）

这的确是一个重要的调整，不再将这个概念的规定性应用于实践，将最容易引起质疑的部分切割出去，解决了二度区隔在具体情境中难以确定的问题。但这似乎与赵毅衡先生最初的观点有些出入。

我们暂且不去考虑应用性问题，仅在基础学科讨论“是什么”和“为什么”的意义上，对“双层区隔”进行再一步探讨。

二

关于二度区隔的另一关键问题，也是较难理解之处是：为何虚构框架必然建立在纪实基础之上，或者说二度媒介化构成虚构的“进一步再现”，这和第一次建立在经验基础上的纪实叙述是否是同一性质？如果是同一性质，如何能说明两次再现就一定构成虚构？

按照谭光辉教授的说法，可以将小说看作对作者在创作阶段想象世界的实录，因而所有小说就都成了纪实体裁（2015，p. 108）。他似乎也接受了第二层区隔也是再现区隔的看法。在这样的理解中，如何将在作家头脑中的“创作阶段想象世界”进行双层区隔呢？想象和虚构的关系到底怎样呢？

的确，所有文本，包括虚构叙述和纪实叙述，都是符号文本。因此，谭光辉教授所说“任何虚构文本，必然首先是一个符号文本。没有符号文本就不可能有虚构”，是没错的。但是这个前提并不能推出“二度区隔必然先经历了一度区隔”（2017，p. 99）这一结论。谭光辉教授认为：“一度区隔中的叙述来源于感知……是符号文本与经验事实之间的区隔……二度区隔中的叙述来源于想象……没有感知就不可能有想象，没有纪实就不可能有虚构，没有一度区隔就不可能有二度区隔。”（2017，p. 99）从普遍意义上谈，先有感知，才有可能存在建立在感知经验之上的想象，纪实叙述的出现早于虚构叙述，这没错。作为虚构文本构成要素的符号是基于人类在漫长进化过程中对事实的感知而形成的，也没错。但为什么某一个具体虚构叙述就是再区隔一次的纪实叙述呢？为什么这个符号文本不能直接虚构呢？如果二度区隔的原理能够确立，至少要说明每一个虚构文本都建立在某个纪实文本之上，由它经过再次区隔形成，且两次区隔必然使得纪实变成虚构。但这个纪实的基础何以存在？为何经历两次区隔之后文本的性质就发生了变化？这些问题似乎仍然没有得到解决。

“二度区隔是否虚构所独有”这一问题也值得讨论。在赵毅衡先生的最初表述中，二度区隔是虚构叙述的本质属性。笔者在书评中提出了照相时区隔了多次的文本仍是纪实叙述的例子。谭光辉教授对此做了修正，认为算命、拍照等虽有二度区隔，却是纪实，这说明“虚构约定”才是问题的关键之所在（2017，p. 101）。他认为多度区隔的确存在，但是对于认识区隔中的实在性问题，再多的区隔也没有意义，因此在讨论虚构问题时最终只能简化为双层区隔。（2017，p. 104）

谭光辉教授在此强调“虚构约定”而非二度区隔是问题的关键，似乎是要指出，二度区隔是虚构叙述的必要条件，但不是充分必要条件。那么，我们要追问的是：纪实的二度区隔和虚构的二度区隔的区别又在哪里？如果纪实叙述也可以是二度区隔，那么它和纪实的一度区隔又有什么样的关联？这些困惑似乎仍然没有消除。

“虚构区隔框架与人格 - 框架二元叙述者是否合一”也是值得讨论的问题。按照赵毅衡先生对于广义叙述者的描述，它具有人格 - 框架二元的性质，在不同的叙述实践中，人格与框架处于此消彼长之中。当叙述由多种媒介呈现出来，有多种表意来源，而有些并不能确认人格叙述者时，可以将叙述者归于这个框架。这一点很精彩地解决了戏剧、影视等叙述者不明确的文本如何解释的问题。

但这个“人格－框架”和“纪实－虚构”意义上的区隔结合在一起时，又令笔者心生困惑。谭光辉教授肯定了“这两个框架从不同的角度看并不是一回事”，但又强调叙述者框架与“纪实－虚构”框架的重合：“叙述者本身既是一度区隔内的内容，又构成了二度区隔的边框。”（2017，p. 101）这个表述和赵毅衡先生的“人格－框架”二元的表述似乎也有出入。

在笔者看来，叙述者的情况可以和纪实与虚构无关，纪实叙述与虚构叙述的叙述者的形态在本人看来并不一定具有差异性。比如，同样是第一人称叙述，可以是自传，也可是第一人称的小说。因而，这个叙述者框架与虚构框架似乎并不能合而为一。将不同视角所观察到的现象归并在一起，这又使得问题变得复杂，容易产生混乱。

另外，在赵毅衡先生看来，这个叙述者人格是从作者自身分裂出来的。但在笔者看来，叙述者和作者的分别在于一个是文本中的，一个是现实中的，二者在立场上可能一致，但也可能不一致，这是讨论不可靠叙述的前提。因此，不必强调这个人格是从作者自身分出的。

可能“双层区隔”原理遇到的最大的挑战是如何解释反模仿叙述的问题。“双层区隔”最精彩的地方就在于解释虚构在什么意义上是“真实的”。赵毅衡先生认为：“虚构叙述之所以可能，就是因为在虚构框架之内，它是纪实性的，否则被叙述世界中的受述者，没有理由接收这个叙述。”（2014，p. 142）“无论何种区隔内的叙述文本，其底线的‘纪实’品格，为这种认知接收心理效果提供了基础。”（2013，p. 86）由此可见，赵毅衡先生认为，虚构是建立在纪实基础之上的，这也是双层区隔论的立论基础。显然这与其旨在建立统一的、整合全部叙述的广义叙述学理论框架是一致的。在《广义叙述学》开篇的“叙述体裁基本分类”表格中，虚构与事实是重要的分类依据，但他更多的是强调纪实性叙述与虚构性叙述的关联，而这一原理在处理非自然叙述时则可能会遇到挑战。

非自然叙述理论是近年来西方叙述学界兴起的后经典叙述学中引起较大反响的分支，美国学者布莱恩·理查森（Brian Richardson）是最为重要的代表之一。他认为经典叙述学理论存在着缺陷和不足，原因在于经典叙述学基于主流叙述即模仿性叙述，意在建立适用于主流叙述的叙述诗学，而非自然叙述因其不同于模仿性主流叙述的特性，被有意无意地忽视或排斥，因而经典叙述学的理论框架和概念体系是不完整的，故而理查森致力于补正已有叙述学理论，大力倡导“超越模仿模式”，推动对非自然叙述的研究。理查森对非自然叙述的界定是与模仿叙述、非模仿叙述相区别的反模仿叙述。模仿叙述是指非虚构叙述或效仿非虚构叙述的现实主义叙述；非模仿叙述是在模仿叙述基础上增加了一些现实中不存在的要素的叙述，如童话、幻想故事等；反模仿叙述则是违背模仿框架的叙述（Richardson，2015；理查森，2019），比如消解叙述（denarration，指文中出现矛盾且无法消除的叙述）、跨层叙述（metalepsis，又译作“叙述转喻”，指一个叙述层次中的人物进入另一叙述层次从而造成混乱）、可选择叙述（叙述为读者提供一系列可选项，故事和叙述话语都是多线索和可变的）等。这种有意破除模仿框架的非自然叙述，通常被视为虚构叙述的一个子集。按照二度区隔的规定，我们搁置了二度区隔，会将虚构叙述视为一度区隔纪实叙述。但这种特别的反模仿叙述的虚构性质恰恰来自对模仿框架的破坏，是依据不能按照纪实方式去理解而得到确认的。按照二度区隔的规定性以及非自然叙述的界定，二者显然不能兼容。理查森还仔细讨论了一系列特意模糊或颠覆虚构与非虚构之间界限的非自然叙述，诸如自传体小说（autofiction）、复合虚构文本（unfictional text，同一文本既作为纪实文本又作为虚构文本出版，比如纳博科夫的短篇小说《O 小姐》后来成为其回忆录《说吧，记忆》的第 5 章）等（Richandson，2015，pp. 67 - 88）。这些叙述中的区隔框架显然也不好确认。

关于虚构框架的性质也同样值得思考。如果我们将“双层区隔”当作对虚构叙述的本质性描述，那么，这种“双层区隔”是附着于文本自身的客观存在呢，还是基于发送者和接收者的主观认定呢？谭光辉教授此前称：“当我们看到了区隔框架时，我们就知道它是虚构。但是如果文本没有区隔框架，或者伪装区隔框架，就需要接收者的解释。”（2015，p. 110）这段话仍在纠结于“双层区隔”的可操作性，也值得推敲：这个区隔框架是客观存在吗？“如果文本没有区隔框架”似乎意味着区隔框架理应是文本的一部分，但是否存在“没有区隔框架”的文本？如果存在着“伪装区隔框架”，我们又如何能做到“看到区隔框架，我们就知道它是虚构”呢？接收者的解释是否会解释出区隔框架来？这种被解释出来的区隔框架是否能被认为是文本中存在的？赵毅衡先生认为：“神话现在被认为是虚构体裁，其基本叙述方式划出了虚构区隔，但对于产生神话时代的人们，口述的神话是历史，写下的神话也是历史。它们当时不可能看出神话的虚构框架。”（2014，p. 142）对于同一个文本，当时看不出虚构框架被视为历史，现在看出了虚构框架就被视为神话，那么虚构框架是否是一种客观存在？而另一种对一度区隔的描述，也同样令人困惑："'一度框架'可以看作一种意向性，它迫使我们按照朝向经验事实的方向理解。一度区隔内的符号文本再现，是符号学、现象学研究的起点和基础。"（谭光辉，2017，p. 99）在此，谭光辉教授又将区隔框架看作了意向性，也就是从叙述文本自身的属性转移到了接受主体之上。那么，到底是意向性确认框架还是由框架产生意向性？这两种立场似乎并不能整合为一。由上述讨论可以看出，尽管"双层区隔"理论产生了较大影响，但似乎还存在着概念上的含混之处。

三

为什么虚构问题如此复杂，以致争论不休？关键问题可能在于，虚构和纪实的分野到底何在。要准确无误地辨认出虚构和纪实的确是比较困难的，主要表现在，同一个文本可能会被不同主体认为是虚构或纪实，也有可能因为语境的变化被同一主体分别认定为虚构或纪实。甚至在理论上，对任何一个文本的接收都可能存在认定为虚构还是纪实的问题，只是有一些文本按照另一个框架解释更为牵强而已。

理想状态中，发送者将虚构或纪实的意愿表现于文本中，接收者明确辨认并按此框架加以理解。但在实际情况中，可能会出现发送者意愿与接收者解释框架的错位，从而使叙述交流情况变得很复杂，见以下示意图：

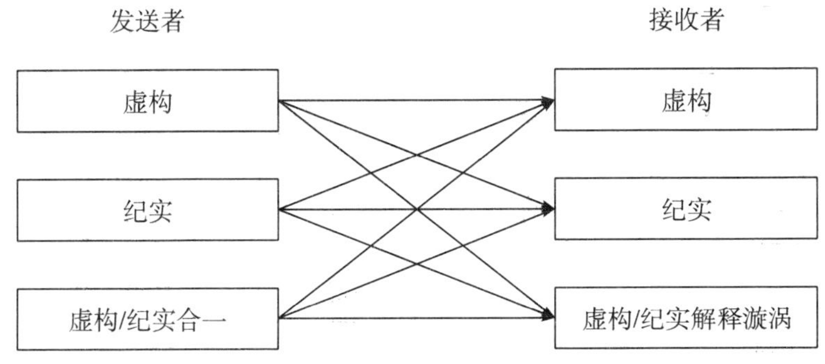

发送者意愿与接收者解释框架的关系

在笔者看来，从发送者意愿方面可以分为三种叙述：虚构、纪实、虚构/纪实合一。前两种常见，第三种指故意混淆虚构与纪实之间的界限，以面对不同接收者，但会偏向某一方。虚构/纪实合一的情况又可以分为以纪实为表象的虚构和以虚构为表象的纪实。在以纪实为表象的虚构中，纪实是达到特定虚构效果的手法和策略。比如《女巫布莱尔》等纪录片风格的恐怖片用纪实的真实感加剧了恐怖效果；新垣平的《剑桥倚天屠龙史》表面上是严肃的历史（非虚构的学术著作），但所写内容来自金庸虚构的小说。在以虚构为表象的纪实中，虚构是为达到更为生动的效果，有时虚构是规避纪实风险的手段，比如历史剧、传记小说、报告文学、影射作品等。

与之相应的，接收者也可以将其接收为虚构、纪实、虚构/纪实同在的“阐释漩涡”（借用赵毅衡先生的术语）。接收者甚至可以否认发送者的（表面）意愿，并将自己的解释归于作者的（真实）意愿，从而强行完成一次叙述交流。在非理想状态中，接收者的判断和发送者的意愿之间会出现错位，这也是现实生活中常见的情形。比如以下例子：

> 9·11 事件时，美国五角大楼起火，焚毁了许多文件。普京对布什表示，可以用俄罗斯拥有的复制件来弥补美国的这部分损失。（转引自徐贲，2018）

理想交流情形中，它会被认定为虚构，是一则笑话，并非实际发生，发送者、接收者都明白这是以夸张、戏谑的方式说明俄罗斯黑客盗取美国情报的情况。在非理想交流情形中，有两种可能：

第一，接收者认定它是纪实，又有两种可能：（a）认定它是真实记载；（b）认定它是谣言，虚假的纪实；

第二，虚构或纪实无从判断，从而陷入或虚构或纪实的阐释漩涡。

由此可见，仅仅从文本进行判断，似乎无法解决纷争，必须考虑到相关指涉以及具体交流过程才能做出判断。

对于戏剧演出、电影等演示性叙述，出现虚构/纪实的阐释漩涡是常见现象。演员和角色是一体的，关键是观众如何接受。正如加拿大学者安德烈·戈德罗指出，任何影片都同时采用虚构和纪实两种体制，“它们既要求‘任何影片都是一种虚构的影片’（麦茨），又要求‘任何虚构的影片……可以从某种观点看作为纪录片’。事实上，观众的解读工作才使一种体制比另一种体制显得更突出”（戈德罗，2005，pp. 38 – 39）。谭光辉教授曾以《快乐大本营》中主持人何炅着古装主持的例子，强调同一个文本中可能内含多种不同层次的区隔，判断纪实与虚构要不断转换视点（2017，p. 104）。在笔者看来，何炅扮演古人主持节目，既不单纯作为古人说话，也不单纯作为主持人说话，和通常虚构与纪实泾渭分明的情况不同的是，我们会时刻意识到这是何炅扮演的古人。这似乎可以是虚构/纪实同时存在并导致阐释漩涡的一个例证。更为典型的情况是有些喜剧演员在扮演古代角色时，故意说出当下的流行语或演员自己的口头禅，奇怪的是，观众不会将其视为穿帮，这样的表演不会引起反感，反而有很好的喜剧效果。为什么会这样？原因或许在于观众很自然地接受了虚构和纪实二合一的接受框架。

此外，在虚构和纪实框架中，都可能出现违规现象，也即在整体的虚构框架中出现局部的纪实，或相反，比如故事片中直接采用历史文献影像。虚构作品中出现纪实片段，通常容易接受，因为很多虚构本身取材于现实，但在纪实作品中出现与事实不符的情况时，有时并不能因此而称它不是纪实而是虚构，只能在接受其纪实性质的前提下判其违规。比如，我们面对《史记》等史书中记载密谋等情形，BBC 纪录片摆拍等，通常会接受它的纪实体裁的规定，认为它弄虚作假，但不是虚构。同样，对于预言、算命，不信者认为它是骗人，是谎言，但不会说它是虚构。

结　语

谭光辉教授将“双层区隔”归于基础学科而非应用学科的范畴，将其内涵从一种可以应用于实践判断的原则变为对虚构叙述与纪实叙述区分的一种抽象性质的描述，使它摆脱了在具体判断中可操作性不足的问题，但这可能与赵毅衡先生的初衷不同。而且，即使将“双层区隔”归于抽象的性质规定，似乎仍有一些可探讨的问题。比如，二度区隔是虚构叙述的必要条件，但不是充分必要条件，纪实叙述中也存在二度区隔，那么纪实的二度区隔和虚构的二度区隔有何区别，以及纪实的二度区隔和纪实的一度区隔之间又有何关联与区别？二度区隔的性质和一度区隔一样也是纪实性的，建立在想象基础上的虚构叙述应以建立在经验上的纪实叙述为基础，但某一作为虚构叙述的二度区隔为何就是再区隔一次的某一纪实叙述？将虚构区隔框架与“人格－框架”二元叙述者这两个从不同视角所观察到的现象归并在一起，又使得问题变得复杂了，而在处理非自然叙述这种特殊的虚构叙述时，“双层区隔”原理似乎也面临挑战。

对于“虚构”或“纪实”的判断困境，笔者认为应该在具体修辞交流语境中进行理解，从发送者和接收者两个维度进行讨论，并且需要考虑叙述交流的理想状态与非理想状态的差异以及在不同框架中违规与否的问题。

引用文献：

戈德罗，安德烈（2005）. 什么是电影叙事学（刘云舟，译）. 北京：商务印书馆.

理查森，布莱恩（2019）. 非自然叙述学概要（王长才，译）. 英语研究，1，154 - 164.

谭光辉（2015）. 论虚构叙述的“双层区隔”原则. 河北学刊，1，107 - 110.

谭光辉（2017）. 再论虚构叙述的“双层区隔”原理——对王长才与赵毅衡商榷的再理解. 南昌大学学报（人文社会科学版），2，97 - 105.

王长才（2015）. 梳理与商榷——评赵毅衡《广义叙述学》. 文艺研究，7，151 - 160.

徐贲（2018 - 03 - 22）. 普京时代的政治笑话. 获取自 http：//www. sohu. com/a/226100901_120776.

赵毅衡（2013）. 广义叙述学. 成都：四川大学出版社.

赵毅衡（2014）. 论虚构叙述的“双区隔”原则. 外国文学研究，2，136 - 144.

Richardson, B. (2015). *Unnatural narrative: Theory, history, and practice*. Columbus: The Ohio State University Press.

作者简介：

王长才，西南交通大学人文学院中文系教授，主要从事叙述学研究。

Author:

Wang Changcai, professor in the Department of Chinese Language and Literature, School of Humanities at Southwest Jiaotong University. He mainly engages in research on narratology.

Email: Wang_changcai@163. com

一般叙述学视野中的叙述定义：与赵毅衡先生商榷

伏飞雄　李明芮

摘　要：赵毅衡先生近年来从符号叙述学视域对叙述所下的定义，极大克服了其他叙述定义的局限，能涵盖尽可能多的叙述类型。但他对叙述类型的判断与解释有时与其定义本身发生矛盾。这主要表现在他对想象与回忆是不是叙述、直接经验与符号文本之间如何区隔的讨论上。现象学对相关问题所做的静态分析与纯粹逻辑层次划分，不能直接运用到上述问题的讨论中。日常生活中的主体对事件的想象与回忆属于叙述，其叙述具有主体自我交流的性质。这说明，"二次叙述"（潜在）预设不同叙述主体具有局限性。另外，叙述还可拓展到日常生活中所发生的处于人们广义交流状态的事件等类型上。

关键词：一般叙述学，叙述，自我叙述交流，日常生活叙述

Definition of Narrative from the Perspective of General Narratology: Discussion with Mr Zhao Yiheng

Fu Feixiong　Li Mingrui

Abstract: In recent years, Mr Zhao Yiheng's definition of narrative from the perspective of general narratology has, to a great extent, overcome the limitations of other definitions to cover as many types of narrative as possible. However, his judgement and interpretation of narrative types sometimes disagree with his own definition. This is mainly reflected in his discussions of two aspects: i. e. Are imagination and memory narrative? And what is the distinction between direct experience and sign texts? The static analysis and pure logic division in phenomenology cannot be directly applied to the discussion of the above problems. In daily life, the subject's imagination and recollection of events should belong to narrative and be considered types of self-communication. As this illustrates, the concept of a "secondary narrative" presupposes that different narrative subjects have limitations. In addition, narrative can be extended to events in daily life that are the subject of widespread communication between people.

Keywords: general narratology, narrative, self-narrative communication, daily life narrative

DOI: 10.13760/b.cnki.sam.202002016

叙述的定义要能涵盖所有的叙述类型，这一直是西方现代叙述学的理想，只是由于西方经典叙述学、后经典叙述学（即"多种叙述学"）两个阶段的理论范式、框架与批评实践的局限，未能真正达成这个目标。所谓"多种叙述学"，其实就是一个"大拼盘"。一方面，它并不固守经典叙述学的结构主义语言学范式、形式论立场，不仅吸纳了其他西方文论思潮，而且吸纳了整个人文社会学科"叙述转向"的诸多成果，引入了新的认识论、方法论。但另一方面，这个时期的理论家主要还是从事"门类叙述学"的研究，要么修正经典叙述学的明显局限，要么试图建构新的理论模式，但总体上并未根本突破"文学叙述学"甚至"小说叙述学"的疆界。而且，他们在对待西方"叙述转向"的成果上，都存在不同程度的暧昧态度。因此，他们无法为各门类叙述学、各种叙述类型提供一套有效、通用的理论框架，一套方法论，一套通用的术语。

与前两个阶段不同，"一般叙述学"的出发点，就是建立一个能解释所有叙述类型的一般叙述理论。这是它不同于"多种叙述学"的根本方面。正因为如此，可把它视为现代叙述学发展历程中一个新的阶段，即第三阶段。这种理解，当然不同于赫尔曼、费伦等西方理论家对现代叙述学历史发展阶段的划分。以戴维·赫尔曼为代表的西方当代主流叙述学界，把自20世纪60年代以来的西方现代叙述学划分为"经典叙述学"与"多种叙述学"两个阶段（Herman，1999，pp. 1－30）。费伦则倾向于把西方现代叙述理论的演变划分为三种形态，也就是他所说的三个不同的"主角"，即"作为形式系统的叙述”“作为意识形态工具的叙述”“作为修辞的叙述”（Scholes & Phelan，2006，pp. 286 - 301）。他并没有明确把这种划分看成三个阶段，但至少包括他自己在内的不少学者，都把“作为修辞的叙述”视为代表现代叙述学新阶段的理论形态。

一般叙述学，主要由中国学者开启与推动，发端于21世纪第一个十年，持续至今。从当代全球叙述实践与理论演变的内在逻辑来说，它会是未来一个时期叙述理论研究的一种主要模式。

一、一般叙述学叙述定义回顾与分析

至少对汉语学术界一般叙述理论研究来说，赵毅衡先生是其最早、最主要的开拓者。2008年，他首次从“广义叙述学”（即一般叙述学）视野出发提出了叙述的“最简定义”，认为只要满足以下两个条件的“思维或言语行为”，就是叙述：其一，“叙述主体把人物参与的事件组织进一个符号链”；其二，“这个符号链可以被接受主体理解为具有内在的时间和意义向度”（赵毅衡，2008，pp. 30 -41）。这个定义，明显不同于其他叙述理论的地方，在于它的理论视野已经扩大到了远比叙述学广阔的符号学。这也算是回到了现代叙述学初创时期以格雷马斯等为代表的西方符号叙述学家的理论初心。格雷马斯一开始就倡导从普通符号学层面研究“符号系统如何以叙述方式来表达意义”，并试图建立适用于不同叙述种类的叙述模型，他尤其强调普通符号学先于语言学，认为“叙述结构模型属于符号学总体经济内部的自主机制”，它的“普遍性完全由其符号语言属性得以保证”，认为“没有完整的符号学理论，就很难建立一套公理系统来支撑叙述结构”。（格雷马斯，2005，pp. 165 -170）。罗兰·巴尔特尤为强调叙述模型对不同符号叙述类型研究的重要性，强调叙述分析之演绎逻辑的必要性（Barthes，1977，pp. 81 - 82）。但是，正如前文所说，他们的结构主义语言学范式，基本以小说作为其理论的试金石或批评对象，在文本内以形式论的立场讨论叙述语法、叙述技巧等的局限，这使他们无法完成宏愿。赵先生的这个定义中“思维或言语行为”这个限定表明，叙述或者是一种语言文字的行为，或者是一种思维行为。所谓思维性的叙述行为，在作者那里主要指心灵媒介类型的叙述体裁，比如白日梦、错觉、幻觉等。这类叙述体裁是思维性的，但不一定经过语言媒介。这一点明显是对现代叙述学狭隘研究范围的突破，即没有局限于口语叙述，尤其是文字书面叙述。思维可以不经过语言，已是当代学界共识。语言学家萨丕尔就指出，“语言和思维不是严格同义的”（萨丕尔，1985，p. 13），现象学家梅洛－庞蒂也强调，“思维并非语言的一个结果”（Merleau-Ponty，2012，p. 198）。

2013 年，赵毅衡先生对这个定义做了两个小改动。第一个小改动，是把“符号链”修改为“符号文本”，即认为“一个叙述文本包含由特定主体进行的两个叙述化过程：1. 某个主体把有人物参与的事件组织进一个符号文本中；2. 此文本可以被接收者理解为具有时间和意义向度”（赵毅衡，2013a，p. 7）。这个小改动，是其符号学理论进一步成熟的结果。“符号链”只表示符号之间的联结，而“符号文本”则表明，它不是符号的任意联结，而是构成一个符号组合，构成一个“合一表意单元”（赵毅衡，2012，p. 41）。另一个小改动，是删除了 2008 年那个定义之“思维或言语行为”这个限定，使叙述范围进一步扩大与明确，即所有叙述性的“符号文本”。无论如何，“思维”一词总是指意模糊。况且，“言语行为”也多少有退回到过去叙述定义狭窄范围的嫌疑。这个“最简叙述定义”，是其“最简符号定义”——“一些符号组织进一个文本中，此符号文本可以被接收者理解为具有时间和意义向度”（p. 43）——的推演式细分。

2014 年，作者对这个定义又做了一点修改：“只要满足以下两个条件的符号文本，就是叙述，它包含两个‘叙述化’过程：1. 有人物参与的变化，即情节，被组织进一个符号组合；2. 此符号组合可以被接收者理解为具有时间和意义向度。”（赵毅衡，2014，pp. 121－127）相对于 2013 年那个定义，该定义强调：这个符号文本必须有能体现时间或事态变化的情节，因为“情节既是叙述文本符号组合方式的特点，也是叙述文本的接受理解方式”。鉴于作者对这个定义所涉及的基本因素都做了较为详细的解释，这里只从笔者所关注的维度做一些不算多余的补充解释。首先，这个定义突出了情节之于叙述的本质规定性，进一步把叙述明确为“卷入人物的情节”的广义符号叙述文本。其次，卷入人物的情节即故事还要求：所述故事或事件必须是有人物参与的事件，至少是有人格化的角色参与的事件。这一点，格雷马斯早在经典叙述学开创时期就强调过。他在对叙述进程所做的形式化描述中，已经明确提出了形象形式，即行为者角色，必须是人或人格化（拟人化）的角色（格雷马斯，2005，p. 406）。对此，他稍早时间所著《结构语义学》一书有着较详尽的解释：

> 叙事被缩简为“考验”序列，后者在话语中显现为一个施动者模型，故在某种程度上使意义人格化，呈现为一连串人类（或拟人

> 类）行为。我们已经知道，这些行为同时包含了一种时间上的连续（它既非邻接又非逻辑蕴涵）和一种连续自由，也就是说包含了人们习惯上据之定义历史的两个属性：不可逆性和选择性。我们还知道，这一不可逆选择（F 在 A 之后）必有一个结果，从而使参与历史进程的人始终负有责任。所以，顾名思义，叙事的基本历史性序列包含了人类历史活动的全部属性，即不可逆转性、自由和责任。（格雷马斯，2001，p. 312）

其表述可简化为：（1）形象形式或施动者模型：人类行为或拟人化行为→意义人格化；（2）叙述的历史性序列（人参与的历史进程）：时间上的连续及连续自由→不可逆转性、自由与责任。这个思考已经不是我们对经典叙述学的通常理解了，即不能仅仅把它理解为受结构主义影响的纯形式论。当然，两者核心都在于作者把叙述进程形式化为“考验序列”。纯粹自然界、动物界、生物界、物理界、化学界等的事件进程变化或状态变化，不可能有所谓“考验”一说。其逻辑，从本质上说在于：他把叙述现象纳入了符号意义视域，符号意义问题，必须对人而言，或者必须人格化。之所以强化这一点，在于热奈特、普林斯等不少西方叙述学家在定义叙述时，都将其忽略了。热奈特曾这样定义叙述：“叙述指用语言，尤其是书面语言对一件或一系列真实或虚构的事件的表现。”（Genette，1976，pp. 1 - 13）普林斯也认为：“叙述是对于一种时间序列中至少两个真实或虚构的事件或情境的表述，其中任何一个事件或情境都不假定或包含另一个事件或情境。”（Prince，1982，p. 4）

接着，作者特别强调，“叙述文本携带的各种意义，需要接受者的理解和重构加以实现”，这是“判断各种意义活动是否为叙述的标准”（赵毅衡，2013a，pp. 7 - 8）。这里所强调的——前面几次对叙述的定义都强调了这一点——是叙述信息的接受与解释：如果没有这一过程，叙述就只是单方面的，只完成了叙述化过程的一半，因而无法最终成为叙述。这个看法，是其符号理论对皮尔斯符号三分之“解释项”强调的延伸。按照赵毅衡先生的理解，符号意义之“存有”，只是符号接收的必要前提，符号发送者的意图意义、符号文本携带的意义，只是轮流在场，它们的在场最终被不在场的解释意义取消，最终在场的，就只有解释意义（赵毅衡，2012，pp. 50 - 51）。这种理解并没有决然取消意图意义与符号文本携带的意义，只是说，这两种意义最终在与符号接收者的交流与解释中会合。当然，这一点不尽合理的潜在理论预设也会引发争论，下文将展开论述。另外，这个定义中使用的“组织”一词，完全避免了其他理论家使用的“叙述”，甚至“重述”“转述”等术语所带来的理论尴尬：要么同语反复，导致循环定义，要么暗示了被叙事件及其发生的时间。在这个定义中，我们完全看不出人物参与的事件到底发生在过去、现在还是将来。这自然避免了过去学术界定义叙述似乎只讲述过去发生事件，甚至一定有一个原本发生的事件等着我们去叙述的陷阱，也避免了“转述”“重述”概念所暗示的叙述必经语言文字的陷阱。

总的来说，这个叙述定义基本上达到了一般叙述学的目标，能涵括尽可能多的叙述类型。当然，与任何系统性理论创构探索一样，该定义也留下一些困惑。这些困惑，更多来自作者对这个定义所做的解释与具体运用。正是这些解释与运用，才使我们从根本上理解了该定义的内涵与外延。这些解释与具体运用，有时与该定义发生了矛盾。讨论这些矛盾，修正这个定义，将是下文的重点。

二、一般叙述学叙述定义的深度解析与修正

赵先生在讨论心像叙述类型比如梦叙述时，特别说到回忆、想象不是叙述，因为它们虽然可能是卷入了人物的事件，而且被心像媒介化，但它们属于“主体主动的有控制的行为”，且不符合叙述定义的第二条：“此文本可以被（另一个）主体理解为具有合一的时间和意义向度”（赵毅衡，2013a，p. 47），即它们只有一次叙述，没有二次叙述。在判断心像叙述属于叙述时，作者还这样说道：“它们是叙述：首先它们是媒介化（心像）的符号文本再现，而不是直接经验。”

应当说，这真正触及作者关于叙述的问题意识：从哲学符号学这个更为原初、基础的理论视野思考叙述问题。归纳起来有两点：第一，叙述信息的产生、发送、接收与解释的主体似乎必须是不同的；第二，直接经验必须与符号文本区分，在此基础上，符号文本与叙述文本的区分。

（一）

先说第一点。按照作者在《论二次叙述》一文的表述，“首度叙述化发生在文本形成过程中，二次叙述化发生在文本接受过程中”，只有“二次叙述才把这些因素真正‘实例化’为一个叙述”。也就是说，联系上文所引，在作者看来，回忆、想象之所以不属于叙述，乃是因为这两种行为只进行了

叙述过程的一半，只有某主体对叙述文本的组织，而没有另外一个主体对这个文本的叙述接受与解释。这一点很难说得通。举例来说，某个人回忆他的初恋时光：一桩桩，一幕幕，或意象（物象），或事件细节，或情景（场景）画面（包括时间、空间），历历在目，回忆、品味、情伤、雾里看花式的美化等意识样式悉数在场。这个过程必然涉及回忆主体对这些卷入人物的事件所做的情节化组织。如果这个人回忆时意识清醒，那么他的回忆性的叙述文本就显得较有逻辑，富于秩序化，尽管也包括不少情感化甚至非秩序化的成分。此时，这个主体不就既是叙述文本的构建者，同时也是其接收者、解释者吗？换一种方式思考，如果这个主体以写日记的方式回忆这段恋情，自己一边写一边咀嚼，或者写好之后供自己阅读，或者再也不看，也不给别人看，直接烧毁它，凡此种种，这个人是否经历了一次完整的叙述过程，完成了一种叙述？答案是显然的。正如我们常常说，一个作家往往是自己作品的第一个读者，即使他写完之后再也不看自己的作品。

不过，从理论上说，这里依然有一些问题没有阐明。作者认为这两种方式是以心像媒介化，只说出了其媒介化的方式之一，而且是胡塞尔现象学所说的想象、回忆的方式。对想象与回忆的思考，在胡塞尔那里经历了较为漫长的过程，其间出现了不少摇摆与变化（倪梁康，2007a，pp. 356 －359）。简单来说，广义的想象本质上属于一种当下化的直观行为，根据是否具有存在设定信仰来说，可分为不设定的想象与设定的想象。前者称为单纯想象或单纯表象、单纯思维。后者在作者的最终思考中，被划分为回忆、期待、真实性想象或感知性想象。感知性想象与回忆属于与感知（知觉）行为对立的行为样式。在感知行为中，对象直接显现，属于当下直观。感知性想象与回忆属于感知的想象性变异（变更），对象以心像（或作“心象”“表象”）的方式显现，是对对象感知的“再造”，属于当下化直观的行为（他也提到了“回忆图像”，但未对“回忆表象”做深入的描述）。（胡塞尔，2015，pp. 861 －871）

胡塞尔这种关于想象与回忆的现象学分析，是否能直接运用到对日常生活中的想象与回忆体验的讨论上呢？换言之，日常生活中一个人的想象与回忆是否只以心像的形式存在呢？胡塞尔在讨论想象表象（心像）时，也把它们看成“图像符号”，它们作为想象的内容，在想象中被“立义”或赋予意义。这似乎表明，这个过程属于符号性的行为。但从胡塞尔的符号意义理论来说，还不能这么看。他在这个时期还没有严格区分图像表象与想象表象。他认为对象以图像的方式显现于想象中，图像与对象具有绝对的、必然的相似性，因此其图像符号似乎还难以完全说是符号学意义上的符号——尽管他也认为，这种图像符号像指示性符号一样，是“对被标示之物的表象”。（胡塞尔，2015，pp. 861－871）这种说法有其意义理论的支撑。对胡塞尔来说，纯粹的知觉立义行为与言语表达含义行为是分割的，知觉立义行为“能独立于言语声音出现”“不需要一点音声语言意义上的表达或任何类似于语言意指的东西”（胡塞尔，2014，p. 219）。而言语表达的含义源自知觉意向体验行为中所获得的意义，是现成的，“言语声音只能被称作一个表达，因为属于它的意义在表达着；表达行为原初地内在于它”（胡塞尔，2014，p. 219）。从哲学符号学的立场来说，这种分割是有严重问题的。从知觉意义行为来说，似乎无需符号，因为事物直接向知觉主体显现，知觉对事物立义。但这并非一种真正的意义行为。真正的意义行为，必需意义载体即符号，哪怕符号载体就是意义发出者的身体行为或者事物本身——也就在此时，行为或事物被看成了符号。没有符号载体，意义就无法外在化传与他人，他人无法接收、交流与确认。纯粹个体性的、单向的意义实在无从说起。简言之，意义必伴随符号，是由意义发生的主体间性或者说公共性决定的。因此，如果我们确认想象与回忆是一种意义性的行为，那么它必然有符号或语言伴随。换言之，日常生活中一个人想象、回忆初恋，不可能只是心像式的体验，因为，日常生活经验已是一种符号意义行为。这一点，下文还会作详尽的解释。

另外，作者之所以把回忆、想象看成纯粹的心像行为，可能受到了胡塞尔“孤独心灵生活中的表达”思想的影响。胡塞尔认为，“在孤独的话语中，我们并不需要真实的语词，而只需要被表象的语词就够了。在想象中，一个被说出的或被印出的语词文字浮现在我们面前，实际上它根本不实存”（胡塞尔，2015，p. 344）。从根本上说，胡塞尔不认为孤独心灵中存在言语表达。在他看来，真正的、交往意义的表达是主体间的。这当然是对孤独心灵话语与表达过分狭隘的理解。狭隘的根源，依然是前文提到的分裂的意义观，即认为言语表达含义的行为与感知、想象、回忆等立义行为是完全分离的。事实上，柏拉图的“心灵与它自己的无声对话”思想，并没有被后世哲学家完全驳倒与放弃。倪梁康先生认为，“对语言的使用常常也可以不带有交往的目的，例如出声的或无声的自言自语”（2007b，p. 285）。问题在于，一旦承认孤独心灵中一个主体的自言自语，即承认存在表达，也就承认了存在一个主体发出叙述信息并自己接收、解释这个叙述信息的情形。因此，不把日常生活中对过去事件的回忆、想象看成完整的叙述过程，认为叙述信息的产生、发送与接收、解释主体必须不同的看法，需要修正。这也说明，二次叙述至少不能对“是否为叙述文本”这个问题潜在预设不同主体这个条件。除此以外，“二次叙述”依然是一个非常有用的概念，因为它经常发生于人类的叙述实践中，只是需要注意其有效适用范围或层面。

（二）

再说第二点。上文对胡塞尔有关感知、想象、回忆等所做的现象学思考的讨论，已经涉及“直接经验与符号文本的区分”这个问题。对这个问题的澄清，涉及叙述的外延扩容，即涉及发生在日常生活中的事件在什么情形下可能是一种叙述。

2013 年，赵先生对叙述做了一个极简定义：“任何符号组合，只要再现卷入人物的情节，即故事，就是叙述。”（赵毅衡，2013b，pp. 139 - 144）这个定义，包括上文对作者判断心像叙述是否属于叙述的引述，两次出现了“再现”这一重要概念。在作者的解释中，所谓“再现”，是指“符号再现”。在他看来，对于人类经验来说，事物呈现表现为直接呈现，但它尚未媒介化为符号，因而无法传达意义。因此，事物要传达意义，必须经过符号再现：“再现是用一种可感知的媒介携带意义，成为符号载体”，通过符号“媒介化”，再现就表现为事物的“重新呈现”——“用某种媒介再次呈现事物的形态”（赵毅衡，2017a，pp. 23 - 37）。就叙述来说，它必须通过符号媒介，或者必须经由符号之媒介化过程，才能成为叙述。

应当说，作者也是在现象学的理论框架中理解直接经验与符号文本的区隔的。对胡塞尔来说，人的知觉与事物的原初关系是知觉朝向事物，事物直接向知觉呈现。此时，知觉与事物之间还没有建立一种意义关系，最多只是建立了一种表象性的关系，即“知觉表象”。康德的先验主体哲学，也大致这样看待这种关系。只是在康德那里，感性中一些先天直观形式，比如时间、空间形式介入了对经验对象的感知，对象对主体成为现象，构成“感性表象”。人的知觉与事物建立的第二步关系才是意义关系。在这个第二步中，知觉行为对杂多的知觉材料（事物向知觉显现的材料，它们成为意向性的意识感知体验的实项内容）赋予一种意义（立义），把事物统摄为一个意识对象，构成一种初级阶段的认识。对此，倪梁康先生这样解释道：“在感知中，杂多的感性材料被统合、被统摄、被立义为一个统一的东西。在这里已经有最基本的认识形成，它可以说是初级阶段的认识。但我们一般还不会把它称为‘认识’，而是至多称作‘辨认’，就像我们不会说，‘狮子把面前的一个动物认识为羚羊’。之所以如此，乃是因为，确切意义上的‘认识’，一般是指在符号行为中进行的认知活动。”（倪梁康，2004，p. 196）在康德那里，则是主体知性自发性的表象能力通过概念或范畴对杂多感性表象进行联结、思维、综合把握，从而达成一定的对现象的认识。当然，正如前文不断指出的，我们这里所说的知觉对对象进行符号立义，已经不再立足于胡塞尔认识论现象学的语言意义论立场，而是立足于哲学符号学的符号意义论立场。

如此看来，作者对直接经验与符号文本的区分（区隔），无疑有着坚实的、有效的哲学基础。但问题是，我们是否能直接运用这种哲学区分去判断日常生活中人们对过去事件的想象或回忆，或者去判断发生在日常生活中有着广义交流性质的事件是否属于叙述这样的问题呢？

应该说，胡塞尔对知觉意义过程所做的现象学区分，有其理论合理性。但这种区分，属于对意向意识行为进行共时性静态分析的结果。胡塞尔本人非常重视这种静态分析与（历时性的）动态分析的区别，认为在动态分析中，认识行为将各个关系环节联系在一起（在时间上则是相互分离的，这与其严格的现象学时间认识有关）（胡塞尔，2015，pp. 911 – 912）。简言之，对对象的知觉和意指与意义的直观“充实”并不截然分离。这与符号哲学如下理解基本一致：对知觉对象直观与赋予意义呈现为一体化的过程。这也与康德对感性与知性在认识一个现象时的关系的理解一致：“康德所谓感性与知性的‘联合’（联结），就不能理解为好像两种要素各自都可以单独存在。并不是感性已经预先提供了个别对象，而后知性才从这个现成的对象出发运用概念去思维它；相反，感觉之成为表象、对象时就已经包含了知性的综合作用了，即使在意识或表象的最简单、最不确定的状态中，概念和直观都已经在共同起作用了。”（邓晓芒，2013，p. 100）这说明，直接经验与符号文本的区分，其有效性是有范围的。在胡塞尔那里，其有效性只能限定在对感知、想象、回忆等基础性的直观意识行为所做的静态分析中，而在动态分析中，这种明显层次化的逻辑区分不再完全有效。同时，正如上文所指出的，胡塞尔的这种区分本身，在意义理论方面还存在着严重局限。对于胡塞尔现象学的知觉意指观，利科早就提出了批评：“现象学讨论的首要问题是能指意指什么，指出这一点是很重要的。不管后来知觉描述得到多么大的重视，现象学的出发点不是意识活动的无声特点，而是它借助各种符号与事物产生的联系，比如像一个既定的文化所建立的联系。”（利科，2010，pp. 3 – 4）另外，伽达默尔对胡塞尔经验思想的反思，也表达了类似的意思：“胡塞尔给出了一个经验的系谱，以说明经验作为生命世界的经验在它被科学理想化之前就存在。不过，我认为他似乎仍被他所批判的片面性所支配。因为就他使知觉作为某种外在的、指向单纯物理现象的东西成为一切连续的经验的基础而言，他总是把精确科学经验的理想化世界投射进原始的世界经验之中。”（伽达默尔，1999，p. 454）他进一步指出：“胡塞尔试图从意义起源学上返回到经验的起源地并克服科学所造成的理想化，他这一尝试显然必须以一种特别的方式与这样一种困难相斗争，即自我的纯粹先验主体性实际上并不是作为这样的东西被给予的，而总是存在于语言的理想化中，而这种语言的理想化在所有获得经验的过程中已经存在，并且造成个别自我对某个语言共同体的隶属性。”（伽达默尔，1999，p. 454）。其实，赵先生也严重质疑胡塞尔把直观行为与符号行为分割开来的做法（赵毅衡，2017b，pp. 1－9）。这种质疑主要基于其符号意义观的符号哲学立场，即“意义必须用符号才能承载（发生、传达、理解），没有无须符号承载的意义”（赵毅衡，2017c，p. 62）。

从实质上说，利科与伽达默尔的上述看法，无非是想说，人类的日常生活经验本身已经是一个符号意义化的世界。对这一点，卡西尔、本维尼斯特等理论家都有着异常直白的强调。卡西尔在对人与一般生物世界的比较中指出，人除了具有一切动物都具有的感受器系统和效应系统外，还具有符号系统这个处于上述两个系统之间的第三环节。正是这个环节，使人生活在远比动物更为宽广的实在之中，也是新的实在之维中：“人不再生活在一个单纯的物理宇宙之中，而是生活在一个符号宇宙之中。……人不再能直接地面对实在，他不可能仿佛是面对面直观实在了。……在某种意义上说，人是在不断地与自身打交道而不是在应付事物本身。他是如此地使自己被包围在语言的形式中……以致除非凭借这些人为媒介物的中介，他就不可能看见或认识任何东西。”（卡西尔，2004，pp. 35－36）对此，当代现象学新锐、丹麦哲学家丹·扎哈维也明确给予了肯定（扎哈维，2008，p. 113）。本维尼斯特也曾指出，人类的基本状况、一个基本事实是，“在人与世界之间或在一个人与另一个人之间不存在自然的、无中介的和直接的关系，中介者是必不可少的”（1966，p. 26；转引自利科，2004，p. 354）。这个中介，指的就是符号或语言。这种理解，更可从利科对晚期胡塞尔提出的“生活世界”观念的反思中得到强化。他认为，人类无法在直接的直观中抵近“生活世界”，而只能通过对符号或语言“迂回的沉思”间接地“回问”，因为“我们一旦开始思考就会发现我们已经‘在’并且‘通过’各种再现的‘世界’、各种空想的‘世界’、各种标准的‘世界’而生活了”（利科，2010，p. 275，p. 285）。“生活世界”为既定的世界，属于界限和他人的根基，同时也只能是一种理想或理论预设，无法完全还原，经验世界已经属于符号象征和规则的世界，已经被符号再现等包围。简言之，人类已然生活在符号意义化的世界中。应当说，这是我们讨论日常生活经验的前提或基础。所有这些，其实也是赵先生在其符号学开山之作开篇第一句所强调的："人的精神，人的社会，整个人化的世界，浸泡在一种人们很少感觉到其存在却没有一刻能摆脱的东西里，这种东西叫符号。"（赵毅衡，2012，p. 1）

至此，可以这样认为，我们不能直接运用胡塞尔现象学对直接经验与符号文本所做的静态区分去理解这两者的关系，更不能用此静态区分去判断日常生活中一个人对过去事件的想象或回忆、日常生活中所发生的处于人们广义交流状态的事件是否属于叙述。如此看来，"直接经验"基本属于一个哲学用语，指认识论现象学对人的直观行为或者客体化行为，如感知、想象、回忆等做静态考察的结果。它与人类在日常生活中符号意义化的生活体验并不相同。简言之，人的日常生活已经就是一种符号文本，而且，日常生活中发生的处于人们广义交流状态的那些事件还属于一种叙述文本。所谓日常生活中发生的处于人们广义交流状态的事件，可以描述为如下一些事件样式：日常生活中发生的具有直接交往性质的事件，一个人自己体验、自己解释的不乏事件性、情节性的生活过程本身，或者一个人在日常生活中对他人生活事件（常态的、偶发的）的持续观看或观察，等等。人类社会的日常生活总是处于各种各样或隐或显的交流中，发生在你、我、他身上的事件总被自己或他者观看、观察与思索。这些叙述类型，到目前为止，都被世界主流叙述学界排除在外。当然，正是由于首次讨论这些事件是否属于叙述，其理论上论证的繁难不同一般，这里只是简单提及，以服务于本文讨论的叙述定义。

综上所述，笔者认为，相比于其他叙述定义，赵毅衡先生的如下叙述定义更具包容性，也更恰切一些："任何符号组合，只要再现卷入人物的情节，即故事，就是叙述。"只是从表述上，似可修改为：叙述，指以符号文本形式存在，以情节化方式所表达与交流的卷入人物的事件或人格化的事件。这个定义，明确了叙述的媒介形式即符号文本，明确了卷入人物的或人格化的事件或事件系列，明确了事件被组织的方式即情节化，也明确了叙述必须是交流的——因而没有特别强调叙述化过程之构造与接收、解释两端——哪怕是自我交流。广义的事件或系列事件，总是时间性的，没有事件不在时间中发生、变化，就如康德所说的，时间与空间总是人类经验认识的先天直观形式。该定义没有特别提到"故事"一词，因为它已被该定义内在蕴含——事件或事件系列的情节化组织的结果就是故事。此时的故事，既有内容，也有形式，是内容与形式的综合体。这个定义，也适合一些日常生活叙述类型。

参考文献：

邓晓芒（2013）.《纯粹理性批判》讲演录. 北京：商务印书馆.
格雷马斯，A. J.（2001）. 结构主义语义学（蒋梓骅，译）. 天津：百花文艺出版社.
格雷马斯，A. J.（2005）. 论意义（吴泓缈，冯学俊，译）. 天津：百花文艺出版社.
胡塞尔（2014）. 纯粹现象学通论——纯粹现象学和现象学哲学的观念（第1卷）（李幼蒸，译）. 北京：中国人民大学出版社.
胡塞尔（2015）. 逻辑研究（倪梁康，译）. 北京：商务印书馆.
伽达默尔，汉斯-格奥尔格（1999）. 真理与方法（洪汉鼎，译）. 上海：上海译文出版社.
卡西尔，恩斯特（2004）. 人论（甘阳，译）. 上海：上海译文出版社.
柯亨，L. 约纳坦（1988）. 语言学的认识论. 载于利科（主编）. 哲学主要趋向（李幼蒸，译）. 北京：商务印书馆.
利科，保罗（2010）. 论现象学流派（蒋海燕，译）. 南京：南京大学出版社.
倪梁康（2004）. 现象学的始基——对胡塞尔《逻辑研究》的理解与思考. 广州：广东人民出版社.
倪梁康（2007a）. 胡塞尔现象学概念通释（修订版）. 北京：生活·读书·新知三联书店.
倪梁康（2007b）. 意识的向度：以胡塞尔为轴心的现象学问题研究. 北京：北京大学出版社.
萨丕尔，爱德华（1985）. 语言论（陆卓元，译）. 北京：商务印书馆.
赵毅衡（2008）. “叙述转向”之后：广义叙述学的可能性与必要性. 江西社会科学，9，31-41.
赵毅衡（2012）. 符号学：原理与推演. 南京：南京大学出版社.
赵毅衡（2013a）. 广义叙述学. 成都：四川大学出版社.
赵毅衡（2013b）. 演示叙述：一个符号学分析. 文学评论，1，139-144.
赵毅衡（2014）. 论二次叙述. 福建论坛（人文社会科学版），1，121-127.
赵毅衡（2017a）. “表征”还是“再现”？——一个不能再“姑且”下去的重要概念区分. 国际新闻界，8，23-37.
赵毅衡（2017b）. 意义理论，符号现象学，哲学符号学. 载于曹顺庆，赵毅衡（主编）. 符号与传媒，15. 成都：四川大学出版社.
赵毅衡（2017c）. 哲学符号学：意义世界的形成. 成都：四川大学出版社.
Barthes, R. (1977). *Image music text* (Stephen Heath, Trans.). London: Fontana Press.
Genette, G. (1976). Boundaries of narrative (Ann Levonas, Trans.). *New Literary History*, 1, 8, 1-13.
Merleau-Ponty, M. (2012). *Phenomenology of perception* (Donald A. Landes, Trans.). New York: Routledge.
Prince, G. (1982). *Narratology: The form and functioning of narrative.* Berlin: Walter de

Gruyter GmbH & Co. KG.
Scholes, R. & Phelan, J. (2006). *The nature of narrative*. New York: Oxford University Press.

作者简介：

伏飞雄，文学博士，重庆师范大学文学院教授，主要研究领域为解释学、符号学、叙述学、西方文学与文论等。

李明芮，重庆师范大学文学院2018级比较文学与世界文学硕士研究生，主要研究领域为西方文学与文论。

Authors:

Fu Feixiong, Ph. D., professor of College of Liberal Arts, Chongqing Normal University. His research fields are hermeneutics, semiotics, narrative theory, Western literature and theory.

Email: 848521545@ qq. com

Li Mingrui, Master candidate of comparative literature and world literature, College of Liberal Arts, Chongqing Normal University. Her research field is Western literature and theory.

Email: 498624905@ qq. com

叙述是自我的“待在”之家：读文一茗的《叙述与自我》*

刘利刚

摘　要：《叙述与自我》一书主要探究了自我如何借由符号化（叙述）进入世界这一问题。该书通过配置“自我－符号－意义”这把三项式关联的钥匙，借由叙述之门，把自我带入了世界。同时除对自我的“文在”形式进行理论推演和深度阐释外，还将自我引入了“身份－认知－现实”的三项关联式中，使得自我的展示扎根于社会，具有了现实意义，不再仅囿于文本中心主义所构建的阐释漩涡中，而是给了自我一个认知的范畴以及将这种认知进行再现的身份。正是借助身份，自我才得以维系和规范，自我意义诸方面的符号化与具身化才得以实现。这种自我分别向文本和现实延展所产生的张力，既是对索绪尔符号观中自我绝对意志的挑战，又是对皮尔斯符号观中自我相对“文在性”的检视。叙述文本不再是自我绝对意志的展示，而仅是展示自我的自由意志之意义链条中的一环而已。

关键词：叙述，自我，身份，待在，无限衍义

Narrative as a Becoming of the Self：An Interpretation of Wen Yiming's *Narrative and the Self*

Liu Ligang

Abstract: *Narrative and the Self* mainly examines how the self enters the world

---

* 本文为重庆市社科基金规划项目“新三峡生态旅游的影视化传播策略研究”（2018YBCB094）、重庆市教委人文社会科学规划项目“新三峡生态旅游的场景传播策略研究（17SKG161）”的部分成果。

through semiotisation (narrative). The book shows how the self enters the world through the door of narrative using the triad of "self-sign-meaning" as the key. In addition to the theoretical deduction and in-depth interpretation of a "texture being" form of "the self", the book also introduces the self into another triadic relation, that is "identity-cognition-reality", which gives practical significance to the rooting of self-display in society. The self is thereby no longer confined to the vortex of interpretation constructed by text-centrism, being also assigned a category of cognition and an identity that reproduces this cognition. It is with the help of identity that the self can be maintained and standardised, thus realising the symbolisation and embodiment of the self from many aspects. The tension created by the self between text and reality is not only a challenge against the absolute will of the self as it appears in Saussure's semiotics, but also an inspection of the relative "texture being" of the self in Peirce's semiotics. The narrative text is no longer a display of the absolute will of the self, but only a link in the meaning chain of displaying self-will.

Keywords: narrative, the self, identity, becoming, infinite semiosis

DOI: 10. 13760/b. cnki. sam. 202002017

引言：一个鸟瞰式全景观照

《叙述与自我》一书，主要探究自我是如何通过符号化（叙述）进入世界并认知自身的。作者通过配置"自我－符号－意义"这把三项式关联的钥匙，借由叙述之门，把自我带入世界。或更为确切地说，作者正是通过叙述所绘制的形式地图，让自我进入了时间之流和意义之域。正是叙述为自我展演提供了形式这个无限的舞台。或许舞台的不同，会使得自我与其生存的形式条件（符号）及其结果（意义）相互分离，但正是这种分离性，让叙述可以展演出自我的多种身份。作者不只是对自我进行文本式挖掘，而且还努力试图进行深层次的理论建构和哲学反思。作者以皮尔斯的符号学理论为操作后台，融合多种理论视域，对小说和电影文本中的多种自我进行了挖掘和理论推演。

除了对自我的"文在"形式进行理论推演和深度阐释外，作者还将自我引入了另一个的三项关联式中——“身份-认知-现实”，使得自我的展示扎根社会，具有了现实意义，不再仅囿于文本中心主义所构建的阐释漩涡中，而是给了自我一个认知的范畴及将这种认知进行再现的身份。正是借助身份，自我才得以维系、规范，自我意义诸方面的符号化和具身化才得以实现。这种自我向文本和向现实延展所产生的张力，既是对索绪尔符号观中自我绝对意志的挑战与反叛，又是对皮尔斯符号观中自我相对“文在性”的检视与拥趸。叙述文本不再是自我绝对意志的展示，而仅是展示自我的自由意志之意义链条中的一环而已。

该书总体上分为四大部分，分别是“理论与缘起”“推进与小说”“类比与电影”“文本与演绎”。第一部分以皮尔斯符号观的核心思想即“解释项”为理论视域，构筑了《叙述与自我》一书的逻辑出发点，即主体性。作者指出自我并不能完全为自己做主，而是一种作为先验实体的自我意识，这种自我意识是一种能够辐射他者的指涉自我，而这种示意者将自我定位为主体的能力，是借由叙述话语的建构来完成的。由于解释项是一套开放的意义机制，同时自我在世的方式就是对意义的感知、阐释与传达，因此解释项成为理解自我通过叙述进行示意的关键环节。

第二部分是在第一部分所进行的理论准备的基础上，探讨了主体如何通过叙述把自己编码、再现、整合为对象（object）。这个被符号化的自我是一种“待在”（becoming），处于未来正在生成的自我即“解释项”（interpretant）当中，这个“待在”的自我生产着叙述与被叙述，以及阐释与被阐释之间的张力，冲向一个尚待生成的意义空间，等待下一轮叙述与被叙述及阐释与被阐释。可以说，第二部分是对自我如何借由叙述落实到文本中的推演。

第三部分在探讨自我叙述化的过程中进行了表达媒介的升级，从小说进入了电影，从文字升格为镜头。在此基础上，作者分析了镜头叙述如何打破常规视觉语法，成为观影者思维展开的方向指示，以及镜头叙述如何被赋予了文学性意义。在镜头语法和叙述语法分析的基础上，作者将电影视作一个复杂的符号化过程，其中包括一部具体的影片从生产到消费的过程，以及观众的参与。这一个过程中必然会卷入主体与示意的问题。作者指出，要理解电影的示意机制，就必须理解符号电影的三元模式。

第四部分主要围绕四个文本展开分析与推演。围绕第一个文本《时间中的孩子》，作者主要探究了从叙述时间到被叙述时间的认知转向；围绕第二个文本《踩影游戏》，作者主要探究了自我是如何被卷入意义和符号漩涡的；围绕第三个文本《欲望教授》，作者主要探究了欲望符号如何在自我的不同阶段进行演变；围绕第四个文本《黑天鹅》，作者主要探讨了彼此否定的身份在当代社会竞争机制中如何挑战符号自我统一不同身份的能力。

上文主要对《叙述与自我》一书做了一个鸟瞰式的全景把握，下文将镜头下移，聚焦于书中四个具体问题的探讨。

一、解释项：为自我"待在"提供理论可能性

《叙述与自我》一书的出发点是主体性，即示意者将自我定位为主体的能力，仅仅出现于叙述话语的根本属性之中。"主体"是一个在人类思想史上存在很多争议的概念。作者从英文"subject"一词的中文翻译引发的歧义谈起，引出了"主体悖论"问题。而对于这一深奥问题的论述，作者却借用了一个非常简单的句子，即"Three years' experience as a salesperson enables me to communicate with people from different walks of life（本人从事销售工作有三年，具备与不同人打交道的能力）"。最为关键的是，对这个简单句子的分析的确也能够说明主体悖论问题。在该句子中，行为的承担者和实施主体确实是"我"，但是在字里行间我们又只能真切地感受到"我"只是一个谦卑的受益者，并不是一个发起整个行为的主体。"我"反倒要感谢这三年的工作经验，是它成就了今天的"我"。这即是说，主体好像是限于主动与被动之间的一个悖论，每当主体采取主动，便同时也是被动的，毕竟主动也是对某事做出的反应。这正像福柯所言，主体因控制与依赖而受制于他人。

作者纵观了几十年的文学和文化研究史，发现学界几乎一致否认文艺复兴时期完全自足的主体，认为主体是一个符号建构、意义建构的过程。作者沿用这一范式，进一步地认为主体拥有一种指涉自我、辐射他者、通达世界的话语能力。这种话语能力让主体从言说中隐退，隐退于所说的话语之中。但是，话语是作者叙述或说出来的，那么隐退之前的这个话语建构者是谁？他与主体是什么关系？该叫他什么？作者将这个既处于话语之外又处于话语之内的人称为"自我"，并认为自我总是处于"说"与"被说"两个世界。

这就既顾及了文艺复兴时期主体完满自足的论题，又顾及了主体栖身于话语之中的说法，笔者认为这是《叙述与自我》一书对先前研究有很大推进的地方。主体既不仅是"在世之在"的自我，又不仅仅是"文在"的自我，而是处于"待在"状态的自我。最为关键的是，作者从皮尔斯的符号学思想中为主体栖居于"待在"找到了充足的理由。这个理由就是皮尔斯符号观中的核心，即解释项。解释项理论涉及一套开放的意义机制，而自我在世的方

式就是对意义的感知、阐释与传达。因此，要理解自我是如何示意的，关键就是要引入解释项理论。

解释项是一种符号，它是可以翻译或发展的原初符号（皮尔斯，李斯卡，2014，p. 159）。在《叙述与自我》一书中，作者把解释项理解为“符号自身的转换与翻译，具有‘无限转换’（endless commutability）属性”（文一茗，2019，p. 14）。既然主体借助叙述话语来栖居自身，而且主体的在世方式就是对意义的感知、阐释与传达，那么解释项作为一种话语的延续，就理当承担系列化地、不断地为主体建构“待在”之家的任务。同时，主体正因为有了这样的“待在”之家，才能生生不息，处于永无止境的示意生成中。

二、叙述自我：自我的具体存在方式

自我是在示意过程中生成的，叙述是示意过程，因此叙述是自我的存在方式。文一茗探讨了自我何以可能及如何可能借由叙述而栖居于小说文本。小说写作是写作者借助叙述技巧与策略，将自我意图注入小说文本的过程。在这一过程中，叙述语言、叙述技巧及策略造就了小说叙述艺术的形式美，而写作者自我意图的注入则赋予了小说叙述艺术精神美。自我并不是一个叙述完成后就在那儿了的客观对象，而是处于叙述话语生成的互动之中。小说文本的生成是“一次叙述化”过程，而小说文本的阅读是“二次叙述化”过程，正是在这两次叙述化的互动过程中，写作者自我与阅读者自我展开了对话，通过对话，写作者与阅读者确立了双方“此时此刻”在这儿的自我主体性。倘若没有“对话”这一召唤自我在场集聚的机制，那么这样的自我就只能是一种“沉默的自我”，它（the self）也许只能存在于写作者自行建构的写作循环中，并不会存在于符号传播过程即这条无尽的示意链条中。毕竟，自我一旦陷入循环，就无法在敞开的社会符号语境中卷入更为深刻的示意活动中。

故此，不妨说，叙述即传播，传播即存在，叙述即存在。故事是讲给大家听的，怎么讲，要靠叙述，而故事讲得效果如何，则由传播决定。在此意义上，叙述学与传播学可以在许多层面上通约。小说写了不是只给自己阅读的，而是要影响他人的，影响他人实质上就是影响他人的主体性建构。但是，写作者只是一个存在于现实语境中的真实的个体，这个个体不可能与每一个读者相遇于现实社会语境中，相遇的最大可能是于虚拟世界（fictional world）中。那么，问题来了：在这样的虚拟世界中写作者到底是如何具体影响阅读者的呢？《叙述与自我》一书回答了这一问题：写作者通过叙述将作者自我分化为了不同的叙述自我，具体包括隐含作者、叙述者、人物。这三类叙述自我，也就是虚拟世界中的不同叙述主体。在小说的传播过程中，叙述主体与接受主体之间展开对话，这一对话建构了双方的交互主体性。

《叙述与自我》一书从修辞和认知两个向度，特别就“不可靠叙述”展开了讨论。这一讨论是对叙述主体与接受主体如何具体展开交互的展示。不可靠叙述是一种叙述展开的策略或技巧，它通过制造隐含作者与叙述者价值取向的不一致，预设了一种不可预期的认知差，这种预设构筑起来的是一种“询唤结构”，它能够引发受众“预料之外的快感”，使受众不自觉地与文中各种主体展开对话，并在对话当中产生对参与各方的认同感。而至于隐含作者是“执行主体”（executive author）还是“推导主体”（deduced author），则各有其合理性。就二者通过叙述建构交互主体性而言，笔者倾向于认同修辞派，认为认知派实质上是给修辞派提供了一种通过关注受众所关注而进行反修辞建构的策略，因为毕竟在实质上小说文本的生成并不是由读者来完成的。

讨论至此，还是要寻根问底，自我到底是如何落实的？文一茗认为，任何叙述都源于那个说事儿的“我”（文一茗，2019，p. 70），也即是说，自我借由说事儿的“我”来落实的，这个“我”就是叙述者。叙述者在叙述文本中既可以显在，也可以隐在，显在到一定程度就是第一人称叙述者兼具主人公，而隐在到一定程度就是第三人称叙述者即隐身“框架”，叙述在显在的“人格”与隐身的“框架”之间的变动形成了不同的叙述角度。叙述角度是叙述文本的指示符号，因为叙述角度是一个符号化的自我的视角，所以它是叙述者的价值选择的指示，引导着接受者从某个角度感知叙述文本，这种引导在很大程度上决定了读者如何理解叙述中隐藏的或显明的主体价值观。换言之，叙述视角直接邻接起了谁在讲、如何讲、讲什么与谁在看、如何看、看到什么。同时，《叙述与自我》一书通过探究小说文本中的引语问题，进一步指出在二次叙述化过程中，接受者感受到的文本中的各种“话语之争”或“抢话”实质上都是在彰显自我的具体存在样态。

不仅如此，《叙述与自我》一书还探讨了如何通过元叙述来反观自我、暴露叙述自我。文一茗认为，“元”（meta-）化意味着通过分离而实现的自我反观与深入，元叙述是一种对原有自我的转向与突破（文一茗，2019，p. 100）。帕克里夏·沃（Patricia Waugh）在《元小说》中认为，虚构作品是对“一种更为彻底的感受的回应，这种感受的关键点是，不再有永恒真实的世界，仅仅存在着被建构的系列、技巧和非永恒的结构”（Waugh，1984，p. 8）。这种“元叙述”观念消解了叙述的传统使命，即对现实世界的再现，让我们明白原来叙述仅仅是一种构成。事实上，我们的现实世界并不比虚构世界更真实。赵毅衡在《广义叙述学》一书中指出，我们所面对的现实世界是由符号构成的，世界不过是一个大文本，符号的边界就是世界的边界。（赵毅衡，2013，p. 291）我们就生活在符号世界这个大文本中，我们之所以是我们，是因为我们通过符号叙述建构了我们的符号自我。《叙述与自我》一书通过对叙述者的自我暴露、叙述机制的自我揭示、叙述意图的自我批评，将我们的意识进行了“元”化，经由这种“元”化的意识，我们认识到了叙述自我的建构性特征。

三、媒介升级：自我的镜像话语

罗兰·巴尔特在论及摄影如何触动观者时说：“要想看清楚一张照片，最好的办法是抬起头，或闭上眼。”旋即，他又引卡夫卡补充道：“拍照是为了把要拍的那些东西从头脑里赶走。我的麻烦在于以什么样的方式闭眼。”（巴尔特，2011，p. 73）巴特尔的这段话看似与我们的日常拍照经验相矛盾，实则揭示了一个深刻的道理，即“看”是为了“不看”。无论一张照片中有多少个能够发人深省的“刺点”（punctum），更深层次的看都不是仅仅为了看见直接意指层面的能指或明示意，而是为了领会含蓄意指层面的所指或神话。从媒介考古学的角度来看，电影是摄影的拓展或更为复杂的延伸，因此巴尔特在《明室》一书中的“观看之道”亦可对电影分析产生积极的启发。在电影镜像话语中，叙述自我的生成并不是完全依照像似规律在运作，有可能叙述自我的“像”借由仿造被植入镜像话语之中，但是更多的是自我精神“意象”向镜像话语的凝缩或移置。电影中的每一个角色看似具体，即“他或她就在那儿”，但实则这些具象所意指的是意义变量，而这些意义变量的基础语义域就是现实社会，或超越现实社会基础的某种超验域。

文一茗认为，“我们可以将镜头的视觉语法理解为电影对观影者接受文本的规范，并通过这一细则，达到与之交流与相互理解的目的”（文一茗，2019，p. 115）。电影的视觉语法是电影工作者经长期修辞实践而做出的总结和理论化概括，它不是最终结局，而是永远处在不断的生成中，只是从某个暂时态来看具有相对的规定性。电影视觉语法本身是一套创作者与接受者发生共谋的机制，其本身的规定性召唤作为解释社群的观众的出现。这套机制是“携带‘语义矢量’的指示符号”（赵毅衡，2017，p.105）的集合，它指示或提醒接受者运用自己的观察能力与影片产生意义的流动。

电影既不是现实生活本身，又不是物质现实的复原。电影的视觉语法常常以创新的方式制造陌生化的感知形式（携带“语义矢量”的指示符号）。具体来说，在视觉形式方面包括空间、线条、形状、影调、色彩、运动和节奏（布洛克，2012，p.2），在声音形式方面包括节奏（有节奏的－无节奏的）、强度（轻的－响的）、音调（低－高）、音色（悦耳的－嘈杂的）、速度（慢－快）、形态（直达的－混响的）和组织状态（有序的－无序的）（索南夏因，2007，p.59）。这两个方面都起到了积极建构视听感知形式的作用，不过对于声音的形式方面的探讨，《叙述与自我》一书并没有拓开言路，尚有待深化。值得肯定的是，作者对蒙太奇做了比较深入的探究后，提出“作为风格的蒙太奇”，并以风格对蒙太奇进行了分类。

诚然，作为风格的蒙太奇是在建构镜像话语，为自我构筑一个可以“待在”的家。在借由蒙太奇生成镜像话语的过程中，无论符号层面的修辞，还是叙述层面的修辞，都既是在为自我“待在”的这个家做装潢，也是在为这个叙述的自我做打扮，以吸引更多的受众。没有受众认知的叙述自我是一种“潜在自我”，只有受众与之相呼应，叙述自我才能进入待在状态；待在的自我不是孤立的，而是融入了社会网络关系的。唯如此，双方的意义才能流动起来，叙述自我与受众之间才能完成交互主体性建构。

《叙述与自我》一书也讨论了由文字叙述转化为镜像叙述的过程，并比较了在这一过程中文字叙述之于自我的符号化过程和镜像叙述之于自我的符号化过程的差异：文字叙述重在塑形，而电影叙述重在体验。作者重点讨论了在后者中自我的分化问题。作者对影片与电影做了区别，前者是指一部具体的影片，后者是指从影片生产到消费以及观众参与的复杂的符号化过程。这一区分可以看作是作者在分析镜像话语时从结构主义向后结构主义的过渡——结构主义注重文本的分析，而后结构主义注重受众及文本的消费。由于叙述主体或叙述自我与示意过程总是彼此依存，且符号示意过程又涉及三个方面，即符号再现体、符号所涉及的对象、符号示意过程中生产的意义解释项，所以作为符号的电影也卷入了三重主体，即作为符号再现体的叙述主体、作为符号指涉对象的建构主体及作为符号解释项的释义主体。文一茗将叙述主体（the speaking subject）解释为包裹着丰富的电影感知形式的电影文本，将作为符号指涉对象的建构主体（the spoken subject）解释为电影观众，将释义主体（the interpreting subject）解释为意义。这种解释既是对电影符号学研究的一种拓展，也表现了镜像话语中主体问题的复杂性。作者对电影中主体分化问题的分析，是一种“元分析”（meta-analysis），是对电影符号表意思想前提的建设性分析，有助于培养作为观众的接受者认知自我、反思自我的能力，使观众不至于在不知不觉中沉溺于电影符号带来的感知漩涡中，经多次镜像反射（电影间性）后迷失自我。

四、可见的时间：作为文本的自我

赵毅衡给“叙述”这样一个底线定义，即一个叙述文本包含由特定主体进行的两个叙述化过程：“1. 某个主体把有人物参与的事件组织进一个符号文本中；2. 此文本可以被接收者理解为具有时间和意义向度。”（赵毅衡，2013，p. 7）这里提出了构成最简叙述的两个基本条件：从修辞建构的角度来看要卷入人物，从认知的反修辞建构的角度来看要能够从中解读出时间和意义向度。这两个条件无非是在告诉接收者，叙述实际上是叙述主体从底本向述本投射事件的组织化过程，这一组织化过程也就是在安排人物有意义的行为，而行为是由序列事件展现出来的，这序列事件的展现就是在使时间可视化和使意义可触化，接受者正是通过感知或意向化地参与序列事件来感受时间和解读意义的。也即是说，就我们所感知到的时间来说，人物所参与的事件是经由叙述化即符号表达的结果。

《叙述与自我》一书对于叙述与时间之间的纠缠问题有着精彩独到的论述。这里，笔者受此书的启发，做了一个简要推导：时间是存在之维，叙述是时间之维，叙述是存在之维。这里，时间不是一个抽象的存在，而是经由叙述具象化的符号，即被叙述的时间。文一茗以伊恩·麦克尤恩的小说《时间中的孩子》（*The Child in Time*）一书为例，分析了从叙述时间到被叙述时间的认知转向。只有在被叙述时间中，自我才能搭上深入缺失之黑洞的时光列车，逃离“成人世界”，回到“孩子世界”。文一茗指出，在《时间中的孩子》中，“如果查尔斯是披着孩子外衣，返回孩子世界的成人；史蒂芬则是披着成人外衣，进入成人世界的孩子”（文一茗，2019，p. 173）。无论穿着何种外衣来到孩子世界，都要借助时间之维，而这里的时间之维绝非“刹那一瞥”或一般意义上的“三年之后”等，而是依据叙述打开的时间之维，这个借由叙述获得了形式的时间，也就是被叙述的时间。

在被叙述的时间中，成人之自我向不在场的缺失（即孩子）进行了反观，试图还原当下不在场的孩子及其主宰自我。文一茗认为，在《时间中的孩子》中，自我为修复缺失或还原为孩子选择了两条路：查尔斯绝望而疯狂地主动出击，希望通过再现孩子的形式，实现孩子的内涵，不过却上演了一出浮士德式的悲剧；史蒂芬虽然保持了沉重而艰难的探索步履，这种有限的主体能动性却意外得到了命运的恩宠。（文一茗，2019，p. 170）两位人物返回童年的叙述过程形成了“互为反向注解的叙述格局”（文一茗，2019，p. 170），成功地把时间建构为自我感知的媒介，接受者正是在时间的悄悄变化中感知到了从成人到孩子的变化过程，而这一过程即是符号化了的时间。自我之所以能够被不停地植入当下、过去及未来的符号文本中，可能正在于时间被叙述形式化后，成了文本本身的一部分。

《叙述与自我》一书在分析了《时间中的孩子》从叙述时间到被叙述时间的认知转向的基础上，继续深入挖掘了符号文本中被叙述时间的分层：对路易斯·厄德里克的《踩影游戏》从三个层面展开叙述分析，发现其中瑞尔利用被叙述时间的可修辞性，在虚实之间把玩的一场踩影般的游戏；对菲利普罗斯的《欲望教授》展开分析，发现当下正在叙述的主我向下沦为一个既定的他者欲望的客体，使自己成为自我符号所指的过去自我，而自我过去的欲望体验反而上升为自我使用的一个符号，它不停地与当下互相置换，充实着自我的符号意义，向未来传达、衍生出尚待形成的自我形象；对达伦·阿罗诺夫斯基《黑天鹅》的分析，向我们展示两个相互否定的身份在当代社会竞争机制中挑战符号自我、统一不同身份的能力；对翁贝托·艾柯《玫瑰之名》的分析，发现了无限衍义正是主体思维方式的本质特征，揭示了主体缺失之存在状态，即主体只能不停地使用符号表达或逼近自己所缺失的那一部分，它永远是主体所追求的精神之家，而当下此刻主体只能不停地使用符号构筑这样一个仅供当下自己暂且“待在”的家。

结语：一个符号学式反思

文一茗的《叙述与自我》一书就放在笔者的书桌上，而笔者之所以还要写这篇解读文章的，目的在于想要把那不在场的意义阐述出来。尽管这种缺席的意义在敲击键盘想要尽情地表达出来时一直往后隐退，但是在当下此刻笔者对自己敲出的文字所携带的意义的领悟确实是真实的。此外，由于解读这种符号化活动可以说在某种程度上是与原著写作活动在同一个意识中发生，即解读是在原著写作印迹上的叠加，所以解读在很大程度上是对原著的重复。这种重复是非常有必要的，它是一种导读，同时也可以说是抛砖引玉，期待后来者对当下所读所写进行检验。这里，笔者拿《论语·为政篇》中那句“温故知新，可以为师矣”为写解读文章进行合理性辩护。解读的确在某种程度上是对原著的“温故”（重复），不过其目的是为了“知新”。温故为什么能够知新？德勒兹主义的回答是：“故”本身已先天地蕴含着无穷的“新”，当眼睛看出来（阅读）时，“新”就形成了。那么再进一步，为什么温故知新，才可以真正为师？请试想：某君的眼睛看同样的对象，却能够看出不同，看出全新的东西，唯此等人才能真正传播新知。（吴冠军，2015）

《叙述与自我》一书对自我或主体的探讨，尽管非常深刻，处处充满着洞见，闪烁着思想的火花，但是这种探讨却并没有完结，而是尚待继续。文一茗在该书引言中说“本书绕了一个大圈”（文一茗，2016，p. 1），这里的“圈”是指先于符号的自我通过叙述进入符号世界，结果由于范式之争，又被从由符号构筑的形式条件及其意义结果中剥离出来，离开了符号世界。搁置《叙述与自我》一书，暂且不论，仅就自我或主体本身而言，也永远是值得探讨、值得演绎的，其所存在的社会语境在变，对其的解释也会不断地发生变化。虽然前期有如赵毅衡、唐小林、伏飞雄、文一茗、颜小芳等学者介入讨论主体问题，但后期可能还会有更多的学者陆续加入其中。这也表明，“主体是一个‘待在’（becoming）的过程，一种指称自我、向他者辐射从而通达世界的话语能力”（文一茗，2016，p. 45）。换言之，自我只有在不停的感知、阐释与叙述话语建构中，或与他者的动态交流中，才能将自己文本化，使自我得以成为主体。

总之，贯穿全书的思想是，主体通过叙述这种话语生成的方式为自我找到了“待在”之家，而这个由叙述话语建构的家园处于不断的扩充和膨胀中，随着这种家园语境的扩充，自我也不断处于更新或生成中，主体对意义的感知、阐释与传达也不断生成。就拿目前非常火爆的“北快手，南抖音”来说，它们都是主体叙述表达自我在场的有力证据，而且这种短视频的数量每日都在暴增，这或许能够充分说明，自我永远处于“待在”状态，要不断地借助“场景叙述”（scene narrative）维持自我的在世之“在”。

引用文献：

巴尔特，罗兰（2011）. 明室：摄影札记（赵克非，译）. 北京：中国人民大学出版社.

布洛克，布鲁斯（2012）. 以眼说话：影像视觉原理及应用（汪弋岚，译）. 北京：世界图书出版公司北京公司.

皮尔斯，李斯卡（2014）. 皮尔斯：论符号（赵星植，译）. 成都：四川大学出版社.

索南夏因（2007）．声音设计：电影中语言、音乐和音响的表现力（王旭锋，译）．杭州：浙江大学出版社．

文一茗（2016）．论符号解释项与主体示意的关联．中国外语，2，41－47.

文一茗（2019）．叙述与自我．成都：四川大学出版社．

吴冠军（2015－04－30）．像德勒兹一样阅读．社会科学报，第6版．

赵毅衡（2013）．广义叙述学．成都：四川大学出版社．

赵毅衡（2017）．哲学符号学：意义世界的形成．成都：四川大学出版社．

Waugh, P. (1984). *Metafiction: The theory and practice of self-conscious fiction.* London: Routledge.

作者简介：

刘利刚，博士，四川外国语大学新闻传播学院编导系副教授，研究方向为符号叙述学、跨媒介修辞与传播。

Author:

Liu Ligang, Ph. D., associate professor of Editing and Directing Department, School of Journalism and Communication, Sichuan International Studies University. His research fields are semiotic narratology, rhetoric and communication across media.

Email: llgtianshui@163. com

综述与书评

日本符号学的发展与中日符号学界的交流

徐 克

摘　要： 中日两国的符号学研究几乎同时起步，发展阶段也相似，都经历了以索绪尔符号学研究为中心的初级阶段，与结构主义的纠缠阶段，以及跨学科融合阶段。同处于汉字文化圈的中日两国，在学理基础上本来就具有深厚的渊源，中日符号学界之间的交流也必将促进双方的学科建设和发展。本文对日本符号学发展历程的探讨，将有助于国内符号学界加深对日本符号学研究现状的了解。

关键词： 日本符号学，跨学科研究，东亚符号学

The Development of Japanese Semiotics and Exchange between Chinese and Japanese Semiotics

Xu Ke

Abstract: Research on semiotics started at almost the same time in China and Japan and has gone through similar stages of development. In both countries, research has gone through the primary stage centred on Saussurean semiology, the stage of entanglement with structuralism and the stage of interdisciplinary integration. China and Japan—in the cultural circle of Chinese characters—are deeply related to each other both academically and theoretically, and exchanges on semiotics between them will certainly be conducive to disciplinary construction and development in both countries. This paper discusses the development of Japanese semiotics to deepen understanding in this field.

Keywords: Japanese semiotics, interdisciplinary research, semiotics of East Asia
DOI: 10.13760/b.cnki.sam.202002018

一、符号学在日本的发展历程

日本自古以来就善于吸收先进的外来文化，这在西方文艺理论的译介上也表现明显。早在 1928 年，小林英夫就以《言语学原论》为名翻译了索绪尔的《普通语言学教程》，使日本成为第一个引入《普通语言学教程》的国家。因此可以说，日本的符号学研究始于 1928 年。在经历了 20 世纪 20 年代至 60 年代的初创期和 70 年代的成长期后，从 80 年代开始腾飞，广泛地与其他学科融合，并取得了丰硕的成果，至今仍然有着旺盛的生命力。

由于小林英夫在《言语学原论》中把“semiologie”译为“記号学”，日本学界就统一把皮尔斯的“semiotics”译为“記号論”。关于“記号”一词，符号学家外山知德曾做过考证，他认为：“在江户时代末期‘記号’作为‘しるし’（记号，标记）的同义语已经被广泛使用。”（1985，p. 36）明治时代初期，日本学者在翻译西方著作时往往把“sign”和“symbol”统一译为“記号”。一直到 1873 年，哲学家中江兆民才第一次把“symbol”译为“象徵”，后来，经过森鸥外和上田敏等文学家和美学家的使用和推广，“象徵”作为“symbol”的译词才被固定下来。同时，“記号”也就成为“sign”的固定译语。

日本的符号学研究在初创阶段，主要围绕索绪尔的语言学模式展开。《普通语言学教程》被引入日本以后，首先在日本的国语学界引起了强烈反响。森冈健二曾在《言语过程说的开展》一文中提到，“在当时如果不学习索绪尔的语言理论，就无法进入国语学的领域”（1968，p. 214）。当时的日本国语学家几乎都受到了索绪尔理论的影响。例如，曾开创了日语“学校语法”的桥本进吉，在索绪尔的影响下创造了“文节”这一语法概念；语言学家松本大三郎则依据索绪尔的“组合关系”与“聚合关系”理论对日语的“格”与“相”做了区分。

然而，时枝诚记却对索绪尔的语言学理论提出了质疑。他认为索绪尔忽视了人的主体性，并在其代表作《国语学原论》中专设了《对费尔迪南·德·索绪尔语言学理论的批判》一节进行批判。时枝诚记是日本近代语言学的泰斗之一，提出了著名的“言语过程说”。他的质疑引发了一场关于索绪尔语言学的大讨论，小林英夫和服部四郎等知名学者也都参与了这场讨论。这场讨论不仅加深了日本学界对索绪尔理论的认识，也为结构主义理论的引入做了铺垫。

日本学界从20世纪60年代中期开始关注西方的结构主义，并在70年代形成了一股结构主义热潮。雅柯布森的《普通语言学论文集》，列维-斯特劳斯的《结构人类学》、马丁奈的《一般语言学原理》、洛特曼的《文学理论与结构主义》、福柯的《知识考古学》等主要的结构主义理论著作都在这个时期被译介到了日本。日本学界也迅速出版了一些讨论结构主义的著作。仅在1968年，就有《什么是结构主义》（伊藤俊太郎）、《结构主义和辩证法》（田岛节夫）、《什么是结构主义——存在主义的继承者》（伊东守男）等著作出版。同年，知名的学术杂志《中央公论》还专门做了题为《什么是结构主义——列维-斯特劳斯及其影响》的特辑，并分为《列维-斯特劳斯及其思想》《结构主义的方法》《结构主义的挑战》三部分出版。同时，罗兰·巴尔特在20世纪60年代末的三次访日以及《符号帝国》在日本的出版，也推动了日本符号学界把研究重心从语言符号研究开始慢慢转移到大众文化研究上来。

因此，日本的符号学研究在该阶段又与结构主义思潮纠缠在了一起。山口昌男、前田爱、矶谷孝等符号学家都深受结构主义的影响。山口昌男还积极地把塔尔图符号学派和俄国形式主义的理论引进到日本。他曾提道：“我的符号学方法，一方面是基于俄国形式主义理论，另一方面是基于我正在研究的文化人类学。”（2002，p. 13）其代表作《文化与两义性》对列维-斯特劳斯和特尼亚诺夫（Tynjanov）的理论做了深入探讨。

前田爱则在洛特曼的影响下完成了毕生最重要的著作《都市空间中的文学》，该著作开创了日本文学研究的新范式，影响深远。文学批评家高桥修认为：“前田氏所尝试的都市论和文化符号学的手法以把作品结构化为切入点，让日本的文学批评从单纯的作品论和作家论突破到了文本论。”（2002，p. 42）此外，前田爱还深受罗兰·巴尔特的影响，开创了“文本分析”理论，并影响了小森阳一、石原千秋、高桥修、岛村辉等学者，形成了文本分析派。

矶谷孝对俄国形式主义在日本的推广功不可没。他于1971年编辑出版了

《俄国形式主义论集——诗性语言的分析》，并对巴赫金和洛特曼的理论做了深入探讨。俄国形式主义文论曾对日本学界带来了巨大冲击，“它作为一种新的‘智识范式’深刻影响了日本的文学和文化研究”（平井正，1985，p. 260）。该时期，符号学家千叶荣一和平井正还对布拉格学派给予了关注，并共同编著了《捷克结构美学论集》，该论集收录了穆卡洛夫斯基（Mukarovsky）的《作为社会事实的美学功能、标准与价值》。平井正认为穆卡洛夫斯基对于语言的美学功能的阐发加深了日本符号学界对于“符号”的认识。

直到20世纪70年代末，日本学界才开始关注皮尔斯和莫里斯的符号学理论。其实，早在1950年，哲学家鹤见俊辅就在其编著的《美国哲学》中对皮尔斯的生平和哲学思想进行了述评。1963年，上山春平在《辩证法的谱系》中也单列一章《皮尔斯的逻辑思想中的辩证法性格》，对皮尔斯的逻辑思想进行了阐述。1968年，上山春平又编译了《皮尔斯·詹姆斯·杜威》，对美国的实用主义哲学进行了详细论述。因此，当时的日本学界只对皮尔斯的实用主义哲学和逻辑学思想给予了关注，其符号学思想则鲜有人论及。对此，符号学家外山知德撰文指出：“在人类学术史上，有很多知识渊博的学者被埋没，在19世纪末20世纪初开创了独特符号学体系的美国哲学家查尔斯·桑德斯·皮尔斯就是其中一位。在日本，皮尔斯的符号学几乎没人探讨，即使偶尔被引用，也是部分的、片段的，并没有触及其理论的核心意义。”（1976，p. 154）这是日本学界对皮尔斯符号学研究的第一声呼吁。

也许是外山知德的呼吁起到了作用，日本学界在20世纪80年代出版了一系列皮尔斯符号学的相关论著。1981年，米盛裕二出版了《皮尔斯的符号学》，是日本符号学界第一部系统阐述皮尔斯符号学思想的专著。1985—1986年，日本劲草书房编译了皮尔斯著作集，并分为《现象学》《符号学》和《形而上学》三卷陆续出版。米盛裕二编译了《现象学》卷。《符号学》卷则由内田种臣编译，主要收录了皮尔斯的《符号的分类》《给魏尔比夫人的书信》《现象与范畴》《心灵的基本要素》《知觉与知觉判断》《思考、符号、试推》《何为意义》《人是象征符号》等论文。内田还对这些论文中的符号学术语进行了详细分析和解说。皮尔斯符号学的引入对日本的结构主义热带来了冲击，也为日本符号学研究打开了广阔的领域。建筑符号学、市场营销符号学、会计符号学、体育符号学等门类符号学也在这一时期迅速发展。

日本符号学会也于1980年成立，汇集了各个领域的专家学者，并迅速成为跨学科研究的平台。20世纪80年代出现的消费热潮让日本学界更加关注消费市场和商品的“符号”问题，星野克美、今村仁司、大塚英志等学者在商品和市场营销符号学领域做出了突出贡献。以上因素让日本的符号学研究在80年代达到了鼎盛时期。但是，随着90年代日本经济泡沫的破灭，以及日本符号学在前期发展过猛所遗留的一些问题，符号学研究在日本出现了一段低潮期。进入21世纪，随着计算机网络技术的迅速发展，各种新媒介层出不穷，网络社群和虚拟世界也造就了很多新的流行文化。日本符号学界紧跟当下流行文化，并在这些领域重新焕发了活力。近些年来日本的媒介符号学和信息符号学也迅速发展，并有可能成为未来日本符号学的主要研究领域。

纵观符号学在日本的发展历程，可以发现日本的符号学研究融合了索绪尔语言符号学模式、皮尔斯逻辑修辞模式以及塔尔图学派的社会文化符号学模式，并把俄国形式主义、英美新批评、结构主义等形式文论也纳入研究体系。因此，符号学在日本不仅打破了东西方的界限，还打通了日本各人文社科各领域之间的隔阂，各领域的学者都在符号学的名义下齐头并进。

二、中日符号学界的对话与交流

现代符号学原生于西方，对于中日两国来说都属于外来学科。但是，中国先秦诸子的思想中已经蕴含了丰富的符号学思想。比如，名实之辩和言意之辩、儒家的正名论都是具有中国特色的符号学命题。“从符号学的角度看，礼其实就是人的符号表意过程中逐渐约定俗成的一套仪式系统，而这套系统形成之后又规范制约着人的表意行为。”（祝东，2014，p. 80）日本自古以来深受儒家思想的影响，水户学派“大义名分”论就是在融合了中国的名实论和正名论的基础上提出的。因此，中日两国在引入符号学之前，就已经开始了符号思想的交流。

日本的符号学研究始于1928年，而中国的符号学研究则可以追溯到1926年，赵元任在《符号学大纲》中提出了“符号学”一词。“符号学”与作为译词的“記号学”和“記号論”不同，它是由赵元任独立提出的。赵毅衡认为“他的确是独立于索绪尔或皮尔斯提出这门学科，应当是符号学的独立提出者”（2012，p. 5）。

在前现代时期，中国学界对西方思想的引进往往借道日本。《普通语言学教程》被译介到日本以后，也迅速引起了中国学界的注意。张世禄的《语言学原理》（1930）和王古鲁的《言语学通论》（1930）都把小林英夫的《言语学原论》列入参考书目。这应该是中日两国在符号学研究领域的第一次对话。此外，对索绪尔学说在中国的传播做出巨大贡献的陈望道和方光焘也都曾留学日本，并通过《言语学原论》接触到了索绪尔的思想理论。

但是，从那以后的很长一段时间里，中日两国的符号学研究一直处于平行发展的状态，都把目光投向了西方。一直到1982年，国内才出现第一篇介绍日本符号学研究状况的文章——《日本的符号学研究》，作者童斌在该文中梳理了日本符号学界对符号学理论的译介情况，并以日本符号学会的成立大会（1980年）和第一次年会（1981年）为中心，介绍了当时日本符号学界的主要研究领域。日本的符号学研究在20世纪80年代正开展得如火如荼，而中国的符号学研究则刚刚度过漫长的黎明期。因此，中国符号学界开始把一部分目光投向日本，中日两国的符号学研究从此有了交集，日本的一些符号学著作也开始被译介到中国。1985年，张晓云翻译出版了池上嘉彦的《符号学入门》，对符号学在中国的推广做出了非常大的贡献。其他的日本符号学译著还有《诗学与文化的符号学——从语言学透视》（池上嘉彦著，林璋译，1998年）和《影像化的现代——语言与影像的符号学》（宇波彰著，李璐茜译，2014年）。

1986年，“日本哲学研讨会”在辽宁大学举办，卞崇道在会上指出：“这些年，日本掀起一股新思潮，叫‘新学院派’哲学，它的主要思想特征是用结构主义、符号学的方法宣传反理性主义、反科学主义。”（1986，p. 46）毛丹青也认为，日本学者把符号学的“基本原理用在具体学科领域的研究上，推动了像语言学、科技美学、文化学等学科的发展进程，使日本学术成为符号学演练的‘实战场所’”（1986，p. 48）。

紧接着在第二年，毛丹青在《符号学与当代日本的文化思潮》中对当时日本符号学界的研究状况进行了详细梳理，并从文化研究的角度分析了符号学热潮在日本出现的文化动因。魏育邻则在《丸山圭三郎对索绪尔语言学手稿等原始资料的研究》（1999）和《索绪尔语言学理论的文化人类学意义——日本著名学者丸山圭三郎的索绪尔研究综述》（1999）中着重论述了丸山圭三郎的符号学思想及其在索绪尔符号学研究领域的突出贡献。这两篇文章是中国学界对日本符号学家研究成果的第一次详细论述。2005年，卢德平在《日本当代主要符号学家及其学术观点》中，对丸山圭三郎、山口昌男、池上嘉彦等几位具有代表性的符号学家的学术观点进行了系统论述。

其他关于日本符号学研究状况的论述主要散见于日本文学和文化研究的论文中。例如，于长敏在《日本学者从语言学角度研究文艺的几种新方法》（1990）中论述了索绪尔的符号学对日本文体学研究的影响，并重点介绍了符号学家篠田浩一郎在文学研究领域的符号学尝试。魏育邻的《“语言论转向”条件下的当代日本近代文学研究》，孟庆枢的《对日本 20 世纪 80 年代以来文学批判的几点思考》和《全球化语境下的日本当代文学理论——从作品论到文本论、超文本论》都对前田爱的符号学研究在日本文学研究领域的影响做了深入阐述。

除此之外，中日符号学界还在汉字符号学研究、先秦诸子的逻辑思想研究等领域展开了对话。1983 年，孙中原在《日本学者对中国古代逻辑的研究》一文中梳理了加地伸行、大滨浩、高田淳、末木刚博等日本学者对墨子、荀子和公孙龙的逻辑思想的研究，并指出，“日本学者在研究中国古代逻辑时，除运用传统逻辑观点外，还常用现代符号学的理论来认识问题”（1983，p. 62）。加地伸行在《中国人的逻辑学》（1977）中运用莫里斯的符号学理论对先秦诸子的名实论进行了深入探讨。而中国学者在此领域的研究则始于 1988 年的《〈指物论〉，文化史上的第一篇符号学论文》（胡绳生、余卫国），并在 20 世纪 90 年代取得了丰硕的成果。

中日符号学界的第一次直接对话也与先秦诸子的逻辑思想研究有关。1986 年，符号学家坂本百大受中国逻辑与语言研究会的邀请来中国讲学，并在湖北大学做了“欧美及日本逻辑学研究动态”“符号学的本质及其现代意义”和“逻辑的先天性和语言生理学”三场学术报告。他在《中国与符号学》一文中描述了当时中国学界对符号学的兴趣：“去中国之前，我向中方报送了逻辑学、符号学、认知科学、言语哲学、第五代计算机等选题。让人感到意外的是中方选择了符号学，去了中国以后，又有很多学校来邀请我去做符号学讲座，可能符号学对他们来说还是个崭新的课题。”（1986，p. 249）他认为符号学研究在中国还处于起步阶段，建议中方首先创建中国符号学会，并表示日本符号学会会给予支持。

通过这次讲学，坂本百大与中国的符号学界建立了联系，并促成了东亚符号学国际研讨会的召开，进而拉开了中日符号学界直接对话的序幕。首届东亚符号学国际研讨会于 1992 年在湖北大学召开。坂本百大率领室井尚、吉冈洋、藤本隆志等 10 位日本学者参加了该次研讨会。中方则有李先焜、陈宗明、王维贤等 40 位专家学者参会。因此，该研讨会实际上是中日两国符号学界之间的一次学术交流会。会议的主题为“汉字文化的意义”，王维贤从语义学的角度对《说文解字》进行了解读，陈宗明提出了汉字符号学的构想，李先焜则从符号学的角度对公孙龙的《名实论》和《指物论》进行了探讨。坂本百大则做了“东亚符号学的可能性”的主题演讲。他认为，“随着符号学变得更加国际化和跨学科化，人们对亚洲文化的兴趣也在迅速增加。事实上，亚洲文化尤其是东亚文化，是符号学研究的一座宝库。而东亚文化的本质特征可以概括为‘汉字文化’”（1994，p. 230）。日方的参会学者从文化人类学、音乐、美学、艺术学、比较文学、翻译学等角度对汉字符号学进行了探讨。

第二届东亚符号学国际研讨会于1997年在华东师范大学举办，并成立了东亚符号学会，坂本百大被推举为主席，李先焜为副主席。研讨会仍然围绕着东亚符号学的传统和未来发展前景展开讨论。坂本百大做了“符号学和亚洲文化的未来状况”的主题报告。外山知德、横手裕、大域宜武、高须俊明、高濑畅秀等日本学者也参加了会议。横手裕讨论了道教和佛教的符号学思想。高须俊明对符号的功能进行了探讨。高濑畅秀则从符形、符义和符用三个方面对法律的概念进行了分析。外山知德对建筑符号学做了深入探讨，并对建筑功能、建筑设计中的符号过程做了阐述。中方的与会学者则主要对《易经》《白马论》《指物论》以及因明学、汉字六书等做了符号学探讨。

第三届东亚符号学国际研讨会于2002年在武汉大学举办。时任东亚符号学会副会长的藤本隆志与桑子敏雄等日本学者参加了该次研讨会。藤本隆志对东亚符号学的发展前景表达了自己的看法。桑子敏雄则对环境空间与人类行为活动的关系进行了符号学考察。与会的中国学者则对中医的阴阳五行思想、汉诗的审美机制、先秦语言的来源等问题进行了探讨。

以上三届东亚符号学国际会议是中日符号学界之间规模比较大的交流活动。除此以外，符号学家谷口勇还参加了第四届中国语言与符号学研讨会，并用皮尔斯的符号学理论对公孙龙的《白马论》进行了探讨。近年来，石田英敬和松本健太郎等日本符号学家也频繁来中国讲学，这也是中日符号学界交流的一部分。

笔者认为，中日符号学界未来在媒介符号学和信息符号学领域将会有更多的交流和对话。随着计算机网络技术的发展，人们面临的媒介环境也越来越错综复杂。手机、计算机、网络等媒介已经不再只是一种传播信息的手段，它们作为人类身体的延伸，正慢慢把人自身也编入信息系统之中。同时，符号与媒介技术的关系也变得更加复杂，媒介技术对人类的思考和认知过程的干涉也越来越深，人与人、人与媒介之间的关系也因此发生了转变。人们在与媒介技术的相互渗透中，不断更新“文化”这个意义之网。因此，如何处理纷繁复杂的媒介环境中的人与人、人与媒介技术之间的关系，是符号学必须面对和解决的问题。

近些年来，中日符号学界都在这方面做出了努力。日本符号学家石田英敬长期致力于信息符号学与媒介符号学研究，并陆续发表了《媒介与政治》《信息符号论的学术体系化和超文本事典的制作》《信息符号学讲义》《新符号学：人脑与媒介的相遇》等论著。他认为，在数字媒介时代，人们的心智（mind）通过身体直接面对计算机的信息处理。人的心智、身体以及计算机的信息处理过程是未来“信息符号学”必须面对和深入研究的三个领域（2019，p. 26）。此外，符号学家松本健三郎在该领域也成果显著，先后发表了《用理论阅读媒介文化》《越境的文化・内容・想象力——跨越国境的流行文化》《数码符号学》等专著，也值得中国符号学界予以关注。

三、结语

中日两国同处于以汉字为根基的东亚文化圈。东亚文化与西方文化有着非常大的区别，在某些世界观和哲思方式上甚至是相反的。原生于西方的符号学在传入中日两国的同时，也带来了它的概念模式和理论预设，这导致人们往往拿西方的理论标准来衡量和判断中日两国的符号学研究，这不利于中日两国的符号学发展，也不利于符号学自身的发展。归根结底，符号学是意义学，对意义的探索是人类共通的追求。因此，西方的符号学研究范式和方法值得借鉴，但没必要套用。中日两国的传统文化中有着丰厚的符号学资源，只有在充分发掘这些资源的基础上坚持对话和交流，才能推动具有东方话语特色的符号学发展。事实上，东亚各国的符号学界同仁正在做这方面的努力，符号学研究阵地也出现了向东方转移的趋势。相信在不远的将来，以汉字文化为根基的东方文化会成为符号学转向的契机。

引用文献：

卞崇道，毛丹青（1986）. 谈日本哲学与文化思潮. 辽宁大学学报，6，46－48.
坂本百大（1986）. 中国と記号学. 記号学研究，6，249.
坂本百大（1994）. The possibility of an East Asian semiotics. 記号学研究，14，230.
高橋修（2002）. 新しい文学研究のために. 東京：岩波書店. 42.
平井正（1985）. 日本における記号学の動向. 記号学研究，5，260.
室井尚，山口昌男（2002）. 記号論逆襲. 東京：東海大学出版社.
石田英敬（2009）. 情報記号論講義：総括と展望. 東京大学大学院情報学環紀要，96，26.
外山知德（1976）. パース記号論についての検討. 現代思想，10，154.

外山知德（1985）. 用語からみた日本における伝統的記号概念 . 記号学研究，1，36.
赵毅衡（2012）. 符号学：理论与推演 . 南京：南京大学出版社 .
祝东（2014）. 仪俗、政治与伦理：儒家伦理符号思想的发展及反思 . 载于曹顺庆、赵毅衡（主编）. 符号与传媒，9. 成都：四川大学出版社 .

作者简介：

徐克，四川大学文学与新闻学院博士研究生，研究方向为中日文学关系与日本符号学。

Author:

Xu Ke, Ph. D. candidate of College of Literature and Journalism, Sichuan University. His research fields are relationship between Chinese and Japanese literature and Japanese Semiotics.

Email: xkshendu@ 163. com

连接自然与文化符号世界的现象学之桥：评《认知符号学：自然、文化与意义的现象学路径》

康亚飞

Towards Phenomenology and Culture ：A Review of Göran Sonneson's *Cognitive Semiotics*

Kang Yafei

书名：《认知符号学：自然、文化与意义的现象学路径》
作者：〔瑞典〕约伦·索内松（Göran Sonesson）
译者：胡易容、梅林、董明来等
出版社：社会科学文献出版社
出版时间：2019 年
ISBN：978－7－5201－5435－2
DOI：10. 13760/b. cnki. sam. 202002019

《认知符号学：自然、文化与意义的现象学路径》是瑞典隆德大学约伦·索内松（Göran Sonesson）教授近 30 年的论文选编，展现了北欧符号学界极具代表的符号学家索内松的学术洞见。北欧符号学界具有欧陆哲学传统，又重视经验科学，呈现出与北美、亚洲不同的符号学研究取向。索内松教授学术背景深厚，曾在巴黎的格雷马斯小组从事十余年姿势符号和玛雅语言研究，回到瑞典后几乎以一己之力引领了瑞典的符号学研究，在以图像为代表的非语言符号领域贡献卓著，也形成了北欧符号学中瑞典的图像与认知符号学的独特研究取向。据译者介绍，此次为中国读者译介的部分论文是索内松教授基本理论和立场的呈现。

本论文集共分上、下两篇，上篇为《现象学与意义理论》（Phenomenology

and Theory of Meaning)，内容偏向于理论原理；下篇为《文化、传播与演化》(Culture, Communication and Evolution)，主要涉及不同领域的应用问题。此种上下篇较为流畅的衔接逻辑，并非索内松教授有意为之，而是译者在选编时为了使读者能从全貌和具体两方面了解索内松的学术观点特意做的独具匠心的编排。索内松的认知符号学研究框架，核心在于将现象学、符号学和认知科学三者进行结合，试图通过现象学融通认知符号学的科学之维与人文之维。在他看来，认知科学需要符号学“意义理论”的灌输，而基于人文传统的符号学也欠缺经验研究的根基，如果想要将这二者完美结合起来，现象学必不可少。若缺乏任何一环，这个框架都将沦为一种“折中拼凑”。

一、现象学作为符号学和认知科学的桥梁

关于符号学的认知转向问题，学界一直存有争议，其中主要的分歧在于符号学和认知科学的关系问题。西比奥克（Thomas Albert Sebeok）认为“‘认知科学’的另一个别名就可以叫做符号学”（西比奥克，拉姆，1987），拉姆也提出“符号学是有关信息系统或结构的研究”（西比奥克，拉姆，1987），二人一致同意将符号学应用于自然科学的极大可能性。但此说法遭到了赵毅衡的反对，他提出：“符号学是意义学，认知符号学也不是一个新的符号学，而是符号学的某个方向得到进一步强调。符号学，尤其是延续至今的‘皮尔斯式符号学’实际上一直是认知符号学。”（赵毅衡，2015）在他这里，符号学原本就是认知符号学，并非是认知科学，更不是符号学的认知转向，学界讨论的认知符号学，实质上是符号学的认知科学化。赵毅衡将符号学定义为“意义之学”（赵毅衡，2011，p. 3），符号学的研究也始终处在文化世界，属于人文学科，而认知科学主要的研究方法来自观察和实验，一般认为属于自然科学。索内松在其研究中也注意到了这个问题，他认为二者长期以来较少交流的原因主要是认知科学和符号学的学科史非常不同(2019，p. 27)。“符号学的基本概念是符号，而认知科学的基本概念是‘再现’”（2019，p. 27），同时，符号学更注重文本分析法，而认知科学重实验方法。由此说来，二者的分歧由来已久，非一朝一夕所就。

面对这个看似不可调和的矛盾，索内松提出了他的方法，这也是他在认知符号学研究中试图解决的主要问题之一。首先，他视符号学为“一门科学”（2019，p. 4）。这并非说符号学要走量化的路子，用自然科学化的方式进行探索。相反，“符号学倾向于从定性的，而不是定量的角度思考所有现

象，但它的目的是系统地阐述规律。而不是被还原为特定对象的阐释”（2019，p. 23）。这即是说，符号学是一门寻求普遍规律的、追求规范性的科学，它强调的是“范畴经验”；其次，他提出“认知科学的符号学转向”（Sonesson，2006），将重点落在了对意义问题的探寻上。最后，他建议用胡塞尔的现象学来进行调和。因为在他看来，符号学的认知转向其本质是自然与人文在意义世界问题上的融通，而现象学恰好提供了方法论的桥梁。

鉴于此，索内松所提及的现象学并非基于认识论层面的研究，而是将其作为一种方法来连接符号学和认知科学。符号学对世界的理解缺乏经验研究的根基，而“现象学的任务是解释人类获得关于世界知识的可能性；作为一种哲学努力，现象学是关于我们经验世界的构成方式”（2019，p. 37）。因此，胡塞尔的现象学正好弥补了符号学方法论层面上的缺失。同时，胡塞尔的现象学方法是理解生命世界理性结构的基础，索内松坚信“自然科学要变得完全理性，就需要现象学”（2019，p. 59）。尽管在《启蒙辩证法》中，霍克海默和阿多诺悲观地认为我们一方面追求理性，另一方面却又免不了最终被理性束缚的命运，但索内松依然认为在人的生存、生活中，理性必不可少，理性是“永远追求更好的知识，同时有标准来确定我们现在所知的至少比我们昨天所知的更接近真理”（2019，p. 59）。

然而，并非所有学者都对现象学和认知科学的结合持乐观态度。2020年，方圆在其《“自然化的现象学”是否可行——从当代认知科学的视角看》一文中对丹·扎哈维的“融通观”提出了批评。在她看来，现象学和认知科学的解释模型并不一致，二者在事实层面上无法相互包容，因此，主观地将其结合缺乏可行性，只能是空谈（方圆，2020）。方圆的观点与胡塞尔的本意有某种相似性。在《哲学作为严格的科学》一书中，胡塞尔明确表示反对自然主义，“对于实现作为严格科学的哲学之可能性而言，仅仅反驳自然主义还不够。我们必须对它的基础、它的方法和它的结果进行积极的批判”（胡塞尔，1999，p. 81）。

对于现象学的自然主义转向之争，索内松提出了他的看法。他将胡塞尔和皮尔斯都看成现象学家，且二人都认为“理性问题真正发挥作用是在科学的舞台上”（2019，p. 59），而“现象学方法发现了作为生命世界之基础的理性结构”（2019，p. 54）。他的意思是，当我们把眼光放在现象学与自然主义的对立中时，应该从中抽身出来，站在更广的视野下去看胡塞尔。因为胡塞尔反对的是用自然科学的方法解释意识，而非用现象学的理性主义去解释科学。相反，科学的快速发展以及人们对于自己深陷其中的狂欢和无知，恰恰十分需要作为方法的现象学的审视。

索内松避免了简单的二元对立，用更具操作性的视角去探索可行方案，从而使得符号学、认知科学和现象学得以融通，解决了关于认知符号学的认知问题的分歧和现象学的自然化转向中的自然主义矛盾，在人文研究与科学研究之间架起了一座桥梁。

二、认知符号学对文化意义世界的探索

下篇的内容主要是认知符号学在文化意义世界的具体实践和应用，涉及的是“生活世界”“人与动物”“文化演化”“全球化情境”等问题，实际上是上篇所提及的方法从微观到宏观、从动物世界到人类文明的解释。其所述核心要义，一方面是对理论有效性的检视，另一方面也是将认知符号学独立应用于诸领域的探索。

下篇的论述始于胡塞尔“生活世界”的概念。索内松认为，“胡塞尔提出‘生活世界’来解释自然科学模式构建的基础。这是一个由事物、人、太阳的升落组成的世界，而不是由细胞、原子和黑洞组成的世界”（2019，p. 162），亦即，胡塞尔将“意识”作为“生活世界”的观照点，正是索内松探讨认知符号学的关键所在。在胡塞尔那里，生活世界是一切意义的起源，我们对于世界的认知起源于生活世界，也要落脚于生活世界，同时，人也只有在生活世界中才能体会到生活的意义。根据索内松的理解，胡塞尔“将生活世界这个概念作为模型研究和转化的首要对象，以及作为科学家们完成他们的工作所处的常识世界”（2019，p. 158）。而且，生活世界并不是一个机械的、客观上完全一致的世界，而是“与主体相对”，这即是说一个事物的全貌不可能被我们的一个视角穷尽，我们所能观察到的，只能是其部分，这一部分成为我们“注意力的中心”，我们可以通过部分推知整体。正如人们虽然只看到水杯的一面，但能够依靠想象对杯子的全貌进行把握，看到了正方体的一面就能够想象正方体的完整形状一样。

对胡塞尔生活世界概念的认同是索内松认知符号学的重要基础，在此基础上，他引入了文化符号学的代表——塔尔图学派。塔尔图学派是20世纪60年代崛起于苏联的符号学派，尤里·洛特曼（Juri Lotman）和鲍里斯·乌斯宾斯基（Boris Uspensky）是该学派的两个重要人物。索内松将塔尔图学派的研究路径称为“标准模式”，根据该模式，“每一种文化都把自身设想为秩序，而与外部的东西相对，这些外部的东西被视作混乱无序和野蛮，换句话

说，作为与文化相对的自然”（2019，p. 163）。这意味着，文化始终是以自我为中心的，这与胡塞尔的提到的“主体相对”的生活世界有异曲同工之妙。

塔尔图学派的另一个重要人物雅各布·冯·尤克斯库尔（Jakob von Uexküll）也在索内松的研究中被多次提到。尤克斯库尔是生物学家，1921年，他在《动物的周围世界与内心世界》一书中提出了“周围世界”（Umwelt，也翻译为“环境界”）的概念。在尤克斯库尔看来，周围世界是生命体从自我出发建构出来的世界，由于每个物种对环境的感知不同，所以周围世界也并不相同。蜜蜂的周围世界和老虎的周围世界不是同一个世界，人的周围世界和动物也不可能相同。周围世界是一种动物所认为理所当然的世界，在其中，动物的感官系统发挥着重要作用。周围世界“包括生命体的感知世界（Merkwelt）和行为世界（Wirkwelt），两者相互融合，形成功能圈（functional cycle）”（王新朋，王永祥，2017）。在阐述意义理论时，尤克斯库尔举了狗的周围世界和人的周围世界是多么不同的例子，比如人可以用来行走的楼梯，在狗看来只能用于爬行，大部分人生活所必备的家具，可能只是狗活动的障碍物。无论动物、人，还是其他生命体，对周围世界所赋予的意义，都是依据自己的认知展开的，每一个周围世界都是主体意识投射下的独特存在。

根据这个思路，具体到文化上，就有“自我文化”“他者文化”和“其他文化”的区分。自我文化是指将自我放在文化的主体位置，他者文化和其他文化都是基于自我视角下的文化关系。索内松对此文化主体性表示赞同，他指出，“我们一直都在关注主体之间的关系，或者更确切地说，关注‘我’的单一主体与所有被指定为他者文化或其他文化的所有主体之间的关系。在自我文化（Ego-cultural）中，成员之间的关系通常是他者文化（Alter-cultural）的，然而，在反对另外的文化占主导地位的程度上，它必须被认为是自我文化的”（2019，p. 178）。

在关于他者文化的讨论中，移情理论经常被用到。从字面可知，移情的过程必然少不了主体和客体，这就涉及索内松前文所提及的“自我和他者之间的关系”（2019，p. 179）。但这个关系具体为何，不同的学者有不同的看法。经典的移情理论将他者看作自我的投射或推理，前者假设自我和他者都是已知的；后者则认为只有自我是已知的，他者需要通过推理创建。巴赫金用“作者”和“英雄”的概念来表达他对移情的看法，在他的话语体系中，自我是在无限的过程中变动的，并没有一个固定的自我，因此，自我永远不能被完整把握，只有他者才是为人所知且完整的整体。这与经典的移情理论恰好相反。在对其他文化进行解释时，巴赫金也秉持此观点，提出“理解不可能通过与另一种文化的完全认同来实现，而只能通过进入另一种文化，然后回到另一种文化之外的位置来实现”（2019，p. 183）。亦即，试图从自我文化的视角来看待另一种文化只能是徒劳，应该采取的是相反的态度。一些现象学家也对移情问题给予了直接或间接的关注，如胡塞尔、梅洛－庞蒂和古尔维奇等。索内松之所以引出一系列学者对移情的探讨，是想说明，自我文化和他者文化的关系有多种类型，但无论哪种都离不开人文学科在其中进行解释的必要性，也离不开“将我们自身作为人的理解，以及将他人作为人的理解”（2019，p. 190）。

到此，我们便知索内松的认知符号学框架是如何探索文化意义世界的了。首先，现象学中关于生活世界的概念，成为解释生命体与周围世界关系的普遍模式；自我处于意识主体，一切经验都是与自我有关的经验，因此，文化即是以“我”为中心的文化，文化不是散落世间的混乱，而是有特定的结构。其次，根据胡塞尔对生活世界层层内涵的划分，对文化也可循此进行不同角度的细分化，从而将文化问题作为类型问题来加以解决。最后，文化并不是机械存在的，也不是一成不变的，文化在进行着演化，借由不同的主体、情境等因素而不断被建构，因此，面对文化问题，用历时性的眼光看待或许更为有效。

三、结语

符号学的认知转向以及现象学的自然化转向问题都是多年来学界争论的焦点，而这两个争论实质也是自然学科和人文学科的边界划分问题。一些学者将认知符号学的“认知”看作经典符号学里对符号意义的认知，也有些学者将认知等同于认知科学，是自然科学的范畴。前者将符号学视作人文学科，而后者则走向了科学化、实验化的路径。对此，胡易容提出：“心灵是个多元体，神经实验只提供了它某个生理维度上的切片。基于生物神经元个体的实验并不负责社会语境下的文化意义，实验室也无法穷尽社会文化中符号意义生成的所有变量。这实际上要求自然科学突破认知和意识的瓶颈，更深刻地理解‘人’，而这正是人文科学的工作领域。”（2015）索内松在研究中对现象学作为方法论的坚守，也正体现了他基于人之主体性的人文关怀。因此，用现象学在符号学和认知科学之间架起桥梁的方式不仅是一次勇敢的探索，更是一次有意义的结合。

在当今国际符号学界，不同国别的符号学研究呈现出各自不同的学术倾向。索内松所代表的北欧认知符号学研究，展现了符号学的哲学深度与经验现实相融通的尝试。这种尝试深具价值的一面，是对“学科范式预设”的反思。在索内松看来，符号学的认知转向并不仅仅是一个单向度的过程。实际上，几乎所有的哲学社会科学都受到了认知科学的影响，进而出现了某种认知转向。符号学的认知转向也是其中之一，但与其他学科不同的是，符号学本身即是以某种“意义认知论”为基础的学科，因此，符号学的跨学科之路恰恰是在“严格遵循自身逻辑体系的基础上与其他科学共同探索现有知识的边界的过程”（胡易容，2015）。

引用文献：

方圆（2020）.“自然化的现象学”是否可行——从当代认知科学的视角看．科学技术哲学研究，2，14－18.

胡塞尔（1999）.哲学作为严格的科学（倪梁康，译）.北京：商务印书馆．

胡易容（2015）.从人文到科学：认知符号学的立场．符号与传媒，1，117－125.

索内松，约伦（2019）.认知符号学：自然、文化与意义的现象学路径（胡易容，梅林，董明来，等译）.北京：社会科学文献出版社．

王新朋，王永祥（2017）.环境界与符号域探析．俄罗斯文艺，4，144－150.

西比欧克，T. A.，拉姆，S. M.（1991）.符号学与认知科学．哲学译丛，2，16－19.

赵毅衡（2015）.关于认知符号学的思考：人文还是科学？符号与传媒，1，106－113.

赵毅衡（2011）.符号学：原理与推演．南京：南京大学出版社．

Sonesson, G. (2006). The meaning of meaning in biology and cognitive science: A semiotic reconstruction. *Sign systems studies*, 1, 135－213.

作者简介：

康亚飞，四川大学文学与新闻学院博士研究生，四川大学符号学－传媒学研究所成员，主要研究领域为传播学、符号学。

Author:

Kang Yafei, Ph. D. candidate of College of Literature and Journalism, Sichuan University, member of the ISMS research team. Her research fields are communication and semiotics.

Email: 294926750@qq.com

符号学视角下的当代幸福研究：评《幸福感符号学：社会文化修辞》

吕思睿

Happiness in Contemporary Context: A Review of *Semiotics of Happiness*

Lü Sirui

书名：幸福感符号学：社会文化修辞
作者：〔英〕阿什利·弗劳利（Ashley Frawley）
译者：谭光辉、李泉
出版社：社会科学文献出版社
出版时间：2019 年
ISBN：978－7－5201－4264－9
DOI：10. 13760/b. cnki. sam. 202002020

幸福感符号研究作为一个新课题，迄今尚未得到充分讨论。而英国学者阿什利·弗劳利（Ashley Frawley）的社会符号学著作《幸福感符号学：社会文化修辞》（*Semiotics of Happiness*: *Rhetoric Beginning of A Public Problem*）作为学科前沿学术成果，为这片新领域开疆拓土，具有标志性的意义。

一、打破消费社会的幸福幻象

让·波德里亚（Jean Baudrillard）在《消费社会》一书中说：“自工业革命和 19 世纪革命以来，所有政治的和社会的毒性转移到了幸福上。幸福首先有了这种意识意义和意识功能，于是在内容上引起了严重后果：幸福要成为平等的神话媒介，那它就得是可测之物，必须是物、符号、‘舒适’能够测得出来的福利。”（2000，p. 33）这就意味着，在资本疯狂扩张的消费时代，幸福常常成为可以看见的指数，来显示身在其中的人们是如何实现“平等”的。阿什利·弗劳利正是在消费时代的大背景下，通过统计、分析纸质新闻媒体有关幸福的文献，拨开重重迷雾，打破消费社会的幸福幻象，向我们揭示幸福问题中所隐藏的修辞逻辑、话语逻辑、政治逻辑和文化逻辑，以及在“财富悖论”即“人们并不会因为财富的增加而感到快乐”（2019，p. 18）背后，是什么样的力量使幸福可以被有效测量，成为潜在的民间神话。阿什利·弗劳利对所谓的“幸福指数”一针见血地指出：“幸福指数成为所有现代社会问题的指标，是对现代性本身的批判。”（p. 22）

阿什利·弗劳利着重强调幸福作为一个问题，引起了诸多发声者的关注，而他们的发声是具有修辞性的，因为幸福是个“有利可图的领域”（p. 130）。

阿什利·弗劳利解释了他之所以选择报纸文献，即新闻媒体印刷文本作为数据搜集和分析的起点的原因：一是如果发声者希望与大众沟通，新闻媒体的报道至关重要；二是新闻媒体的报道给予了这些发声一定程度的可信度；三是新闻媒体的覆盖范围和潜在有效性意味着无数发声者争相获取“最大可能的受众”，使媒体行为成为社会问题“市场”。麦克卢汉（Herbert Marshall McLuhan）在《理解媒介》一书中说：“所谓媒介即是讯息只不过是说：任何媒介（即人的任何延伸）对个人和社会的任何影响，都是由于新的尺度产生的，我们的任何一种延伸（或曰任何一种新的技术），都要在我们的事务中引进一种新的尺度。”（2000，p. 33）“媒介即信息”的说法表明了媒介的本质。麦克卢汉还说：“站在与任何结构或媒介保持一定距离的地方，才可以看清其原理和力的轮廓。因为任何媒体都有力量将其假设强加在没有警觉的人的身上。”（p. 42）传播是一项系统性的活动，在各个环节都不可避免地会受到人为因素、主观性的影响，造成传播活动传者和受众信息的不对称，而媒介的修辞效果即是通过符码来象征、传达其形而下的能指，掩盖或者深化某些意义，使受众更易于接受他们的观点。阿什利·弗劳利认为要深入研究幸福如何在新闻媒体中成功地问题化，纸质新闻媒体已然成为公共权威的主要发声者的切入点，从纸质新闻媒体中可以了解幸福话语的主要特征和进展，然后再对其他公共领域发声者的活动和发声进行考察，这就提供了一种比较好的理解方式。让·波德里亚“承认麦克卢汉‘媒介即信息’确实是消费分析的一个基础特征”（2014，p. 130）。“大众传播的这一技术程式造成了某一类非常具有强制性的信息：信息消费之信息，即对世界进行剪辑、戏剧化和曲解的信息以及把消息当成商品一样进行赋值的信息，对作为符号的内容进行颂扬的信息。简而言之，就是一种包装。”（p. 130）阿什利·弗劳利打开了发声者对幸福问题的“包装”，清晰地描述出幸福成为一个问题是社会构建的结果：正如在书的前言中，弗兰克·弗雷迪（Frank Furedi）所说的：“幸福成为一个问题，令人深感不安，它不断传达着这样一个观点——除非某些政策和治疗手段干预，我们就注定要陷入不幸福的状态。”（2019，p. 1）

这本作为关注当今热点社会问题的社会符号学著作，在符号活动与社会意义这一既庞杂繁芜又微妙难传的结合点上，通过解释新闻媒体提出为幸福发声的历史文化语境，分析发声者，并精准把握符号修辞作用，深度剖析了三个时间段中纸质新闻媒体呈现的大量社会活动和社会现象，“试图在非政治化的背景下帮助读者更广泛地理解社会问题的表现”（p. 37），展示了符号学的阐释力量。

二、打开媒介时代的话语盒子

幸福是一个伦理问题，也是一个哲学问题。人类关于幸福的讨论由来已久，西方哲学对幸福的讨论可以追溯到古希腊时期。德谟克利特认为人的自然本性决定了人是趋利避害的，人活动的目的都是为了追求快乐；苏格拉底强调德行与幸福的关系；亚里士多德则提出“幸福是心灵的活动”，将幸福定义为“自给自足”；伊壁鸠鲁将快乐主义融入于他的幸福观，认为幸福始于快乐、终于快乐，构成了以至善为最终目标的快乐主义幸福观。17 世纪英国经验论哲学家约翰·洛克（John Locke）指出，“极度的幸福就是我们所能享受的最大快乐”；近代英国功利主义哲学家杰里米·边沁（Jeremy Bentham）把快乐主义幸福观进一步发展为功利主义幸福观；大卫·休谟（David Hume）高度关注幸福所具有的超越性意义，提出“一切人类努力的伟大目标都在于获得幸福”；卡尔·马克思（Karl Marx）的幸福观认为实践是现实的人实现幸福的基础。阿什利·弗劳利说：“虽然人们习惯于把幸福的历史追溯到古希腊，或者追溯到一些普遍的、永恒的人类探索，但我认为，目前对幸福的兴趣产生并不久。”（2019，p. 17）“符号学资源与社会问题发声关联使用是最近才出现的。”（p. 16）因此，阿什利·弗劳利正是将幸福视作社会问题并以社会符号学来解读幸福的先驱。正如谭光辉所言：“西方哲学史对幸福的讨论烦琐，基本上都在伦理学、社会学、心理学领域内进行，但是都能在符号学理论中得到解释。幸福感符号研究可以解决自我危机问题，有助于找到自我的精神核心，完成自我重建。”（2012）

《幸福感符号学》将“幸福”（及其各种相关术语）的兴起视为一种社会和政治符号学，把语言看作发声活动。罗兰·巴尔特（Roland Barthes）认为“符号学符号与它的语言学原型一样，也由能指和所指组成，但它在实体的层面上又与语言学符号有分别”（巴尔特，1999，p. 31）。“幸福”作为一个特定的能指，其意义结构是被利用的。幸福具有独特的能力，既可以作为一个自由浮动的能指，又能够达成规范的联盟。在资本主义时代，人们对“幸福”这个名词的关注，暗含了对社会制度框架内汇集的各类社会问题的思考——“幸福”恰恰是一个很好的切入点。作者坦诚他的兴趣点既不是抽象的幸福，不是它更深层次的、“真实”的或哲学的意义，也不是它在世俗个体日常生活中的用法或追求，而是聚焦于幸福的问题化，即声称幸福构成严重社会问题的幸福发声之兴起及其随后的成功。这些幸福发声认为个人和政府在追求幸福或其他目标时误入歧途，认为这些问题以及诸多相关问题都可以根据幸福科学的发现，通过“和谐”地调整行为及政策而得到改善。所谓“改善”，即降低对幸福的期待值。阿什利·弗劳利以其冷静而客观的分析、严谨而有条理的重构，向我们展示了幸福问题背后的深层意味。“一个符号，随着它的展开，是指向其他东西的任何东西。”（2019，p. 3）阿什利·弗劳利深度剖析纸质新闻媒体呈现的现象，从而引出对幸福问题背后的政治制度、经济发展、社会文化等一系列问题的思考。以往学界对幸福的研究，大多集中在探讨影响幸福感的因素、不同阶层人群的幸福感状况、政策实施对人们幸福的影响、收入差距对幸福感的影响机制，等等，而阿什利·弗劳利则深入探究幸福发声中的修辞，“为了把幸福作为一个社会问题来理解，就要理解修辞和修辞选择在构建问题形象中起的重要作用”（p. 46）。阿什利·弗劳利打开了媒介时代的话语盒子，向我们敞开了这个盒子中的话语权。

三、打造多元视角的研究方法

阿什利·弗劳利在书中以开阔的视野、多元的视角、严密的论证，抽丝剥茧般将已成为“社会政策对象”的幸福的真实状况呈现在我们面前。全书逻辑清晰、结构合理、科学严谨、图文并茂，对大量纸质新闻媒体资料做了科学的数据分析，为结论提供了有力的支撑。书中一共展示了 21 个图表，包括 14 张表格、1 幅示意图、3 幅饼状图、3 幅柱状图。

本书以纸质新闻媒体上的文章作为分析材料，运用统计法，主要在以下几个层面对幸福这一问题进行梳理与统计。这些统计归结起来为：

（1）分析发声者及其在发声过程中的角色，1 幅示意图清晰地显示了个人和团体之间的相互联系，展示了某些潜在关系以及这些关系被认可与制度化的途径，并对知情人发声者与局外人发声者做了比较。

（2）列举了诸多批评派别对幸福发声的批评与反对意见，以及决策者们对幸福发声的接受。

（3）试图识别问题发声、发声者及其彼此关系的突出来源，通过探讨自认为幸福者在幸福被问题化最关键时期出现的最频繁的活动来揭示幸福的生成过程。作者通过 2 幅饼状图来显示样本中确定的个体发声者的类型和样本中确定的机构类型。

（4）作者用列表对 1993—1995 年幸福问题化的第一批发声者进行分析，指出他们的公共幸福发声在 1993—2002 这十年后的其余时间影响力很小。2003 年初出现大量的文章，其中伦敦的经济学家莱亚德的一系列幸福发声工作产生了重要的影响。作者列出了 1 幅柱状图和 1 张表格来说明莱亚德的重要性，并罗列了对数据库中 9 个最常见个体发声者的描述、身份类别及发表的相关文章数量。

（5）作者用了 2 张表格来说明“幸福是什么”：最常见的专家领域的发声认为幸福是什么，还有一些发声者将幸福的含义指向了道德。作者列出图表展示有关“财富问题化的原因”“对幸福的威胁”的文章数量。

（6）对幸福发声提出的变革建议进行了梳理，以柱状图的形式展示各类推论（即为发声所提出的问题提供解决办法的发声）类型的文章百分比，目的是显示修辞推论的关注中心。作者还对推论类别中最常见的发声做了表格梳理，认为其倡导把降低期望值作为通往幸福的道路。

阿什利·弗劳利以从时间上分段梳理资料的方式为我们厘清了幸福问题的发现、幸福研究的介绍，将涉及“幸福”这个关键词的讨论划分为三个时间段，即从随意把幸福作为自由浮动的空洞的能指，到去语境化和幸福研究的引入（始于 20 世纪 80 年代），再到 20 世纪 90 年代的话语状况。阿什利·弗劳利对这三个时间段的报纸进行了细致梳理，以《泰晤士报》为例：一是报纸中所出现的关于“幸福”和“繁荣”文章的篇数；二是对所有英国全国性报纸进行了搜索，列出了新闻全文数据库中关于幸福的三种专家意见；三是对提出幸福悖论的文章数量的增长做了图表说明。对 2003 年这个时间点作了重点强调，说明直到 2003 年以后，幸福发声问题才开始在公共议程上占有一席之地。对 20 世纪初到 90 年代第一次“发现问题”期间公共讨论中关于

“幸福”一词使用情况变化做了历时性概述，呈现了有关幸福问题时间线性的逻辑关系。

阿什利·弗劳利着重描述了修辞在新社会问题发声中的作用，以此提供一些用于解释幸福问题的基本理论工具。作者用“发声”这个术语，指代“为进一步实现某个实际目标而设计的解释或故事”（米勒［Miller］）。对于发声，“发声者必须意识到他们的受众，以及哪些发声可能在各种媒介中都有吸引力”（2019，p. 43），因此报纸上对同一个社会问题所采用的言辞都是不同的；“成功的发声往往是设法避免最大的反对”（p. 44），所以，发声有可能是被精心设计的；“在次要发声受到空间限制和媒介需求制约的程度上，它们必须足够有说服力，才能吸引目标受众的关注”（p. 44），为了吸引人们的注意力，成功的发声往往是一个“引人入胜的故事”（p. 45）。对于幸福问题来说，发声就是一个有吸引力的策略，“发声不仅仅告诉我们现实，而且必须说服我们相信它们的现实。于是，问题发声就成了一种修辞形式”（p. 45）。阿什利·弗劳利认为，社会问题是一种社会实践，它根植于文化和历史语境。一个发声者可以以其所选择的任何方式发声，但若要自己的主张被广泛接受，就需要和这个时代的图像和想法存储库一致。那么，对于幸福问题，独特的修辞方式就会显得“有效”，这也就是“幸福可以被测量”的原因。

《幸福感符号学》关注的幸福问题，可以说是全世界共同的社会热点话题。幸福感是一种社会心理，社会心理作为社会意识的一种低级表现形式，折射出社会制度、经济形态、政治文化。符号学在社会学领域的交叉实践，充分体现了符号学对人类活动的阐释力量。《幸福感符号学》正是对幸福这一社会问题背后的根源进行了追溯，大量的客观事实与数据表明，发声者对幸福问题的描述表面上热情、积极、轻松，实质上这种关注最终是保守的，希望通过降低期望值来获取幸福，这种幸福实质上是决策者的权宜之计，非常适合于（对资本主义而言）“别无选择”的时代。阿什利·弗劳利跳出了幸福学家的视野，他不仅以符号学介入对当代幸福问题的研究，还提及大量心理学、文化学、经济学、社会学等对幸福的论述；他不止于揭示纸质新闻媒体现象背后的问题根源，还对这种根源做了客观的描述。幸福感符号学作为一个新课题有着充分的阐释空间，它也将成为幸福学研究的一个重要视角和维度。

引用文献：

巴尔特，罗兰（1999）．符号学原理（王东亮，等译）北京：生活·读书·新知三联书店．

波德里亚，让（2000）．消费社会（刘成富，全志钢，译）．南京：南京大学出版社．

弗劳利，阿什利（2019）．幸福感符号学（谭光辉，李泉，译）．北京：社会科学文献出版社．

麦克卢汉，赫伯特·马歇尔（2000）．理解媒介（何道宽，译）．北京：商务印书馆．

谭光辉（2012）．幸福感符号研究的现状与未来．贵州社会科学，12，29.

作者简介：

吕思睿，四川师范大学文学院中国现当代文学专业 2019 级博士研究生，主要研究方向为中国现当代文学与文化。

Author:

Lü Sirui, Ph. D. candidate in modern and contemporary Chinese literature, School of Literature, Sichuan Normal University. Main research direction is contemporary Chinese literature and culture.

Email: 857151302@ qq. com

本书在编辑过程中，得到了四川大学人文社科期刊资助项目、四川大学中国语言文学与中华文化全球传播双一流学科群，以及教育部人文社科重点基地四川大学中国俗文化研究所的支持，特此感谢。